Shared Differences

Shared Differences

Multicultural Media and Practical Pedagogy

Edited by

Diane Carson and Lester D. Friedman

University of Illinois Press   Urbana and Chicago

1 2 3 4 5 C P 5 4 3 2 1

This book is printed on acid-free paper.

Library of Congress Cataloging-in-Publication Data

Shared differences : multicultural media and practical pedagogy /
    edited by Diane Carson and Lester D. Friedman.
        p.   cm.
    Includes bibliographical references and index.
    ISBN 0-252-02150-9 (cloth). — ISBN 0-252-06450-X (paper)
    ISBN 978-0-252-02150-3 (cloth). — ISBN 978-0-252-06450-0 (paper)
    1. Minorities in motion pictures. 2. Multiculturalism—Study and
teaching. I. Carson, Diane. II. Friedman, Lester D.
PN1995.9.M56S52   1995
791.43'08'693—dc20   94-29251
                                                                 CIP

Printed and bound in Great Britain by
Marston Book Services Limited, Oxford

For Willis, for everything
  —D.C.

For the little ones:
Jessica Pitt, Dylan Walter, TJ Walter
  —L.D.F.

Contents

Part 3: Multicultural Media as Product

Preface:
Commitment and Action

Diane Carson

In "Pied Beauty," Gerard Manley Hopkins exclaims, "Glory be to God for dappled things— / ... / All things counter, original, spare, strange." For the cleric Hopkins, diversity, the "freckled" world, provided yet another reason for praising a God beyond change, proclaimed in a world ever in flux. Such celebration of variety in creation is one theme of multiculturalism in American education. It also signals diverse, even contradictory, definitions, interpretations, and applications as academics have envisioned, discussed, and debated the issue. Aware of its multifaceted nature, we, the coeditors and contributors to this anthology, must define multiculturalism and delineate its place in education. And because we are committed to enriching our own lives and those of our students, we want to provide suggestions to colleagues engaged in a similar enterprise.

This anthology grew out of numerous formal and informal dialogues among teachers, exchanges in which the need and desire for some innovative ideas and their practical, direct applications emerged repeatedly. A sense of urgency motivated our work as we noted the projections of America's demographics into the next century, as Lester Friedman summarizes. A teacher's inclusion of multicultural pedagogy and an active engagement with diverse ethnic, racial, and national issues is critical to America's social well-being then and now. We must put our beliefs into practice, aware that the defining characteristics and enabling understanding of ethnic, racial, and national groups can and ought to be taught. Teachers must acknowledge uniqueness and difference as they also applaud similarity, for the strength of small communities and also society at large derives from celebrating our diversity.

Moreover, in a continually and dramatically interdependent world, we recognize that intercultural contact will inevitably occur. People from a variety of backgrounds within a given culture will increasingly encounter people from other cultures. Inclusive multiculturalism encourages positive, honest interactions among individuals who differ in some significant ways but have worked to develop strategies for sharing, understanding, and enjoying their diversity. Progressive, energizing receptivity is a condition of survival. A recognition of the strength gained from positive, open responsiveness is embedded in our political and social ideologies and in the nation's motto "E pluribus unum" (from many one). The stress is on unity, but with equal attention to the dynamic inclusion of the many.

We must, as a community, commit to action. Therefore, thorough integration of diverse cultural content must become an ongoing part of the educational process, for effective education empowers students. Multiculturalism, a central element in that empowerment, acknowledges and values difference while recognizing when experiential particularity limits the insight that any one individual or discipline can offer into another culture. Because multiple perspectives help to truly broaden our horizons, the topics included in this volume address a wide range of variables—gender, class, ethnicity, race, and religion—because multiculturalism implicates and intersects with socioeconomic, intellectual, and conceptual differences as it moves from local to national to international perspectives. This particularly complex area of multiculturalism cuts across all disciplines and a multitude of variables.

To achieve the goal of offering multiple perspectives, we encourage selecting educational material that has well-defined multicultural representations, and we attempt to model workable approaches with specific suggestions. We realize that we cannot realistically address all the distinctive academic demands that our readers encounter. However, we trust that resourceful and committed teachers will find numerous ways to adapt the suggestions in this book to individual circumstances. And so, in the articles collected here, we include a range of disciplines taught at both two- and four-year colleges and universities. The following chapters include exercises designed for classes of all sizes (anything from a dozen students to a full lecture hall) and describe short- as well as long-term projects. We hope that these multicultural activities will aid in curriculum reform, because we endorse multicultural education as a liberating ingredient at all educational levels and in all subjects.

The following essays represent topics from English literature to African-American cinema, from anthropology to writing, from ethnography to health and social well-being, and from video production to filmmaking. Across the entire curriculum, we all have a stake in integrating, examining, and applying a multicultural perspective. All disciplines can and must confront the pressing need to examine ethnic, religious, and gender biases. It is to all those teachers who deal with such issues daily and upon whom, increasingly, society depends. We encourage all teachers to join with us in this undertaking.

The Anthology

Although all the authors in this anthology do not agree in their perspectives or advocacy, they do concur on the idea that action must be taken to foster multiculturalism. To aid in our endeavor to educate a diverse student population, each chapter offers a pragmatic approach for curricular development. Each contributor's syllabus is included to provide a context for the explanation and discussion. Acquaintance with the specific details of each syllabus, such as texts, weekly readings, and assignments, will establish an informed perspective from which to grasp how each author integrates multicultural content into his or her courses.

After presenting a brief theoretical position and then describing their academic setting, each author elaborates on specific experiences and courses in which she or he uses media—film, television, videos, and advertising—directed toward a multicultural audience. The variety of subjects, settings, and suggestions will prove provocative to teachers and, implicitly if not explicitly, will recommend ways to adapt the strategies and techniques to a wide range of educational institutions.

In order to clarify the often-contentious issues and define our perspective, we begin with Lester D. Friedman's overview "Struggling for America's Soul: A Search for Some Common Ground in the Multicultural Debate." Teaching, as Friedman explains, is not a politically neutral act, and teachers have a great deal of power that must be wielded for the good. The vituperative debates over political correctness and multicultural education should not sidetrack teachers into either silence or divisive arguments. In an attempt to define and seek out that common ground that teachers must share in order to move forward, Friedman explores seven major premises.

Believing that our greatest tradition is change and our greatest value is respect for individual difference, Friedman argues that recognition of these seven principles will enhance multicultural methods of education and solidify teachers' resolve to pursue them. We can agree, he hopes, that knowledgeable, well-trained teachers can impart information about cultures other than their own to all students, not only those of ethnic minorities; that one monocultural approach should not replace another; that the core of values and ideals of Western culture, a central influence on American political, intellectual, and social thought, should be taught; that individual and cultural groups contain multiple components; and that white ethnic groups constitute part of the multicultural spectrum. An understanding of the nature and import of these principles will empower teachers and students alike and lead to constructive learning environments. Friedman believes that the goals endorsed are necessary and achievable in an educational community that strives for the best, most dynamic classrooms possible. Friedman recognizes that the ideal evolves continually and that constructive engagement is ongoing and should be embraced enthusiastically.

Following Friedman's introduction, the chapters are grouped into three categories: "Multicultural Media as Tool," "Multicultural Media as Text," and "Multicultural Media as Product." Our distinction is straightforward. In most classes, multicultural media can serve as a tool to introduce an array of topics for analysis and discussion. In other courses, media itself—film, television, videos, and advertising—provides the subject matter for investigation; it functions as the text for the class. Still other courses focus on the production of film and video work as a central activity. To keep these distinctions, we designate separate sections.

However, we hasten to add that often courses, even those quite different from our own, offer provocative units or approaches that can be incorporated into dissimilar situations. For example, although media may serve as the text for some classes, some of the films discussed might prove directly relevant and productive in another, more general class that uses media as a tool. Similarly, courses that use multicultural media as text might benefit from one or more activities that ask students to apply their theoretical understanding to a specific product. Although we hope that our classification scheme proves useful, we encourage teachers to browse throughout the chapters for valuable techniques and exercises.

In "Film as Ethnography and Cultural Critique in the Late Twentieth Century" Michael M. J. Fischer suggests further exploratory possibilities for many of his ideas, for beliefs that Friedman espouses, and for those in succeeding chapters. Fischer investigates the changing dynamics of transnational cultures tied to domestic diversity. In his course he explores the ways ethnographic methods focus attention on the multiple perspectives of cultural reality. Through what he calls "cultural hermeneutics" he uses films to unpack the cultural information carried in the languages of varied discourses.

In describing his theories and explicating numerous examples drawn from filmic cultural discourse, Fischer explains analytical ways of moving toward multicultural revelations. Citing distinctive examples from journals, critical papers, and discussions, he models ways to open consciousness about American and transnational diversity. Discussing cultural codes in Japanese, African, and European film traditions, exploring documentary, ethnographic, and narrative forms, Fischer demonstrates the powerful work that can be achieved through his critical approach. He concludes by expressing our shared hope: with more active, more analytical awareness, behavioral change will follow and make the problems of multiculturalism the strengths of a new pluralism.

Margaret Himley and Delia C. Temes, in "Cultural Rhetoric, Difference and the Teaching of Writing," describe how they use multicultural material. Ideally, they want to develop their students' rhetorical skills as readers and writers, guiding them to achieve an understanding of the demands, the injustices, and the possibilities of a complexly multicultural and divided world. To this end, Himley and Temes use cultural rhetoric and theories of difference as organizing frameworks for the design and development of their writing studio, teaching from and toward an understanding of how difference is constructed. Avoiding the trap of merely adding new voices without challenging hierarchies, they examine the inequitable power relations reflected across gender, race, class, and ethnic variables.

To guide students to an increasing awareness of their position within history and culture, Himley and Temes's course, The Study and Practice of Narrative, draws on popular culture, especially television, video, and film, for material. They clarify their approach to student writers as a social subject, constituted within and expressed through language. Writing thus becomes an inherently political activity through which students participate in public arenas of meaning. Quoting from student essays, Himley and Temes particularize their course's empowering effect. They also provide a provocative and informative interpretation of a "Roseanne" episode that reveals strikingly different responses. They conclude with suggestive questions and evidence from students, illustrating the sophisticated critique emerging from such approaches. Overall, their approach to writing demonstrates the positive, engaging analysis possible using media, television in particular, to generate new ways for students to recognize and articulate their cultural contexts.

Housed in an English department and using film to stimulate dialogue about multicultural issues, Linda Dittmar addresses institutional resistance as well as individual uncertainties to a still relatively new approach—the integration of multicultural material into a course called Narrative Form in the Novel and Film. Within a universitywide curriculum hospitable to multicultural and interdisciplinary teaching, she recognizes that teachers move away from staid canonical frameworks when they embrace and promote progressive course designs. In "Letting Go: Resistance and Transformation in the English Curriculum," Dittmar describes the past and present dialogics of her Narrative Form class and delineates a course committed to considerations of social justice and social transformation, offering specific examples of literary and filmic subject matter conducive to furthering her goals.

Dittmar's orientation and commitment to infusing multicultural considerations into the themes of the course open the possibility of addressing the intersections of feminist, class, ethnic, and other such concerns without segregating the subject matter. Interweaving multicultural concerns through the fabric of the entire course, she normalizes awareness of cultural specificity, dialogue, and conflict as an attribute of all thinking and directs attention to the technical and ideological operations of any medium. Through a brief commentary on selected novels and films, Dittmar models the connections and cultural insights that she leads her students to consider. Always cognizant of the potentially unsettling learning situation that her materialist, historic, and dialectical reading of self-reflexive texts might create, she reminds teachers that useful syllabi must lead to developing a sensitivity to social inequities and difference. Relying on multicultural perspectives promotes such awareness by unmasking the ideology that informs all representations of communities.

All of the authors provide implicit arguments for and would agree with Clarence Spigner's thesis that popular film imagery reveals the social, psychological, and physical well-being of some minority group members. Further, commercial cinema contributes to the development and reflection of social norms and attitudes. In "Teaching Multiculturalism from the Movies: Health and Social Well-being," Spigner pursues precisely these issues, using his courses on health and social well-being as the vehicle. He aims to foster a learning environment that promotes greater understanding of multiculturalism through classroom interaction, written expression, and opinion exchange using as content racial imagery in movies. Drawing on an expansive range of films, he considers the roles of minorities and the nature of their social interaction and wonders whether "art imitates life or life art."

To answer the many important questions that this investigation prompts, Spigner incorporates images of African Americans, Latino Americans, Asian/Pacific Americans, and Native Americans, providing additional ways to evaluate the many images described in the other chapters. He pursues his announced intent of interrogating the racism, stratification, and inequality that continue to be the status quo. He inventories various revealing elements within mainstream narrative films: social interaction, primary versus secondary characters, micro and macro behavioral interactions, and psychological characteristics. He also scrutinizes the limited depictions and devaluation of minorities in most popular films and the effects and implications of such representations as they influence mental and social well-being. In the process of delineating the psychosocial forces and political economy that reinforce a dominant ideology, Spigner provides students with strategies to move toward more positive social, psychological, and physical well-being.

In "Media and Education in a Multicultural Society: A Historian's Perspective," Carlos E. Cortés further expands the perspective on media by using it as an unconventional tool in a conventional humanities course. In contrast to some of the teachers discussed previously, those whose goals include developing their students' media scholarship, Cortés never intends to mold media studies scholars. Rather, as a historian, he uses multicultural media to achieve several other aims: to chart the evolution of the relationship between media and society; to develop students' ability to think analytically when dealing with history; to sensitize students to the nuances and complexities that racial, ethnic, cultural, gender, and other kinds of diversities raise; to open discussion of controversial historical and contemporary racial and ethnic issues; and to teach students to write and speak in clear, comprehensible, jargon-free English. In his History of the Mass Media course, as well as others in his area, Cortés approaches moving-image media as historical evidence, a springboard to multicultural considerations.

Through his courses, media literacy workshops, and global education research work, Cortés interrelates academic and personal domains, moving beyond classroom to community arenas and role modeling his direct, unwavering attention to multicultural issues. Through an exploration of various examples, he shows how media functions as evidence for social and cultural history, past and current, academic and personal, for teacher and student alike. He leads students to greater recognition of the nuances and complexities of diversity by openly discussing controversial historical and contemporary racial and ethnic issues.

In "A Different Image: Integrating Films by African-American Women into the Classroom," Gloria Gibson-Hudson advocates a similar analytical study. Maintaining that films made by African-American women are critical to contemporary film pedagogy because they communicate the unique visions of this group, she surveys the possibilities and the insights that such works provide and contends that analysis from a cinematic, historic, cultural, and political perspective profoundly enriches our collective consciousness, as demonstrated in Gibson-Hudson's examination of black women in mainstream and African-American cinema. Her discussion shows how such works impart a unique cultural reality and affirm black womanhood in ways that conventional representations ignore.

Gibson-Hudson provides a black feminist theoretical perspective as well as an informative explanation of black women's contributions and viewpoints. The articles, books, and films she describes substantiate her claims for the inclusion of such subject matter. She cites works that counter negative, one-dimensional societal attitudes and stereotypes and create a new discourse of black female identity. These alternative images reaffirm womanhood and, through a liberating pedagogical approach, promote students and teachers to embrace difference daily.

With a complementary aim, in "Put Some Brothers on the Wall! Race, Representation, and Visual Empowerment of African-American Culture" Todd Boyd focuses on African-American men and outlines a complex survey of African-American cinema that engages questions of history, culture, politics, and the overall function of race and representation in American society. He discusses the submissive posture that most African-American cinema courses have adopted when dealing with Hollywood's racist past. To counter this, Boyd argues for a movement away from stereotypes to a new black esthetic that opposes the mainstream yet empowers African Americans' cultural production. Further, Boyd contends that one must have knowledge and experience of this culture to articulate the discourse rooted in its African-American context.

Culturally specific, politically daring, and imaginative cinema moves beyond previous boundaries by foregrounding its existence and structure without imitating dominant cinema. Boyd supplies examples from television, music, and film to explain and apply this esthetic. Discussions such as his mute cinema's function as a discursive institution using stereotypes and "rhetorically powerful visual images to reinforce the power hierarchies explicit in a racist society." The ultimate question concerns who wields the power to represent culturally specific perspectives through cinema. Creating one's own representations yields a vital tool for intellectual and political struggle.

Charles Ramírez Berg, who also considers strategies for investigating stereotypes and presenting ethnic film, teaches a course analyzing Latino stereotypes in film and television. He hopes that teachers will add stereotyping units to courses in areas ranging from the specific (Latin-American studies, ethnic studies, and Spanish) to the general (anthropology, sociology, and government, as well as literature and communication). In "Analyzing Latino Stereotypes: Hispanic Images/Counterimages in Hollywood Film and Television," Berg argues that any sensitive, well-prepared, open-minded teacher, regardless of race, class, or ethnicity, can and should address such concerns. To aid in doing this, he provides specific grading strategies that he uses in his course, ways to use the course as a writing workshop, and also an annotated description of the films he uses. Berg invites teachers to grapple with and learn about racism, prejudice, stereotyping, and ethnocentrism in all their perplexing, confounding, and gut-wrenching dimensions through a supportive environment.

Rounding out the analysis of ethnic images, in "Cultural Screens: Teaching Asian and Asian-American Images" I interrogate the stereotypes of Asian Americans in Hollywood films and contrast them to images presented in cinema from mainland China. Calling for an intellectual diversity that will complement my multicultural reach, I argue that progressive education begins when learners become receptive to radically different ways of storytelling. In the film units that I teach, this means first moving from a critique of Hollywood's largely negative representations of Asians and Asian Americans to a more productive consideration of independently produced Asian-American films. My class then embraces even more challenging fare, films made in the People's Republic of China, works that often present both a considerable challenge and an exciting alternative to everyday cinematic experiences. Employing less traditional narrative patterns and cinematic conventions, the Chinese filmmakers selected refused to be colonized by Hollywood, either thematically or stylistically.

Moving from familiar stereotypes to more enlightened, diverse representation, my students work intellectually and emotionally to grasp the esthetic, historical, and sociopolitical differences among contrasting modes of production—studio versus independent, individual versus state, and capitalist versus communist. In the process, the commonplace becomes new, and students learn to accommodate new concepts of filmic styles and culture, to incorporate new dimensions into their perspectives. Shifting focus to the unknown makes it possible to reconsider the known, to feel less sure of the "naturalness" of how we interpret and see, and thereby invites an ongoing reconsideration of all Hollywood images.

Also encouraging a thorough media critique, and finding oral histories a productive way to accomplish this, Serafina Bathrick and Louise Spence discuss their classes, which encompass both film and related media studies. Bathrick and Spence embrace intimacy and distance, safety and insecurity, fascination and criticism through close examination of print, film, and broadcast media. They use these to question the multiple, even contradictory, experiences we encounter daily. Because contemporary culture is media-saturated, Bathrick and Spence ask students to investigate their relationship to the images they consume. Through provocative pairings of slides, videos, and films, they explain how an idea of struggle enhances learning through individual differences, diversity, and even disagreements in a secure classroom environment. Within this community, they encourage and find strength in difference, especially by engaging students in oral history projects that personalize subject matter and engage the students in unexpected and unprecedented ways. Quoting several student examples, Bathrick and Spence illustrate the value and creative learning possible through this and similar assignments.

With a firm grasp of theoretical constructs and a desire to apply this knowledge to media production, three authors direct students to do more than critique the images already produced for their consumption. They guide students in creating their own film and video works. This intriguing next step, from analysis, to insight, to production, may either be a unit in a class or, as in the case with these three authors, the focus of the entire course.

In "Multicultural Learning through Documentaries: Focus on Latin-American Women," Julia Lesage chooses documentaries that center specifically on images of Latin-American women. She immediately foregrounds the financial constraints under which these documentary filmmakers work, acknowledging as well the urgency that many Latin-American intellectuals feel in dealing with acute social problems and political oppression. The documentaries she discusses enable examination of larger ethical and multicultural issues that involve ethnography, oral histories (as with Bathrick and Spence), and personal narratives. Lesage advocates the use of the creative resources from other cultures and subcultures to investigate what multicultural education might be. Like Boyd and Berg, she questions dominant media representations that reinforce oppressive institutions and ideology. Artistic expression by representatives from other cultures offers a rich alternative to common images, and Lesage explains how to facilitate students' engagement with such new offerings. She then describes and discusses many excellent alternative films and videos that reassess images of Latin-American women.

Also hoping that theory moves into practice, both Steve Carr and Patricia Zimmermann offer a theoretical overview of a production classroom and make specific recommendations for assignments and content analysis. Wanting to liberate students from institutionally based education, Carr examines film and video pedagogy in the hope of encouraging exploration and creativity that confronts racism, sexism, and heterosexism. In "Multiculturalism in the Production Classroom," Carr uses his classroom experience as a case in point, discussing the strengths and pitfalls of inviting works that critique conventional mainstream media. He explains his theoretical underpinnings and the struggle to escape representations that stereotype, to establish a learning community, and to devise projects that yield technically and ideologically challenging content. In documenting successes and failures, Carr grapples with the hierarchical class structure and the power dynamics that intrude into class interactions. He concludes by offering suggestions for improvement in such courses and applauding antidotes to mainstream media.

On the same theme, Patricia Zimmermann outlines her complementary approach in "Good-bye Hollywood: Introductory Filmmaking and Difference." Indicting institutional resistance to progressive ideology and overdetermination of dominant ideology as perpetuated through mainstream media, Zimmermann advocates making films within students' means and in their voices. Multiculturalism emerges as an offensive strategy to produce films out of students' own experiences, a welcome alternative to expensive and impersonal filmmaking, which is neither financially possible nor thematically relevant for the students. Charting a confident and pragmatic course between dreams of a pluralized paradise and regressive, mainstream narratives, Zimmermann encourages students to see the larger educational and social context of film production. Using her college's program as a case study, she forthrightly addresses the mindless privileging of Hollywood norms over opening the classroom to diverse models and personal expression. Zimmermann discusses feminist media theory and political documentaries, as well as text selection, as avenues to her goals. She acknowledges the pressure on students for industry success and jobs, as well as more authentic alternatives. Like Carr, she explains how to establish a functional production environment and describes the organization, film selection, and battles that have occurred over her film production classes.

It is easy to conclude, from the breadth and depth of these articles, that possibilities are limited more by time and space than by imagination. Perhaps this anthology will prompt secondary and post-secondary teachers to be creative in implementing some of the strategies enumerated herein. Integrating multicultural subject matter into courses, either as a tool in the service of various curricula or as a focus for study in its own right, enables individuals to emerge from their educational milieus better prepared for a rapidly changing world. As all the contributors prove, the empowerment of students through the integration of provocative subject matter can only enliven the classroom and improve the futures of everyone.

Acknowledgments

Diane Carson thanks Lynda Krenning and Beth Dotson, St. Louis Community College at Meramec, for their hours of quick and accurate secretarial work; as important are their positive, can-do attitudes and buoyant good spirits. The constructive atmosphere fostered by President Richard Black at St. Louis Community College at Meramec is crucial and deeply appreciated, especially his commitment to professional growth and increasing multicultural offerings. As always, the many discussions with colleagues helped immeasurably in working through difficult concepts, and valuable librarians sped research. Also important were the National Endowment for the Humanities 1993 Summer Institute on Chinese Culture and Civilization and the 1993 summer seminar devoted to infusing Asian studies into the curriculum, both cosponsored by the East-West Center and the University of Hawaii, Manoa. Elizabeth Buck, Roger T. Ames, and Steve Goldberg provided inspirational guidance in both the institute and the seminar and gave generously of their time and expertise. Without the insightful guidance of Lester Friedman, this anthology would never have seen print. Without his fine sense of humor, it would never have been so thoroughly enjoyable and rewarding a project. Finally, Willis Loy engaged in hours of discussions about every phase of this anthology and always discerned the difference between information and knowledge.

Lester D. Friedman gratefully acknowledges the assistance of the following people who made this book possible. As usual, Eva and Eugene Friedman endowed the project with their love and support. At the SUNY Health Science University, Sharon Osika-Michales provided expert secretarial support far beyond the required skills of typing and editing. President Gregory Eastwood, Provost-Dean Donald

Goodman, and Department Chair Margaret Braungart have created an atmosphere that encourages all types of scholarly activities, even those outside the common boundaries of medical research. At Syracuse University, the Art Media Studies Department also includes supportive colleagues, particularly Owen Shapiro and Dana Plays. The expert research skills of Denise Stevens of the E. S. Bird Library saved much time and considerable effort, and Delia Temes and Tony Bucci forced the consideration of multicultural issues and provided insights and suggestions. Ann Lowry at the University of Illinois Press first suggested the topic and worked hard to make this book a reality, while Mary Giles's expert editing made us all better writers. Carolyn Friedman, as always, provided a sane and reasonable voice. Diane Carson brought humor, common sense, and patience to the project and made working on this book a pleasure.

Shared Differences

1

Struggling for America's Soul:
A Search for Some Common Ground
in the Multicultural Debate

Lester D. Friedman

> The political challenge is to articulate universality in a way that
> is not a mere smoke screen for someone else's particularity. We
> must preserve the possibility of universal connection. That's the
> fundamental challenge. Let's dig deep enough within our heri-
> tage to make that connection to others.
> —Cornel West

The intense hostility among various factions housed within educational institutions represents just one example of a contemporary American society shredded by strident accusations and dogmatic defens-
es. We live in the midst of a rancorous cultural struggle, a vituperative
clash of ideologies that resonates from the highest levels of public
policy to the most intimate aspects of private life. We live, as James
Davison Hunter describes it, within "political and social hostility rooted in different systems of moral understanding. The end to which
these hostilities tend is the domination of one cultural and moral
ethos over all others. . . . They are not merely attitudes that can
change on a whim but basic commitments and beliefs that provide a
source of identity, purpose, and togetherness for the people who live
by them. It is for precisely this reason that political action rooted in
these principles and ideals tends to be so passionate" (42).

Surely Hunter's comments describe the debate over abortion as
well as over literary canons; they characterize equally well the con-
troversies over gays in the military and Murphy Brown's illegitimate
son. But before I'm accused of practicing sociology without a license,
let me hasten to invoke a fundamental belief that underlies this an-

thology: The teaching of texts, like the creation of those texts, occurs within a dynamic cultural context. Therefore, to characterize teaching as a politically neutral act ignores the power of teachers' positions and the privilege of their status; it also insults the intelligence of students. Words and images have consequences. After all, their intrinsic power to affect people's lives in real and concrete ways is one critical reason why they are analyzed and studied.

Although this book examines a broad range of approaches that successfully incorporate multicultural media into various academic disciplines, my primary focus is not on that topic. Instead, I will investigate some of the broader conflicts within multicultural education and offer a personal response to several of the more troubling issues confronting scholars and teachers. Anyone reading the literature surrounding the multicultural debate—whether in academic journals or daily newspapers—must be struck by the bitterness that pervades almost every discussion. Indeed, competing moral visions and antithetical versions of truth now polarize many segments of American society: "Whatever else may be involved, cultural conflict is about power—a struggle to achieve or maintain the power to define reality" (Hunter 52). To understand the gulf that separates various cultural positions, consider the discussion about cinema as simply a starting point. For those on the right of the multicultural debate, the products of the Hollywood film industry represent a sustained frontal attack on individual morals, family values, and national ethics; for those on the left, the same films reinforce sexist stereotypes, racist portraits, and middle-class conventions.

Put generally, the attitudes toward the issues that define the multicultural debate run the gamut of the political spectrum, usually envisioned within a series of Manichaean alternatives: civilization versus barbarism, oppression versus equality, authenticity versus appropriation, self-esteem versus self-abnegation, and assimilation versus identification—the list is virtually endless. Such binary thinking results in diametrically opposed visions of America, what it has been and where it is going. At its crudest, the debate pits self-righteous thought police who insist that multicultural sensitivities must structure our public and private worlds against equally sanctimonious sloganeers who view such a demand as anathema to the essential character of American culture. Nowhere has this battle been more bitter, more divisive, than on college campuses. There, constant fire fights between the fervent defenders of canonical barricades and the zealous eradicators of European culture leave precious little common ground for those caught in the acrid cross fire. But it is precisely this territory between the academic incarnations of "America—love it or leave it!" and "Amerika" that I wish to explore.

Such common ground must be adamantly claimed by those deeply committed to multicultural education but who firmly reject the call to annihilate the traditional curriculum. Our silence permits an unacceptable dichotomy to define the parameters of the argument. It forces a choice between two equally unacceptable positions: to support either puritanical conservatives such as Dinesh D'Souza or intolerant pedants such as Leonard Jeffries. This assertion of common ground rests on a series of premises shared by many people involved in multicultural education. I would not expect everyone who feels trapped between the rigid conservatism of the right and the revolutionary fervor of the left to embrace all of the following positions. (Academics are, after all, bred to disagree with each other.) Yet, I do hope that many who sense the dream of an inclusive multicultural education slipping slowly away, who refuse to get sidetracked by the straw man of political correctness, and who reject silence as an alternative to ideological bludgeoning can agree on a majority of the following propositions:

1. that knowledgeable, well-trained teachers can generate discussions about cultures other than their own, acknowledging that such information is mediated through their own social identities and that they are accountable for their words;
2. that demographic statistics should not force multicultural curricula to be taught only, or even primarily, to members of ethnic minorities;
3. that multiculturalism does not mean replacing one monocultural approach (e.g., Eurocentrism) with another monocultural methodology (e.g., Afrocentrism);
4. that Western culture, despite its myriad faults, remains a crucial influence on American political, intellectual, and social thought and, as such, should play an important role in classrooms;
5. that a core of American values and ideals exists, and although such values and ideals have not always been implemented, they cut across racial and cultural boundaries;
6. that multiple identities construct individuals as well as cultural groups; and
7. that white ethnic groups should be part of the multicultural spectrum.

I will explore each of these premises, realizing that each in itself might form the basis of an article.

> *Knowledgeable, well-trained teachers can generate discussions about cultures other than their own, acknowledging that such information is mediated through their own social identities and that they are accountable for their words.*

The legitimacy of teaching elements—history, literature, sociology, and anthropology—of a culture to which a teacher does not belong remains one of the most intricate and volatile questions of multiculturalism. Some argue that teachers can speak authentically only about their own ethnic identities and should refrain from giving classes, presenting lectures, or writing articles about other cultures. Instructors who do teach, lecture, and write about other cultures, the argument goes, put on intellectual blackface; they masquerade as part of a tradition they can never fully, or perhaps even adequately, understand. The problem about "speaking for others," as Linda Alcoff points out, arises from two sources: (1) the recognition that "systematic divergences in social location between speakers and those spoken for will have a significant effect on the content of what is being said"; and (2) "the practice of privileged persons speaking for or on behalf of less privileged persons has actually resulted (in many cases) in increasing or reinforcing the oppression of the group spoken for" ("Problem" 7). Yet another problem concerns the so-called turf issues, which hold that allowing others to speak for a group will significantly decrease the hiring of that group's members within the academy.

I take as a starting point that when one teaches about another culture classroom, information is mediated through the psychological, sociological, and ethnic identities that constitute each teacher's particular consciousness. The same sort of mediation occurs when we deal with elements of our own cultural beings. Everything we comment upon, therefore, we interpret from our own perspectives, assuming a point of view created by our relationship to society. Yet bearing this in mind, as well as the harm that speaking for others has done over the centuries, I still maintain that a demand for what Werner Sollors calls "biological insiderism" (13) will ultimately doom the spread of multiculturalism. Such a tactic imposes a separatist mentality that militates against the guiding spirit of this movement. Clearly, someone from one culture will not experience things as will someone from another. For example, a Christian teaching about the Holocaust will never have the same visceral response to that subject matter as a Jew whose parents perished in Nazi death camps. Yet to deny a well-trained Christian instructor the right to teach about the Holocaust violates one of the central goals of liberal arts education and one of the most important aims of multiculturalism—to move beyond personal experiences and grasp the realities of another person's existence.

This insular intellectual position ultimately results in even more dangerous consequences: It limits scholars and teachers to their own ethnic enclaves. Taking this argument into the field of literary studies, Reed Way Dasenbrock concludes that "such a view logically leads away from—not toward—the incorporation of non-Western literature in an American curriculum, as in this view the only literature most of us could know well enough to teach would be American literature" ("Teaching" 37). Equally dangerous, this position severely circumscribes teachers of color. If whites cannot teach about black history, does that mean that blacks cannot teach about whites?

Some multiculturalists try to avoid this quandary by explaining that minority group members, such as blacks, experience both the majority culture (white) and their own culture. Such a response, however, misses the point. On at least the intellectual level, a white person may be as deeply immersed in black culture as a black may be in white culture. Henry Louis Gates, Jr., speaks for a common ground position when he criticizes "ghettoized programs where students and members of the faculty sit around and argue about whether a white person can think a black thought" (quoted in Schlesinger, "Disuniting" 30). He further argues that we should not "remain hostage to the ideology of authenticity. . . . The distasteful truth will out: like it or not, all writers are 'cultural impersonators'" (Gates 1:29).

Granting cross-cultural presentations, what special preparations does it take to teach materials that fall outside one's own culture? In his essay "The New Cultural Politics of Difference," Cornel West searches for "intellectual and political freedom fighters" who "avoid ethnic chauvinism and faceless universalism" (46). To that end, he issues a call to arms: "The time has come for critics and artists of the new cultural politics of difference to cast their nets widely, flex their muscles broadly, and thereby refuse to limit their visions, analyses, and praxis to their particular terrains. The aim is to dare to recast, redefine, and revise the very notions of 'modernity,' 'mainstream,' 'margins,' 'difference,' 'otherness'" (46). To do this, teachers should express themselves freely without the inhibition of an enforced party line. Among the more damaging aspects of the multicultural debate remains the linguistic quibbling that passes for political engagement. As Barbara Ehrenreich warns, we should not "mistake verbal purification for genuine social reform" (84).

Clearly, teachers who undertake the daunting task of presenting cultures other than their own must build an appropriate knowledge base, always remembering that such information arrives from the outside in. The teacher must also present a broad approach to a particular cultural text, revealing, where appropriate, both the blemishes and virtues of a given multicultural situation. My impulse, therefore, would be to discourage the spread of so-called therapeutic courses, which draw their rationale from the need for student "self-esteem." Such an approach rests on a layer of very thin ice and places the teacher in perpetual danger, from the fear of including anything negative, to the blunting of critical abilities, to the charge of lying.

In the final analysis, teachers of multiculturalism must rely on the characteristics and abilities that underlie the most effective teaching in any field: reading the best sources available, preparing as well as possible, understanding the scope and focus of the subject matter, maintaining interest in the field, communicating with enthusiasm, and keeping current with the latest research and interpretations.

Demographic statistics should not force multicultural curricula to be taught only, or even primarily, to members of ethnic minorities.

Discussions about the need for multiculturalism within various school settings, from elementary through university programs, often begin with a statement about demographic imperatives, claiming that educational programs must be relevant to the increasingly large number of nonwhites who comprise current and future student populations. Certainly, the majority of new immigrants to the United States come from non-European countries. U.S. Bureau of the Census figures indicate that between 1981 and 1989, 89 percent of America's legal immigrants came from non-European nations (including 47 percent from Asia and 38 percent from Latin America), mostly from the Philippines, Korea, China, Mexico and Cuba. By the year 2000, according to a report issued by the Commission on Minority Participation in Education and American Life, one-third of the population will be nonwhite, a basic fact that will profoundly influence all our lives. Take, for example, the world of business. As the Bureau of Labor Statistics has estimated, by the year 2000, from 26 to 30 percent (some twenty-two million people) of the American work force will be comprised of persons who are not white (*Syracuse Herald American,* August 4, 1991, C1).

Such forecasts spur business leaders to consider how they might effectively manage an increasingly diverse cadre of workers, leading them to hire diversity consultants, institute sensitivity training sessions, and establish cultural differences seminars. Most CEOs readily admit that the main motivation to spend millions on such consultants and programs rarely springs from civic, moral, or ideological motives; rather, such initiatives offer the most productive method of maintaining corporate competitiveness within the realities of a rapidly changing work force.

Equally affected by a changing America will be the country's educational system, for schools inevitably react to society. In a 1989 article exploring the ramifications of the demographic statistics cited earlier, Pallas, Natriello, and McDill concluded that by the year 2020 whites will make up only 54.5 percent of the nation's students (in 1982 the number was 73 percent); in public schools in the twenty-five largest American cities, half (or more) of the students will be nonwhite (quoted in Banks 30n9). A September 1991 study conducted by the College Board and Western Interstate Commission for Higher Education predicted that by 1995 one-third of American public schools would be comprised of minorities: 13.7 million, or 34 percent of enrollment.

Such dramatic statistics will obviously reverberate within higher education, particularly as the make-up of the traditional college-age population changes drastically. By the year 2000, to take the New York State Education Department's example, almost 30 percent of this eighteen-to-twenty-four age group will be nonwhite. The number of Hispanics will increase from 8 percent to 11 percent of the population, blacks from 14 percent to 15 percent, and other races from 3 percent to 4 percent. By the year 2050, the nonwhite segment of American society between eighteen and twenty-four will jump to almost 45 percent. By contrast, in 1950 only 12 percent was not white— a leap of 33 percent. Such a demographic revolution will substantially alter not only who attends college but also what is taught and who teaches it.

Yet a closer look at this information yields some startling counterpoints to the cry for multiculturalism based mainly on demographic statistics. Even given the sweeping changes that such figures portend, America will clearly remain predominately white. According to the U.S. Census Bureau, in 1992, 83.8 percent of the population was white, 12.6 percent black, and 3.6 percent "other." The bureau's projection is that by 2025 about 79 percent of the population will be white, 14.6 percent black, and 6.5 percent other.

Where are the dramatic changes occurring? To few people's surprise, urban areas will be most affected by population shifts in the coming years, and, given this fact, one must admit the persuasiveness of Louis Menand's position: "What is happening is not demographic change but demographic skewing" (381). Digging deeper, he provides some statistics of his own, noting that almost 80 percent of public school students are white. But, he continues, in New York City, Houston, Dallas, Baltimore, San Francisco, Cleveland, and Memphis, two-thirds are nonwhite; in Los Angeles, Chicago, Philadelphia, Detroit, San Antonio, El Paso, New Orleans, and Washington, D.C., three-fourths are not white. "This skewing is a social disease no curricular reform is likely to cure," argues Menand, "despite the apparent belief of educators that a more integrated reading list will lead to a more just society" (381).

Whether one agrees with Menand's conclusions or not, the fact remains that demographic imperatives form an unstable foundation upon which to build a case for multicultural classes. For better or worse, public schools have never been particularly responsive to the changing colors, religions, and customs of students. In fact, immigrant parents traditionally praised such schools for "socializing" (some would say indoctrinating) them and their children into American society. By compelling newcomers, however systematically painful, to learn a common language, to abide by generally accepted customs, and to internalize primary values, the public school system forced them to adopt the ways of their new country, to fit in with those already here. Children might have spoken Yiddish or Chinese or Spanish at home, but at school they spoke English, learned about George Washington, and studied Mark Twain. Such classes demonstrated little concern for those who struggled with the new language or had little context for a story about the first president and a cherry tree. They never dwelt on the negative side of American history, for example, how many of the Founding Fathers owned slaves or what this land was like before Columbus "discovered" it. Perhaps not surprisingly, the schools' biggest supporters remained the immigrant parents who sent their children to learn one thing and learn it well: how to become American.

But the need for multiculturalism in schools goes far beyond knee-jerk responses to shifts in demographic patterns. If diversity programs are admitted only under the pressure of student numbers, then such classes can be eliminated via the same reasoning. Rather, I would strenuously argue that it is as important for overwhelmingly white schools to incorporate multicultural classes as it is for schools in more integrated areas. Thus, students who interact with relatively few racial or ethnic groups will gain a broad range of information about the cultures of people they might never encounter otherwise. The responsibility of teachers to provide their students with experiences about a variety of cultures may, at times, be more important than having them read works by someone of their own culture. As the educator James Banks puts it:

> All students, regardless of their race, ethnicity or social class, should study about the cogent and complex roles of ethnicity and ethnic conflict in American society and culture. Most Americans are socialized within ethnic or cultural enclaves and are ethnically illiterate. Within their communities, people learn primarily about their own culture and assume that their life-styles are the legitimate ones and that other cultures are invalid, strange, and different. The schools should help students to break out of their cultural enclaves and to broaden their cultural perspectives. Students need to learn that there are cultural and ethnic alternatives within our society that they can freely embrace. (12)

To put it another way, if whites remain unexposed to many different facets of black culture in America—from literature, to sociology, to history, to anthropology, to painting, and to medicine—we abandon the field to simplistic media portraits and bigoted stereotypes. Why limit white students' perceptions of black people to sit-coms, gangster films, or movies of the week, particularly when they might gain valuable insights from the works of Alice Walker or Toni Morrison? Conversely, I feel equally strongly about the fact that white authors, even dead European males, have much of importance to offer all readers. Why, therefore, would we deprive black students of the wisdom of John Milton or William Shakespeare? Again, we need to search for some common ground, a curriculum that provides necessary space for both Morrison and Milton.

Multiculturalism does not mean replacing one monocultural approach (e.g., Eurocentrism) with another monolithic methodology (e.g., Afrocentrism).
One group of educators strongly supports what I would label a separatist approach to multicultural education. Such thinkers define every person by his or her racial, cultural, or ethnic group and see little to be gained by interactions among groups. For them, the dream of integration, of diverse groups working together to form a better nation, has turned into a nightmare of racism, discrimination, and rejection. For example, separatists would support black student unions and organizations that determine membership only by skin color or ethnic group. In essence, they believe that racial bigotry is

inherent and basically irremediable. They teach members of their group to take pride in their heritage, in their difference, and as Molefi Kete Asante asserts, to resist the bewitching siren call for brotherhood and racial harmony: "Do not be captured by a sense of universality given to you by the Eurocentric viewpoint; such a viewpoint is contradictory to your own ultimate reality" (as quoted in Ravitch, "Diversity" 342).

Often these separatist attacks, as Asante's quote indicates, characterize traditional classes as Eurocentric smoke screens that see the world exclusively from a white perspective and ignore alternative interpretations of events. For example, history classes that celebrate the democratic ideals of the American Constitution and Bill of Rights often disregard the unpleasant fact that both documents exclude women and blacks. Much of the time in literature classes is given to analyzing American and European writers, oblivious to the power of Latin-American, Middle-Eastern, and African authors. Medical schools ignore the insights of Native-American or Asian healers and rely instead on ways of thinking validated by Western tradition.

The most vocal separatists often insist that we replace Eurocentrism with Afrocentrism. Exchanging points of view with Diane Ravitch, assistant U.S. Secretary of Education, Asante, one of the leading proponents of Afrocentrism, clearly articulates his approach to education (*American Scholar* 1991). Beginning by paralleling American education with the South African regime, he argues that both supported "an educational kingdom built to accompany the era of white supremacy" (268). He then outlines the key points in his program: (1) "more fundamental than eliminating racial segregation has to be the removal of all racist thinking, assumptions, symbols, and materials in the curriculum" (269); (2) "the idea of 'mainstream America' is nothing more than an additional myth meant to maintain Eurocentric hegemony. . . . mainstream is a code word for white" (268–69); and (3) "we do not seek segments or modules in the classroom but rather the inclusion of African American studies in every segment and in every module" (270). Initially, most educators would disagree with Asante's simplistic equation of American and South African culture, pointing out that clear differences exist between a regime that murders and jails dissenters with one that often awards them book contracts and professorships. But even more problems appear when his three major points are examined in depth.

First, after overt examples of violence and discrimination, vast disagreement exists among various definitions of racism, enough that what might be racist to some would be quite acceptable to other reasonable people within academia. (A good example would be the debates about welfare and affirmative action.) Second, what constitutes "mainstream" American thought remains a hotly contested issue in every debate from abortion to advertising to movie ratings. Asante's claim that the concept is a "code word" for white, however, is true in a great variety of situations, although *white* and *Eurocentric* are not necessarily synonymous. Yet because whites remain the vast majority of the population in the United States, it stands to reason that their views (which I see as far less monolithic than Asante) constitute a mainstream position. After all, commentators often label positions as mainstream precisely because a majority of American citizens holds them.

Such a common-sense admission, however, doesn't mean that mainstream views are necessarily moral, correct, or workable. It doesn't mean that everyone who disagrees with them must stop demonstrating, criticizing, or trying to change the views of others. It simply means that a seeming majority of people hold that particular belief in common. Even more important, Asante fails to consider that mainstream views shift constantly and must always be taken within the context of the issue under discussion. Finally, his demand that African-American studies permeate the curriculum seems both oversimplified and ethnocentric. First, scholars estimate that, if the next U.S. Census adds a box labeled "multiracial," at least "seventy-five to more than ninety percent of the people who now check the Black box could check multiracial because of their mixed heritage" (Wright 47). So incorporating a definitive African-American perspective risks setting up one point of view within that community as official and all others as tangential. But suppose we could arrive at an acceptable perspective. How would it function in hard science classes, for example, in a chemistry course? Equally important, would not such a perspective be as oppressive to people who are not African American, including many people of color, as Asante claims the Eurocentric approach is to blacks?

Yet even those who reject these assumptions must admit that most traditional history, social science, and humanities classes obliterated African Americans, making them victims of widespread curricular neglect and distortion. In history courses, as many educators have pointed out, little is taught about blacks before the slave trade, and only a few exemplary individuals (Frederick Douglass, Martin Luther King, Jr.) make it into American classrooms. Even in the literature classes that deal with modern American writers, students read relatively few black authors. Magazine journalism courses rarely cover black periodicals or newspapers. Even film classes pay little attention to the history of black independent films and, with the exception of a Spike Lee picture now and then, rarely include works by black writers and directors.

But a curriculum that fundamentally excludes blacks should not be replaced with one that reifies them. To posit Eurocentrism or Afrocentrism as the only possible alternative blunts the entire thrust of multiculturalism. First, as Dasenbrock argues, "this way of framing the issues ignores the degree of acculturation already undergone by minorities in this country. Most African Americans are no more culturally African than I am culturally German" ("West" 208–9). No teacher of good conscience could possibly deny that including a black point of view within a curriculum provides students with a long-overdue and sorely needed corrective that acknowledges the uniqueness of African-American culture and explores its construction by using predominately black voices. Yet as Ronald Walters, a political scientist, claims, "Afrocentrism should be one aspect of a multicultural curriculum. . . . [but it] can't be entirely Afrocentric. It needs to be multicultural, meaning that it must deal with some number of the important events, personalities, and ideas of the major racial and ethnic minorities in this country" (27).

Even Asante has softened his position, agreeing with more moderate claims that "there is space for Eurocentrism in a multicultural enterprise so long as it does not parade as universal. No one wants to banish the Eurocentric view" (268). Such a position bodes well for the future of multiculturalism, because it understands that ethnic groups within America must always be seen in relation to each other. The relationship may incorporate conflict or cooperation, antagonism or harmony, but it forces people to speak with and learn about each other—and, maybe, to respect each other. It brings people closer to common ground.

Western culture, despite its myriad faults, remains a crucial influence on American political, intellectual, and social thought and, as such, should play an important role in classrooms.

In this section, I will assert the importance of Western culture in American society, although I am mindful that the role European, or for that matter African or Asian, culture occupies in a particular class will fluctuate according to such determinants as subject matter, time, teacher knowledge, student interest, classroom goals, and other variables.

The need to defend Western culture would, only a few short years ago, have seemed quite unnecessary. Now, however, those who reject this tradition have convinced many educators that texts derived from European society remain so permeated with racism, sexism, and a colonialist mentality that they constitute only negative examples. As such, they offer little of value to students, particularly minority students. For example, a passionate advocate of multiculturalism, Wahneema Lubiano, who is a sophisticated scholar and understands the inherent problems of creating simple polarities like "the West" and "non-West," argues that "if 'the West' establishes exactly what 'America' is to mean, and if 'America' established the direction of much of the world's resources, then the work of multiculturalism that breaks up the hold 'the West' has on our respective imaginations is part of the work of changing the world" (19). Similarly, Henry Giroux warns educators against summarily dismissing "a curriculum steeped in Western tradition outright," then calls for a "postcolonial discourse [that] rewrites the relationship between the margin and the center by deconstructing the colonialist and imperialist ideologies that structure Western knowledge, texts, and social practices" (*Border Crossings* 236–37).

For both Lubiano and Giroux, exploding Western texts to reveal inherent evils remains an important concern within the multicultural agenda. They would surely agree with Rousseau, ironically an author whose writing figures heavily in the European canon: "The science, letters and arts . . . cover with garlands of flowers the iron chains that bind them, stifle in them the feelings of that original liberty for which they seemed to have been born, make them love their slavery, and turn them into what is called civilized people" (quoted in Trey Ellis, B2).

Yet many who seek a common ground within the conceptualizations of multiculturalism view Western culture as elemental, a position that the history of American culture supports. Anyone even faintly aware of the evolution of America must admit the obvious: Our fundamental ideals were framed by a group of men, mainly descended from British ancestors, who drew predominately upon European ideas to formulate principles and policies. As the historian Kenneth T. Jackson observes, "The dominant American culture might have been German or French or Chinese or Algonquin or African, but for various historical reasons the English language and British political and legal traditions prevailed" (39).

Because the primary language of most Americans is English, British society provides an immediate point of reference through which Western culture spills over into the realms of politics, business, music, literature, and even fashion. Yet, I fully agree with Michael Berube, who observes, "It's Tolson [author of the poem 'Harlem Gallery'] who reminds me now that the canon revisions of the past fifteen years have not attacked Western culture; they have, above all, *enriched* our sense of Western culture. But precisely because we've done so much to recover some of the West's suppressed heterogeneities, we cannot stand mutely by while the West is defended by a phalanx of conservative journalists and political hacks who apparently only read one another" (236). Berube strikes precisely the right note for those who see multiculturalism as neither the destruction of civilization by the barbarians nor a holy war to annihilate all traces of oppressive Western culture from schools and life in general.

Perhaps the most fascinating defense of Western culture comes from Dasenbrock, who shows how European ideals, as is the case with all culture, were created by ideas imported from other cultures. Constructing the notion of culture as something learned, something "we share with and take from others" ("West" 202), Dasenbrock demonstrates how some of the main elements of what we characterize as Western culture, including Christianity, science, and technology, are not exclusively Western. Building upon this model of hybridization and syncretism, he asks readers to consider that "a historical perspective shows how culture was itself formed at some earlier point out of a multicultural context" ("West" 206).

To develop Dasenbrock's ideas even further, Western culture is far from a monolithic entity, as even many extremists point out. In an attempt to demonize it, critics lump together a group of countries that have been at each other's throats since ancient days. Such attacks also ignore the diversity of intellectual positions that come from Europe, a multifarious series of works that stretches from Machiavelli to Marx, from Luther to Sartre, from Rousseau to Nietzsche, from Lévi-Strauss to Chekhov. Certainly, many of the great European thinkers spent their careers attacking the very culture they inhabited. Even Gayatri Chakravorty Spivak, a scholar clearly in the more radical wing of the multicultural movement, warns against "homogenizing" the West to gain rhetorical advantages (quoted in Lubiano, 14).

The attack on Western cultural ideas springs from the idea that courses that incorporate works from such a position of power are simply part of the imperialistic philosophy that informs Western political activities. In addition, some multiculturalists posit the wholesale elimination of Western values as a necessary, although admittedly radical, corrective to years of monocultural indoctrination. Yet using such arguments to "denigrate and reject the whole heritage of Western civilization," according to C. Vann Woodward, ironically ignores that it is "this common culture to which they owed their very right to protest" (33).

Striking a similar vein, Arthur Schlesinger, Jr., in a dissenting opinion of the Report of the New York State Social Studies Review and Development Committee (June 1991), calls attention to the origin of our democratic ideals, citing Europe as the "unique" source of these ideals and claiming this is precisely why students need to be acquainted with the "western history and tradition that created our democratic ideals" ("Dissenting" 47). Schlesinger goes on to decry the "Europhobia" that underlies so many attacks on the traditional curriculum:

> Certainly Europe, like every other culture, has committed its share of crimes. But, unlike most cultures, it has also generated ideals that have opposed and exposed those crimes. This report, however, plays up the crimes and plays down the ideals. Thus, when it talks about European colonization of Africa and India, it deplores "the eradication of many varieties of traditional culture and knowledge." Like infanticide? slavery? polygamy? subjection of women? suttee? veil-wearing? foot-binding? clitorectomies? Nothing is said about the influence of European ideas of democracy, human rights, self-government, rule of law. Even Karl Marx was fairer to European colonization than that. (47)

According to Schlesinger and others, we must neither downplay nor ignore the sins of the Western world. Yet the crimes of Western culture are no less or greater than those of Africa, Asia, or the Middle East. Many, however, argue that a critical difference exists: Western traditions, unlike those in many other parts of the world, spawned movements to fight the injustices of racism, sexism, and a host of other social ills. Schlesinger argues that "whatever the particular crimes of Europe, that continent is also the source—the *unique* source—of those liberating ideas of individual liberty, political democracy, the rule of law, human rights, and cultural freedom that constitute our most precious legacy and to which the world today aspires. . . . The Western commitment to human rights has unquestionably been intermittent and imperfect. Yet the ideal remains—and movement toward it has been real, if sporadic" ("Disuniting" 32). Put even more strongly, as does John M. Ellis, "In seeking an end to racism and sexism, we automatically ally ourselves with certain *Western* values" (B2).

A core of American values and ideals exists, and although such values and ideals have not always been implemented, they cut across racial and cultural boundaries.

Scholars who reject the European heritage of American culture often claim that, as it is now constructed, American culture has little relevance to one's ethnic identity. Indeed, some multiculturalists—and some white supremacists—maintain that the idea of an American national identity that incorporates immigrants from almost every country in the world represents a cruel hoax perpetrated on desperate people. Some scholars view such platitudes as savage delusions. So, for example, Lubiano characterizes them as the "triumph of mythic imagination over material reality—[it] ignores the relation of these ideas to the continual marginalization of many people, many groups, many knowledges" (11). Similarly, Asante asserts that "there is no common American culture as is claimed by defenders of the status quo. There is a hegemonic culture to be sure, pushed as if it were a common culture" (269).

If no common cultural elements exist, if what historically passed as shared American values really only included and perpetuated white European perspectives, then multicultural diversity dooms any sharing of American ideals or values. Pushed one step further this line of reasoning means that even those nonwhite Europeans who were born here, or whose parents lived here for decades, have more in common with their ancestors than with their next-door neighbors who belong to another ethnic group. Conversely, if they do identify more with their neighbors, then long-time American citizens betray their cultural legacy. In Schlesinger's words, this position equates assimilation with "Angloconformity" ("Dissenting" 46).

Such claims often result in one of the most common charges against multicultural educators: that by stressing ethnic and racial ancestry they inevitably balkanize American culture. The sociologist Nathan Glazer worries about the

> hypostatization of race, ethnic group, culture, people.... When we speak of "multiculturalism," we should be aware that there are no fully distinct cultures in the United States, aside from American culture. We should not make of something labile, changeable, flexible and viable—the cultures people bring with them to the United States or develop as variants of our common American culture— something hard and definite and unchanging, something that establishes itself as a distinct and permanent element in American society and polity. That is not the way our society works, or should work. (35–36)

Glazer's remarks seem quite tempered, particularly when compared with others who engage the issue of divisiveness by calling multicultural educators a variety of epithets (new segregationists, ideologies of authenticity, or sensitivity fascists) and leveling charges against them (creators of a modern Tower of Babel, a New Age caste system, and cultural reservations).

The charge of divisiveness, at least up to a point, seems to be a classic red herring. After all, American society has always been characterized by a great deal of separation among ethnic groups. No college administrator ever told Jews that their Hillel organizations must admit Gentiles or Catholics that they should open Newman Clubs to Protestants. Ethnic clubs for almost every immigrant group still form part of the social life of America's towns and larger cities. In relatively benign instances like these, ethnic enclaves always subdivided American society. Of course, prejudice and bigotry divided (and still divide) America in far less benign ways, as when Jim Crow laws enforced racial segregation until the civil rights protests of the 1960s.

Still, whatever their ethnic identities, most people celebrated the Fourth of July and Thanksgiving as enthusiastically as they did any religious or ethnic holiday. They understood that for all their pride in their ethnic heritage, they were now Americans, a title that conferred upon them a series of rights and responsibilities. Furthermore, many ethnic groups made accommodations to what seemed to be a consensus of values that informed American life, including learning a new language, modifying their religious beliefs, and attaining educational objectives. Although one could obviously agree with Horace Kallen's observation that we "cannot change our grandfathers" (quoted in Chametzky, 7), the prevailing notion was that cultural identities were fluid and, for the most part, could be adjusted to the circumstances found in the United States.

Such a flexible position, as noted in Glazer's quotation, seems absent in modern identity politics, where race often seems to be the sole determinate of culture. So, for example, Ravitch attacks the "your ancestor oppressed my ancestor" school of thought, maintaining that this approach "encourages a sense of rage and victimization in those who are the presumed descendants of victims and a sense of resentment in those who are the presumed descendants of oppressors" ("Diversity" 20). A sense of shared American values thus crumbles in the face of ancient animosities, creating what Schlesinger calls "a nation of groups, differentiated in their ancestries, inviolable in their diverse identities" ("Disuniting" 14).

An approach that only stresses the differences among people of various ethnic origins can certainly ferment hatred that boils over into violent conflict. The problems in Yugoslavia, Northern Ireland, the Middle East, and the new republics carved out of the Soviet Union attest to how dangerous such attitudes may become. In the dire words of John Ellis, "Anyone who thinks . . . the celebration of ethnicity must lead to egalitarianism is sadly mistaken: the lesson of history is that they are more likely to unleash dangerous forces of the extreme right" (B2). On a less dramatic level, the tactic of defining people solely by race and then encouraging them to define themselves only by values outside American culture clearly alienates huge numbers of people from the very culture that surrounds them.

But if a common American culture exists, what are its hallmarks, its ideals? In general, I would agree with Kenneth T. Jackson when he warns that "it is politically and intellectually unwise for us to attack the traditions, customs, and values which attracted immigrants to these shores in the first place" (39). Among these traditions and values, although certainly not fully realized, must be included democracy, regard for individual rights, freedom to practice the religion of one's choice, and justice under the law. Certainly, critics can cite chapter and verse to point out how all these ideals have been subverted from the formation of the United States until the present. The treatment of Native Americans as simply an impediment to manifest destiny surely violated all four of these ideals, as did the incarceration of Japanese-American citizens following the bombing of Pearl Harbor, and the Rodney King trial provided a new low in American legal history. But the idea of America remains fundamentally, inextricably, bound up with these ideals, no matter how tarnished they might become in the practice of everyday existence. The freedom to teach multiculturalism results from these common principles, as does the right to debate it so fiercely. Multicultural concerns need not be taught in opposition to these common principles. As Ronald Walters aptly puts it, "We need to realize that in each of the ethnic and racial experiences there are core values, and they have to be linked to the larger experience and to our common values" (21–27).

Schlesinger, in his dissent to the Sobol report, claims that the central theme of American history is "to move the American experiment from exclusion to participation" (53). Although such a theme both tempts and flatters Americans, it seems far too self-congratulatory for a nation still lacerated by bigotry and racism. For me, a more accurate theme would place multicultural issues at the heart of the American experience but would cast them slightly differently: the delicate balance between individual rights and group demands. I would certainly perceive such a balance in ethnic terms, but I recognize that such an interpretation would be only one of many possibilities. After all, it might behoove even those who are deeply committed to multicultural education to remember that in survey after survey millions of citizens, when asked to state their ethnic affiliation, simply write in "American." Again, I think that Walters strikes a common-ground position when he argues that "all students, regardless of their race or ethnicity, need a certain common education about the history of America and the world. But it is also true that students from different backgrounds may be especially interested in pursuing in more depth the history of their own cultural identity" (21–27).

Such a position strikes me as eminently sensible, one that combines the individual demands of multicultural education with the communal needs for a collective knowledge base. "Our project," observes Alice Kessler-Harris, a historian, "can be neither a false universalism, nor the reification of pieces of the culture at the expense of the whole. Rather, we need to explore how people become part of, not separate from, that unified whole called America" (311). In this way, multiculturalism can provide students with a sense of their own unique identities while at the same time connecting them to a shared sense of traditions, ideals, and values:

> Far from undermining the search for unity, identity, and purpose, the multicultural enterprise has the potential to strengthen it. It provides a way of seeing relationally. . . . If it redefines identity from a fixed category to a search for a democratic culture, if it refuses to acknowledge a stable meaning or precise unchanging definition of America, multiculturalism nevertheless opens the possibility of conceiving democratic culture as a process in whose transformation we are all invited to participate. (Kessler-Harris 311)

Such conceptions of multiculturalism demand that a broad-based notion of inclusion inform our efforts, change the parameters of the debate, and explore some common ground; these efforts underscore the belief that we can do justice both to the ethnic multiplicity and the cultural unity of American society.

Multiple identities construct individuals as well as cultural groups.
Along with considering the notion of common American ideals, multicultural educators must recognize that each individual is shaped by many factors that define his or her response to any particular situation. Even more to the point, more than one set of cultural fac-

tors constructs each individual, so the notion of a stable identity must be challenged constantly. One might honestly question the possibility of separating "pure" ethnic strands in American culture, especially given the rate of intermarriages between members from different ethnic groups and races. In a similar fashion, the historian Barbara Epstein theorizes that identity politics remains problematic because the concept of identity remains so fragile. She notes that everyone occupies various categories at once, and emphasizing difference, although it can provide a sense of security, "can also get in the way of efforts to find common ground for action. . . . I am arguing that a politics that is organized around defining identities based on race, gender, or sexuality forces people's experience into categories that are too narrow and makes it difficult to speak to one another across the boundaries of these identities—let alone create the coalitions needed to build a movement for progressive change" (153–54).

Directly related to this issue of self-definition is one of group definition: "On what basis can we justify a decision to demarcate groups and define membership in one way rather than another" (Alcoff, "Others" 8)? History reminds us that many victims were dragged off to the Third Reich's gas chambers claiming each step of the way that they were good German Protestants. Unfortunately for them, being a German Protestant for two generations was not sufficient for the Nazis, who adhered to a far more stringent definition of ethnic purity and group definition. Our American version of racial purity, the so-called one-drop rule, defined as black anyone with a single drop of "black blood," assuring that "each race had its own blood type which correlated with physical appearance and social behavior" (Wright 48).

Equally important, a member of a particular group may have a weak (or nonexistent) commitment to the beliefs and values that the majority of the group's members espouse. Certainly this remains true with religious affiliations. One can be Jewish or Catholic and have little formal or informal attachment to the belief system espoused by these religions' leaders. From the perspective of class consciousness, a black professional making $100,000 a year may have more in common with his or her white neighbors, may share more of their same values and beliefs, than that person does with poorer blacks in another part of the city. In addition, the issue of gender may downplay that of race. A Hispanic female advertising executive, for example, may relate more to her Anglo female co-workers than to a Hispanic man with a different status. Ethnic culture, then, is one element within a person's overall identity. As such, it may be more or less important than other components such as gender, physical attributes, socioeconomic class, status, or age. Lubiano puts this rather nicely when she observes that, within intersections, multiculturalism "helps us to think about and predict where identities converge and diverge, about how the instability of identity is played out as well as where strategic activation of identity does specific intellectual, cultural, and/or political work" (16). Such a use of multicultural perspectives manages to find the "interstices between cultures as well as their overlap" (14) and gives teachers a powerful tool for understanding and teaching their students.

As individuals incorporate many traits that combine to form an identity, so, too, cultural groups incorporate many different components within their formation of a group identity. Glazer aptly warns that "the groups we refer to when we speak of 'multiculturalism' are not monolithic and unchanging realities. Each is made up of different classes with different interests, each has been marked by differences created by the time of arrival of different waves under different circumstances, each has undergone various degrees of assimilation, acculturation, intermarriage, and each carries different attitudes to its past" (35). Being part of a cultural group does not automatically endow one with the right to speak for all its members. As Scott argues, too often "personal testimony of oppression replaces analysis and explanation and comes to stand for the experience of the group. The fact of belonging to an identity group is taken as authority enough for one's speech; the direct experience of a group or culture—that is membership in it—becomes the only test of true knowledge" (220). Such a position excludes anyone outside the group and perhaps even those within the group who have a different conception of reality. This mantle of authenticity denies not only the dynamic nature of cultural experiences but also the breadth of experiences within any one group. Thus, multicultural scholars need to explore various components within cultures as well as among cultures, understanding that even so-called authentic voices present only partial and highly subjective perspectives.

White ethnic groups should be part of the multicultural spectrum.

"What happened to the WASP?" asks Dasenbrock, musing that "in one generation the crucial distinctions between Protestant and Catholic, between Protestant and Jew, between Anglo-Saxons and other European ethnic groups have ceased to matter: all of these groups are seen as part of a homogeneous 'Eurocentric' tradition" ("West" 203). Certainly, these ethnic enclaves within so-called white groups did not disappear magically overnight. Similarly, James Banks, an early and prolific writer about the issues of multicultural education, argues the necessity of challenging the assumption that ethnic studies deals only with people of color: "To conceptualize ethnic studies exclusively as the study of people of color is inconsistent with how sociologists define ethnicity. Conceptualizing ethnic studies as the study of ethnic groups of color also promotes a kind of *we-they* attitude among many white students and teachers. Many students think that ethnic studies is the study of *them,* whereas American studies is the study of *us.* Many educators believe that ethnic studies has no place within an all-white classroom" (11–12). Furthermore, the designation of all people via racial groups (most commonly African Americans, Asian Americans, Native Americans, Hispanic Americans, and European Americans) simply replaces the large American melting pot with five separate melting pots that ignore the multitude of differences within vast categories.

To examine this issue of white ethnicity in a bit more detail, I will focus on the placement of American Jews in the spectrum of multicultural studies because I bring a personal perspective to this discussion. Also, I will shift to a fictional construct, a television program, to demonstrate how multicultural media can help illuminate contemporary ethnic dilemmas. In an episode of "Northern Exposure" that aired on November 28, 1992, the Native Americans of idyllic Cicily, Alaska, celebrate Thanksgiving by throwing tomatoes at the town's white residents. Because Cicily represents a multicultural utopia, the tomato hurling is done and accepted with good-spirited comradery, but the gesture explicitly protests the exploitation of Native Americans at the hands of Puritans and their descendants. Yet when Dr. Joel Fleischman, the Jewish physician sentenced to pay off his medical school loan by practicing in Cicily, finds himself the target of a tossed tomato, he protests, explaining to his secretary: "Ed made a very serious mistake. He got the wrong guy, an innocent bystander. I'm not white. I may look white, but I am not. I am Jewish, ok, Jewish. A fellow person of color. A victim of oppression. . . . In Eastern Europe, in the Pale of Settlement, Jews were herded into squalid villages. We were ostracized, segregated. And the Cossacks would ride through regularly raping, pillaging, and murdering. So you see Marilyn, I may be a lot of things, but I am not white, definitely not white." Clearly, Fleischman deeply feels his direct connection with the people of color, even though they view him simply as another white man. In fact, he is a white male with distinct privileges because his medical degree confers immediate prestige and status upon him.

The fictional Joel Fleischman's situation coincides quite nicely with the real-life status of Jews on American campuses. On the Champaign-Urbana campus of the University of Illinois, for example, Jewish students were specifically voted out of a student coalition on culture and color during April of 1992. Around the same time, the University of Washington at Seattle decided not to allow courses related to Judaism or Jewish history to fulfill an ethnic studies requirement. Ironically, these decisions occurred as the Anti-Defamation League of B'nai B'rith reported that the number of anti-Jewish incidents had risen to a thirteen-year high, that Jews were by far the most targeted religious group for hate crimes, and that anti-Semitic incidents on college campuses had increased by 72 percent over the preceding three years (*Jewish Observer,* February 20, 1992). The latter includes swastikas and anti-Semitic slogans sprayed on the Hillel house at Rutgers University, a fraternity party that mocked the Jewish New Year at Pennsylvania State University, and severe "JAP baiting" at Syracuse University, as discussed in *The Chronicle of Higher Education* on February 7, 1990. So while most campuses in the United States engage in heated discussions about multiculturalism, diversity, and inclusiveness, Jewish students find themselves lumped together with the white establishment, often being seen as part of a political agenda they do not particularly endorse. At the same time the multicultural alliance eliminates Jews as legitimate partners in the struggle, Jewish students increasingly find themselves the target of hate crimes.

The reasons for the decisions at Champaign-Urbana, Seattle, and other schools stem from four hotly contested issues: (1) the continued animosity of many African-American professors who view the traditional black-Jewish coalition, in the words of the historian David Levering Lewis, as "an apparent rather than a real soul fellowship that was minimally beneficial to the Afro-American" (*Jewish Observer,* December 12, 1991); (2) the continued perception of Israel as an outpost of Western imperialism in the Middle East, a counterpart of Jewish exploitation of blacks in American ghettos; (3) the rising prominence of the Muslim religion among American blacks, a conversion that spiritually and politically ties them to the Arab populations in the Middle East who oppose Israel's existence; and (4) the fact that the relative economic success attained and the positions of power occupied by Jews unites them more with the perpetrators than the victims of oppression.

David Friedman, author of *African-Americans and Jews: What Went Wrong* (1992), characterizes university campuses as the new battle-grounds for conflict between blacks and Jews: "Black intellectuals are challenging old dogmas and strategies and some are creating the emerging overt bigotry," he said in the *Jewish Observer* on December 12, 1991. Because this rhetoric inevitably spills over into the multicultural alliance, Jewish students who share the goals of multiculturalism feel alienated and unable to join peers in any sort of political organization. Not accepted as legitimate partners, Jews become part of the enemy establishment; they emerge as willing participants in a system that has abused people of color throughout the history of the United States, aligned with Puritans not Native Americans. In this conceptualization, Dr. Fleischman deserves to be pelted with tomatoes.

What a profound irony! Many Jews, no matter how successful, still see themselves as defined by their religion, as never being part of mainstream America because they are not Christian. (Somehow, the hegemony of Christian culture within the United States rarely gets explored, or even mentioned, in the dialogues about oppression and persecution.) Knowing that their ancestors were hounded out of various countries over the centuries precisely because they rejected total assimilation, modern Jews recognize their vulnerability in any society dominated by another religious group. Indeed, one reason Jews traditionally march in the forefront of movements that fight discrimination against other minority groups is because they remain exposed to attacks. Yet many in the multicultural alliance envision American Jews as the status quo, the oppressor. Scholars note the dark absurdity of lumping Jews together with Russians, Germans, and Poles—groups that traditionally rejected and murdered them.

In perhaps a less dramatic fashion, most Euro-American ethnic groups have suffered similar oppression. For example, anti-Catholic prejudice reached its apex in America during the nineteenth century (Hunter 36–37). Similar stories of exclusion and persecution can be told by Polish Americans, Armenians, Italian Americans, and others. If we persist in making oppression a status symbol and defining oppression only in terms relevant to people of color, we construct a parochial perspective inimical to any sort of balance between common concerns and individual differences. As such, to eliminate the notion of diverse ethnic groups within European culture, groups that may have more in common with people of color than with other white ethnic cultures, is intellectually narrow, emotionally numbing, and politically disastrous.

Conclusion: The Challenges of Multiculturalism

My desire to write this introduction stemmed from a need to find some common ground between the extreme positions on multicultural curricular reform evident on college campuses, realizing that neither side had a monopoly on moral stances or ethical actions. On a personal level, this piece challenged me to defend my answers, as well as some of my deepest beliefs, to a complicated set of questions that rests at the heart of the multicultural enterprise. I come to the end of this essay with my faith in multicultural education—or at least a vision of it shared by many other teachers—strengthened. I firmly believe that the question facing education is not whether to institute changes in traditional courses and departments that reflect an awareness of multicultural issues; rather, teachers must decide how to make structural and fundamental changes that will produce a genuine multicultural perspective, an altered understanding of cultural diversity. As my colleague Delia Temes put it recently, "We need to change the suit, not just add some fringe."

The multiculturalism I support celebrates, rather than denigrates, the differences of others. It listens to voices of dissent rather than demands a standard of linguistic purification; it seeks commonalities as well as differences. I know that many find these changes disturbing. I understand that the stakes in the reconceptualization of America demanded by multiculturalism are high and, for some, represent an uncomfortable reformulation of cherished, long-held ideals: "Put simply, the truth is changing, and a lot of people don't like that" (Jay B1). Indeed, the multicultural debate remains the clearest example of the ongoing battle over how we envision America and what it means to be an American.

Yet to be truly educated in the modern world means to study the ideas of past as well as present thinkers, to have a knowledge of one's own culture as well as those of others. The type of multicultural perspective I have outlined should challenge both white students and those of color to question the basic assumptions that characterize their lives. At the very least, it should clearly demonstrate how seemingly objective concepts of knowledge are constructed by issues of power, gender, sexual orientation, class, race, and religion. Thus, the multicultural classroom could become an exciting focus of deep and meaningful explorations of both the private self and the public culture. Banks articulates some goals of a multicultural education and provides concrete objectives when he argues that the multicultural curriculum should:

1. develop the ability to make reflective decisions on issues related to ethnicity;
2. help individuals to develop cross-cultural competency;
3. provide students with cultural and ethnic alternatives; and

4. help students expand their conceptions of what it means to be human. (25–27)

Such goals seem both necessary and achievable. I would add that such a curriculum should also teach students and faculty the need to respect as well as to argue, to listen to rather than dismiss, the ideas with which they disagree. Perhaps, as Frank Wong argues, "It is not a multicultural community that we seek; it is an *intercultural* community" (53). Whatever term teachers choose to describe their endeavors, they should strive to make students (and themselves) multiculturally literate, a goal that envisions students as thinking, creative, knowledgeable individuals who make decisions based on a fundamental respect for diversity as well as commonality.

For me, multiculturalism represents the best, the most dynamic, aspect of American culture. It is not, as some conservatives tend to characterize it, something that guilt-ridden liberal professors invented to appease minority group members. Neither does it represent the last hope of sixties' radicals who, defeated in the streets, converted America's colleges into hotbeds of subversive activities. Indeed, multiculturalism, at its most basic level, acknowledges the broad range of cultures that constitute the United States. It recognizes that the homogeneity of the past resulted as much from silencing as from assimilating minority voices, downplaying contributions by cultures outside the West, and denying the legitimacy of competing visions—a selective process of myth-making that excluded many more people than it included.

The fact that most of our ancestors came from different countries and brought with them a wide variety of cultures is not a sidebar to the main story of America. It is the central—the defining—fact of American history, the predominant element that makes the United States different from most of the other countries in the world. The creation of the United States remains an ongoing process that will evolve from decade to decade—indeed, from year to year. Yet if our common history teaches anything it teaches that the same essential truths underlie all multicultural education: Our greatest tradition is a commitment to change; our greatest value is respect for individual difference. Such principles mark the basic starting points for the search for common ground.

Note

I would like to thank the following colleagues for their help and guidance with this chapter: Delia Temes, Tony Bucci, Carol Japha, and Diane Carson.

Part 1

Multicultural Media as Tool

Like the writer who holds onto the scraps of her mother's life and who has borrowed her great grandmother's name as her signature, I share the sense that my own identity is an unstable patchwork of crosscutting and often contradictory associations. Yet, like almost everyone else, I always act as though I were in fact a subject—a stable human unit defined in space and time. My work consists of knitting together patches without obliterating seams.

   —Jonathan Boyarin

2

Film as Ethnography and Cultural Critique in the Late Twentieth Century

Michael M. J. Fischer

Background: The Pedagogical Setting

The Course

Currently offered at MIT, the course Film as Ethnography and Cultural Critique in the Late Twentieth Century began as one of the series of initiatives of the Department of Anthropology and the Center for Cultural Studies at Rice University—including the volumes *Anthropology as Cultural Critique* (Marcus and Fischer), *Writing Culture* (Clifford and Marcus), *The Unspeakable* (Tylor), *Lifetimes and Beamtimes* (Traweek), *Debating Muslims* (Fischer and Abedi), and the periodical *Late Editions: Cultural Studies for the End of the Century*—that explores the changing nature of our cultural worlds in the late twentieth century.

These changes include the ethnic composition of the United States and the changing dynamics of transnational cultures to which this domestic diversity is tied. The initiatives explore how ethnographic methods can bring to attention multiple perspectives on cultural reality, which circulate and rub against each other in the world, and that already operate as critique and stimulant to the making of explicit theories, explanations, descriptions, and understandings about the worlds we inhabit. Film is an important ethnographic tool in this endeavor, but it is underexploited and too often viewed and used naively and uncritically.

One important technique of cultural critique that film can exploit (often more easily and more powerfully than textual description) is the juxtaposition of different socially grounded points of view, as, for example, in the opening classroom scene in *Boyz 'N the Hood* (1991), where a black class is being taught a New England Anglo version of American history. A similar technique is used in *Europa Europa* (1991), in which Communist and Nazi ideologies are dramatically deconstructed simply by viewing them through the eyes of a young Jewish boy forced to hide his identity while parroting these catechisms. Cultural critique in this sense, as was argued in *Anthropology as Cultural Critique,* can be read in everyday discourses and juxtapositions as often as in the analyses of intellectuals.

A second technique of cultural critique that film wields powerfully is what I call "critical" or "cultural" hermeneutics, the unpacking of the cultural information carried in the languages of different cultural discourses. This makes films from other cultures interesting challenges to think through. Consider, for example, three films. *Wend Kuuni* (Gift of God, 1982) draws on and critiques African forms of narrative. *Az Volt Hoi Men Volt* . . . (1986, called in English *Hungarian Fairy Tale* but literally the title is the formula with which fairy tales begin ["once there was where there wasn't"]) is an allegory about the illegitimacy of the state and uses *The Magic Flute* of Mozart as a reference for the story line and as a reminder to Hungarian viewers of the value system of their Hapsburg past as a critique of the present. *Surname Viet Given Name Nam* (1989) works best if one knows a bit about the Vietnamese national epic *The Tale of Kieu.*[1]

A third technique of cultural critique is also particularly well suited to film. Borrowing a pun from Michel Serres, I call this "cultural interreferences." On the one hand, any given culture is constituted out of references and sources from other cultures (all cultures are hybrid formations). On the other hand, discourses in one culture block the ability to perceive reality from the perspective of another culture—inter-reference/interference. Films about hybrid migrants, exiles, diasporas, immigrants, displaced groups, and intercultural marriages, as well as about pasts constructed through various layers of ideology, can all explore this technique. One thinks, for example, of films like *Coffee Colored Children* (1988), *Mississippi Triangle* (1983), *Sammy and Rosie Get Laid* (1987), *Jungle Fever* (1991), *Mississippi Masala* (1992), and *Bhaji on the Beach* (1994) in which much of the cultural critique resides in the wealth of ethnographic details that film can photograph, as well as the behavioral and ideological implications these details represent metonymically. Yet these films also contain a conflict at plot level or an argument about the values and ideologies that constrain the choices by which we live. More complicated films and videos like *The Life and Times of Rosie the Riveter* (1980) and *History and Memory* (1991) explore the ways in which various forms of media, propaganda, and memory layer consciousness. Even more complex films like *The Body Beautiful* (1991) interweave themes of hybridity, politics, and the discourses of body image, beauty, age, and desire.

The course was mounted for the first time in spring 1992. Offered twice at Rice and so far once at MIT, it remains in an experimental but seemingly fertile phase. The first class, containing fourteen undergraduates, five graduate students, and five auditors, was considerably more ethnically and culturally diverse than the general student body at Rice. The attraction for culturally hybrid students was also the case at MIT. The requirements of the course included keeping a journal and writing a paper. We suggested that the journal be conceptualized in three parts: notes on the films as they were watched; personal reactions to the films; and an analytic section in which the questions of the course and readings were to be applied to each film and the films either integrated with or played against each other.

The journals proved quite interesting. Some people adopted the tripartite suggestion, but others moved on to more synthetic and evocative formats. One journal, for instance, contained short autobiographical interludes reflecting upon how the film worked for the author at various points in his life—his changing sense of what "exoticism" was, his first interactions with subtitled films, and the coolness with which other blue-collar workers received his knowledge of black music.[2] Another journal usefully drew upon films from outside the course that paralleled or related to films shown in the course. A linguistics student elaborated a theme of the difference between Saussurean linguistic analyses and symbolic analyses of the films.

Some students who adopted the strict tripartite format effectively vented their frustrations against films they did not like and then shifted gears dramatically and, with cool analytic skill, applied the questions of the course to tease out cultural codes, highlight cultural critiques that the films performed, or dissect the cine-writing rhetorics of the films, those formal techniques that can be manipulated rhetorically in ways analogous to rhetoric in written forms of ethnography for particular kinds of cultural critique effects.

The final papers ranged from the experimental to the scholarly. One of the more experimental took the form of a video that imitated Pasolini's *Notes towards an African Orestes* (1970), overlaying normal activity in a Texas shopping mall with a commentary that deployed Texas mythology. The effect was to draw attention both on the myth and the kinesthetic aspects of the shoppers. By mismatching cultural, racial, ethnic, and gender attributes in the mythic story to the real attributes of the shoppers, the video drew attention to the cultural constructedness of the categories and to alternative possibilities in the myth itself. The myth, quite appropriate to a Texas shopping mall, was that of the Alamo, with the shoppers representing the various famous characters involved in that event. Another paper juxtaposed a 1974 documentary on a Mexican pilgrimage town (Jon and Natalie Olson's *We Believe in the Nino Fidencio*) with the student's experiences studying with musicians in the same town in 1991 and 1992, thereby raising questions about changes over time and the rhetorical editing devices of the film.

A third paper, written by a student who came to America from India as a child and was raised here, explored how during her upbringing Indian movies provided some of the emotional and linguistic root experiences about what it means to be Indian. The first Hindu wedding she ever saw, in Shashi Kapoor's 1973 *Kabhi Kabhi* (Sometimes), was followed only a year later, reality following filmic art, by a real-life Hindu wedding. It was her desire to understand the films that stimulated her to learn more than household Hindi. Language in the films was more complex than routine household questions (a matter of "I have to make certain that I win the election so that I will be able to raise the rent on the lands of the peasants, heh, heh, heh" versus "What's for dinner?"). Like Rea Tajiri's exploration in *History and Memory,* the student also commented on vivid memories from before her birth: "I have never actually seen my father buying *paan* from the *paanwallah,* but I 'remember' him doing it in my mind's eye."

A fourth paper, like the second, contrasted a film with personal experiences in the same setting. It argued that despite the overbearing ethnocentric structuring of *City of Joy* (1992), elements of "the real India" still came through, an example where the descriptive camera exceeds the constraints of the narrative apparatus.[3] A fifth paper, somewhat like the first, put lessons into practice by producing a film script about a Nachez, Mississippi, mother and her big-city returned daughter, drawing on the insights of *The Body Beautiful, History and Memory,* and *Postcards from the Edge.*

Two papers analyzed *Ju Dou* (1989) in quite different ways. A Chinese-American woman analyzed the film's gender critique, paying detailed attention to the kinesthetics, the agency, and the revolts against the three Confucian obediences (to father, husband, and adult son) by the lead female character. Another student examined the camera-work techniques, use of color, and staging of the most dramatic scenes. He scrutinized issues of gender, both the greater strength of the woman compared to the men (impotent old men, cowed younger men, and the blind rage of youth—the political allegory) and the way sexual desire is powerfully rendered by the falling, red-dyed cloth that functions as a clever take-off of the traditional Chinese rain and clouds imagery for sex. The student's journal systematically commented upon the camera work in a number of the films we saw.

Perhaps the most ambitious and detailed paper was a Japanese-American student's analysis of Akira Kurosawa's *Macbeth, Kumonosu-jo* (The Throne of Blood, 1957), taking up Noel Burch's challenge in *To the Distant Observer* to look for Japanese esthetics. The paper concludes, "Within this work, Akira Kurosawa reveals how culture-bound the act of viewing is. By returning to the tradition of 'medieval aesthetics' (*Noh* theater, *sumi-e* composition), Kurasawa discloses the difference between word and image, matter and spirit." Yet another paper was by a student just returned from a term in Germany. By analyzing *Die Weisse Rose* (The White Rose, 1982) and *Das Schreckliche Madchen* (The Nasty Girl, 1991), she took up the challenge in *Stranded Objects,* Eric Santer's volume on German films that attempt to address the Nazi period but fail to work through the resistances to a true ability to mourn and the relation of these themes to the violence against new immigrants to Germany.

Through such papers the class successfully drew out a variety of multicultural experiences, cross-culturally comparative perspectives, and cultural critiques generated through the juxtaposition of moral systems in change. The papers elicited the experiences of individuals in their American settings and showed those experiences to have depth in traditions abroad. They also showed that those traditions were undergoing the hybridizations and reorganizations associated with modernity and the creation of new pluralist conditions of existence.

The following section presents the analytic framework of the course: lecture format in the first two sessions; a handout containing a pastiche of quotes from leading film theorists; notes on each film that were handed out in each session; and discussions and debates before or after each film. Due to space limitation, I cannot present the film notes, which provide the meat of the course. The following section, however, describes the initial handout which outlines a cognitive map for the course. We found the pastiche of quotes to be a useful device to focus initial attention and for repeated reference.

The pastiche of quotes consisted of five double-sided pages (single spaced) in easily accessible outline form. The many quotes in the following pages trace that format. Because it needed some verbal elaboration, I include the quotes here in a discursive format. But the organizational outline is quite simple: There are four sets of questions: (1) cine-writing techniques or rhetorics; (2) cultural codes; (3) genres; and (4) reception and social functions. Each of these can be subdivided, represented here by the subheadings.

In each session we asked all four questions about the films viewed but focused on one particular question or subaspect (as listed in the weekly headings of the syllabus). The unifying theme for all four sets of questions is cultural diversity: Are there culturally different ways to handle these areas? Do changes in conventions of film making within a cultural tradition question the assumptions of that society? For instance, regarding cine-writing, Is there a Japanese esthetics? Does the altered order of sequencing events in *Wend Kuuni* raise questions about the stability of village life as told in traditional tales? Does the camera work in *Ju Dou* or in Mohsen Makhmalbaf's postrevolution Iranian films introduce radically different gazes or styles of viewing? Do the hybridized tactics of Michel Kheleifi's *Canticle of Stones* (1990) provoke Arabic-speakers and English-speakers differently? Regarding cultural codes: What difference does it make whether viewers know about the Sufi symbols in *A Door to the Sky* (1988), the rain and clouds symbols in Chinese poetry for viewing *Ju Dou,* or the role of the epic *Tale of Kieu* for Vietnamese in California in *Surname Viet Given Name Nam?* What difference does it make if, in viewing that film, one pays attention to the uses of the lotus image; of the counterpoint on the soundtrack of Vietnamese poetry, Chinese-style song, and translated English prose; or the counterpoint on the visual track between photographs, newsreels, staged interviews, and candid shots of California life and celebrations? We suggest that critique occurs most powerfully through the juxtaposition of different cultures (or strata within cultures), and that film has been a powerful medium of such juxtapositions and critique in ordinary people's consciousnesses across the globe throughout the twentieth century.

Having students from different cultures is a tremendous resource in working out the cultural resonances and functions of multiculturalism in film. Simply hearing quite different opinions expressed opens the eyes of many students: those who were irritated by Trinh Minh-hà's film versus those who were receptive to elements of it; those who were simply bored by the Iranian film clips versus those who were riveted by them. It is perhaps a little harder if classes do not contain such living resources, but then background readings, such as the introduction to *The Tale of Kieu,* can be helpful. Many students were fascinated by the picture of Morrocan women presented in *A Door to the Sky* and recognized it as undoing the standard stereotyping of Muslim women in American popular culture. This ability to recognize elements of the film was aided by readings from two leading Muslim women academics. Watching the films thus becomes like learning a foreign language; the dictionary meanings remain necessary but not sufficient. The idioms, the allusions, the resonances, the emotional patterns, the tropes, the stories, and the philosophies constitute the culture (cultural hermeneutics) that the language carries.

This course is intended to open consciousness about diversity in America and show how this diversity is linked to the dynamics of transnational cultural change. Such courses contribute to discussions about multiculturalism and identity politics; they are equally important for Americans who contemplate careers that involve the cultures and societies with which America interacts abroad. Part of the agenda, therefore, is to develop more sophisticated ethnographic techniques through film and film reading skills.

The Local University Setting

Rice University is the smallest of the nationally ranked elite universities; it has a student body of approximately 2,600 undergraduates and 1,000 graduate students. The Rice Media Center was founded in the late 1960s with help from Dominique de Menil and for a short period was a center of vigorous activity. Roberto Rossellini was a founding presence and helped attract a stream of people. The MacDougalls, ethnographic filmmakers, were at Rice for a time, as was the documentary filmmaker James Blue. During the 1980s, the Media Center seemed to have fallen on leaner times despite various connections to the Southwest Media Project (SWAMP), the local Public Broadcasting channel, and the large Houston International Film Festival. Nonetheless, Brian Huberman of the Media Center, together with the anthropologists Michael Reese and Jon McGee, produced two films on the Lacandon Indians (in Chiapas, Mexico) and a film on the changing myths of the Alamo. SWAMP has organized a series of screenings and lectures on the Texas myth in Hollywood films. The Rice Media Center also programs an extensive regular offering of film showings, as does the nearby Houston Museum of Fine Arts.

Initiatives to reinvigorate film and media studies at Rice University are underway. During the spring term of 1992, a half dozen film courses were in the curriculum. In the art and art history department, Thomas McEvily taught Third World Film and Brian Huberman taught the Western; in the German department, Margaret Eiffler taught about contemporary feminist German film; through the Center for Cultural Studies, Roger Simon taught a course on film noir; in anthropology, Kathryn Milun offered a course on politics and film;

and George Marcus and I co-taught the course described here. As a visitor during 1992, we had in residence the Polish documentary filmmaker Maria Zmarz-Koczanowicz, and in 1992–93 we had as Rockefeller postdoctoral fellows two specialists in Asian and African film: Teshome Gabriel and Hamid Naficy. Naficy has joined the Rice faculty, and I have moved to MIT, where I have continued the course.

Introduction to the Course: Film as Ethnographic Tool

Although film functions as a central medium of modernity throughout the twentieth century, anthropology until very recently has paid surprisingly little attention to it as an object of study in the transformations of consciousness of populations across the globe, a tool of ethnography, or a vehicle for critical reflection on cultural processes. This pilot course makes film central to ethnography and anthropology by reframing past ethnography and anthropology, considering how the tools of cine-writing can be used for ethnographic cultural critique, and examining the interplay of narrative and documentary genres, paying particular attention to those films that people make about themselves rather than those that stereotype others. We deal with multiculturalism in the United States as part of larger transnational dynamics of cultural interaction and massive demographic movements in the late twentieth century, as well as part of the comparative perspective that film fosters as a mind-set of people across the globe.

Modern fieldwork anthropology was born into an environment in which film was changing the spatio-temporal-visual dimensions of social life (including this comparative multicultural mind-set).[4] Film, for example, was brought to India—produced in India and disseminated not only in urban cinemas but also by rural traveling shows—long before the Malinowskian revolution that created modern anthropology.[5] And yet, oddly, until very recently, anthropology has largely ignored this perceptual world.[6]

Traditional ethnographies made surprisingly little use of the visual, even of photography. They usually contained only an illustrative "documentary" photograph or two, preferably in black and white. So-called ethnographic films (whether in black and white or color) seem to have been patterned after these black and white photographs, suppressing cultural narratives in favor of the explanatory voice-overs of the filmmakers.[7] The vibrant search by people for reliable information amid experience, school-learning, travel, myth, religion, prejudice, and reason was usually suppressed into pastorals of ecological cycles, stagings of depoliticized rituals, ritualized stagings of conflicts, and frozen art forms.

Despite such pioneering work in contemporary cultural processes as James Peacock's *Rites of Modernization,* which is about popular theatrical forms in Indonesia, few ethnographers attempted an anthropological reading of the production of the films and advertising that vast numbers of people have consumed during the course of this century, that is, a reading in their multiple registers: for the ethnography they display, for the future-oriented cognitive work they encourage, for the comparative perspective on life that people make of them, for the forms of perception they foster, and for the modes of agency and political action they constitute.

For purposes of this course, we group these areas of interest into four sets: (1) cine-writing; (2) the cultural codes and genre forms used in different cultural traditions as vehicles for (and objects of) critical thought, moral critique, political action, and esthetic judgment; (3) the genres of filmmaking as conventionally labeled (ethnographic, documentary, narrative) and their utilities and limitations, crossover possibilities, ability to generate new hybrid forms and present understandings that exceed, subvert, or get around the genre constraints; and (4) the reception and cultural-historical functions of films in changing psychology, perceptual frames, expectations, and comparative understanding of others, paying particular attention to the positionality of filmmakers and audiences (e.g., the difference between ethnicity as used by Hollywood and films by ethnics about themselves).

Cine-Writing and the Double Realities of Real and Reel

Film rarely simply records reality; rather, it creates and constitutes reality through various techniques. (As Federico Fellini put it, "People think of cinema as a camera loaded with film and a reality out there ready to be photographed. Instead one inserts him[her]self between the object and the camera" [Grazzini 16].) What are these techniques and how might one best analyze them? Keith Cohen (*Film and Fiction,* ch. 3) reminds us that film provides a double reality. It operates as *eikon* (iconic, mimesis) and as phantasma (fools the eye, montage, and trompe l'oeil effects). Two kinds of models are often suggested to analyze cine-writing: linguistic and psychodynamic.

Linguistic Models   A number of film theorists take the model of film as a kind of language quite seriously, looking for minimal units of meaning and formal grammars or syntax; others take the ideal of film language more metaphorically. Some, such as Jean-François Lyotard in "The Dream-Work Does Not Think" and "Figure Foreclosed," argue that visual figurations operate by a logic quite different from linguistic grammar and that in both visual and linguistic fields two types of logic—figuration and grammar—are "blocked together" in uneasy tension.[8] In any case, we are interested in the formal means—grammars, syntaxes, logics, rhetorics, and figures—that films manipulate.

Pierre Rouve, producer of Antonioni's *Blow-Up*, takes the linguistic metaphor seriously, arguing that the film object does not mirror or repeat the visible, but makes it visible, citing Paul Klee, "gibt nicht das Sichtabare wieder, sondern macht Sichtbar (does not repeat the visible, but makes visible)." Rouve also says there is a film grammar that is a "techno-semantic co-reality." The minimal units of this grammar, he argues, are a space-time (*Zeitraum,* or chronotype) unit, not just single photograms or shots. It is the viewpoint and relation among photograms that semanticizes or creates meaning. Rouve cites Lev Kuleshov's famous demonstrations in the early 1920s: The same facial expression of the actor Mosjukine was read alternatively as lust, horror, and hunger when juxtaposed respectively to shots of a scantily clad girl, a decaying corpse, and soup. Another example of "techno-semantic coreality" occurs when, in Sergei Mikhailovich Eisenstein's *October* (1928), a tilted camera shot is conditioned not by the actual gradient of the road, but by the intent to signify obstacles, as if portraying the figure of speech, "an uphill struggle." Similarly, Jean Epstein's *The Fall of the House of Usher* (1928) uses multiple exposure as a rhetorical way to create an enigmatically strange, macabre appearance: Candles are superimposed on trees (and look equally as tall) and frame three silhouetted figures on the horizon. Rouve makes the linguistic analogy explicit: "Pointing the camera at a given target in a given direction is a technosyntactic equivalent of the verbal recourse to demonstrative pronouns. High or low key lighting is parallel to the use of adjectival qualifiers. The quantifiable duration of a screen image acts as a variable intonational stress. Dissolves act[ed] as punctuation codes." He concludes, "Semiotically enriched, the Reel enriches the Real" (106).

As an example of one sequence of films, drawing on multiple cultural codes and foregrounding cine-writing tactics, the class watched parts of Parviz Kimiavi's film *Moghul-ha* (The Mongols, 1974), which is not only an allegory about the destructive invasion of television in Iran but also a meditation on film techniques and the differences among traditional storytellers, poetry, film, and television. It begins with a history of filmmaking techniques. The primary argument is not that film and television kill off traditional storytelling and poetry, but rather that television is the antagonist of film.

Kimiavi's film is part of a sophisticated film tradition both in Iran and among Iranians living in Europe and the United States. We sampled the genres and cine-writing techniques of this tradition through films made about Iranians in the United States (Ghassem Ebrahamian's *The Suitors,* 1988) and films made in postrevolutionary Iran that draw on narrative structures and filmic devices of Alfred Hitchcock and Alberto Moravia but pose social questions about the dispossessed in Iran (Mohsen Makhmalbaf's *The Peddler,* 1986). More specifically, during the first two weeks of the course the class viewed films that foregrounded cine-writing techniques: Gaston Kaboré's *Wend Kuuni,* Trinh T. Minh-hà's *Surname Viet Given Name Nam,* Jorge Furtado et al.'s *Illha das Flores* (Island of Flowers, 1989), and Pier Paolo Pasolini's *Notes towards an African Orestes.*

Psychodynamic Models   Raymond Williams, in his essay "Cinema and Socialism," argues that film must not be left to the few to manipulate and suggests that film has a particular efficacy in the realm of identity politics and psychology. He observes, for example, that Strindberg's plays of the 1890s "are effectively film scripts: involving the fission and fusion of identities and characters; the alteration of objects and landscapes by the psychological pressures of the observer; symbolic projections of obsessive states of mind; all, as material processes beyond the reach of even his experimental theater, but all, as processes of art, eventually to be realized in film" (115).

Slavoj Zizek pursues this sort of suggestion further in *Looking Awry,* arguing that film stages the circuits of desire and that desire is not an object but a process of continual deferment, operating (like dreams) along a dual logic that appears to fit rational means-ends schemas but actually works according to a quite different economy, one illustrated in Zeno's paradoxes. "What fantasy stages is not a scene in which our desire is fully satisfied, but on the contrary, a scene that realizes, stages, the desire as such. Desire is not something given in advance, but something that has to be constructed: through fantasy we learn how to desire" (6). For example, the story line of Zeno's first paradox, that of the race between Achilles and the tortoise, crosses Aesop's fable of the hare and the tortoise with the story in *The Iliad* of Achilles trying to catch Hector (XXII:199–200). *The Iliad* explicitly invokes a libidinal economy, the common-dream paradox of continuous approach to an object that preserves a constant distance: "As in a dream, the pursuer never succeeds in catching up with the fugitive whom he is after, and the fugitive likewise cannot ever clearly escape his pursuer; so Achilles that day did not succeed in attaining Hector and Hector was not able to escape him definitively" (7).

If Zizek explores the libidinal economy of desire that film often invokes, Robert Stam ("Hitchcock and Buñuel" 1989) reminds us that desire can also be dealt with in different formal ways. Stam argues that Hitchcock and Buñuel have the same concerns: law and desire, authority and revolt, the rational, the irrational, and guilt. Both men were Jesuit-educated Catholics, but Hitchcock fosters emotional suspense, the thrill of empathy, and anxiety, whereas Buñuel triggers intellectual surprise, shocks of recognition, and doubt. Buñuel refuses the use of empathy-inducing techniques such as point-of-view editing, shot-countershot, and eyeline matches. Hitchcock loves to position spectators through point-of-view editing to move them to a point of catharsis. A number of the films and videos we showed in class (Rea Tajiri's *History and Memory,* Ngozi Onwurah's *The Body Beautiful,* Trinh T. Minh-hà's *Surname Viet Given Name Nam,* and Farida Ben Lyazid's *A Door to the Sky*) foregrounded libidinal economies and also raised the question of ways in which different cultures might figure, code, allegorize, or symbolize distinctive emotional circuits.

Cultural Codes and Cultural Critique

Under this rubric, we explored cultural traditions that might influence the formal techniques of cine-writing and sedimented historical content of different traditions of film industries. As a shorthand, we used national or geographical labels without accepting Fredric Jameson's argument ("Third World Literature" and "Regarding Postmodernism" 1987–88) that film in the twentieth century is necessarily part of an allegory of political nationhood.[9] Cultural codes might exist in several forms. There could be, as Noel Burch suggests for Japanese film, something in the esthetic style of a cultural tradition that makes its films quite distinctive. There could also be images or narrative figures from traditional poetry or iconic symbolism that are distinctive, for example, rain and clouds in Chinese poetry as figures of sexuality, reworked in the filmic iconography of Zhang Yimou's films as suggested by Yuejin Wang. There could be narrative forms rearranged in films, as Manthia Diawara ("Oral Literature and African Film" 1989) suggests for Gaston Kaboré's *Wend Kuuni.* And, of course, there are the historical and cultural references that constitute a cultural tradition as well as the citations and conventions of a national film tradition itself.

We began the course with the play of these forms, interrogating, for example, Trinh T. Minh-hà's *Surname Viet Given Name Nam* for its poetry, imagery, and esthetic stagings as well as the central evocation of Nguyen Du's *The Tale of Kieu* by the narratives of women in Vietnam and narratives about Vietnamese in California. These are all things that Trinh refuses to make explicit in her conscious narrative and essays but give her work its romantic coherence and sense.

As background, for this sort of interrogation, we began with Noel Burch's arguments about Japanese film. *To the Distant Observer* is a classic statement of the possibility that different cultural traditions may have esthetic codes as well as historical and political references that inform their films and make them distinctive. Moreover, like an anthropologist, Burch remains convinced of the importance of comparative work, of a detour through the East, in order to be able to understand the distinctiveness of one's own cultural conventions in film:

> It is beyond doubt that Japan's singular history . . . has produced a cinema which is in essence unlike that of any other nation. This essential difference between the dominant modes of Western and Japanese cinema is the main concern of this study. It is intended, furthermore, as a step in the direction of a critical analysis of the ideologically and culturally determined system of representation from which the film industries of Hollywood and elsewhere derive their power and profit. It consequently may be understood as part of a much broader . . . approach to art, initiated by Brecht and Eisenstein, and which involves a detour through the East. (11)

To make this argument, Burch sketches the development of the "Western" system of illusionism (a.k.a. classical Hollywood style). It took a decade to develop rules of match-cutting: contiguity matching through exits and entrances with matching directions from shot to shot, reverse field cut, and eyeline matching, with the spectator as mediator between two interlocuters (by the end of World War I). Initially, filmmakers feared that any violation of single frontal theater point of view and distance would lead to a breakdown of the illusion of reality and that the audience would become confused. For instance, in Edwin S. Porter's *The Great Train Robbery* (1903), a medium close-up of the cowboy shooting into the camera was delivered to theaters in a separate roll that could be spliced onto either the beginning or end of the film. The fireman saving a mother and child from a second-story bedroom was shot first from the street then from inside a studio reconstruction of the room. But, fearing that the audience would be confused by intercut shots, Porter juxtaposed two complete versions of the action.

These editing techniques of the West were acknowledged, mas-
tered, and used by the Japanese, says Burch, but not adopted. For
example, in Makino's *Chushingura* (The Forty-seven Ronin, 1913), the
camera runs without interruption through the entire sequence, front-
on, like a spectator at a play, seeming to ignore Griffith's editing
concepts. But Makino did not ignore them; the film contains several
match-cuts (concertinas) and lateral reframing pans. Although such
devices become banal in the West (not signifiers of anything beyond
continuity and contiguity), Makino made them dramatic signifiers,
like signs in Japanese theater (e.g., an *oyama* tugging with her teeth
at her kimono to signify weeping). Burch lists the visual traits of
Kabuki theater that appear constantly on the screen: stylized fighting
sequences in which no blows are exchanged; backward somersaults
to signify the death of a fighter; action-stopping *mie* (tableaux vivants);
theatrical makeup (in the West, theatrical makeup is used to height-
en expressiveness; in Kabuki, makeup is purely graphic, reducing
both expressiveness and singularity); and multiple roles played by the
same actor (in Kabuki, certain plays call explicitly for double roles
and spectacular stagings).

Invoking our methodological principle of trying not to rely solely
on cultural outsiders as guides, we also turned to the distinguished
Japanese film critic Tadao Sato for further suggestions about how
Kabuki theater influenced Japanese film. Kabuki has two main kinds
of leading men, and Japanese cinema inherited them. The *tateyaku*
is the noble, ideal samurai, educated in the Confucian and Bushido
(warrior) code that requires sacrificing love before loyalty to one's
lord. The *tateyaku* stars in tales of sacrificing his wife or child out of
loyalty to his lord and, despite inner pain, he watches them suffer
without betraying emotion. The *nimaime,* in contrast, can whisper
sweet words of love. He is handsome if not strong, pure if not clever,
kind to the heroine, and would commit suicide with her. Sato wryly
observes that one does not tend to get Gary Cooper or Clark Gable
types, who are strong and intelligent as well as successful romantically,
although he argues that perhaps John Wayne is something like a *tateyaku,* whereas Marcello Mastroianni is something like a *nimaime.*

For our discussion of African film, we began with Gaston Kaboré's
Wend Kuuni and Diawara's argument that it uses materials of the oral
literature of Burkina Faso to reflect the changing ideology of the time
and critique the oral tradition as favoring values that cannot be sustained and are detrimental in the contemporary world. Diawara suggests that this is done, in part, by a formal procedure of retelling a
familiar form of story in a different order or sequence.

We began our discussion of films of North Africa (the Maghreb) with the articulate goals of cultural critique set by Maghrebian film-makers themselves. Moumen Smihi, in "Moroccan Society as Mythology," argues that "cinema is the product of Western bourgeois society . . . it is integrated in a novelistic, theatrical, dramatic tradition. From the moment when the same means of expression, the cinema, is manipulated in another cultural atmosphere, it is necessary . . . to interrogate the forms and cultural traditions of this different atmosphere" (81). Asked, for instance, about the title of his film *El Chergui, or the Violent Silence,* he invokes political, psychological, folkloric, historical, and Georges Bataille-style cultural critique registers:

> There are several meanings. A multiple title. . . . "East wind," "levante" . . . often blows in the region of the Straits of Gibraltar and particularly in Tangier where—a somewhat mysterious feature—it has the effect of dividing the population into two opposing groups: some are distraught, the others go crazy. There is also the Chinese proverb, "The East wind will prevail over the West wind." . . . "The violent silence" is a phrase of Georges Bataille, but turned back on itself. It is a precise reference to the historical situation of the Maghreb societies. (81)

Merzak Allouache, director of the wonderful film *Omar Gatlato* (1977), invokes and critiques the oral world, as does Gaston Kaboré in *Wend Kuuni,* "I wanted to pursue the narrative of adventures as a fable, in the style of our grandmothers' stories . . . The dramatic sequence keeps on being slowed down by a series of digressions. Right in the midst of his adventure, Mehdi is stopped by a series of situations and characters which deflect him from this path. He endures history rather than lives it. . . . I've tried to show throughout the film *how the predominance of speech works to befog and not to illuminate*" (97, 96, emphasis added).

European Film Traditions   In considering European film traditions, we reviewed comparative notes on the material conditions in which films are produced. The films of Burkina Faso were encouraged by a political regime that wanted to use film as a vehicle of democratization; the Maghrebian films often struggle with the necessity of obtaining French coproduction funding and then must design their appeal to European audiences as well. In *European Cinemas,* Pierre Sorlin describes the history of film in Europe as a counterpoint to Hollywood film: Europeans wanted a depiction of indigenous themes related to their own cultural and historical experiences.

This desire both sustains and inhibits national studios, providing the content and audience for nationally addressed film but also appealing to limited markets restricted to the nation and not necessarily to other Europeans. Fewer than 10 percent of films shown are from other European countries, and 40–75 percent are American, although after World War II European production nearly equaled American production and the cinema industry has been internationalized from its beginning, with technicians, directors, actors, and capital moving easily from country to country. Sorlin uses films about World War I and about resistance in World War II to explore the differences among different European film traditions.

In the 1930s—it took a decade until the painful memories of war could be dealt with—there were a flood of World War I accounts, from autobiography and photo exhibits to novels and films. Europe produced more films about World War I than Hollywood did. They were not only different from Hollywood films but also from one another. Espionage, ignored by Germans and Italians, fascinated the democracies (it was the theme of half the British films and a third of the French ones).

In the 1950s, resistance films in each nation depicted the secret war as a private domestic activity, downplaying help from others and thereby comforting national pride and deepening prejudices about other Europeans. The films are usually pessimistic (partisans are killed, not rewarded) and introduce new images of cruelty, sadism, and death as dirty and degrading. By contrast, death in World War I is portrayed as quick, dramatic, and clean. (These observations are suggestive of current debates about the three-way relation between experience in war, propaganda and other discourses about war and shifting public expressiveness about death, cruelty, and other passions and behaviors. After all, the machine gun in World War I is often cited as causing a massive change in public consciousness about the mindless, industrial killing fields of modern warfare, in which heroism is an increasingly archaic trope.) Discussion about recent warfare in Vietnam and the Persian Gulf has thematized the increasing role of visual technologies in weaponry, experience, and moral consciousness.

Antonia Lant provides a reminder in the context of European film of how gendered genres construct audiences. She also expands Sorlin's comments on the European genres of the national subject: "National identity is nothing if not internationally defined. No cinema *has* national identity; rather it is secured cross-culturally, by comparison with other national outputs, formed as part of a circuit of reciprocated exchange" (3). In particular, women in Britain during World War II rejected Hollywood as not addressing local conditions or their self-perceptions. Lant cites an interview in one of the mass observation surveys after the war: "Look at the maids in Hollywood films. Do they look as if they've ever done a hard day's work—they're all glamorous girls dolled up to the nines. You can't just sit there pretending" and comments that this woman "perceives the rhetoric of Hollywood now as historically specific and national, rather than universal and natural" (11).

> National identity is not a natural timeless essence, but an intermittent, combinatory, historical product, arising at moments of contestation . . . the stuff of national identity had to be winnowed and forged from traditional aesthetic and narrative forms, borrowed from the diverse conventions of melodrama, realism, and fantasy, and transplanted from literature, painting, and history into cinema. National identity could never be straightforwardly and permanently stated, but instead could emerge only partially, from an insistence on a specifically British nature, definable only through difference from another identity. . . . In the cinema, this other place was above all America. (31)

Lant focuses on films "that can provisionally be called the genre of the national subject: that is, they are linked through an address to their audience as nationally defined," and argues that "if there is one area on which these films wish to stake their identity as British, it is their representation of women . . . the maimed, wartime female body as the quintessential sign of recent historical events in Britain" (14). She notes the atomization of the British, a process that Paul Virilio has addressed on a global scale but that in Britain took the form during the war of some 34.7 million changes of address in a civilian population of 38 million. This, and the arrival of first Free French and Polish forces and then the American GIs, meant that "representations were needed to pull together these differences, to emphasize that the most important divide was between Britain and Germany" (6). Moreover, "Focussing on the home front . . . meant emphasing the psychological . . . and this forced (or allowed) an emphasis on narratives about female experience" (13). In other words, Lant argues, British cinema constructed itself around a specific style of realism that was initially constructed around British femininity contrastive to American femininity.

Virilio takes a broader account of the atomization of war-induced disruption and cinematic address: "A mass industry, basing itself upon psychotropic derangement and chronological disturbance, was directly applying cinematic acceleration to the realism of the world. This new cinema was particularly aimed at the ever wider public which had been torn from its sedentary existence and marked down for military mobilization, exile and emigration, proletarianization in the new industrial metropolises . . . and revolution. War had everyone on the move, even the dead" (28).

Genres: Documentary, Ethnographic, and Narrative

It was not only in Britain that, as Lant argues, war "blurred the distinction between documentary and feature filmmaking. . . . There was now a freer exchange of personnel between the two limbs of the industry. . . . The war was also causing film's entertainment and informational roles to merge" (34).

It is also on principled grounds that documentary strategies can interact with narrative ones. Ana López describes several important experiments in Latin-American film. *Memories of Underdevelopment* (1968) uses inserts of documentary footage not as proofs of authenticity or "realism," but rather the fiction and documentary discourses relativize each other, disallowing any single indisputable truth. *The Jackal of Nahueltoro* (1968–69) "parodies the mechanisms of 'reporting' or documenting by highlighting the dialectic between the [story] *telling* and *showing* the functions of narratives and documentaries in an explicitly dialogical fashion. . . . Positioned as a second order discourse on an already existing discourse about 'the jackal' . . . a *commentary* rather than a *documentary*. . . . The sound track . . . is used to give voice to four different kinds of text, four different interpretations" (66–67). What is important here is that most discourses today are second-order commentaries on already-existing discourses, and this film operates as a reminder that ethnography, like reporting, need not always pretend to an "originary" relation to history or reality.

Reception and Cultural-Historical Functions of Film

Perceptual Change, Reflexivity, Cultural Critique, and Parallel Texts   If films often operate as second-order commentaries on already-existing discourses (and through references to previous films), there is an important historicity to chart. As Sorlin puts it, "Films beget films. . . . Each film could be considered a small bit in the huge text of all the already shot movies, but images evolve with societies, and we do not see our surroundings with the conceptual tools people used even half a century ago" (10). Noticing this change in conceptual tools can work as a component of cultural critique in the same way that simply re-viewing can spur self-reflection. "When seeing images of their daily life, people understand and appreciate it differently" (Sorlin 20). For example, Sorlin suggests, "Partly because youth was staged as such in so many movies in the 1960s, the concept of 'youth' (and youth culture) emerged" (20).

The phenomenon of the desire of some audiences for an erasure of distinction between actors' off-screen lives and their characters on stage often amuses critics. Vijay Mishra, Peter Jeffrey, and Brian Shoesmith, in "The Actor as Parallel Text in Bombay Cinema," suggest that only some actors take on this function of being a parallel text and that the elements of what constitutes the parallel text are interesting in their own right and can provide access to wider processes of social change.

> Devanand and Shashi Kapoor, Vinod Khanna, and Rajesh Khanna have been great stars in Bombay cinema but have not generated parallel texts. To find that parallel text which vies for place with the film itself (as character to plot), we must go to K. L. Saigal and Ashok Kumar, Dilip Kumar and Raj Kapoor, and finally and most recently, of course, to Bachchan who, we suggest, may well be the last of the parallel texts. . . . the mode of production of Bombay cinema . . . itself is undergoing such radical changes that no single actor can become either exemplary or emblematic of Bombay cinema in the near future. . . . We therefore advance the idea that the parallel text is both constructed and carried by the song and dialogue situation. In other words, the star so defined is represented as a feature of the "labor" of memory, a product of the essentially oral traditions of the Indian as well as a production of the industry. (57)

The second-order nature of much film discourse can lead to dead ends, but it can also be used in new rewritings that constitute a powerful kind of cultural critique. If Wim Wenders finds himself in a vicious circle, wanting but unable to stop quoting from other movies ("Whatever film you went to see, it had its nourishment or its life or its food, its roots, in other movies . . . I didn't see anything anymore that was really trying to redefine a relation between life and images made from life" [cited in Kinder 75]), Marsha Kinder argues that the ideological parody characteristic of New German cinema works by rewriting stories and genres: "Each new text sacrifices at least one of its central characters through castration, murder, suicide. Such characters are both victim and embodiment of destructive ideological forces. They are double agents, not unified subjects who invite emotional identification, but rather they are ambivalent signifiers whose meanings slide between two systems of signfication" (74).

Class, Gender, and Social Background   As a start, we cite only two sets of suggestions contrasting Japan with the United States. The way the Japanese class structure evolved, Burch argues, allowed plebeian tastes to inform film longer than in the United States. "In the West, plebeian tastes were formed by vaudeville, circus, magic lantern, etc.; these were viewed by dominant bourgeois taste as archaic forms suitable only for children and nannies and as in contradiction to the developed 'illusionism' of dominant theater. While early cinema has traces of the plebeian forms of art, the introduction of naturalism is in part a class strategy" (6). Burch wonders whether there is something inherent in the cinema that pulls it toward realism: "In Kabuki when a prop is no longer needed, a black clad stage assistant retrieves it. In film, one often sees the prop disappear at the end of an invisible thread. Why is the stage assistant not retained, given the other practices of stage artifice that were retained? Is this one sign of conflict over the next two decades of defining cinema as more realistic than stage?" (6).

Larry May's *Screening Out the Past* (1980) provides a rich ethnic, gender, and psychological map of the functions of the cinema in America as it shifted from appeals to immigrant working classes to homogenizing middle classes:

> With the Jewish moguls on top [in the third stage of the industry's growth], and a large ethnic component among the rank and file, the creative personnel were already one step removed from the Victorian restraints holding earlier film makers. . . . Those who created the aura—producers, directors, cinematographers, and set designers— came largely from European or Canadian backgrounds. . . . Those who provided the models—actors and actresses—were overwhelmingly young. Two-thirds of them were under thirty-five. Moreover, three-fourths of the industry's female performers were under twenty-five. This suggests that the youth cult so necessary for uplifting "foreign" elements concentrated most heavily on women who were responsible for making sensuality innocent. (188–89)

Women in the 1920s comprised from one-third to one-half of the screen writers. "From the memoirs of several, we can see they were in the vanguard of moral experimentation, forging into dress reform, new sexual styles, and consumption. . . . Their plots overwhelmingly revolved around heroines like themselves" (189). Ethnically, May observes that "Jewish film moguls were ideal middle men for a fusion of styles . . . Zukor . . . capitalized on the star . . . who could synthesize moral experimentation with traditional virtues. . . . Wall street bankers hedged, and Zukor . . . turned to ethnic financiers. . . . With the help of A. H. Gianini's Bank of Italy (the future Bank of America) and the German-Jewish firm of Kuhn and Loeb" (176). But it was not just ethnics who were important: Cecil B. DeMille was the scion of an eastern elite family.

His father was descended from a long line of Huguenot planters in South Carolina . . . took orders to become an Episcopal priest, but shed the clerical collar and turned to writing domestic dramas. His mother came from a German-Jewish family and apparently converted to her husband's religion; she was active in the circles of New York reformers . . . DeMille pioneered a set of marital ethics that the Protestant churches would not sanction until ten years later. . . . The director knew that this rebellion held a strong appeal for women. In fact, over 90 percent of DeMille's films in the late teens and twenties were written by female scenarists. (May 206–9)

Effects on the Arts and Philosophy   Cohen reminds us that modern fiction writing is tremendously dependent upon a cinematic way of seeing and telling; that Marx and Freud among other shapers of the intellectual concepts of modernity used cinematic metaphors for fundamental concepts (ideology as camera obscura, dreams as screen projections); and that Bergson is only one of the twentieth-century efforts to examine the similarity between thought processes and cinematic processes to show the constraints fostered by mechanistic epistemology. Lawrence Rickels (1991) has attempted to reread "California" through the Freudian and Marxian cinematic metaphors latent in the Frankfurt School's social analyses of modernity. His book is brilliant, mind-expanding, and hilarious for those who wish to be challenged but probably too elliptical and dense for undergraduates without considerable coaching.

Consumer and Industrial Economy   Mary Ann Doane provides useful starting points, at least for Hollywood films, touching on the relations among gender, film, and the commercial circuits; how workers were incorporated through film and advertising into a consumer economy (deflecting resistance to the industrial and corporate structures); how commodity tie-ins were closely associated with film releases by film studio publicity departments; the ways in which women might be moved in and out of the labor force (as in *Rosie the Riveter*); and, above all, how the gaze cultivated in the movies and advertising is quite different from that of the literary or art critic. It is a gaze that "hovers over the surface of the image, isolating details which may be entirely peripheral in relation to the narrative" (29) but not to the consumer economy. Attention to advertising and film in India suggests that a whole new process of social stratification is occurring around the markers of middle-class commodity consumption but involving ethnicity, class, and caste in new ways (Appadurai and Breckenridge 1991; Fischer, "Figuring (Indian) Ads").

Conclusions: Multiculturalism, Ethnography, and Cultural Critique

Various ways exist in which multiculturalism might be addressed in the classroom. A sufficient variety of films that American ethnics (African Americans, Asian Americans, and Hispanic Americans, for example) have made about themselves are becoming available and could provide the syllabus for a thematic course on ethnicity and diversity. We included some of these films in our syllabus. However, because what is at issue is multiculturalism understood not as old-fashioned identity politics with essentialized ethnic cultures with their own values, but rather multiculturalism as the creation of new pluralisms and hybridities—multiple individual identities, overlapping socialities, and enriched multiple cultural resources available within American society for domestic use and as bridges abroad—it seems more important for us to throw our analytic net more broadly than mere ethnic or ethniclike groups (e.g., gays or gender-defined groups).[10] Above all, it is important to include in discussions of multiculturalism in America some access to the cultural resources encoded and carried in ways not immediately available through English and the conventions of Hollywood and some access to a comparative perspective on how film changes perceptions and forms part of the constituting of modernity.

Discussions of multiculturalism tend to be overly localized and need a comparative perspective. Anthropology's greatest strength derives from the dual focus of grounding in concrete historical and ethnographic contexts and, at the same time, maintaining a comparative perspective. Film provides a similar comparative perspective for many across the globe. Although Hollywood tended to be a homogenizing and parochializing force for many Americans, the influx of foreign and ethnic self-defining films has begun to help change consciousness along with the demographic forces changing the social composition of America.

Out of this comparative perspective, which can be powerfully transmitted in intelligently constructed films, cultural critique can be fostered and turned to creating societies in which we want to live. The film industry in Hollywood, from its beginning, was multicultural. The recovery of that fact through the kind of work cited by May may help reconsiderations of film's role in America, how film apparatuses can work ideologically, and the fact that film apparatuses (the way they are made and how they lock into circuits of the economy, politics, psychology, and gender relations) can be reconstructed in various ways.

As people become more film literate, more film critical, film can become a tool rather than a passive means of consumption and entertainment. There are many examples of how film can be active: the use of video by the Kayapo to appeal to international audiences against the destruction of their lands by Brazilian state hydroelectric dams; the psychoanalytic transferencelike presence of Claude Lanzmann in *Shoah* (1985); the ways in which some filmmakers in Germany try to provoke audiences (e.g., *The Nasty Girl*); and the fine line that the new generation of young black filmmakers in the United States finds themselves treading between mirroring the violence of the streets and finding a way to turn such mirrorings in positive rather than negative directions (e.g., the remarkable series of films that presaged the 1992 Los Angeles riots: *Do the Right Thing, Boyz 'N the Hood, New Jack City,* and *Juice*). Film is not just a passive consumption-entertainment form; it is active in asserting political agency, as in the Kayapo case, and in provoking thought and possible behavioral change in the other examples. These all invoke the problems of multiculturalism and the creation of new pluralist civil societies, both in the United States and abroad, under conditions of transnational migration and transnational cultural exchanges of an intensity and pervasiveness that will change everyone's lives.

Appendix: Syllabus for Film as Ethnography and Cultural Critique in the Late Twentieth Century (Rice University)

DISCUSSION TOPICS, READINGS, AND SCREENINGS

Week 1

Introduction: Goals of the Course

Readings: Noel Burch, *To the Distant Observer: Form and Meaning in the Japanese Cinema* (Berkeley: University of California Press, 1979), 11–17 (Japanese film esthetic) and 61–66 (Hollywood illusionism); M. M. J. Fischer, "Collage of Quotes from Film Theorists on the Themes of the Course" (handout, 1992); Tadao Sato, *Currents in Japanese Cinema* (Tokyo: Kodansha International, 1982), 15–30 (two types of male role); and Slavoj Zizek, *Looking Awry: An Introduction to Jacques Lacan through Popular Cinema* (Cambridge: MIT Press, 1991), 3–6 (Zeno's paradoxes and staging desire).

Week 2

Cultural Codes: Critiquing Oral Tradition, Using a National Epic

Films: Gaston Kaboré, *Wend Kuuni* (Gift of God, 1982); and Trinh T. Minh-hà, *Surname Viet Given Name Nam* (1989), (supplementary: Trinh T. Minh-hà, *Naked Spaces* [1985]).

Readings: Manthia Diawara, "Oral Literature and African Film: Narratology in *Wend Kuuni,* " in *Questions of Third Cinema,* ed. Jim Pines and Paul Willemen (London: BFI Publishers, 1989); and Huynh Sanh Thong, "Introduction" to *The Tale of Kieu* (New Haven: Yale University Press, 1983).

Week 3

Cine-Writing: Montage, Fishing for Images
Films: Jorge Furtado, *Ilha das Flores* (Island of Flowers, 1989); and Pier Paolo Passolini, *Notes towards an African Orestes* (1970), (supplementary: Fax Barr with George Hickenlooper, *Hearts of Darkness* [1991]).
Readings: Peter Brooks, "Fictions of the Wolf Man: Freud and Narrative Understanding" in *Reading for the Plot* (New York: Random House, 1984), ch. 10 (four orders of narration in Freud); and William Burroughs, "Screenwriting and the Potentials of Cinema," in *Writing in a Film Age: Essays by Contemporary Novelists,* ed. Keith Cohen (Niwot: University Press of Colorado, 1991).

Week 4

Constructing Documentaries
Films: Rea Tajiri, *History and Memory* (1991; Japanese-American internment); Raul Ruiz, *De grands evenements et des gens ordinaires* (Of Great Events and Ordinary People, 1979), (supplementary: Michael Apted, *Thirty Five Up* [1992]; *Incident at Oglala* compared with *Thunderheart* [both 1992]; Connie Field, *The Life and Times of Rosie the Riveter* [1980]; and Agnieszka Holland, *Europa Europa* [1991]).
Readings: Bill Nichols, *Representing Reality: Issues and Concepts in Documentary* (Bloomington: Indiana University Press, 1991), 18–23 (supplementary: ch. 2); and Jonathan Rosenbaum, "Mapping the Territory of Raul Ruiz," *Cinematograph* 3 (1988): 166–78.

Week 5

Cultural Codes and Cultural Critique
Film: Farida Ben Lyazid, *A Door to the Sky* (1988).
Readings: Merzak Allouache, "The Necessity of a Cinema which Interrogates Everyday Life," in *Film and Politics in the Third World,* ed. John H. Downing (New York: Autonomedia, 1987), 93–98; Pat Aufderheide, "The Maghreb," 6–7; Victor Caldarola, "Reading the Television Text in Outer Indonesia" (1991, handout); Fedwa Malti-Douglas, *Women's Body, Woman's World: Gender and Discourse in Arabo-Islamic Writing* (Princeton: Princeton University Press, 1991), 3–10 (supplementary: ch. 1); Fatima Mernissi, *The Veil and the Male Elite: A Feminist Interpretation of Women's Rights in Islam* (New York: Addison-Wesley, 1987), 1–2, 9–11, 63–81; Miriam Rosen, "Cinemas of the Arab World," Arab Film Festival (handout); and Moumen Smihi, "Moroccan Society as Mythology," in *Film and Politics in the Third World,* ed. John Downing (New York: Autonomedia, 1987), 77–87.

Week 6

Constructing Documentaries, Surreal Realism under Communism

Films: Maria Zmarz-Koczanowicz, *Kazdy Wie Kto Za Kim Stoi* (Everyone Knows Who's Standing behind Whom, 1982); *Jestem Mezczyzna* (I Am a Man, 1986); and *Urzad* (The Office, 1987).

Readings: Janusz Anderman, *The Edge of the World* (New York: Reader's International, 1988), 94–96; and Charles Eidsvik, "Mock Realism: The Comedy of Futility in Eastern Europe," in *Comedy/Cinema/Theory*, ed. Andrew Horton (Berkeley: University of California Press, 1991), 91–105.

Week 7

Cultural Critique, Hybridity

Film: Ngozi Onwurah, *The Body Beautiful* (1991), (supplementary: Ngozi Onwurah, *Coffee Colored Children* [1988]); Christine Choy et al., *Mississippi Triangle* (1983); Jamil Dehlavi, *Towers of Silence* (1975); Ann Hui, *Song of the Exile* (1989); Stephen Frears, *Sammy and Rosie Get Laid* (1987); Spike Lee, *Jungle Fever* (1991), and Mira Nair, *Mississippi Masala* (1992).

Readings: Homi Bhabha, "Signs Taken for Wonders," *Critical Inquiry* 12, no. 1 (1985): 144–65; and M. M. J. Fischer, "Ethnicity and the Postmodern Arts of Memory," in *Writing Culture: The Poetics and Politics of Ethnography*, ed. James Clifford and George Marcus (Berkeley: University of California Press, 1986).

Week 8

Engage Documentary and Narrative

Film: Michel Kheleifi, *Canticle of Stones* (1990), (supplementary: Michel Kheleifi, *Fertile Memory* [1980] and *Wedding in Galilee* [1987]; and Marguerite Duras and Alan Resnais, *Hiroshima, Mon Amour* [1959]).

Week 9

Allegorical Codes

Film: Zhang Yimou and Yang Fengliang, *Ju Dou* (1989), (supplementary: Gyula Gazdag, *Az Volt Hol Men Volt* [Hungarian Fairy Tale, 1986]).

Readings: Yuejin Wang, *"Red Sorghum:* Mixing Memory and Desire," and Tony Rayns, "Breakthroughs and Setbacks: The Origins of the New Chinese Cinema," both in *Perspectives on Chinese Cinema,* ed. Chris Berry (London: BFI Publishers, 1991); Chen Xian, "Shadowplay: Chinese Film Aesthetics and the Philosophical and Cultural Fundamentals"; and Bai Jingshen, "Throwing Away the Walking Stick of Drama," in *Chinese Film Theory,* ed. G. Semsel, Xia Hong, and Hou Jianping (New York: Praeger Publishers, 1990).

Week 10

Modernity and Iranian Codes

Films: Parviz Kimiavi, *Moghul-ha* (The Mongols, 1974); Ali Nasirian, *Agha-ye Holu* (Mr. Gullible, 1971); and Mohsen Makhmalbaf, *The Peddler* (1986), (supplementary: Jamil Dehlavi, *Towers of Silence* [1975]; and Gassem Ebrahamian, *The Suitors* [1988]).

Readings: M. M. J. Fischer, "Towards a Third World Poetics: Seeing Through Short Stories and Film in the Iranian Culture Area," *Knowledge and Society* 5 (1984): 171–241; and Hamid Naficy, "Exile Discourse and Televisual Fetishization," *QFRV* 13, nos. 1–3 (1990): 85–116.

Week 11

Bombay Film, Popular Genres, and Cultural-Political Critique

Films: Kundun Shah, Sudhir Misra, and Renu Suluja, *Jaane Bhi Da Jaaro* (Who Pays the Piper, 1991), (supplementary: Raj Kapur, *Awaara* [Vagabond, 1951]; Ramesh Puri, *Tejaa* [1990]; Ramesh Sippy, *Sholay* [Flames, 1975]; and Ramgopal Varma, *Shiva* [1990]).

Readings: Wimal Dissanayake and Malti Sahai, *Sholay: A Cultural Reading* (Delhi: Wiley Eastern, 1992), 9–28, 64–67; Vijay Mishra, Peter Jeffrey, and Brian Shoesmith, "The Actor as Parallel Text in Bombay Cinema," *Quarterly Review of Film and Video* (1988): 11; Ashis Nandy, "An Intelligent Critic's Guide to Indian Cinema," *Deep Focus* 1, nos. 1–3 (1987–88): 68–72, 53–60, 58–61; and Rosie Thomas, "Melodrama and the Negotiation of Morality in Mainstream Hindi Film," in *Orientalism and the Postcolonial Predicament,* ed. Carole Breckenridge and Peter Van der Veer (Philadelphia: University of Pennsylvania Press, 1994).

Week 12

Kayapo: Controlling the Medium

Films: M. Beckham, *Disappearing Worlds: The Kayapo* (1987), *The Kayapo: Out of the Forest* (1989), *Video in the Villages* (1989), *A Fesa Da Moca* (1987), *The Spirit of T.V.* (1990), and *The Fruit of Forest People's Alliances* (1990).

Readings: Vincent Carelli, "Video in the Villages: Utilization of Video-Tapes as an Instrument of Ethnic Affirmation among Brazilian Indian Groups" (photocopy); Terence Turner, "Representing, Resisting, Rethinking: Historical Transformations of Kayapo Culture and Anthropological Consciousness," in *Colonial Situations: Essays on the Contextualization of Ethnographic Knowledge,* ed. George W. Stocking (Madison: University of Wisconsin Press, 1992); and Terence Turner, "Visual Media, Cultural Politics, and Anthropological Practice: Some Implications of Recent Uses of Film and Video among the Kayapo of Brazil," CVA.

Week 13

Bushmen, Trobrianders, Australian Aborigines

Film: John Marshall, *N!ai, the Story of a !Kung Woman* (1980), (supplement: *Trobriand Cricket* [1976] and *Waiting for Harry* [1980]).

Readings: Robert Gordon, "People of the Great Sandface," 1990; Richard B. Lee, "Art, Science, or Politics? The Crisis in Hunter-Gatherer Studies,"

American Anthropologist 94 (March 1992): 31–49; and Keyan Tomaselli, Teshome Gabriel, Ntongela Masilela, and Amie Williams, "People of the Great Sandface," *Visual Anthropology* 5 (1992): 153–66.

Notes

1. This film (*Surname . . .*) by Trinh T. Minh-hà is an interestingly problematic limit case because it—and her equally problematic polemical writings—attempts to deny the utility of presenting information that would allow serious cultural critique to occur. She seems very much a traditional romantic esthete in this sense.

2. Compare the opening chapter of Theodore Roszak's novel *Flicker* (1991), which could be used as class reading as a model of such exercises; Part 3 of Dissanayake and Sahai (1992), which provides a simple research example of reception differences among viewers; and the paper by the Indian-American student described subsequently.

3. From my own perspective, having interviewed both leads, Shabana Azmi and Om Puri, *City of Joy* poses a series of interesting contradictions and film industry negotiations, beginning with, on the one hand, the incongruity of such stars, with their exceptionally healthy bodies and upper-class accents, portraying destitute Bihari peasants in Calcutta. On the other hand, the meaning of Shabana Azmi's performance cannot be separated from her highly visible involvement over the years in making film socially responsible. Her early career was devoted to creating serious roles for women; she now heads the government bureau for children's films and is one of the few superstars who has maintained careers in both the parallel and commercial cinemas. Her role in *City of Joy* thus functions as a statement of the interplay between the power structures in the Indian film industry and in the international film industry. Her lead role in *Madame Sousatzka* (1988), by contrast, did not raise such issues. Still, the life portrayed in the film, particularly the exquisite old godfather and the magnificent little cripple, exceeds the film's constraints.

4. For one insightful review of the background to the reorganization of the visual to which film contributes, see Crary. For a survey of the effects of the filmic imagination on modernist European writers and thinkers in the early twentieth century, see Cohen (*Film and Fiction*).

5. Tamil film was consciously used as a political organizing device, with fan clubs serving like ward organizations. Lead actors, who later became chief ministers, selected roles and lines with careful attention to their political image. This all predated M. N. Srinivas's introduction of British social anthropology into the more census-sociological and social work styles of analyses in colonial and postcolonial academia and administration.

6. See the collections on anthropological film and video in the 1990s, *Anthropological Film and Video in the 1990s*, ed. Jack Rollwagen (Brockport: The Institute Press, 1993) and in *Visualizing Theory: Selected Essays from Visual Anthropology*, ed. Lucien Taylor (London: Routledge, 1993). The two key

journals in the field are the *Visual Anthropology Review* and the *Commission on Visual Anthropology (CVA) Newsletter.* Books analyzing ethnographic film traditions and filmmakers are now also beginning to appear, for example, Rosalind Morris, *New Worlds from Frangments: Film, Ethnography and Representation of Northwest Coast Culture* (Boulder: Westview Press, 1994); Peter Crawford and David Turtoor, eds., *Film as Ethnography* (Manchester: Manchester University Press, 1992); Jay Ruby, ed., *The Cinema of John Marshall* (New York: Harwood, 1993); and Paul Stoller, *The Cinematic Griot: The Ethnography of Jean Rouch* (Chicago: University of Chicago Press, 1992). As these works make clear, the visual has not been well integrated into more general ethnographic work, and indeed for the purposes of the present course, work on rational cinema and television are at least, if not more, important, for example, James Lull, *Turned On: Television, Reform, and Resistance* (New York: Routledge, 1991).

7. The visual record used as documentary by ethnography might have contributed to a sense of essentializing and temporal distancing of the sort that Johannes Fabian indicts in his now widely cited *Time and the Other: How Anthropology Makes Its Object* (1983). The point is to look for the alternative visual tracks that exist in the world rather than always coming back to those constructed by any particular set of commentators.

8. See Lyotard's "Figure Foreclosed" and "The Dream-Work Does Not Think," both reprinted in Benjamin; for an introduction to the argument, see *Reader.*

9. See Jameson ("Third World Literature" and "Regarding Postmodernism") and Aijaz Ahmad's critical response ("Jameson's Rhetoric").

10. The recent emergence of queer politics in contrast to gay identity politics parallels the argument here.

3

Cultural Rhetoric, Difference, and the Teaching of Writing

Margaret Himley and Delia C. Temes

> The choice of language and the use to which it is put is central
> to a people's definition of themselves in relation to their natu-
> ral and social environment, indeed in relation to the entire
> universe.
> —Ngugi Wa Thiong'O (Giroux *Border Crossings,* 19)

The following discussion comes out of work done in our collaboratively designed and taught upper-division composition course at Syracuse University, a private university in upstate New York. Syracuse
has about ten thousand undergraduates, most of whom are enrolled
in professional colleges and schools. Advanced composition courses
typically take up an aspect of language use—a genre, the composing
process, classical rhetoric—and treat it in depth while also extending that knowledge to other fields or disciplines.

Ideally, our course, The Study and Practice of Narrative, enables
students to develop further their rhetorical skills as readers and writers of texts of all kinds and discover, through writing, a way to question, challenge, and even rethink the ways they interpret, act in, and
respond to the world. For it is in language use that our selves are inscribed, our worlds constructed, and our possibilities enacted.

Writing becomes one means by which students may achieve an
understanding of the demands, the injustices, and the possibilities
of a complexly multicultural and divided world; for locating their
position and responsibility within the social order of things; and for
communicating that understanding effectively with others for the
betterment of all. To act within this horizon of hope, we have turned
to cultural rhetoric and the theories and politics of difference as
organizing frameworks for the design and development of our writing course, or "studio," as such courses are called at Syracuse.

We want to teach from and toward an understanding of how difference is constructed through various representations and practices in culture that name, legitimate, exclude, and marginalize gender, race, sexuality, class, and ethnicity. And we want to do so with an awareness of the power struggles involved in those representations and practices, without falling into the trap of a liberal notion of multiculturalism that merely wants to add on new voices without challenging the power relations at stake in having suppressed those voices.

Writing 305: The Study and Practice of Narrative

Our studio examines narrative as both theory and act. Storytelling is a fundamental use of language for ordering and understanding the world, and the stories we tell (and that are told about and for us) have powerful implications for us as individuals trying to write our own lives and as social actors striving to participate in professional and public spheres. The topic of storytelling particularly interests us because, as educators, we are deeply implicated in the production of individual, disciplinary, and cultural narratives. The course gives us a chance to listen carefully and dialectically to students as they tell their narratives and also shows the partiality and particularity of all our stories.

To introduce the topic, we read about narrative from the perspective of literary theory and semiotics, write and interpret our own stories, and explore cultural narratives (of gender and class, for example) as they are represented in television, film, and fiction. We introduce and explain the course to our students in the following introduction to the syllabus.

> WRT 305 is an "advanced" writing course. As such, it makes certain assumptions about your writing abilities and background: that you are familiar with studio practices (groupwork, peer response, conferencing, informal writing), that you have attained a measure of organizational, stylistic, and mechanical fluency in your writing, and that you are willing to work your way through complex ideas, in writing and reading, to analyze and understand how arguments and claims are made and supported, and that you are also willing to enter into an intellectual conversation with other writers as you formulate and develop your own arguments.
>
> The topic of this section of 305 is narrative. People tell stories all the time—in conversation, newspapers, advertisements, literature, academic lectures and research, and in professional settings such as law

and management. Starting from the premise that constructing narratives is a fundamental act of the human mind, we will explore several questions: how is narrative an important means for constructing a sense of identity; in what ways does narrative function within communities and disciplines; how and in what ways does popular culture such as television shows, movies and literature create narratives that both are and are not our stories? In order to understand how and why stories come to mean, we will examine the cultural stories told about us and to us, investigate the uses of narrative in media and disciplines, then design individual projects that extend our understanding of narrative in specific, individually chosen topics of inquiry.

The course looks at a range of narratives, from folktales, for many of us our first introduction to fictional narrative, to contemporary movies and television shows. We will read scholarly articles by narrative theorists, analyzing them rhetorically as well as discussing their approaches to narrative. In your own formal and informal writings, you'll try applying these theories, arguing for—or against—their use. As we seek to understand more fully the role of narrative in our lives and culture, we will be talking and writing about questions of gender, race, sexuality, class, and ethnicity. You may have seen these terms in the press lately, describing something called "politically correct" (PC) thinking. It is neither the purpose of this course, nor our intent as teachers, to indoctrinate you into the ideology of marxism or feminism, or any other "ism." We look at various viewpoints and systems of belief as a way to open up the possibilities for thinking and writing about issues, ideas and cultural artifacts we take for granted more often than we examine. Ours is a culturally diverse world in which power is distributed unequally. That statement contains two premises that will guide our investigation of narrative in culture.

We don't have a monolithic destination we expect us all to arrive at. Rather, we would like you to be able to entertain viewpoints and positions that may be new, or very different from your own, without simply dismissing them as not relevant. You may, indeed, end up countering claims and arguments, but through a reasoned and thoughtful analysis of the original position that provides support for your own equally reasoned argument.

Cultural Rhetoric

Cultural rhetoric means first 'reading' the world—looking at the relations of culture and ideology as enacted through and enabled by language and other practices of signification. Cultural rhetoric also refers to a method for doing that reading—for using theories of rhetoric and culture studies to have students and teachers develop that critical ability together. Our pedagogical use of cultural rhetoric is a reimagining of Dewey's call for "citizenship education" as realized in a postmodern world. It shares Dewey's emphasis on schools as a key cultural site but differs in its focus not on pragmatism but on critical literacy and civic courage. This move also requires a consideration of the questions and politics of difference in relation to achieving those educational goals by calling for a pedagogy that acknowledges the multiplicity and constructedness of the subject and the complex subject positions people occupy within different social, cultural, and economic locations. Citizenship that acknowledges difference educates people in the Gramscian sense of becoming agents who can and do locate themselves within history and culture.

Cultural rhetoric enacts the aims of a critical pedagogy by helping students and teachers alike learn how to 'read' the world and their lives critically, to understand their interdependence and potential mutuality, and to act in or 'rewrite' that world in order to better it. This aim does not eliminate either individual development or professional training, but rather embeds those goals within the larger context of culture and democratic life and results in a focus on the interrelationships of the individual, the social, and the professional. "The notion of being able to think critically on the basis of informed judgment and to develop a respect for democratic forms of self- and social-empowerment represents the basis for organizing school programs around the principles of critical literacy and civic courage. In other words, schools should be seen as institutions that prepare people for democracy" (Aronowitz and Giroux 205).

In our course, we take cultural rhetoric to be the study and practice of texts of all kinds—from short stories to editorials in the student newspaper to the latest popular movie—as semiotic or ideological events that function within culture to produce meaning, pleasure, power, knowledge, and the very conditions of subjectivities.

The Teaching of Writing

Difference

We consider the student writer as a social subject—that is, not casually or behaviorally social, but deeply, originally, and ontologically social. From this premise, the individual is understood as constituted within culture through the shared territory of language use and other semiotic practices (Himley). Oriented toward and drawn into the social and the public, the individual emerges within her or his reciprocal relationship with the world and with others in what Berger calls "the social function of subjectivity" (*Another Way of Telling* 100).

Irreducibly social, the writer is I/other or, as Trinh T. Minh-hà represents it, "I/i"—"the differences grasped both between and within entities, each of these being understood as multiple presence" (*Woman, Native, Other* 94).

The writing subject is a particular and positioned response to the world, multiple and complex, an answerability, changing, struggling, permeable to history, culture, and setting—and especially permeable to language. Learning to write, therefore, is not a simple or unilateral process in which an autonomous individual acquires new ways to express private and single-voiced intentions, but is rather a complex act of appropriation, assimilation, and resistance in which the individual learns the very meanings "s/he" can have. "I live in a world of others' words. And my entire life is an orientation in this world, a reaction to others' words (an infinitely diverse reaction), beginning with my assimilation of them (in the process of initial mastery of speech) and ending with assimilation of the wealth of human culture (expressed in the word or in other semiotic material)" (Bakhtin 143).

Because writing is a way to individuate through participation in public arenas of meaning, it is also an inherently political activity that involves differences in social power. People act in classed, racial, and gendered settings. To write is to make claims about what those settings are and how they should be, to enter into public discourses, and to locate oneself within and against those settings and discourses. People are, therefore, better able to be effective writers when they have an understanding of how difference and language work in culture and how their varied, complex, and often contradictory positions as particular language-users both allow and disallow them a public voice.

'Difference' replaces 'multiculturalism' for us. We do not often use the concept 'multicultural,' nor do we teach in what could be termed a "multicultural classroom." Our students are predominantly white and middle- to upper-middle class, although Syracuse has a significant Jewish population and a fairly active African-American student organization. An average writing class of twenty would have few, sometimes no, students who are not European American. In such a classroom we risk merely bringing in and potentially romanticizing the voices of others, while never calling into question the dominating aspects of European-American, or 'white,' culture or never questioning the norm of 'whiteness' itself.

As students become more critical readers of cultural narratives, particularly those of television and the movies, they also become more aware of themselves as constructed and positioned in and against culture in complex ways. As they come to recognize (and, to differing degrees, believe) the dominant culture to be one that suppresses and, at times, excludes nondominant narratives, they start becoming aware of "otherness," often because of its very absence. They are likely, then, to see a television show such as "Cheers" as offering few subject positions for any viewers who are not white men, heterosexual, or Christian. Their awareness of issues of difference comes through an acknowledgment of the sort of false homogeneity or limited diversity represented through our culture's popular media—and some awareness of the power dynamics and privileges in that representation. "Difference holds out the possibility of not only bringing the voices and politics of the Other to the centers of power, but understanding how the center is implicated in the margins" (Giroux 58).

As a theory and politics, 'difference' is not easy to work with, for us or for our students. The term can reinscribe racism and sexism, for example, when it is read as locating difference within people in essentialized and dualistic ways, or when it results in boundaries that border on separatism, or when it risks commodifying the other as spectacle, voyeurism, and entertainment. Difference cannot simply be read as identity, but must remain fluid, situated, contradictory, political, and historical.

So we move slowly. We start our course with the expectation that students will come to recognize, analyze, and respect difference, but we are also scrupulously careful to see that difference does not reside in the individual students in the class, who would become tokens. Having taught these issues many times, we have learned to be particularly conscious of the vulnerability of African Americans, women, lesbian and gay students, and, at Syracuse, working-class students to becoming spokespeople for their positions simply because their positions are more or less visible. We think of our classroom as one in which a Jewish man might actually learn to speak or read cultural artifacts from the subject position of a Latin-American woman. In other words, we try to teach, through a carefully designed sequence of reading and writing assignments, a relatively sophisticated way of being multicultural that goes beyond attending the events of Celebrate Diversity Week.

As a final project, a senior journalism major, a black woman, chose to investigate how blacks are included or excluded from the educational life, the "narrative," of Syracuse University, in particular its Newhouse School of Communications. She came to the class with a strong and obvious position but never stepped into the role of racial spokesperson. Her interest cut across all the issues. In her final assessment essay, she wrote:

> But more than my writing, my attitude has changed. I see my position in culture as multidimensional. I look not only at my race but also gender and how people view me. I am more aware of other people's positions, that though they are not my position, I am aware of what it means to be in those positions—such as working class and homosexual. These are positions that are considered inferior in our society, and now I am more conscious of how people in other "subordinate" groups are treated, and not just my own group—black woman.

Her final research paper contains eloquent and convincing evidence that reminds us, as teachers of multicultural issues and students, of the need for proceeding with utmost care and respect:

> [I was] the only black student in Newhouse's required "Introduction to Communications" course. When I took the course, the only black journalist we ever spent time on was Janet Cook, a woman who confessed to fabricating a story about a child drug addict after it was printed in the *Washington Post* and after she won a Pulitzer Prize for the piece. Not only was she mentioned, but shown to the class on a taped show of Donahue which exposed Cook's history of lying. Showing only the journalism career of Cook in this class gives students a false impression of blacks in the media. . . . Dean Rubin . . . said that if he says something that offends a black student, misrepresents blacks in media, or fails to recognize blacks in his discussion, black students should tell him so that he can make change. And students do have to speak up, according to Dr. Alvin Pouissant [who spoke on campus during Celebrate Diversity Week, November 1991]. "If you're quiet," he says, "you become accomplices in your own denigration." However, many of the black students I spoke with felt this imposed duty is sometimes frustrating.
>
> I'm taking a course this year in which the professor, whenever referring to black people, says for example, "Mr. Anderson, a black man or African-American, or man of color, whatever you want to call him," then continues his story. Perhaps this professor is trying to cover all bases as to not offend, when actually this is offensive to me as the only black student in the class. Whenever he says this I feel like white students are looking at me and thinking my race is so confused that we can't decide on what to call ourselves. (Michelle V. Mitchell, "White Classrooms and the White Agenda," December 1991)

There are risks in teaching this sort of course, and although we do not have a solution to every scenario, we have learned to expect certain kinds of opposition to what we do. Each semester reminds us of how deeply ingrained is the assumption of some students that they are still the standardbearers of culture. This has been expressed in essays that include all the "isms" the course investigates, most notably racism, sexism, and anti-Semitism. For example, one student wanted, for an early paper, to narrate stories about ethnic groups and blacks to show why such stories were or were not funny. He maintained that telling them was okay as long as no members of the specified group were in the audience.

We tell students early on that respect for difference is part of the academic requirement for the course, and although we do not force our politics on them, we do insist on ethical classroom behavior that grants space to all positions. In the few instances when a student uses a slur or epithet, we turn it into a subject of discussion. We remind them that this is a course in language use and that sometimes language uses us in ways in which we are not aware. Often students at Syracuse casually talk about "JAPS," the acronym for Jewish-American princess, a nasty stereotype particular to campuses with large Jewish populations. Neither of us hesitates to locate student comments like this within larger discursive and political patterns.

Popular Culture

As we have developed the course, we have turned more and more to popular culture, especially television and film, as a shared territory where meaning and pleasure come together. Watching "Roseanne" or *Full Metal Jacket* or feminist videos provides an immediate and compelling way to see how values, ideologies, and subjectivities are represented in cultural narratives. Media offers us as writing teachers a way of teaching both the content and the critical methods of the course. We do not explore these popular texts as evidence of the authentic voice of the masses or as illustrations of passive consumption and robotlike false consciousness. We explore these texts as open, multiple, contested sites of meaning and power.

> The basis for a critical pedagogy cannot be developed merely around the inclusion of particular forms of knowledge that have been suppressed or ignored by the dominant culture, nor can it center only on providing students with more empowering interpretations of the social and material world. Such a pedagogy must also attend to the ways in which students make both affective and semantic investments as part of their attempt to regulate and give meaning to their lives. (Giroux et al. 3)

Popular culture, especially television and film, is a theoretical choice, not a pandering to student apathy or a cheap shot at teenage appeal for an otherwise laborious course. Teaching begins in the lived experiences of ourselves and our students—"the cultural terrain of everyday life" (Giroux and Simon 10)—where meaning and pleasure work to shape the identity, politics, aims, and cultures. Students do not doubt that television and film, for example, exert profound influences on their lives as well as provide pleasure and comfort. They have a stake in popular culture that gives the course its political force. They investigate and argue about cultural narratives: how they are represented, what they mean, who benefits, what is told and what is not told, and how they themselves are constructed in culture. Their commitment creates a context in which they come to understand their positions. Their skills as thinkers and writers deepen, resulting in increasingly effective essays that make sophisticated claims and put forth genuine and persuasive arguments. "The production of subjectivities and of particular ways of life offers a point of intersection between cultural studies [rhetoric] and critical pedagogy" (Giroux and Simon 177).

One of the main theoretical texts we use in the course is John Fiske's essay "British Cultural Studies and Television," an accessible neo-Marxist analysis of culture as ideological production. Fiske defines cultural studies as the generating and circulating of social meanings through media like television and film, particularly along such axes of difference as gender, race, class, and sexualities. Drawing on the concepts of ideological state apparatuses (ISAs), subjectivity as social construction, interpellation, and hegemony, Fiske provides a heuristic for analyzing, for example, the intersection of race and masculinity in shows such as "Magnum, P.I." and the ways Madonna plays with conventional representations of women. He claims that cultural texts are open, the sites of struggle, and capable of being read in different ways by different people and that the meaning of texts is negotiated rather than transmitted. Fiske draws upon Stuart Hall's reading strategies to demonstrate how different meanings can be produced from the same text, depending on the viewer's social position in relation to the dominant ideology. He names these positions "dominant," "negotiated," and "oppositional."

We use a particular episode of the popular television show "Roseanne" to introduce the concept that a single meaning does not reside a priori in the show. In this episode, Roseanne and Dan's youngest daughter, the tomboy Darlene, gets kissed for the first time by one of her boy "pals." Secondary events include Becky's preparations for a date with a college boy, Roseanne's "facts of life" talk with Becky, and Roseanne and Dan's evening out with her sister Jackie and Jackie's boyfriend Gary. It is easy to watch the show as a humorous coming-of-age narrative and dismiss it. Asking students to apply Fiske's reading strategies to an analysis of the show, however, pushes them toward some more complex cultural interpretations. After a discussion of "what Fiske would say," we summarize and give back their theoretical analyses as Fiske might.

The Dominant Reading   This reading is produced by a viewer positioned to agree with the dominant ideology. The viewer enjoys the show because he or she identifies with certain dominant narratives of gender, class, race, and sexualities that reaffirm his or her way of seeing the world and making sense of social experience. This viewer adopts the social position the program constructs for him or her. Thus:

- Roseanne as the mother does the serious sex talk with the girls, highlighting mother's role as primary child-rearer.
- Dan, confronted with the evidence of his daughters' maturing, can only respond with anger, threats of revenge, and outrage. He is the authority figure.
- Both sets of sisters, Becky and Darlene and Jackie and Roseanne, are competitive and quarrelsome, whereas Dan and Gary bond over beer and their dismissal of "women's movies." Women can't get along with one another, whereas men are rational and detached.
- The parents are portrayed as dumb and out of it (after the sex talk, Darlene and Becky exclaim, in unison, "Oh, *lame*"), whereas kids are smart. It is, however, the parents' values, especially pertaining to sex, that are upheld in the end.
- This is how the working class lives—shared bedrooms, tacky furniture and decor, and one telephone and television set.
- Men are not trustworthy in their intentions to women. Dan tells Roseanne the story of his college buddy who slept around.
- Women manipulate situations to get men. Becky and Darlene discuss dating rituals and proper feminine dissembling. They also need to be careful about showing how much they know. Jackie can let the girls know what she knows about birth control but must be careful when Gary walks in.
- Women must look a certain way to be attractive, that is, thin and feminine. Becky wears a tight, short, flounced dress and heavy make-up; "Wow, you look great," exclaims Roseanne before hauling her into the kitchen for the sex talk.
- It is okay for Darlene to have a tomboy phase as long as there is an indication that she will grow up and move on to more conventional activities. She goes back to watching football with Dan after her

initiation into heterosexual behaviors. Their conversation about Joe Montana signals this change. When Dan comments on his powerful arm, she retorts, "Yeah, nice butt, too."

The Negotiated Reading   This reading is produced by a viewer situated to agree with some of the representations more strongly than others. It is the typical reading because different viewers will find different ways into the text based on their various individual positions. For example, women will find things that reflect and affirm their social positions; they will shift the text slightly toward their own interests, one of which might be, in our course, the narrative portrayal of strong women. Thus:

• Roseanne is a strong and assertive woman. She has very aggressive lines in this episode, and it is clear that she, not Dan, makes the major decisions about the family. Her wise-cracking humor keeps her on top of situations and seems to empower her both as a mother and as a woman. It is hard to get the last word in on Roseanne.

• Roseanne is unabashedly fat and sexual at the same time. She presents women with a way of contesting the feminine ideals of culture. Roseanne defies the patriarchal standards of beauty: She is not thin or blonde, she does not wear makeup or stylish or alluring clothes, and she does not defer to men in her demeanor.

The Oppositional Reading   This reading is produced by the viewer who is unwilling to negotiate with the text and instead deconstructs the dominant ideology. The text often angers and annoys the oppositional viewer, possibly to the point of stopping watching the show altogether.

• Left to a different course of events, Darlene might come to a different awareness of her sexuality, but she gets taken up by the dominant culture before she has a chance to be aware of alternative sexualities. Clearly, a lesbian child would not be acceptable to this family. The first hint that Darlene has that her development lags behind "normality" is when Becky accuses her of being "such a virgin." Then later Brian agrees that it would be a real joke if Darlene were to go out for cheerleading. The cues from the dominant ideology are so strong that Darlene is moved out of her developing lesbianism to kiss her friend, admire Montana's butt, and generally assure both family and viewers that she will be heterosexual forever.

• By the end of the episode, the whole Connor family has been disrupted. Roseanne cannot play basketball well enough to join Dan in a consoling game of hoops, and he withdraws into the masculine world of sports while she goes into the feminine one of the home. The girls giggle over their parents' ineptitude.

• As the credits role, Darlene is once again watching football with Dan, but now from her "normal" position of lusty female, looking at "butts."

It is easy for students to see how they can extend this beginning knowledge of theory to more ambitious projects that pull together narrative theory and popular culture. From the sort of informal analysis of "Roseanne," they can write on topics such as the following or design their own, often from something they have found interesting but never had the opportunity to write about:

In this paper [we tell the students] try looking at cultural narratives from a viewpoint influenced and shaped by the theoretical reading we did. You need to begin from a premise, explore and argue your way through some evidence you accumulate from watching your text, and reach some general conclusions. These are meant to be suggestive, not prescriptive.

1. Watch an evening of television (e.g., 8–11) on one channel. What cultural values seem to be set out and reinforced by the shows? Commonalities? Differences? How do commercials work to reinforce or contest the shows' texts? What kinds of gender, class, race, ethnic, sexuality narratives are unfolded? What subject positions are offered? What ISAs are operating?

2. Pick one television show (new, current, or in syndication) and argue for a positioned reading from one of Fiske's strategies. Take into account roles of gender, class, etc. Examine the range of subject positions offered by the show.

3. Watch a movie from this era or another one (1940s, 1950s musicals, mysteries, etc.) and analyze it from a perspective shaped by your reading in White and Fiske. How do master narratives get structured and reinforced? How are these "read" differently now than they might have been in the past? Or how are they indicative of some values, narratives, that don't change?

4. Watch a Saturday morning of children's programming (or several mornings of "Sesame Street," "Captain Kangaroo," "Mr. Rogers' Neighborhood"). Discuss the subject positions offered to children— how are they constructed by the shows they watch, what assumptions are made about their values? What role do commercials play in reinforcing or contesting the values represented by the shows?

Theory and Writing Development

Most importantly, students develop as writers through cultural rhetoric. Theory gives them ideas and claims that move beyond personal opinion or experience. They can take a concept—interpellation, for example—turn it into a question about who gets hailed and how, and open a text like "Roseanne" or a short story such as Katherine Mansfield's "Bliss" from this larger perspective. Some students claim that these concepts allow them to name and understand how they read a text, something they are used to doing, but in less articulated ways. Maybe. Certainly, the theories produce an ongoing heuristic for interpreting a wide range of visual and written texts. They also draw students into the details of the text to examine questions of how various readers construct it.

The theory also draws students into the cultural context by raising questions about a particular episode in relation to other episodes and other similar shows. Discussions of "Roseanne" lead easily into discussions of other family sitcoms and then to changes across time in gender role and class representation. Concepts such as hegemony and ISAs come out of a larger body of theory, so students develop more coherent arguments from all the material generated. Their claims hang together. Furthermore, if they have even vaguely followed the general argumentative moves of any of the theoretical articles they read, they, too, have an effective organization for their essays.

Perhaps, too, the theory gives both distance and ground, that is, students can take the safer or more rhetorically distant position granted (or enforced) by the theory ("what would Fiske say?") and yet they also have an authority for what they want to say located within a discipline and not dependent merely upon their own experience. Theory offers a rereading and respeaking of that experience within new terms. After awhile, in fact, it is unlikely that students will speak from personal opinion. It does not matter so much what the author or television show producer intends, or how individual viewers respond in the "I did/didn't like it" way. That becomes irrelevant unless it serves as evidence for how the student is positioned in culture as a reader or viewer.

A story from one of Delia Temes's classes illustrates how one student actually did move from narrating experience to reading and critiquing culture. We thought it useful to describe in detail the actual process, especially for those unaccustomed to teaching courses where writing is the content rather than an adjunctive or summative activity.

An African American woman (M.) wrote about fairy tales as exclusionary narratives (we had discussed in class how some stories bring us in and others hold us off). In her predrafting conference she mentioned that, as a little girl, she had loved the stories of Snow White and Sleeping Beauty, fantasizing how her life might be similarly changed by Prince Charming's arrival. When she was about eight years old, however, she realized that all the pictures in the stories showed white men and women and she began to feel very differently about them. It seemed likely that she would have a pretty good essay that could make some claims for both race and gender in fairy tale narrative.

The paper she turned in, however, was completely different from anything I anticipated. The first three pages were an analysis of Snow White (even the title of the tale became offensive to her) and Sleeping Beauty, then she suddenly moved into a brief discussion of Jack and Jill as reinforcing cultural stereotypes of women as inferior by having Jill come "tumbling after" and Jack breaking his "crown," showing that in this world, the man is king. That led her into telling a story about when she was seven years old and her aged minister died and her mother took her to see him in his coffin. She remembered him teaching them in Sunday School that death was a wonderful release and took you straight up to heaven, so when she saw him lying there so peacefully, "like he was sleeping," she felt very reassured. From this story, she moved to one that took place when she was older and went on a trip with a church group. One of her friends, a bright, popular boy, was run over by a car while crossing the street. This sudden introduction to the randomness of death put her at odds with the minister's teaching. Then in her last story she related the violent death of another friend from her neighborhood who had been shot in a drug-related argument.

The paper seemed to be two essays, one a conventional analysis of fairy tales without too much passion except when she talked about how she felt after reading them, and the other some very passionate personal narratives. The academic paper was, of course, the first one and the second one was the one we were worried, when we designed the course, that all the students would prefer to write—their personal stories. But I liked both papers, particularly the individualized voice in the second one, and I didn't want to shut down the passion in that second one for the objective analysis of the first. While she was revising and meeting with me about the paper, we began the unit on narrative theory .

It was the discussion of reading which claims that it is the reader who ultimately assigns value and meaning to narrative that opened a world of possibility to M. The claim that meaning exists between the narrator and the reader as a shared enterprise shaped by literary and cultural assumptions of particular communities in history was something she could understand. Ultimately, it was this theory that provided M., still struggling to complete the revision on her first paper, with the link between fairy tales and the narratives of her personal experience. In talking about certain cultural codes, what we came in the class to call "master narratives," she was able to move to a slightly more abstract analysis of both sets of narratives, seeing them as presenting her with cultural stories of happy-ever-after endings that ultimately left her feeling excluded and cheated as both a woman and as an African American.

Though we met several times over this first paper, M. actually only rewrote it entirely once. She was more interested in talking through places where she felt stuck and grew very adept at pinpointing the things she was unhappy with. After our last talk about the paper she announced that she was ready to go and write it up. The final version brought personal and literary narrative into a broader cultural framework and was also strongly written, much freer of the grammar and syntax problems in her first essay. I think that once she had a language—in this case the language of narrative theory—she also felt more assured about what she was writing. I had used the metaphor of learning theory as putting on special "narrative glasses" that let us look at the stories around us in new ways. For M., the glasses focused the seemingly disparate elements of her paper into a unified whole.

She continued to turn away from easy or accessible topics, constantly putting herself at risk (and, as she mentioned in her final reflective essay, always expecting to get a bad grade) in the drive to "figure this stuff out." Her second paper was a very insightful narrative analysis of Spike Lee's difficult film, *Do the Right Thing*, for which she viewed the movie four times and, using her new language of theory, very persuasively took on several of the movie's critics for not understanding it. The voice in the paper was assured and convincing, though she did stick in one "it's just my opinion" toward the end. Her final project was a very well-written examination of three events in American history as they were narrated in a standard high school history book and as they were narrated in an African American history book. Her discussion of exclusionary narrative and marginality was outstanding—the paper was one of the best ones in the class. Each time she took on something new and difficult and each time used theory in more sophisticated ways until, in the last paper, theory became the informing principle of the inquiry rather than just the language through which it was pursued.

It was not, I think, merely serendipitous that the leap from experience to theory was made so dramatically by a African-American woman in a class of students who were, in the main, profoundly unlike her in both background and outlook. In fact, her difference and her insistence on our recognition of it was what made her voice ultimately so powerful. M. never allowed the class to bring her into what she felt was a false community. When one student told a story about adolescence that marked him as privileged in certain ways, others wanted to accept it as a universal "rite of passage" tale that they all could "relate to." M.'s response was, "Well, maybe that's how it was in your neighborhood, but in mine you didn't go out after dark because you could get shot." Over and over she demanded we acknowledge and respect her difference, that we hear her stories as NOT necessarily like ours. Once she had the language to talk of "master narratives" in culture, she also had ways of being intellectual rather than merely personal about her difference. The "I" in her final paper was one that was both sophisticated and informed, rather than the personal and tentative "I" that characterized her first essay.

Earlier, we said that we hope that a course such as ours might help students discover, through writing, a way to raise questions about things that matter and to challenge and rethink the ways they interpret, act in, and respond to the world. This is exactly what M. and other students like her are often able to do. The course asks students to confront the reality of a world that isn't simply multicultural, plural, or diverse, but is rather a place where inequity and injustice are the quotidian. To understand and then, perhaps, object to the representation of difference and otherness in such popular culture artifacts as "Roseanne" is the first step to challenging a system that doesn't really provide equal justice or opportunity for all.

Appendix: Syllabus for Writing 305: The Study and Practice of Narrative (Syracuse University)

For teachers who might want to build a course of their own on the foundations of the one we've described, we include the contents of the reader we compiled, suggestions for extended writing assignments that integrate course readings with projects and topics proposed by students, and, for everyone who wants to know what to do on Monday, a syllabus. Each teacher supplements the core text with whatever she or he chooses—short stories, fairy tales, other essays, television shows, or films.

REQUIRED READING

Margaret Himley and Delia C. Temes, eds., *The Study and Practice of Narratives* (Boston: Copley, 1991). *Contents:* Wallace Martin, "Narrative Structure: A Comparison of Methods," from *Recent Theories of Narrative;* Katherine Mansfield, "Bliss," from *Recent Theories of Narrative;* Robert Scholes, "Semiotic Approaches to Joyce's 'Eveline,'" and James Joyce, "Eveline," both from *Semiotics and Interpretation;* Susan Jeffords, "Fact, Fiction, and the Spectacle of War," from *The Remasculinization of America: Gender and the Vietnam War;* Susan Lanser, "Toward a Feminist Narratology," *Style* (Fall 1986); Annette Kuhn, "Real Women," from *Women's Pictures: Feminism and Cinema;* Mimi

White, "Ideological Analysis and Television," and John Fiske, "British Cultural Studies and Television," both from *Channels of Discourse,* ed. Robert Allen; Donald McCloskey, "Storytelling in Economics," from *Narrative in Culture,* ed. Christopher Nash; and Robin West, "Jurisprudence as Narrative: An Aesthetic Analysis of Modern Legal Theory," from *New York University Law Review* (1985).

SUGGESTIONS FOR RESEARCH PROJECTS
Narrative in Culture

1. Extend the kind of analysis Rabine does and/or supplement it with ideology critique and cultural studies to examine "male" texts such as those by Ludlum, Follett, Clancy, or others you think of. Or, take the same approach and extend it into a consideration of "female" texts—movies, television, and "supermarket checkout line" novels.

2. Using the theoretical essays, work out what you think is your critical position as a reader of cultural narrative and use it to examine a television series over time, or to look at television series of a different time (1950s, 1960s). This would involve some research, perhaps historical.

3. Use a reading strategy and your critical position to explore the meaning in and interpretations of "genre" narratives, for example, Harlequin Romances and books by Danielle Steele and Stephen King. Or choose a popular magazine and examine the ways in which it may or may not inscribe dominant ideology. Be sure to acknowledge your position.

4. Use the Jeffords article as a "seed" piece and analyze a Vietnam narrative from a defined critical position. This could be a movie or a television show such as "China Beach" or a work of fiction.

5. Look at, among other things, how dominant ideology is inscribed in children's literature—the Hardy Boys, Nancy Drew, or someone more current like Judy Blume. Or, take up the idea of "masculinist/feminist" texts we developed from looking at the Jeffords and the Rabine articles and apply it to children's narratives—film or text.

6. Use a gendered position and ideology critiques and/or cultural studies to compare and contrast specifically gendered texts. Or, use feminist analysis to analyze the characters and themes in a novel.

7. Consider issues of class, race, gender, sexualities, and ethnicity as you investigate a large body of cultural narratives—MTV, a day-long session of network television, or shows on a specialized channel (the Black Entertainment Network, for example).

8. Find yourself a partner of the gender you aren't and explore gendered subject positions and reading strategies by choosing a film, book, or television show and critiquing it collaboratively. Collaborative projects should be roughly twice as long as single-authored papers and usually earn one grade for both partners.

9. For the creatively thwarted: Reread the Rabine article and write a short

romance. Then write a separate, brief essay in which you discuss the work critically in terms of its inscription of ideology (race, class, gender, sex roles). You could also do this in pairs, critiquing each other's stories.

10. For the really adventurous: Write a narrative essay that details your own intellectual growth as a subject in culture. Talk about ISAs, ideology, and how an understanding of what all that means helps you determine your cultural position.

Narrative and Disciplinarity

1. Discuss marketing (retailing or consumer studies) as studying, reproducing, or resisting dominant ideologies. Don't do this through advertising alone. Look at the texts in the field.

2. Read the article on narrative and the law by Robin West in the reader. Are there ways your discipline is open to a narratological analysis suggested by West?

3. The West article and one by Donald McCloskey on storytelling in economics (also in the reader) look at narrative in disciplinarity. What about disciplinarity in narrative? West suggests that Kafka and Melville are "legal" writers. Can you think of other narratives that are shaped, informed, or dependent on a view of your particular discipline or profession? How is that view unfolded? What subject positions are offered? How is culture encoded? What dominant ideologies are reinforced or contested? (For example, as an academic, I might want to read a novel about English teachers and examine the view of my profession and the academy created there. Would I contest it? Accept it? Or, as a finance or marketing major, what do I think about the ideology and the ISAs inscribed in narratives by Donald Trump and Lee Iacocca?)

4. Examine your discipline in terms of ISAs. What kinds of narratives does it value? What subject positions? How are you interpellated? As ways of research, you can look at the texts, the courses, and interview practitioners and teachers.

5. After reading the articles on disciplinarity and narrative, "try on" one of those approaches to identify and analyze the types and uses of narratives in your profession or discipline. You could tell the story of your discipline across time and in terms of major heroes (thinkers) and battles (issues).

DISCUSSION TOPICS AND ASSIGNMENTS

Week 1

Introduction to course and to cultural narrative.

Week 2

Read "The Twenty-Something Generation," *Time,* July 16, 1990, a cultural narrative about your generation. Locate two or three claims in it and write briefly on whether you agree or disagree; be prepared to read your essays and discuss your responses in class.

Week 3

Discussion of *Time* essay as cultural narrative. Revise and extend your informal responses to the essay into a three-to-five-page paper that uses specific evidence to back its claims.

Week 4

Introduction to narrative and narrative theories. Read Robert Scholes's "Semiotic Approaches to Joyce's 'Eveline'" and "Eveline" (in reader). Write on study questions for essay, noting particularly how Scholes structures his argument for interpreting "Eveline." Then read selections (to be discussed in class) from Lang, *The Blue Fairy Book*. Pick one of the folktales you read and write an informal essay that tries out one of the approaches Scholes outlines. Be prepared to share the essay in class.

Week 5

Discussion of folktales, informal essays, possible topics for paper number two. Selections from Lang, *The Blue Fairy Book*. Begin thinking (in writing) about what you might want to try in a formal paper. Discussion of folktales and paper topics.

Week 6

Conferences on formal paper number two, an analysis of a fairy tale or tales from some perspective suggested by the reading and class discussions.

Week 7

Mimi White, "Ideological Analysis and Television" (in reader). Write on the study questions and come prepared to talk, with specific references to the text, about her position, the claims she makes, and how she makes them. If you disagree, look for specific points of entrance in her text where you might argue.

Week 8

Begin reading John Fiske, "British Cultural Studies and Television" (in reader). Use study questions to guide your responses and think about the essay in rhetorical terms as for White. Video viewings: "Roseanne" and others. Discussion of Fiske, White, and videos. Write an informal essay (handwritten) in which you try applying some of the claims of Fiske and White to some aspect of one or both of those videos we watched. Be prepared to share your essay in class.

Week 9

Discussion of informal essays and how to extend this kind of analysis into formal paper number three—possible topic, ideas. Draft a brief proposal for paper number three (one page) that outlines an area to investigate, defines the argument, and suggests what evidence or support might help.

Week 10

Individual conferences (bring proposals).

Week 11

Susan Jeffords, "Fact, Fiction, and the Spectacle of War" (in reader). Write on the study questions and come prepared to discuss them in class. Write an informal essay on issues raised in class discussion.

Week 12

Video viewing: *Die Hard 2.* Write a brief, informal essay on the movie as particularly "masculinist" in light of the viewpoint expressed in Jeffords's essay (two to three pages). Read Leslie Rabine, "Romance in the Age of Electronics," in *Feminist Criticism and Social Change,* ed. Judith Newton and Deborah Rosenfelt (handout). Looking back at your informal essay on masculinist narrative, write briefly on what you think feminist elements in narrative might be, especially with regard to the movie we watched.

Week 13

Review all the positions we have considered, thinking about the language and concepts you would use to define your own position. Write a brief (one-page) "freethinking" paragraph about what you might like to explore for a final project, to what might you like to apply your developing consciousness of narrative. Draft a one-to-two-page preliminary proposal for your final project that includes not only what you will do but also how.

Weeks 14 and 15

Individual conferences and independent research.

Week 16

Oral presentation of research; draft of project for peer review. Final projects due, twelve-to-fifteen pages, typed.

Note

We would like to acknowledge the others who sometimes joined us in teaching the course—Faith Plvan, Molly Voorheis, and Bronwyn Adam. Our classes were enriched by their contributions.

4

Letting Go: Resistance and Transformation in the English Curriculum

Linda Dittmar

Teaching film within an English department, and doing so multiculturally on top of that, requires delicate negotiations. The use of any nonliterary materials can raise more than a few eyebrows, and the tendency is to dismiss all film courses, even the most canonic, as lacking intellectual rigor. Curriculum committees often distrust proposed film courses, and some faculty who teach literature in relation to the "high" arts do not accept film as an equal partner. When films find their way into literature courses, they usually function thematically, along the lines of, "Here is another story about. . . ." Exceptions do exist, of course. Drama (notably Shakespeare's plays, for which filmic adaptations abound) and fictional adaptations facilitate analyses of performance and interpretation. But a review of English course offerings nationally, of the annual programs of the MLA and similar organizations, and of available grant support reveals an overwhelmingly conservative definition of the discipline as focused on the written word and as qualified about multicultural teaching in either medium.

This situation creates special problems for those instructors most likely to teach film and least able to risk it—young and untenured faculty. They face the double burden of having to legitimize teaching film in principle and having to address their colleagues' fear that a multicultural emphasis will dilute the field of its standards and rigor. Ostensibly at issue is the choice of texts to be taught during the all too brief life-cycle of a course. But underlying that question remains a debate concerning the egalitarian social vision that motivates the challenge that multicultural teaching poses to the canon. At stake on both sides are deeply felt commitments and, at times, the life work of individuals. In this respect, the anxiety and defensiveness that film studies and multicultural concerns evoke have to do with the permeable boundaries and changing nature of English as a discipline, including its current receptiveness to cultural studies, and new historicism, legal studies, psychoanalysis, and other poststructuralist approaches.

I review these obstacles because it is helpful to sort institutional resistance imposed from above from the anxieties and misgivings teachers may experience when flying in the face of accepted practice. The following discussion mainly concerns the latter, precisely because internalized resistance is the hardest to dispel. Rather than describe courses hospitable to multicultural considerations (e.g., my Woman's Image on Film, Women Film Directors, America on Film, and The Politics of Film—none of them literature courses), I will focus on a course that seems resistant to a multicultural perspective—Narrative Form in the Novel and Film. As I have come to see, the problems this course raises have more to do with my own expectations than with institutional barriers. I will return to this issue of internalized resistance shortly, but should first explain that in my case there was no one to blame but myself. I teach in a department that allows my film work to flourish and in a university that welcomes multicultural approaches.

Founded in the mid-1960s, the University of Massachusetts–Boston is an urban state university that serves an adult, commuting, self-supporting, ethnically and racially diverse student body. With an average age of twenty-seven and often the first generation in their family to go to college, these students include adults considering career and life changes, Armed Forces veterans, retirees, and immigrants, as well as recent high school graduates. They bring to the classroom not only complicated feelings about ways their education may reposition them socially but also a fresh, diverse responsiveness to a universitywide curriculum that has been hospitable to multicultural and interdisciplinary teaching.[1] Our English department has been particularly active in shaping and implementing this curriculum and in developing a major that accommodates both canonic and nontraditional course work.

In this context, multicultural teaching in courses that include film is mainly a question of course design. In fact, some courses encompass it quite naturally, particularly a thematically organized course such as Literature of the Working Class, which always included film and was taught from a feminist perspective attentive to race and ethnicity. But my colleagues also incorporated multicultural perspective into courses ranging from Introduction to Shakespeare to Science Fiction. Science fiction, for example, teems with thinly disguised recreations of gender, race, class, national, and ethnic relations, and Shakespeare's *The Tempest* makes a fascinating case study in racial and colonial ideology on top of class and gender issues. Other literature courses offered in my department—Modernism, for instance, or Images of Women in Literature, Modern Drama, Introduction to Fiction, or African American Literature—are all similarly amenable to including filmic texts, and they are all open to multicultural perspectives.

In contrast, Narrative Form in the Novel and Film strains under the weight of its dual allegiance to two distinct media. Conceived in the early 1970s as an advanced undergraduate course in narratology, not themes or adaptations, it emphasizes style, structure, point of view, and self-reflexivity as discursive practices that foreground intersections of esthetics and epistemology. The original syllabus included some of the mainstays of art cinema—*Battleship Potemkin* (1925), *The Cabinet of Dr. Caligari* (1919), *Rashomon* (1950), and *Hiroshima, Mon Amour* (1959), for instance. The readings included Henry James's *The Turn of the Screw* (1898), Nathaniel West's *Miss Lonelyhearts* (1933), Vladimir Nabokov's, *Invitation to a Beheading* (1934), and William Faulkner's *The Sound and the Fury* (1929).[2] Although the course earns students five credits and meets for some six hours a week, the comparative work across media on top of the formalist and conceptual preoccupations of the modernist canon make it hard to interweave a multicultural perspective into this already demanding agenda.

Although some may argue that the diverse geographic, historic, and national origins of this course's materials automatically make it multicultural, my own definition of the term resists this view. As I understand it, the goal of multicultural teaching is to analyze diversity politically, as embedded in unequal power relations. It includes considerations of social class, gender, and sexual orientation, as well as ethnicity in shaping cultural and political identities. Seen in these terms, multiculturalism does not point to a melting pot model of social development. It does not suggest a horizontal continuum of differences wherein African Americans and recent Haitian immigrants to the United States, working-class heterosexual women and middle-class lesbians, or second-generation Japanese Americans and recent Cambodian immigrants are perceived as so many snowflakes, each unique and all ultimately alike. Instead of a pluralist notion of human variation, I propose a materialist, historic, and dialectical reading of cultural difference. Following Wahneema Lubiano's discussion of multiculturalism as negotiations of politics and knowledge

(11–12), my use of the word presupposes a socially transformative approach to education.

In terms of this definition, Narrative Form in the Novel and Film is not necessarily a multicultural course. Once the term *multiculturalism* is taken to entail considerations of social justice and social transformation, the course's international reach does not itself make it multicultural. After all, the original syllabus, dating back to the early 1970s, set forth a formalist agenda: It was mainly concerned with the semiotics of form and the ways narrative design help structure readings. In this respect the current syllabus has not changed much. Within a fourteen-week allotment, the sequence of novels and films guides the discussion further and further away from realism and narrative verisimilitude. Focusing mainly on narrative operations as epistemological and esthetic constructs, this work continues to subordinate theme-propelled readings to considerations of forms.

At least initially, and often until midsemester, students struggle to accommodate this unfamiliar perspective. Most of them have never had a course in film analysis, and they usually feel more comfortable discussing plot and character than analyzing scrambled chronology or camera angles as signifying practices. Most have never considered the function of film editing or mise-en-scène, and although they grasp the notion of point of view in fiction, they still have trouble understanding, say, how Virginia Woolf's syntax may affect her readers' construction of meanings. The very fact that the texts in the course are so self-reflexive about processes of expression and reception, so resistant to suture (Silverman 1983), and so committed to devices that foreground distanciation and "strange-making" effects, creates an unsettling learning situation further strained by the fact that most of our films are black and white and many either have subtitles or are silent. And matters get worse! Not only do students need to develop strategies for reading such materials but also the course keeps upping the ante as it progresses over the semester further and further away from the comforts of mimetic representation.

Such priorities do not necessarily mesh with a multicultural agenda, and they certainly leave little time for it within a crowded syllabus. Thus, even though a film like *Rashomon* comes out of a culture different from our own and is open to a historical-materialist reading in these terms, its place in my course (and in the film canon generally) has been more allied to Western art cinema and narrative theory than to studies in cultural difference. Similarly, *Pather Panchali* (1955) mainly functioned as an introduction to lyrical humanist realism, and only incidentally as a cultural artifact specific to its social and historic origin. Along similar lines, although *Hiroshima, Mon Amour* concerns extreme instances of nationalist and racist violence, in the context of the course I emphasize the way its cinematography shapes spatial, temporal, and therefore conceptual dislocations. This film's heightened self-referentiality encourages this reading despite its thematic focus on atomic holocaust and love across enemy and racial lines, but the choice ultimately remains the instructor's. Not surprisingly, until recently the last film screened—the course's apogee, so to speak—has been *Last Year at Marienbad* (1961), a film obsessed with the claustrophobic and self-referential activity of producing narrative materials. The novels interwoven into the course follow a similar trajectory. From *The Turn of the Screw* (1898) to *To the Lighthouse* (1927) and *The Sound and the Fury* (1929), the course's unfolding problematizes the notion of realism and foregrounds formal considerations.

As this overview suggests, introducing a multicultural perspective into a course as indifferent to thematic unity as this one requires careful reorientation. In part, this reorientation means seeking out novels and films which, at once, satisfy the course's emphasis on formal aspects of narrative discourse and infuse it with multicultural considerations. Less obviously, this reorientation also means working with any and all texts differently. This understanding that multiculturalism includes all diversities, including social class, gender, and sexual orientation, has proven particularly helpful in unprying Narrative Form in the Novel and Film from its seemingly neutral stance. The easiest first step for me as a white, middle-class woman was to open the course to women writers and directors (e.g., Virginia Woolf, Germaine Dulac, and Maya Deren) who at once fit squarely into the modernist tradition and introduce into it feminist perspectives that uncover cultural and political differences.

This move taught me that the course's roots in the patriarchal canon are not its inalienable essence. It showed me that the syllabus's progression toward subjectivity, self-referentiality, and formal abstraction was not as politically neutral as I had supposed. It also demonstrated that it is possible to modify the course's original agenda by introducing another trajectory into the syllabus. In this instance that trajectory extended from *To the Lighthouse* to *Hiroshima, Mon Amour* (text by Marguerite Duras), and from *The Smiling Madame Beudet* (1923) to *Meshes of the Afternoon* (1943).

On its face, this change is modest, for the new cluster consists of self-referential novels and films that blend easily into the course's original plan. But once one singles out women's social and material inscription as a subject matter in its own right, one foregrounds attention to gender as a social construct. In this respect female authorship can function oppositionally precisely because it is so often overlooked within the canons of literature and film. Its very presence denaturalizes existing power relations in ways that can be extended to other groups that gather under the multicultural umbrella.

Inserting into the course an awareness of difference and social marginality, these new works cleared the path to considerations of what Linda Alcoff calls "positionality" (405–36), including white positionality, as Richard Dyer argues ("White" 44–64). Key here is the idea that identities and texts get constituted within historical processes and bear the imprint of such external processes. At this point in the evolution of Narrative Form in the Novel and Film the emphasis happens to be on the imprint of history on women, but the awareness it fostered became available for dialogue with other multicultural concerns. Although not yet truly multicultural, this modest first step created a potential for developing the course in that direction.

Especially helpful was my decision to avoid inserting a discrete unit on women or, by extension, on any other group. As I have suggested elsewhere ("Inclusionary Practices"), such units necessarily segregate their subject matter and thus risk coming across as tokenist inclusions of devalued materials. Brief units, in particular, are likely to be tokenist (making one representation stand in for diverse actualities), in contrast to extended units that can frame a body of materials for in-depth study. My course America on Film does have a successful unit on African-American representations. In this case, segregation becomes an opportunity for an in-depth study that accords its subject matter considerable respect. It allows for singling out racism and pursuing it complexly in ways that are appropriate to this particular American studies course. But this structure is not useful in Narrative Form in the Novel and Film, which is more vulnerable to tokenism because it casts such a wide net. Here, in contrast, weaving multicultural concerns into a course's other agendas normalizes awareness of cultural specificity, dialogue, and conflict as an attribute of all thinking.

Each of these models has its own logic. In the case of Narrative Form in the Novel and Film, the interwoven model was dictated by the fact that I adapted a preexisting course where a new unit would have been the easiest but worst option. The course's formalist agenda and wide-ranging syllabus essentially reject a theme-driven unit. The solution was to find works that fit into the course's original conception and infuse it with multicultural awareness. In its present form, multiculturalism is, like the figure in the carpet, an orientation that can lay claim to our attention at any moment.

The feminist revision of Narrative Form in the Novel and Film proved useful to me, both as an intervention in the patriarchal presumptions of the canon and as a first step toward opening the course to other perspectives that register cultural difference. Approaching all texts from a feminist perspective, and weaving women's writing and filmmaking into the course as equal partners, of interest both formally and culturally, students learned to notice ways in which the relation between narrative discourse and the production of meanings is culturally specific. To recast John Berger's position in *Ways of Seeing,* they learned that our ways of reading, teaching, and studying shape the substance of what we read, teach, and study. What is important here is not a dichotomy between thematic and formalist approaches, as I had originally imagined, but the need to develop a course that puts its formalist concerns at the service of a socially motivated inquiry into the material origins and ideological functions of specific narrative discourses.

Seen this way, the course proved flexible enough to accommodate variation and adjustment. The feminist model alone can be much more multiculturally complex than mine was, regardless of whether one adopts a national or international definition of multiculturalism. Once the group sees ways in which Dulac, Deren, Woolf, and Duras fit in with the course's formalist concerns, it is possible to include films by Sarah Gomez, Julie Dash, Su Friedrich, Sally Potter, or Yvonne Rainer, to name just a few. It is also possible to incorporate novels by Djuna Barnes and Gertrude Stein, Toni Morrison, Gloria Naylor, Maxine Hong-Kingston, Leslie Marmon Silko, Monique Wittig, and others.

Forms and cultures clearly intersect in the work of these women, as they do in equivalent works by male novelists and filmmakers. Morrison, for one, can be studied in relation to William Faulkner, Ralph Ellison, and Ishmael Reed as well as in relation to Virginia Woolf. The thematic and formal preoccupations that energize *Beloved* (1988), for example, criss-cross the semester, linking this novel not only to *The Sound and the Fury, To the Lighthouse,* and *The Cabinet of Dr. Caligari,* all currently on the syllabus, but also to potential alternatives like *Invisible Man* (1947), *The Other Francisco* (1975), and *Daughters of the Dust* (1991). The possibilities, it turns out, exceed what any one semester might accommodate.

With options proliferating, the issue is less whether such a course can be taught multiculturally than the way one might approach this teaching. One can, for example, infuse it with a historical emphasis. One can gear it toward a broadly inclusive view of diversity or toward in-depth scrutiny of particular kinds of cultural expressions. One might focus narrowly on a country or a region and, within that framework, pursue multicultural questions chronologically, or one might inflect the issue through gender or social class as an organizing principle. Whatever the choice, it helps to approach multicultural awareness as a grid that lies over the entire semester. Vigilant to note connections and draw comparisons routinely, if sometimes only in passing, teachers can naturalize this perspective as an intrinsic aspect of the inquiry at hand.

In this respect, my decision to start Narrative Form in the Novel and Film with *Pather Panchali* (originally *Viridiana* [1961] occupied this position) proved fortuitous. The film's cinematography makes for an excellent introduction to the audio-visual operations of the medium and to an awareness of realism as an artifice made up of conventions, and the fact that it is an Indian film, black and white, subtitled, and accompanied by non-Western music, showcases and normalizes the discourse of the other. Screened on the first day of class, with only the briefest introductory lecture, the film and its position in the syllabus make an uncompromising demand for acceptance.

Learning to read the medium, students learn to read the construction of its subject matter. The other is not automatically readable, they discover, but difference does not preclude knowledge, identification, and analysis. Difference, they also learn, is a construct, the product of social relations and representations that cover a range of personal and social inscriptions. Male and female, young and old, insiders and outsiders, these identities and more are inscribed dialectically within this narrative, their interactions subtly inflected by the residues of British colonialism as well as indigenous cultural markings.

It is Satyajit Ray's lyrical treatment of these materials that makes *Pather Panchali* useful at this early point in the course. Third World directors whose work resists an affectionate, sympathetic Western gaze would necessarily play a more confrontational role were one of their films to serve as the entry-point into the course, and the same applies to any one of several independent filmmakers within the United States (e.g., Heile Gerima or Charles Burnett). But *Pather Panchali* eases students into the course gently, opening a safe space for both an affectional and a political reading of difference. Thus, my use of *The Turn of the Screw* as the first literary piece is not as great a leap as it might seem. Each work provides an excellent introduction to its medium, with the former to read film as an audio-visual medium and the latter teaching us to read literature verbally. Scrutinizing James's syntax, punctuation, and word choices and analyzing his use of narrating personae and framing narratives, students gradually uncover the role of conjecture and obfuscation as a central narrative ploy.

Taken together, this unlikely pair lays out the semester's agenda. *Pather Panchali* introduces the film medium, it questions realism as a representational discourse, and it normalizes attention to cultural difference (caste, class, nationality, and gender) as an ongoing political consideration for the course as a whole. *The Turn of the Screw* introduces the verbal medium, elicits a heightened skepticism about narrative as representing actuality, and allows us to continue normalizing the inclusion of cultural difference (class, gender, and sexual orientation) as ongoing considerations. Precisely because each is a canonic work within its discipline, admired and in this sense uncontroversial, each, once read against the grain, lays a foundation for the course's effort to unmask the ideology that informs all representations of communities and to promote a multicultural awareness. By the time we reach the end of the semester, students are more than ready for the two final works—Manuel Puig's novel *Kiss of the Spider Woman* (1976) and Sergio Giral's film *The Other Francisco*.[3] Coming as they do at the end of a long sequence of texts that increasingly reject mimesis and verisimilitude as models of knowledge, the two works foreground a self-referential attention to narrative practices as essential to reading difference in terms of power relations.

As a pair, the two share a Latin-American connection and thus a measure of cultural continuity, especially given their shared critique of repressive political regimes.[4] In my course, though, the main task for *Kiss of the Spider Woman* and *The Other Francisco* is to foreground the discursive practices of narration as complicit in framing and sustaining the dominant ideology. Thus, both Puig's novel and Giral's film put diverse fictional and nonfictional discourses into a dialectically conflicting interaction that invites a Brechtian reading. Interspersing simulated documentary, fiction, and authorial comment (voice-over in the film), both works question and recast formulaic narrative conventions.

Most immediately, *Kiss of the Spider Woman* protests the brutal repression of political dissidents in Argentina, linking it to a critique of fascism on the one hand and misogyny and homophobia on the other. *The Other Francisco* puts forth a historical-materialist critique of both slavery and abolitionism in Cuba, implicitly extending to contemporary capitalism and liberalism as propelled by economic motives. But coming as they do at the end of the semester, the political and formalist self-referentiality of the two works makes for a particularly good summing up of the semester. In terms of multiculturalism, their importance goes beyond historically informed national specificity. It includes analysis of the conflictual nature of difference and the abuses widely perpetrated in its name, notably regarding race, class, gender, and sexual orientation. *The Other Francisco* explores differences among slaves, for whom social class and national origin, and thus culture, prove as divisive as they are within the ruling class. *Kiss of the Spider Woman* does so in terms of social class, gender roles, and sexual identity as these come into play between the protagonists and across the stories told within their framing narrative.

This final summation pivots on my choice to have *The Other Francisco* replace *Last Year at Marienbad* as the course's concluding film. As long as *Last Year at Marienbad* occupied that position, the course's evolution stressed processes of discourse formation as an almost abstract idea. Even *Kiss of the Spider Woman* fit into this paradigm, encouraging us to see the maze of narrative options constructed by Puig and his narrators as a postmodern exercise like Vladimir Nabokov's *Pale Fire* (1962) or Italo Calvino's *If on a Winter Night* (1981). But with *The Other Francisco* occupying this position, postmodern conceptual play gives way to political urgency. Similarly, with *Kiss of the Spider Woman* now paired with *The Other Francisco*, the novel also becomes available for a different kind of reading—less playful, more focused on ways narrative procedures can sustain ideology, and more aware of how reception can question it. What is important is the idea that texts can become available to certain readings. Rather like Kuleshov's early experiments with cinematic montage, the configuration of works within our syllabi inflects their meanings.

This idea that texts become available to certain readings, and that meanings emerge out of the sequences and proximities that occur across each syllabus's progression, is further born out by the following examples. *The Other Francisco*, for instance, functions somewhat differently in my thematically focused course, The Politics of Film (this one not a literature course) than it does in Narrative Form in the Novel and Film. Now placed between *Salt of the Earth* (1954) and *Bush Mama* (1976), its current applicability and revolutionary urgency emerge starkly, partly because the course's syllabus already sequences films that address race, ethnicity, gender, and social class from an increasingly activist perspective, and partly because the documentary footage and treatment of *Bush Mama* combine with the inspirational authenticity projected by *Salt of the Earth* to encourage such a reading.[5]

In another theme-oriented course, America on Film, *Bush Mama* occupies a somewhat different position. Focused exclusively on U.S. cinema, this American studies course includes an extended unit on African-American representations that starts with *The Birth of a Nation* and goes on to versions of *Imitation of Life* (1934 and 1959), *Nothing but a Man* (1964), and *Bush Mama*.[6] Within this sequence, and building on previous work done during the first two-thirds of the semester, *Bush Mama* addresses the needs of contemporary African-American communities more pointedly than it does in The Politics of Film, where it is placed after *Salt of the Earth* and *The Other Francisco*. Meaning, then, gets defined by the configuration of each syllabus. The African-American sequence of America on Film tends to raise the question of what's to be done. Were we to rearrange the sequence of The Politics of Film and place *Malcolm X* (1992) after *Bush Mama,* that question would begin to get answered.

In the case of Narrative Form in the Novel and Film, careful attention to sequences and proximities within the syllabus helped me infuse the course with multicultural concerns. Although the course's syllabus may seem dispersed, in practice it is held together by a grid of dovetailing, mirroring, and echoing works. The course may not have shed its origins in art cinema and the modernist literary canon, but now it is also guided by an overarching effort to come at such materials from a multicultural perspective. Rather than substitute a new course, I redesigned this one so as to critique and reclaim its heritage. Abandoning *Viridiana* and *Last Year at Marienbad* as its framing works and extending, instead, from *Pather Panchali* and *The Turn of the Screw* to *The Other Francisco* and *Kiss of the Spider Woman,* the course now unfolds through a flexible sequence of works that create a climate hospitable to the reading of difference as an ongoing activity.

This new elasticity is evident in the way two short South African novels functioned in a recent version of the course. Taught early in the semester, Nadine Gordimer's *July's People* (1981) and Michael Coetzee's *Waiting for the Barbarians* (1980) extended the preceding discussion of literary narration. Building on the groundwork laid during work on *Pather Panchali* and *The Turn of the Screw* (notably our initial analysis of realism, referentiality, and reading as an epistemological inquiry), students were ready to discuss Gordimer's realism in relation to Coetzee's allegory and expressionism in ways that deepened their evolving grasp of the constructed nature of fiction. At the same time, given Gordimer's and Coetzee's subject matter, this juxtaposition helped them bring this new awareness to bear on questions of difference. In particular, the pairing introduced the concept of racial, gendered, and class difference as the site of cultural, economic, and political conflict. Setting this conflict in colonial history, the two works laid the groundwork for the subsequent study of *The Heart of Darkness* (1910), *Apocalypse Now* (1979), and *The Things They Carried* (1990) on the one hand and also *The Cabinet of Dr. Caligari* on the other. Explicitly or metaphorically, questions of imperialism, colonialism, racism, and totalitarianism criss-cross these works in relation to narrative realism, expressionism, and allegory.

Although this sequence has interesting possibilities, I am not inclined to repeat it in the course. Among the various drawbacks to the sequence, the most important in terms of multiculturalism concerns the preponderance of Western perspectives in the multicultural sense. I do assign Chinua Achebe's essay on *The Heart of Darkness,* but that essay has become just about obligatory in this context, and as the sole articulation of black African response to Joseph Conrad and white racism its efficacy has become greatly compromised. Instead, one would need to pair Conrad with an African writer, like Bessie Head, for instance, picking up on Conrad's formal and epistemological preoccupations. If anything, in its present form the sequence is further weakened by the fact that *Apocalypse Now* is a poorly conceived film and a racist one to boot. It is marginally useful as an exercise in the pitfalls of adaptations and as a segue to Tim O'Brien's complexly self-reflexive book *The Things They Carried,* but not in this course's already crowded syllabus. Taken as a whole, the one benefit of this sequence is that it challenges the West's hegemony, thereby making it possible to envision a more multicultural configuration of the syllabus.

As the preceding suggests, after twenty years Narrative Form in the Novel and Film remains a course in formation. Its most recent syllabus merely captures a point in its evolution, while this discussion already supersedes it. Rather than propose a ready-to-use model, this essay raises the question of whether the underlying goals of such a course leave it enough flexibility to accommodate multicultural perspectives and begins to answer that question provisionally. I deliberately chose a difficult, even recalcitrant, course as the focus of this discussion in order to bring into the open the less acknowledged and harder to eradicate resistance the project is likely to meet within the discipline. But the worst resistance is personal, partly because teachers remain imbued with the social and professional values that surround them and partly because attention to multiculturalism can, and often does, stir up conflict and pain.

In its classroom application, multiculturalism can prove divisive, all the more so when students and faculty recognize ways it impinges directly on their lives. This is certainly the case at my university, where the prevalence of nontraditional students makes one question daily the cozy multicultural companionability of the melting pot ideal. At issue is not only the professional belief that multiculturalism simply does not belong in this kind of course, but also the anxieties that necessarily arise whenever considerations of social justice call into question the neutrality of our academic pursuits.

In this respect, devising a useful syllabus is just a first step. The challenge that multicultural teaching poses does not only concern using the right materials, but rather teaching and learning in an affirming manner. In part this means becoming aware of how reading across a variety of novels and films can reach beyond the study of inequities to include empowerments latent in multicultural perspectives. In part—indeed, crucially—it also means developing a sensitivity to students' reception of this subject matter and the stakes that teachers have in it. Without awareness of such resistance and vulnerability, teachers risk causing alienation and hostility.

Students sometimes criticize multicultural teaching as irrelevant to their lives, deflecting from mainstream academic pursuits, and politically coercive. Some find themselves singled out and misperceived, especially when they are among the few representatives of a group under discussion. (Students of color find themselves all too often called upon to be spokespeople for their particular group, regardless of their individual identities and positionalities.) The pains and denials that go into this resistance are too complex to discuss here, but the fact that they occur must be noted. At least at a school like mine, which serves students whose relation to higher education is extremely precarious, the need to shore up hope is paramount.

Although the lessons that the University of Massachusetts–Boston taught me about teaching multicultural content may not seem applicable to other student populations, in many ways they are. The grounds for resistance to a multicultural perspective may vary, but I think it is generally true that neither blithe optimism about cultural diversity nor a dead-end view of inequalities works. As Paula Rothenberg argues in "Integrating the Study of Race, Gender, and Class," it is necessary to use multicultural perspectives in an enabling manner. For me, what works best is to teach attentively, caringly, and humbly. Being open to suggestions and criticisms, willing to learn and change, and being flexible and committed to students' individual well-being builds a foundation of trust that students learn to appreciate. Guiding students toward extending the same kind of respect and empathy to each another is the second half of the process.

This is not to suggest a privatized, depoliticized nurturance. Especially in the context of course materials organized multiculturally, an approach to teaching attuned to individual positionalities necessarily registers the relation between the personal and the political. When social awareness informs such respect and empathy, alternative social possibilities begin to emerge. The trust that such teaching requires is great and needs to be reestablished every time a teacher faces a new class. It takes self-confidence, strong nerves, and true commitment to repeating this process without feeling burnt out. The rewards of teachers occur when they find students willing to risk thinking about the inequalities and injuries bound up in cultural differences as open to political action and social amelioration.

Appendix: Syllabus for English 325: Narrative Form in the Novel and Film (University of Massachusetts–Boston)

COURSE REQUIREMENTS

Writing Assignments

Ungraded: (1) a short exercise in textual analysis; and (2) a film-viewing journal.

Graded: (1) four short papers (750–1,000 words each), each with a narrow focus; and (2) a written final exam (students choose between a take-home and an in-class examination) stressing interrelations among works studied during the semester.

Critical Readings

Louis Giannetti, *Understanding Movies,* 6th ed. (Englewood Cliffs: Prentice-Hall, 1993).

E. M. Forster, *Aspects of the Novel* (New York: Harvest, 1954).

Handouts gathered from diverse sources.

Note that in-class discussions and student writing assignments mainly focus on the course's primary texts—the assigned novels and films.

READING ASSIGNMENTS AND SCREENINGS

Week 1

Introduction to the course.
Film: *Pather Panchali* (Ray, 1955)
Reading: Giannetti, *Understanding Movies,* chs. 1–2.

Week 2

Novella: Henry James, *The Turn of the Screw* (1898).
Reading: Percy Lubbock, "The Craft of Fiction: Picture, Drama, and Point of View" (handout); Wayne Booth, "Types of Narration" (handout); and

George Bluestone, "The Limits of the Novel and the Limits of Film" (handout).

Week 3

Film: *The Love of Jeanne Ney* (Pabst, 1927).

Reading: Andre Bazin, "The Evolution of the Language of Cinema" (handout); Giannetti, *Understanding Movies,* chs. 6–7; selection from Ilia Ehrenburg's novel *The Love of Jeanne Ney* (handout); Robert Richardson, "Verbal Language and Visual Language" (handout); and George Linden, "The Storied World" (handout).

Week 4

Film: *Battleship Potemkin* (Einsenstein, 1925).

Reading: Forster, *Aspects of the Novel;* Giannetti, *Understanding Movies,* chs. 5, 11; David Mayer, *Eisenstein's* Potemkin: *A Shot-by-Shot Presentation* (New York: Grossman Publishers, 1972); Sergei Eisenstein, *The Film Sense* (New York: Harvest, 1947).

Week 5

Novels: Nadine Gordimer, *July's People* (1981); and Michael Coetzee, *Waiting for the Barbarians* (1980).

Week 6

Film: *The Cabinet of Dr. Caligari* (Wiene, 1919).

Reading: Siegfried Kracauer, "Caligari" (handout).

Week 7

Film: *Rashomon* (Kurosawa, 1950).

Reading: Ryunosuke Akutigawa, "In a Grove" and "Rashomon" (handout); Mark Schorer, "Technique as Discovery" (handout).

Week 8

Film: *Apocalypse Now* (Coppola, 1979).

Novella: Joseph Conrad, *The Heart of Darkness* (1910).

Stories: Tim O'Brien, "The Things They Carried" and "How to Tell a War Story" in *The Things They Carried* (1990); other stories highly recommended.

Week 9

Film: *Hiroshima, Mon Amour* (Resnais, 1959).

Reading: Andre Bazin, "Marginal Notes on Eroticism in the Cinema" (handout); and Christian Metz, "Story/Discourse (A Note on Two Kinds of Voyeurism)" (handout).

Week 10

Novel: Virginia Woolf, *To the Lighthouse* (1927).

Reading: Virginia Woolf, "Professions for Women" (handout).

Week 11

Films: *The Smiling Madame Beudet* (Dulac, 1922); and *Meshes of the Afternoon* (Deren, 1943).

Readings: Lacassin, "Out of Oblivion: Alice Guy Blaché" (handout); Jay Leyda, "Esther Schub" (handout); and Richard Abel, *"La Souriante Mme. Beudet* and *L'Inondation"* (handout).

Week 12

Novel: William Faulkner, *The Sound and the Fury* (1929).

Week 13

Film: *The Other Francisco* (Giral, 1975).

Readings: Leon Edel, "Novels and Camera" (handout); Seymour Chatman, "What Novels Can Do That Films Can't" (handout); J. Hillis-Miller, "Ariadne's Thread: Repetition and the Narrative Line" (handout); and Teresa DeLauretis, "Through the Looking Glass: Women, Cinema, and Language" (handout).

Week 14

Novel: Manuel Puig, *The Kiss of the Spider Woman* (1976).

Readings: Roland Barthes, "Upon Leaving the Movie Theater" (handout); and Walter Benjamin, "The Work of Art in the Age of Mechanical Reproduction" (handout).

Notes

1. This is evidenced by a variety of courses we offer across the curriculum, by extensive faculty scholarship and professional activity in this area, by our universitywide diversity requirement, and by a Ford Foundation grant we received to this end.

2. The current syllabus differs from that early version.

3. One could pair the novel with its film adaptation as an object lesson in the problems of adaptation and the distinct languages of each medium. Given time constraints, I find the film sufficiently complex to justify this exercise.

4. Latin-American literature and film yield a wealth of materials that can be used at this juncture. Most obviously, Morrison's writing has already been compared to "magical realism," but there are other veins to mine. One can also turn to Sarah Gómez's film *One Way or Another* (1974), or novels like Manlio Argueta's *One Day in Life* (1980), or Marta Traba's *Mothers and Shadows* (1981). Linda Ty-Casper's *Awaiting Trespass* (1985) applies a similar formal treatment to the Philippines.

5. *The Jazz Singer* (1927), *Imitation of Life* (1934), *My Darling Clementine*

(1946), *On the Waterfront* (1954), and *Matewan* (1987) bring up considerations of race and ethnicity in conjunction with considerations of gender, social class, and, in some of the films, organized labor as well.

6. This list is open to variation and extension, especially to the by-now prolific work by African-American directors from Oscar Micheaux to Melvin Van Peebles, Charles Burnett, Ayoka Chenzira, Spike Lee, and Julie Dash. My emphasis has been on racism; a more interventionist approach would foreground the work of independent filmmakers. As an American studies course, America on Film included readings in social and political history as well as in film and cultural studies. Although such contextualizing readings are always illuminating, they are indispensable to the teaching of *The Birth of a Nation* in particular.

5

Teaching Multiculturalism from the Movies: Health and Social Well-being

Clarence Spigner

Teaching and learning about multiculturalism in the United States presupposes acknowledgment of cultural diversity. Fawcett and Thomas describe the regions and people of the United States as "a rich and varied sameness" (11). Once thought of as a melting pot, the country is more accurately described as a diverse assemblage of racial and ethnic communities that form the basis for its strength, unity, and cultural richness. In fact, the United States is becoming more racially diverse than ever. The 1990 Census revealed that one in four Americans (roughly 60 million of 250 million) reported having racial minority ancestry. Major racial minority groups include African Americans, Hispanics and Latinos, Asian and Pacific Americans, and American Indians and Alaskan Natives. However, these categorizations have both conceptual and methodological problems; biological and social classifications do not always clearly delineate the categories indicated (Wilkinson and King; Omi and Winant).

Despite unclear demarcations among ethnic-cultural groups, Hatchett and Miller, in separate analyses of race relations and race in the health of America, have both cited W. E. B. Du Bois's prophetic declaration that "the problem of the twentieth century is the problem of the color line." Despite minority ancestry in nearly a quarter of all Americans, social and health status inequalities exist between minority racial groups and the white majority. The social and individual pathologies found in ethnic minorities reflect the racism, stratification, and inequality that continue to be the status quo as America approaches the twenty-first century.

Health, Race, and Imagery

Health is not just the absence of disease, it is a state of social, physical, and emotional well-being. Not simply a biological phenomenon, health is defined within the parameters of social and economic conditions as well as racial attitudes (Miller). The health problems of minority racial groups in the United States are disproportionate to their numbers in the population. Excess morbidity and mortality exist within most minority groups, excesses attributable to factors other than physical or biological ones.

African Americans comprise 12 percent of the total U.S. population. Government statistics show that one-third of them live in poverty, compared to one-tenth of white Americans. More than one-half live in densely populated urban areas, where they are exposed to high levels of crime, unemployment, stress, and disease.

Hispanics and Latinos, the fastest growing minority group in the United States, make up 8 percent of the total population. Eighty-seven percent live in urban areas and are exposed to inner-city pathologies. For example, the death rate for twenty to twenty-four-year-old Hispanic and Latino men in the southwestern part of the United States is four times higher than for whites.

The diverse group of Asian and Pacific Americans represents nearly 4.5 percent of the total U.S. population. They speak more than thirty languages and range from having very high incomes (largely the Japanese) to living in dismal poverty (mostly Laotian refugees).

American Indian and Alaskan Natives make up about .6 percent of the population. Representing more than four hundred federally recognized nations, one-third live on reservations, and about 50 percent live in urban centers. Income and education levels tend to be low; 25 percent of this group live in poverty, and fewer than 8 percent have college degrees (U.S. Department of Health and Human Services).

The political, economic, and social conditions under which many racial minorities live are determinants of significant inequalities in health and social status. The imagery of popular film reflects these disparities and can be studied and examined within the parameters of role expectations, social interaction, and demographic indicators. These themes can be conceptually drawn together in an analysis of whether the imagery constitutes a construction or a reflection of social reality (DeFleur and Ball-Rokeach; Greenberg; Jewell).

Omi and Winant report that "film and television have been notorious in disseminating images of racial minorities which establish for audiences what people from those groups look like, how they behave, and who they are" (63). The depiction of African Americans, Latinos, Asians, and Native Americans affects how they are perceived and treated; the perceptions and treatment, in turn, affect health and social well-being. Cause and effect are not argued here; however, notions about race, ethnicity, social and self-image, and physical and emotional health are consequences of social processes dictated largely by the dominant white power structure to which film images contribute.

Theoretical Rationale

DeFleur and Ball-Rokeach provide general theoretical paradigms to explain relationships among media, society, and individuals. These paradigms are structural functionalism (social stability), social evolution (social change), conflict (social struggle), and symbolic interactionism (interpersonal interaction and symbolic meaning). All are relevant to the study of multiculturalism via popular film imagery. Symbolic interactionism is especially appropriate, however, in light of one of its central assumptions as expressed by DeFleur and Ball-Rokeach: "The bonds that unite people, the ideas that they have of others, and their beliefs about themselves are personal constructions of meaning emerging from symbolic interaction; thus, the subjective beliefs people have of one another and themselves are the most significant facts of social life" (21).

Thus, as underpinned by symbolic interaction, the examination of racial imagery through popular films can (1) show how perceptions of racial minorities are largely social constructions internalized by society; and (2) illustrate how this internalization can manifest itself in the well-being of individuals, groups, and society.

The Teaching Environment

The University and Classroom Setting

The immediate teaching environment is a 250-acre campus founded in 1876 in the Pacific Northwest. The University of Oregon is an accredited comprehensive research university with more than seven hundred full-time faculty, nearly four hundred part-time faculty, and more than 1,100 teaching and research assistants. As of May 1991, a total of 16,725 students included 12,778 undergraduates, 51.4 percent of whom were women. Only 9 percent of the total student enrollment is not white. The Office of the Registrar reports that African Americans comprise 1.3 percent of the student body; Hispanics and Latinos, 1.7 percent; Asians and Pacific Islanders, 5.1 percent; and Native Americans, .8 percent. The monochromatic complexion of the classrooms reflects the Pacific Northwest's white dominance; it also reflects the need to prepare students for an increasingly multiracial world.

About half of the students in my class, Race, Mass Media, and Health, are undergraduate health majors. The rest represent a myriad of majors ranging from business to biology to liberal arts. Total course enrollment is kept to fewer than thirty students, 70 percent of whom are female. The racial makeup of the class usually reflects the makeup of the student body, that is, more than 90 percent white.

The Community

Eugene, Oregon, a community of 112,669 people, is located midway in the western region of the state, approximately fifty miles from the Pacific Ocean and about 150 miles north of the California border. It is the second largest city in a state of nearly three million people, 92.8 percent of whom are white. The community's racial makeup is 94.4 percent white, 1.3 percent black, 2.7 percent Hispanic and Latino, 3.5 percent Asian and Pacific Islander, and 1 percent Native American. Asians and Pacific Islanders represent the fastest growing group in the city and the state, followed by Hispanics and Latinos. Approximately a hundred miles to the north is the state's largest urban center, where 15.4 percent of the residents are racial minorities. African Americans make up one-half of the minority population. In 1988, Eugene was the scene of a racist murder of a black man by neo-Nazi skinheads.

Overall, whites dominate the university, the community, the state, and the region. However, the white population group is experiencing the smallest growth rate. From 1980 to 1990, it increased by only 5.9 percent, compared with a 25 percent black increase, a 70 percent Hispanic increase, a 99.2 percent Asian and Pacific Islander increase, and a 40.9 American Indian increase.

The environment for teaching about diversity is hardly diverse and reflects a regional culture which, in many ways, is a frightening microcosm of race relations in the United States. Although liberal in some ways, the Pacific Northwest is touted by the Far Right as the last geographical bastion and final battleground for white supremacy. The region was featured prominently in such films as *Betrayed, Malone, Dead Bang,* and *Talk Radio.*

Pedagogic Issues

There has been much ado about how shifting demographics have increased minority representation in schools and created tensions between scholarship and ideology. Diane Ravitch, professor at Columbia University's Teachers College, and Molefi Kete Asante, chair of

African Studies at Temple University, have been prominent in their expression of multiculturalism's opposing polemics. My position is generally in line with that of Ronald Takaki, Henry Louis Gates, Jr., and Barbara Ehrenreich, who argue for the need to counterbalance prevailing Eurocentric perspectives within educational institutions with more racial and gender sensitivity.

As prominent forms of communication media, movies express the various aspects of cultural pluralism in a variety of ways. Popular film, a medium with which virtually all students are familiar, provides an educational tool that can be used to facilitate students' analysis and understanding of "E pluribus unum."

Course Requirements

Students in Race, Mass Media, and Health are required to write four five-to-six-page essays (typewritten, double spaced, with references). Each of the first three essays should focus on three different films and examine and analyze them in terms of one of the three recurring themes of the course: roles of minorities, social interaction, and demographic characteristics. The fourth essay, a synthesis paper, should bring together all three themes and all of the movies in an attempt to determine whether life imitates art or vice versa. The focus of the final essay is on social and individual well-being of racial minorities in the United States.

Teaching Strategies

Use Popular Films   I suggest using mostly popular films and fewer of the independent productions because commercial movies are more likely to speak to the dominant ideology. The production of films with mass appeal stems largely from political economy, which is a lesson in itself. For example, in 1987, 23,555 movie theaters operated in the United States. Box office receipts were $4,252,900,000, representing 1,088,500 admissions. According to the *Universal Almanac,* since the industry's inception at the turn of the century, movie-making costs have skyrocketed, attendance has decreased (since the 1930 and 1940s), and ticket prices have soared. Nevertheless, commercial film-making, in conjunction with the technology of VCRs and cable television, continues to exert a powerful influence on mass culture (De-Fleur and Ball-Rokeach). Commercial filmmaking also continues to reflect race and class hegemony.

Use Only Films That Are Available on Videocassette   Only popular movies that are available on videocassette should be assigned for review.

In 1988, 98.2 percent of U.S. households had television sets; in 1987, videocassette sales revenue was $1,103,000, with an average purchase price of $17. Videocassette rental revenue was $4,608,000, with an average rental price of $2.04 (*Universal Almanac*). The enormous mass appeal of video movies, along with commercial and cable television and their use as important sources of information and entertainment, contributes to the "subjective and shared constructions of reality" (DeFleur and Ball-Rokeach 22).

All assigned films should be available in local video rental outlets for review on personal VCR machines or the machines available in most school libraries and media centers.

Provide an Extensive List of Titles   I provide a list of at least a hundred film titles released within a certain time frame (e.g., 1980–90) for review. Films should reflect a broad appeal and cover a variety of topics. In 1987 alone, 478 new films were released; quantity and topic variety are not a problem. Films that the instructor has not viewed should not be included on the list. I also include several classics, such as *Birth of a Nation, Gone with the Wind, Sapphire, Fort Apache, Bad Day at Black Rock, Flower Drum Song, The World of Suzie Wong,* and *The Pawn-broker* in order to give students a sense of race in film history. The extensive and varied list of films gives students greater choice and allows for wide-ranging lectures and discussions.

Do Not Show Films in Class   Commercial movies should not be shown during class time. I am sure that others differ with me on this, but I believe that film viewing assignments are comparable to reading assignments in other classes. Class time should be devoted to lecture, discussion, and exchange. I recommend using slides, which can easily and inexpensively be made from movie scenes in the print media and advertisements, to help guide lecture and discussion points.

Coordinate Lecture and Discussion Topics with Essay Assignments   Essay assignments should be completed at various times during the course. The essays should demonstrate critical and conceptual analysis of the themes addressed in classroom lectures and discussions and should apply this analysis to the films reviewed. Having to address specific themes in each essay will discourage students from "borrowing" from published film reviews. Essay requirements will result in the instructor having to evaluate 80 to 120 papers. This necessitates allotting sufficient time and energy for critical assessment and feedback. (Such a commitment can be burdensome in a comprehensive research institution where teaching is not necessarily valued or rewarded with merit pay or tenure.)

Reinforce Class Participation   Attendance, active participation, and good writing skills are requisite for the class. They can be reinforced via taking attendance, encouraging office visits, providing corrective feedback, and learning all students' names. These practices encourage instructor-student interaction and the creation of a learning environment where students can honestly explore the socializing process that shapes racial perceptions.

Examples of Course Content

The first three areas for lecture and discussion, and which coordinate with the topics to be covered in the essay assignments, are role expectations, social interaction, and demographics. The fourth area is a synthesis of the first three. The overriding theme for all of the assignments is the analysis of how each area impacts the social, emotional, and physical well-being of the characters involved. The topic areas can be addressed, for example, using films that emphasize female-male interactions and power relationships between minority groups and the white hegemony.

The Role of Minority Characters

In focusing on the role of minorities, particular emphasis is placed on norms, values, and expectations, that is, the socialization processes that shape a society. Here the class focuses on behaviors associated with expectations of a given status. The status can be ascribed (inherited traits) or achieved (acquired).

Racially biased expected and assigned roles are seen in the character of the Chinese-American television anchorwoman portrayed by Ariane and her attraction to the racist and sexist policeman played by Mickey Rourke in *Year of the Dragon*. The film's depiction of an Asian woman's sexual attraction toward a despicable (and married) white racist is seen as a reinforcement of white male hegemony. Moreover, *Year of the Dragon* depicts Asians unidimensionally, as either benign or malevolent, "model" minorities (a Connie Chung-like newscaster and a passive Asian policeman) or stealthy gangsters involved in the drug trade and enemies left over from the Vietnam War (Jeffords).

What do such limited depictions imply about society's perception of and reaction toward Asians? Tajima expresses the frustration of constantly viewing the media's depiction of Asians as one-dimensional, sexually estranged, and passive toward white males. In the *Year of the Dragon, China Girl, Come See the Paradise,* and *The Karate Kid,* Asian or Pacific Americans are generally stereotyped in either servile or deviant roles. In the seemingly benign *Karate Kid* and *Karate Kid, Part II,* for instance, Japanese-American Noriyuki "Pat" Morita plays a gardener who becomes a mentor to a jobless young white man (Ralph Macchio). It is Macchio who is promoted as the star of both films. In the second film, a young Japanese actor, Yugi Okumoto, depicts a brute and coward while Macchio's character is strong, adept, sensitive, and has a romantic interest (Tamlyn Tomita). In both films, the Asian men are diminished and the myth of white desirability to Asian women is reinforced, as Weiss and Tajima have pointed out (1973).

Another example of secondary role status assigned to minorities are popular black-white "male-bonding" police films such as *48 Hours, Lethal Weapon,* and *Off Limits* in which the black is always subservient to the white regardless of status. For example, in *48 Hours* and *Another 48 Hours,* a policeman (Nick Nolte) and a criminal (Eddie Murphy) are not equal. Murphy portrays a subservient, horny, foul-mouthed, petty thief given to one-night stands, while the cunning, independent white policeman is in a rocky but committed romance. Such black-white "Huckleberry Finn" pairing is also evident in *Lethal Weapon* and *Lethal Weapon 2,* in which Danny Glover plays a family man in a stable relationship but is still secondary to the more dashing, individualistic, and smarter white man (Mel Gibson).

In addition, the historically incorrect *Mississippi Burning* and self-serving *Dances with Wolves* promote the concerns of whites at the expense of African Americans and Native Americans. Like *Mississippi Burning, Come See the Paradise* (by the same director, Alan Parker) takes a significant Asian-American experience—the Japanese internment—and pushes Japanese Americans into the background in order to promote a white male protagonist (Dennis Quaid). A similar observation could be made about *Cry Freedom* and *A World Apart,* films about South Africa in which the emphasis and focus remain on whites.

Such films typically represent whites in primary, multidimensional roles in which they engage in mutual relationships and minorities in secondary roles featuring limited, nonreciprocal relationships. These portrayals send false and demeaning messages that minorities are monolithic, lack the ability to control their own destinies, and need whites to lead them.

Social Interaction

Here the class focuses on the behavior patterns among minorities and between minorities and whites. Examples of intraracial interaction are the marital turmoil that Whoopi Goldberg's Celie endures in *The Color Purple* and the spouse abuse that Elizabeth Pena's character suffers in *La Bamba*. The message sent to viewers is that black and Hispanic women face greater risk to personal health from their male counterparts; little or no contextual explanation is given of the external racism and oppression that all minorities, regardless of gender, experience.

In both *The Color Purple* and *La Bamba,* the harsh domestic brutality of black and Hispanic men (Danny Glover and Esai Morales) magnifies a stereotype of crude, sexually aggressive minority males. Both films raise questions about role expectations in marriage partners as well as the real problem of spouse abuse, but neither addresses the social, political, and economic determinants of the problems.

Bobo (*The Color Purple*) and Guerrero have examined some of the social, political, and cultural consequences of black female-male antagonism made explicit in *The Color Purple*. Diawara, in "Black Spectatorship," has addressed the historical and psychosocial issues involving spectator identification in the film, and I have discussed the structural-functionalist dimensions in *The Color Purple* and other Hollywood films. Discussions of these analyses are included in the classroom.

Classroom discussion and assignments can also address the various dimensions of micro and macro behavioral interactions. The class can examine how behaviors that occur day to day between people (micro-order) can stem from speculations about psychological states that spawn brutal treatment on the part of minority men toward women (Jewell; Campbell). Large-scale, societywide behavior patterns (macro-order) can underpin classroom discussion on the dynamics of race, stratification, and power relationships, as suggested by Jewell and Bobo. Two years before *The Color Purple* was released, Jewell described how demeaning imagery of African Americans maintains a white status quo. And, in reference to *The Color Purple,* Bobo has described how Hollywood's biased depictions of dysfunctional black families help reinforce an ethnocentric white ideology of welfare dependency.

These negative, one-dimensional depictions suggest that minorities have only their own life-styles to blame for health and social problems. Such blame-the-victim scapegoating has its roots in culture of poverty theories initially posed by the anthropologist Oscar Lewis (*The Children of Sanchez*, 1961) and politician Daniel Patrick Moynihan (*The Moynihan Report*, 1965). Very few films, among them *Do the Right Thing* and this decade's *Boyz 'N the Hood* and *Straight Out of Brooklyn*, speak equally to individual responsibility as well as to the social determinants that produce the high prevalence of pathology among African Americans.

Analysis of movies' depictions of individual and social behaviors must take into account the two operatives engaged concurrently—the psychosocial forces operating within the film plot and the political economy of film production. These forces do what Jewell sees as maintaining the status quo and Bobo refers to as reinforcing a dominant ideology. The social consequences of mass-producing negative images of minorities impact directly on individual and social well-being.

Demographics

The analysis of demographic characteristics includes examining how age, gender, place of residence, occupation, and socioeconomic status are presented in film plots. The demographic factor builds on the previously addressed concepts of role and social interaction and adds another dimension to students' assessment of the relationships between cultural and ethnic diversity and personal and social well-being.

In the movie *Diva*, Wilhemina Wiggins-Fernandez, playing a black opera star, refuses the romantic advances of a young white French letter carrier. What roles do the setting (the city of Paris), the achieved elite status of the opera singer, and her ascribed status (black female) play in the portrayal of race relations? As a response, students might compare Wiggins-Fernandez's portrayal (using role, interaction, and the demographic parameters) with that of the white upper-class woman that Mimi Rogers portrays in *Someone to Watch Over Me*, which is set in New York, and her romantic relationship with the white working-class policeman played by Tom Berenger, or with the relationship of the prostitute that Julia Roberts plays in *Pretty Woman* to Richard Gere's Los Angeles millionaire. In these films, race and ethnicity as well as class and occupation, within the setting of the urban environment, are key factors for understanding race relations.

Role status, nature of interaction, class status, and population demographics are all important factors in the depiction of black women in films and influence the perceptions of black women in reality. Campbell reports that "the image of Black women as depreciated sex objects causes psychological damage and feelings that we are less worthy of marriage or honorable relationships with men" (72). Recall that when *Diva*'s high-class opera star rebuffs the French postman, he solicits a black street prostitute as her surrogate.

The devaluation of black women is evident in films such as *52 Pick Up,* which depicts Vanity as a porno model; *Fear City,* with Rae Dawn Chong as a topless dancer; *Mona Lisa,* with Cathy Tyson as a London call-girl; *Angel Heart,* with Lisa Bonet as a voodoo-influenced sexual nymph; and *Street Smart* and *Internal Affairs,* with black and Hispanic women as street hookers. These films are explicit in their treatment of black women only as detached, alienated sexual objects. Far fewer films cast white women in purely sexual roles. In the few recent exceptions, *Pretty Woman* and *Street Smart,* Julia Roberts and Kathy Baker both play prostitutes but, unlike the black women, experience mutual love and affection with their male counterparts.

One of the demographic factors to be studied is life in the big city, whether it be Paris, New York, New Orleans, London, or Los Angeles. Social interaction and role expectations can be assessed in the context of urban environments, where African Americans, Hispanics, and Asians are overrepresented. Lecture and discussion could examine social and behavioral theories grounded in Ferdinand Tonnie's anomie (alienation and social support), Thomas Merton's functionalism (social stability), or Karl Marx's social conflict (social change) in modern urban life.

The study of demographic factors in conjunction with role status and social interaction provides a framework for the critical analysis of population distribution and composition, economic stratification, and social trends, and also of their impact on societal and individual health. Most of the films mentioned thus far suggest, in part, how urbanization, racial stratification, and continued stereotyping about sex and race can produce stresses affecting quality of life (Stember). The next step is to assess the extent to which the films' depictions reflect reality or are constructs of reality.

Does Art Imitate Life or Life Imitate Art?

At this point in the course, we integrate themes and concepts and synthesize their implications into a summary thesis about individual and social health in the United States. The summary represents common constructions of social reality derived from the films that have been viewed. Readily apparent in the films are dichotomies of superiority and inferiority—depictions that favor white control over minorities and men over women. The racism and sexism inherent in such representations suggest a denial of attributes of self-reliance and empowerment, so critical to determining an individual's health and well-being, among racial minorities. Real-life implications stemming from such celluloid depictions are suggested.

Lack of Healthy, Stable Endogamous Relationships   Jewell and Campbell observe that black women are left sexually stranded from their male counterparts, largely as a result of negative imagery from Hollywood cinema. A similar argument can be made for other minority women. For example, the Latina actress Maria Concita Alonso is rarely cast opposite a Latino counterpart, but often paired with Anglo males. In *Touch and Go,* her romantic interest was played by Michael Keaton; in *The Running Man,* it was Arnold Schwarzenegger; in *Extreme Prejudice,* Nick Nolte; and in *Colors,* Sean Penn. Conversely, Hispanic men are either alone (as are Asian men and black women) or hopelessly infatuated with "gringas," as seen in Andy Garcia's character's infatuation with Rosanna Arquette's in *Eight Million Ways to Die* and with Nancy Travis's in *Internal Affairs.* Another example is Lou Diamond Phillips, who as Ritchie Valens in *La Bamba* sings love songs to Danielle von Zerneck.

This is not an argument against interracial romance in the movies. Films like *My Beautiful Laundrette, Jungle Fever,* and *Mississippi Masala* treat interracial romantic relationships with sensitivity and depth. But most other films make Jewell's and Campbell's conclusions—that damaging psychological effects result from the internalization of negative imagery—highly relevant. Continuous and consistent role devaluation of minority women and men undermines personal worth and social well-being.

Reasserting White Male Dominance   Sylvester Stallone, who as Rocky beat up a series of black men in boxing rings, symbolized a Great White Hope. This can be further interpreted as the white backlash from the 1960s' black power thrust and the 1970s' and 1980s' affirmative action. The white ethnic Rocky, through hard work and will power, triumphs over Apollo Creed (Carl Weathers), a black who symbolizes government intervention programs and the welfare state. During the boxing match, Creed, dressed in Uncle Sam attire, is battered into the canvas.

What Stallone's depiction has in common with those of Arnold Schwarzenegger, Steven Seagal, Warren Beatty, Tom Cruise, Bruce Willis, Clint Eastwood, Harrison Ford, Mickey Rourke, Dennis Quaid, and Chuck Norris is a need to reinforce the image of white male supremacy to a post civil rights generation of movie-goers who had been led to believe that affirmative action was oppressing white males. The racial inequality in health and other social indicators cited earlier, however, provides overwhelming evidence of the falsehood of any such notions of minority advantages or reverse discrimination. For example, Keith et al. report the positive effects of affirmative action programs helping to meet the health-care needs of minorities and the poor. Yet African Americans and Hispanics remain under-represented in the health professions, in part because whites tend to be less supportive of such government interventions as affirmative action programs in medical schools.

Promoting Neo-imperialism   The arrogant, self-serving need to reassert U.S. authority after losing a war in Vietnam and being held hostage in Iran was embarrassingly evident in Michael Douglas's Dirty Harry-type portrayal of a tough New York cop in Japan in *Black Rain*. Japan-bashing is manifested in the myth of a superior American-manufactured Harley-Davidson motorcycle out-pacing a Japanese-made Suzuki. Throughout the film, reality is distorted in order to promote an image of the United States as being white, male, and superior in all aspects to other countries and their peoples.

Other films that reflect racism against Asian Americans include *Rambo: First Blood, Part II, Missing in Action,* and *Uncommon Valor,* which reconstruct history so that heroic white men win the Vietnam War (Jeffords). Even in the politically correct *Under Fire, Salvador,* and *The Year of Living Dangerously,* the concerns of dark-skinned people of the southern hemisphere are only backdrops for addressing the comparatively petty anxieties of the whites cast in the leading roles (Powers).

Such revisionism and racist imagery could have played a role in the 1982 death of the Chinese-American Vincent Chin, who was murdered by two white unemployed auto workers who blamed their layoffs on the Japanese. And was fatigue-clad Patrick Purdey imitating Stallone's Rambo, Schwarzenegger's Terminator, or Norris's Braddock when he fired 105 rounds into a Stockton, California, playground in 1989, killing five Southeast Asian children?

Conclusion

Omi and Winant point out that "the power of the media lies not only in their ability to reflect the dominant racial ideology, but in their capacity to shape that ideology in the first place" (63). Because films reflect images, portrayals, and interpretations of reality that audiences internalize, the ideas that people have about each other evolve, in part, from the imagery of mass communication. The current proliferation of popular films reinforces a status quo of white racial and gender superiority, thereby lending support to the negative determinants of social, psychological, and physical factors affecting the health of racial minorities.

The use of the critical analysis of film as a pedagogic approach to the study of the status of multiculturalism in U.S. society enables students to see the ubiquity of white ethnocentrism. It provides a vehicle for the study of the relationships between the media's imagery of cultural diversity and the realities of minority life and enables students to examine the connections among medium, message, and individual and social well-being.

Appendix: Syllabus for HEP 350: Race, Mass Media, and Health (University of Oregon)

PURPOSE AND OBJECTIVES

The course's general focus is on race, mass media, and health, which are viewed interactively. A society's perception of racial minorities (and, consequently, minorities' perceptions of themselves) affect how they are treated and their consequent well-being. Therefore, the course has a threefold purpose: (1) to show how popular films impact on the social, psychic, and somatic well-being of African Americans, Hispanics, Asian Americans, and Native Americans; (2) to articulate the relationship of cinema, which is a major aspect of popular culture, a leisure activity, and a socializing agent, to the development (and reflection) of social norms and attitudes regarding racial minorities in American society; and (3) to allow an objective analysis of the image of minorities by articulating factors that define perceptions of well-being.

COURSE REQUIREMENTS

Essays

Four essays on (1) "The Role of Minorities"; (2) "Social Interaction"; (3) "Sociodemographics"; and (4) "Does Art Imitate Life or Life Imitate Art?" Each will integrate the following sociohealth aspects: demographics (race or ethnicity, age, sex, and residence); diet, nutrition, and body image (eating, drinking, and smoking); occupation (type of job, employment status, or whether a criminal); and stress and coping patterns (social support and mental health).

Readings

This course does not have a structured reading schedule; therefore, the readings should be done as quickly as possible. During the course, we will reiterate themes as they are reflected in these required readings. Although the articles are sequenced to follow the lectures, students are responsible for integrating the appropriate materials into essays from these readings. They should not wait until a particular reading is covered in class before reading it.

1. Melvin L. DeFleur and Sandra J. Ball-Rokeach, "Media and Society," in *Theories of Mass Communication,* 4th ed., 1–27 (New York: Longman, 1982).

2. Bradley S. Greenberg, "Minorities and Mass Media," in *Perspectives on Media Effects,* edited by J. Bryant and D. Dillman, 165–88 (Hillsdale: LEH Publishers, 1986).

3. Todd Gitlin, "Prime-Time Whitewash," *American Film* 9 (Nov. 1983): 36–38.

4. Gary Indiana, "Out of Sight, Out of Mind," *Village Voice,* Dec. 5, 1989, 99. Also in the same issue: Ted Jojola, "Corn, or What We Indians Call Maize"; Renee Tajima, "I Just Hope We Find a Nip in This Building Who Speaks English," 104; Coco Fusco, "All We Need Is Ganas?" 106; and Michele Wallace, "I Don't Know Nothin' 'bout Birth'n No Babies!" 112.

5. Manthia Diawara, "Black Spectatorship: Problems of Identification and Resistance," *Screen* 29 (Autumn 1988): 66–76.

6. Jacqueline Bobo, *"The Color Purple:* Black Women's Responses," *Jump Cut,* no. 33 (Feb. 1988): 43–51.

7. Ed Guerrero, *"The Color Purple, Brother from Another Planet:* The Slavery Motif in Recent Popular Cinema," *Jump Cut,* no. 33 (Feb. 1988): 52–59.

8. K. Sue Jewell, "Black Male/Female Conflicts: Internalization of Negative Definitions Transmitted through Imagery," *The Western Journal of Black Studies* 7, no. 1 (1983): 43–48.

9. Renee Tajima, "Lotus Blossoms Don't Bleed: Images of Asian Women," in *Making Waves,* edited by the Asian Women United of California, 309–17 (Boston: Beacon Press, 1989).

10. John Powers, "Saints and Savages," *American Film* 9 (Jan.–Feb. 1984): 38–43.

11. S. Robert Lichter et al., "Prime-Time Prejudice: TV's Images of Blacks and Hispanics," *Public Opinion* 10 (July–Aug. 1987): 13–16.

12. Jack G. Shaheen, "The Hollywood Arab: 1984–1986," *Journal of Popular Television* 14 (Winter 1987): 148–57.

13. Marline Glicksman (television), "Black Like Who?" *Film Comment* 25 (May–June 1989): 75–76.

14. Patricia Raybon, "A Case of 'Severe Bias,'" *Newsweek,* Oct. 2, 1989, 11.

15. Manning Marable, "Do the Right Thing," *Black Issues in Higher Education* 6, no. 11 (1989): 64.

DISCUSSION TOPICS

Weeks 1, 2, and 3

The role of minorities: The depiction of minorities as presented in the particular film. Specific areas addressed should be aspects of socialization, role expectations, status within the social structure, societal norms, values and expectations regarding the views of minorities expressed in the film. Examples are psychological and social consequences arising from superior or inferior status.

Weeks 4 and 5

Social interaction: The particular or unique character of the depicted minority with whom she or he interacts. Addressed are the nature of the interaction (love, sexual, platonic, antagonistic, subservient, and criminal) and between whom (male and male, male and female, female and female). Examples are concepts of self-worth and psychosocial consequences from the internalization of negative imagery.

Weeks 6 and 7

Sociodemographics: Such factors as socioeconomic status, race, ethnicity, age, gender, and place of residence should be assessed relative to the overall theme of interaction and socialization. Examples are situations of stress from living within an inner-city environment.

Weeks 8, 9, and 10

Does art imitate life or life imitate art in films?: Specific sociobehavioral aspects (aggression, subservience, independence, exploitation, racism, and sexism). Students will critically determine whether the particular minority depiction is either stereotyped or a valid characterization for the time and place of the film and the real world. An example is expressing the links between acts of racism and social upheaval.

6

Media and Education in a Multicultural Society: A Historian's Perspective

Carlos E. Cortés

The historian Barbara Tuchman once observed that "bias is only misleading when it is concealed." So I will unconceal my bias in order to provide a context for my approach to both media and multicultural education. I am a historian. I am not involved in media studies as a discipline. Although I do teach courses on media and history, and although I do use multicultural media in my teaching, my goal is not to develop media studies scholars. Rather, I use media for four reasons:

1. To help students gain a better understanding of the ways in which the media have evolved, including the historical relationship between media and society;

2. To help students develop their ability to think analytically when addressing the media and dealing with history;

3. To help students become more analytical about and sensitive to the nuances and complexities raised by racial, ethnic, cultural, gender, and other kinds of diversities, as well as become more comfortable and open in discussing controversial historical and contemporary racial and ethnic issues; and

4. To help students learn to communicate their ideas, both orally and in writing, in clear, comprehensible, jargon-free English.

Many of my students go on to become elementary and secondary school teachers or to pursue other careers that involve multicultural factors. I try to help them become more self-aware and self-critical about their interactions with the media and their ways of thinking about race and ethnicity. Speaking jargonistically, I want them to learn how to operate more metacognitively, avoiding the trap described by T. S. Eliot: "We had the experience but missed the meaning." Moreover, I want students to understand, to become more adept in dealing with, and to develop greater ease in talking about diversity-related issues. I try to help those who enter the K–12 ranks become better able to teach multiculturally and improve their own students' media literacy.

How did I arrive at these pedagogical goals? As far as I can tell, they have been the somewhat logical, somewhat serendipitous, somewhat fatalistic result of the confluence of three imperatives—contextual, disciplinary, and personal.

A Tale of Three Imperatives

First, the contextual imperative. I teach at the University of California, Riverside (UCR), a nine-thousand-student public university nestled at the foot of the Box Springs Mountains some sixty miles east of downtown Los Angeles. Teaching in Southern California, I seldom suffer the misfortune of confronting ethnically homogeneous classes. Diversity forms an omnipresent campus and classroom reality, not a celebratory exhortation, an ominous premonition, or a demographic projection. Students named Chen, Bhaga, Niwa, Aviles, Matsui, Ohadi, Ramoran, Naghshineh, and Nanthathammiko far outnumber those named Cole, Christopher, or McCune. Moreover, the wonders of intermarriage increasingly provide me with Latino-descent and Asian-descent students with names like Braun, Feld, Morris, Seibert, and Franklin.

Second, the disciplinary imperative. Presently our campus does not have a film studies major, although it does offer a film and visual culture minor and a journalism minor. Most of my UCR teaching involves nonmedia-based history courses on Latin America (my doctoral specialty) and Chicano history (an avocation). In addition, I offer a variety of media-based history courses.

My annually taught course, History of the Mass Media, is structured chronologically from the "optical telegraph" of smoke signals and "oral telegraph" of ancient Persian megaphone shouters to HBO, MTV, *Grit and Steel,* and Oliver Stone. I also teach Introduction to Film and History (which I offer periodically as an upper-division elective) and a senior research seminar on media and history (our department requires each undergraduate to take at least one senior research seminar, in which students must present both oral and written research reports). Introduction to Film and History is organized thematically around the types of uses that can be made of moving-image media as historical evidence (O'Connor), while the seminar focuses on individual research projects that the students select. Finally, I occasionally offer thematic film and history courses on such topics as Latin America, human migration, law and justice, frontiers, and, occasionally, race and ethnicity. Classes usually range from about fifteen to fifty students.

Except in my lower-division Introduction to Chicano History, most of the students in my courses major in history. While all have concerns and experiences with race and ethnicity, not all have an overriding interest in the topic. Moreover, because of the designation of my Chicano history course as an option for satisfying the campus's ethnic studies requirement (one course taught by or cross-listed with the ethnic studies department), even that class now includes students who have no particular interest in ethnicity, as well as some who resent being required to take any ethnic studies course. In short, few of my students want to become media specialists, while they vary widely as to their interest in diversity.

Finally, the personal imperative. I stumbled through the back door into teaching and research with media. Trained in the history of Latin America and with both educational and professional background in the mass media, I arrived at UCR in 1968, a time of national ethnic resurgence. As one of only two Mexican-American faculty members, I immediately became involved in local Chicano affairs, including serving as Chicano studies chair (1972–79), as well as in K–12 education, particularly its multicultural aspects. This included developing cross-cultural curricula, conducting teacher training workshops, and writing about multiethnic, global, and bilingual education. In attempting to assess and explain the sources of intercultural learning, attitudes, and perceptions, I developed the metaphor of the "societal curriculum" to describe the informal process of intentional and unintentional nonschool education emanating from such forces as family, community, peer socialization, religious institutions, youth groups, and a myriad of other societal elements including, of course, the mass media (Cortés, "The Societal Curriculum").

Through these and other activities, I became increasingly concerned with and fascinated by the role of the mass media, particularly the entertainment media, in influencing intercultural perceptions. Responses to lectures, workshops, and exploratory essays on my societal curriculum conceptual framework—from readers and from educators at my lectures and workshops—encouraged me to develop a research project to examine that idea. I chose to focus on feature films, beginning with the following general research question: How, why, and with what effect have movies communicated ideas concerning race, ethnicity, culture, and foreignness?[1]

While conducting this research, I also became involved in three types of teaching involving multicultural media. First, I present the aforementioned series of media-based history courses here at UCR. Second, I give media literacy workshops, primarily for K–12 teachers, students, and parents, and also at the college level and in the community. Third, I work continuously in the areas of multicultural, bilingual, and global education, not only at the college level but also, and even more intensively, at the K–12 level.

This ongoing mixture of academic and nonacademic teaching has profoundly influenced me and affected my goals, not only as a teacher but also as a scholar and as a person. Moreover, working simultaneously in these various sectors has become a dialectical process. Call it, if you will, "pedagogical intertextuality." My academic work, including research and classroom teaching, influences my noncampus teaching. My noncampus teaching, K–12 curriculum development activities, and intercultural experiences influence my academic research and teaching. So when I talk about teaching multiculturally with media, I cannot separate the university, K–12, and nonschool teaching realms.

By working simultaneously with a wide range of school and nonschool audiences of varying ages, educations, and ethnic backgrounds, I have determined the importance of emphasizing three basic factors—comfort, accessibility, and restraint. To be able to discuss race and ethnicity, participants need to feel comfortable, even if the topic is not. They need to learn to present their ideas with accessible language. And they need to develop restraint in applying value judgments and imposing contemporary categories. This means that when teaching multiculturally with media, three language-based problems must be addressed:

1. the language of race and ethnicity;
2. the language of media; and
3. the language of categorization.

The Challenges of Language

The subject of race and ethnicity can be explosive and controversial, even when dealing with distant eras (ask Columbus, Cleopatra, and Custer about that). In a multiethnic classroom environment, plenty of toes can be stepped on, while some students, teachers, and others seem eager for that experience. Increasingly, moreover, both students and teachers are spinning from the bombardment of self-righteous pronouncements by the "culture cops" (the hyperventilating PCologists, who have etched or revived careers by accusing multicultural educators of catechizing students with supposed "political correctness") and the "word cops" (those hypersensitive sleuths dedicated to chastising anyone for using any language that they can possibly construe as racist, sexist, homophobic, ageist, or any other kind of "ist"). In this PC (politically charged) climate, I find that the best way to be sensitive is not to be too Sensitive. The quicker, more direct, and more straightforward you can be—in language, in ideas, in examples, in questions, and in answers—the more effectively you can engage students in analyzing this potentially explosive topic.

While I realize that "role-modeling" has become a pedagogical and certainly an ethnic cliché, it really does apply to the historical examination of multicultural media in the classroom. The quicker that students see you addressing controversial media without apology or trepidation, and the quicker that they hear you discussing the evolution of derogatory racial and ethnic epithets discussed by placing them in historical and social context without quivering with anxiety or pulsating with piousness, the more liberating it becomes to engage in forthright discussion. The quicker that you set an example by examining a historically important piece of media—for instance, *The Birth of a Nation* (1915) or *The Jazz Singer* (1927)—without either bashing it with presentist claims of contemporary moral superiority or excusing it merely as a product of its time, the more rapidly students are drawn into this analytical enterprise. To illustrate how I attempt to role-model for students so they can talk openly and safely about controversial multicultural ideas and try to involve them in such discussion, I will describe three examples from my History of the Mass Media course.

Early in this course, I alternate lecture, discussion, questions (mine and by class members), and media excerpts (I seldom show a complete movie in class). As I wend my way chronologically through history, I constantly bring in multicultural examples and perspectives. For example, in my lecture on the history of silent movies, I show a brief excerpt, including the title card, from *Broncho Billy and the Greaser* (1914). After the predictable laugh I flip on the lights, provide additional perspective by reading other movie titles of the era—such as *That Chink at Golden Gulch* (1910) and *The Wooing and Wedding of a Coon* (1905)—and explain the societal and industry context in which those films were made. In this way I show students by example that, for purposes of discussion, racial and ethnic epithets are not always out of bounds.

In my class on media during the Great Depression, I read aloud various sections of the Motion Picture Production Code, including the one cautioning filmmakers to "take cognizance of the fact that the following words and phrases are obviously offensive to the patrons of motion pictures in the United States and more particularly to the patrons of motion pictures in foreign countries: Chink, Dago, Frog, Greaser, Hunkie, Kike, Nigger, Spig, Wop, Yid" (Stanley and Steinberg 83). Because many of my students have never even heard some of these epithets, I usually stop and explain those terms and their derivations. Moreover, I engage them in a discussion of the commercial (as contrasted with moral) implications of this section, because the Code's words suggest that the sensibilities and pocketbooks of foreign movie patrons ranked as a greater Hays Code and movie industry concern than the sensitivities of American ethnic groups.

In my class on media during World War II, I give illustrations of the ways that both the Allies and the Axis used racial, ethnic, and religious scapegoating in their mobilization efforts. For example, I play a recording of the popular wartime song "Remember Pearl Harbor," with its repeated references to "Japs" and our "Little Brown Brothers." Although once again the recording seems anachronistic and laughable to young students, I explain that the song expresses that era's national rage over the bombing of Pearl Harbor, illustrates the racialist nature of the U.S.-Japanese war, and demonstrates how racial epithets and stereotypes are used by nations when their governments deem it appropriate for implementing national policy. So students can examine this issue in greater depth and recognize that racialism was not just an American phenomenon, but that other nations, such as Japan, Germany, and England, viewed the world through racialist lenses, I sometimes assign Sam Keen's *Faces of the Enemy: Reflections of the Hostile Imagination* (1986) or John Dower's *War without Mercy: Race and Power in the Pacific War* (1986).

These three examples illustrate the importance of addressing multicultural issues directly and without wavering. If students or workshop participants sense that the teacher is uncomfortable with certain words, ideas, or media, that discomfort will likely prove to be contagious, casting a pall over forthright analysis and discussion. Likewise, if the teacher gives any hint of being a rigid ideologue or a "word cop"—thereby making students unduly worried about their choice of words or ideas—he or she either restricts discussion or encourages mimicry. However, if the teacher immediately, successfully, continuously, and calmly—maybe almost matter-of-factly—uses these words and ideas to provide a range of possible media interpretations, students feel more free to use such words in their analyses, to express their ideas and interpretations, and maybe even to be a little daring. As Jonathan Swift wrote, "He was a brave man that first ate an oyster."

Second, the language of media: Because so much of the insightful material about film and television remains riddled with cinema studies jargon and few of my students have any background in media studies, I need to equip them with a minimalist working knowledge of the language of media. For example, in my senior research seminar, I use Arthur Asa Berger's *Media Analysis Techniques* (1991) because it concisely presents four frameworks for examining media (semiological, Marxist, psychoanalytic, and sociological) and exposes students to a variety of media analysis terms not usually encountered in the study of history.

Although few of my students pursue futures in media studies, many become K–12 teachers or move into other "communicating" professions. I want them to learn some basic film terms—for example, *cut, fade, dissolve, pan, tilt, track, shot, sequence,* and *scene*—and to become at least passingly familiar and even somewhat comfortable with film studies language without acquiring the habit of relying on the latter to express their media ideas. My goal is not to train them to communicate their ideas to the film studies in-crowd, but to the rest of the thinking and thought-developing world, such as K–12 students. Therefore, I greatly restrict the use of film studies and other academic jargon in their research papers. My research paper guidelines insist, quite dogmatically, "Write your papers in clear, comprehensible English, not in 'academese.' Without ceremony or grief, please bury, for the duration of this course (and longer, I hope) such overused and abused jargon as paradigm, parameter, model, prioritize, interface, problematize, discourse, hegemony, and privilege (as a verb)."

Over the years of giving seminars and teaching courses, I have learned what techniques and language work and do not work with folks outside of the academy, especially the media studies academy. I have found that reasonably well-educated community people and K–12 teachers become ideal "reality therapy" testing grounds for language. My neo-Descartian rule of thumb is simple—if they think it is jargon, it is, in fact, jargon. This means that I need to seek clearer, crisper, nonjargonistic explanations.

Finally, we must confront the language problem of the wild, woolly, and indiscriminate use of such terms as *racism, sexism,* and *stereotype.* I constantly struggle to keep students from assuming that media stereotyping is occurring or from leaping prematurely from the observation of ethnic depictions to the conclusion that those ethnic depictions necessarily add up to stereotypes. Moreover, students seem magnetized by the dichotomous idea of positive and negative images, so I push them into defending why they consider particular depictions to be positive or negative or maybe even a mixture, considering the social contexts in which those media selections were created and the possible reception by audiences of those eras.

A similar problem arises with such powerful but overused terms as *racism* and *sexism*. Using presentist thinking, many students tend to impose current lenses on historical examples of the media, which often leads to blanket condemnations of old media as racist or sexist. Although the label sometimes fits, I caution students to use these concepts with care, lest they eviscerate their strength by indiscriminate overuse, and to save these strong, sweeping words until they have marshaled sufficient *historical* evidence to support their arguments. The often-random brandishing of these terms sometimes reminds me of Floyd Abrams's warning, "Nothing is more dangerous than an idea when it is the only one you have."

Media Analysis and Research

In contrast to my History of the Mass Media class, which follows a chronological lecture-discussion format, my other two major media courses and my media workshops emphasize nonchronological media analysis. The first step in both settings is to increase student awareness of the power of the media and the role that recipients play in constructing meaning during the media experience. Based on my own research, I concluded that both fictional and nonfictional media educate, intentionally or unintentionally, in five basic ways (Cortés, "Pride, Prejudice, and Power"):

1. media provide information;
2. media organize information and ideas;
3. media influence values;
4. media affect expectations; and
5. media provide models for behavior.

To dramatize the active role that the viewer/reader/listener plays, I sometimes have students close their eyes, listen to a movie soundtrack, and then tell me what they "see." This works beautifully with some multicultural media. For example, *The Man from Laramie* (1955) opens with James Stewart wandering through a desolate canyon in the late-nineteenth-century Southwest. Before starting the film, I give students that information and then ask them to close their eyes. The music begins nostalgically and then shifts into an ominous theme, underscored by simulated drumbeats. At that point I stop the film, tell students to open their eyes, and ask them what they have "seen." Almost without exception they indicate danger and the presence of Indians, often suggesting that Indians may be lurking in the background waiting to attack. (In fact, no Indians appear in the scene.) They then reclose their eyes and the film continues with the ominous music and drumbeats, but now interlaced with a bugle playing taps. Once again I stop the film, and students usually now explain, quite correctly this time, that Indians have already attacked and wiped out an army unit, which Stewart's character has just discovered. Occasionally, a student suggests that it may be Custer's Last Stand.

I then stop the film, rerun that segment for the students, this time with their eyes open, and ask them to explain how they succeeded in describing the scene so well without having seen it. By then they recognize the power of media to affect organizational frameworks and expectations, as well as how a continuous parade of Indian-and-army movies have influenced their personal organizational frameworks and sensitized their expectations. They point out that they have learned over time that minor-key music means danger, that drumbeats mean Indians (usually menacing), and that the playing of taps means death, usually military death. By juxtaposing these sound elements, the filmmaker enabled them to "see" the movie through sound—or manipulated them into "seeing" the movie—even without their actually having viewed the film. They also realize that they have played an active role in constructing meaning from the music and sound effects. As the old Chinese proverb goes, "We see what is behind our eyes."

I then build upon this experience to explain the idea of encoding. After this, I never again have to convince them of the long-term teaching power of media and of the receivers' historically influenced role in constructing personal meaning from the media. So, on to my two research courses.

Introduction to Film and History is structured around four evidentiary uses of moving-image media, an approach to historical inquiry developed by film-and-history guru John E. O'Connor in *Image as Artifact*. The four frameworks are moving-image documents as (1) representations of history; (2) evidence for social and cultural history; (3) evidence for historical fact; and (4) evidence for the history of the moving image as industry and art form. Although all of the themes in O'Connor's typology offer opportunities for multicultural analysis, the "representation of history" and "sociocultural documents" approaches prove particularly provocative.

The theme of moving-image documents as representations of history raises a number of fertile issues. Filmmakers have developed a variety of approaches to historical re-creation, including documentary films, fictional documentaries, docudramas, feature films about real historical figures, and feature films about historical events but using fictional characters (O'Connor and Jackson; Rollins).

Trained to analyze historical monographs, history students tend to focus on the question of the accuracy of the historical re-creation, using the tenets of monographic re-creation and use of evidence as their model. I posit for them some of the special challenges and complexities of film re-creation, the unique possibilities and limitations of such re-creation, and the need to establish appropriate nonmonographic guidelines for judging accuracy or validity in a historical film. Fortunately, the *American Historical Review* and other history journals increasingly carry articles and reviews addressing these issues (Rosenstone; Toplin, "Filmmakers and Historians").

After discussing analytical guidelines in general, the nature of different historical film genres, and some of the problems of evaluating these different genres for accuracy and validity, I show students various types of movie historical re-creations. For example, I have used a combination of D. W. Griffith's *The Birth of a Nation* (1915), Laurence Olivier's *Henry V* (1945), and the fictional documentary *Northwest from Tumacácori* (1972), which I coauthored and for which I was the coexecutive producer. All three deal with cross-cultural themes; although *Henry V* does not address the issue of race, it does engage cross-national perspectives.

I use *Northwest from Tumacácori* because it provides a sharp contrast to the two expensively mounted feature films and because it offers students the opportunity of discussing with me how I dealt with the issues of making a historical film. An attempt to provide a Chicano perspective on the 1976 American bicentennial, the movie focuses on a 1776 Mexican event in the territory that would some day become part of the United States. We (R. Alex Campbell, Mario Barrera, and I) used Juan Bautista de Anza's 1776 founding of San Francisco as the pivotal event. By using my film, I give students the opportunity of engaging me in the discussion of such filmmaking issues as establishing goals and choices in attempting historical re-creation within severe budgetary limits. This helps them understand, as Ingmar Bergman put it, "Making a film is like laying tracks in front of an express train."

In addressing the final theme, moving-image media as evidence for social and cultural history, I often use films with multicultural elements (Toplin, *Hollywood as Mirror*). For example, for comparative purposes I have used *The Blackboard Jungle* (1955) and *The Principal* (1987). Each deals with a white male hero—one a teacher, the other a principal—who attempts to grapple with the disciplinary problems of a multiracial, multiethnic school. Moreover, these films have comparable structures and even some parallel scenes, such as a school assembly. In retrospect, the "shocking" (for its time) opening assembly of *Blackboard Jungle* looks squeaky clean, particularly when contrasted with the violence-laden school assembly in *The Principal*.

This leads students to the consideration of the many ways that film evidence can be used to gain insight into the eras in which selected movies were made, as well as the industry guidelines and moviemaking restrictions during those different eras. In addition, we explore issues of audience reception, to which students contribute through their reactions to the two films and which I augment historically through reviews, contemporary articles, and my own exposure to *Blackboard Jungle* when it was first released. This also leads to open, sometimes soul-baring discussions of the students' personal experiences in their own high schools, which in California are usually multiethnic and multiracial. Prospective teachers sometimes raise and discuss the larger question of how other movies have dealt with the theme of teachers in multiracial schools and the images of teachers—maybe even stereotypes of teachers—that emerge from Hollywood movies.

Finally, in class and in workshops, I use films as sociocultural documents to provoke discussions of contemporary issues. One of my favorite opening sequences in recent years is from *China Girl* (1987). As the credits roll, the film shows a Chinese immigrant family remodeling an Italian-American bakery into a Chinese restaurant in an old Italian-American neighborhood of New York City. While the Chinese family beams with pride, long-time Italian-American residents watch with looks that range from sadness and nostalgia in the case of the elderly to hostility and rage in the young. That scene becomes the launching pad for class discussion of immigration and internal migration, particularly the movement of Asian-American small businesses into older ethnic neighborhoods. This topic has particular timeliness and topicality, considering the current tensions between Korean-American grocery and liquor store owners and African-American communities, as well as the spring 1992 explosion that rocked south central Los Angeles.

In my final course, the senior research seminar, each student chooses a topic on the history of the mass media. As a result, many of them do not deal with multicultural issues. However, in order to make certain that all engage questions of race and ethnicity, I use the first seminar session to demonstrate how to develop a research project. To do so I take them through the discovery process by which I decided to work on the history of the motion picture treatment of race, ethnicity, and foreignness, focusing particularly on how I developed the research framework for my book-in-progress on the history of the movie treatment of interracial love (Cortés, "Hollywood Interracial Love"). Topics include the changing nature of the questions that I ask, the evidentiary issues with which I contend, and the intrepretive problems that I continue to encounter. By engaging students in a dialogue—posing for them a series of research dilemmas and getting them to join me in grappling with these problems—I quickly draw them not only into historical and media research, but also into a discussion of race and ethnicity in American society.

As events of 1992 demonstrated, issues of race and ethnicity are attaining renewed visibility in American life, thought, and public discussion. Learning to think, talk, and teach about these issues in honest, open, and comfortable forums will not resolve the nation's racial and ethnic problems. However, the failure to develop this ability to think introspectively, to discuss comfortably, and to deal openly with these ongoing issues is a sure formula for societal disaster. Teaching with multicultural media provides one avenue for helping students engage in closer self-examination, develop better understanding of the historical evolution of racial and ethnic relations and perceptions, and grapple more effectively with our multicultural future.

Appendix: Syllabus for History 187: History of the Mass Media (University of California, Riverside)

SCOPE

History 187 will address selected aspects of the development of newspapers, magazines, motion pictures, radio, and television. The course will focus on such themes as media theory, changing media technology, impact of the media, media-government relations, media freedom and responsibility, the international dissemination of ideas, and ethical dilemmas involving the media.

COURSE REQUIREMENTS

Each student will select, closely follow, and critically analyze media coverage of one current news story as it develops during the period of the course.

There will be one question on the final examination concerning media treatment of the topic. In addition, the final examination will include the following question: "Select one argument that I have made in class and disagree with it. In making your case, please provide evidence for your position."

REQUIRED READING

Erik Barnouw, *Tube of Plenty: The Evolution of American Television* (New York: Oxford University Press, 1975).

Philip Knightley, *The First Casualty: From the Crimea to Vietnam: The War Correspondent as Hero, Propagandist, and Mythmaker* (New York: Harcourt Brace, 1975).

Wm. David Sloan, James G. Stovall, and James D. Startt, *The Media in America: A History* (Worthington: Publishing Horizon, 1989).

DISCUSSION TOPICS AND READINGS

Weeks 1 and 2: Establishment of the Mass Media

1. Introduction: Approaches to the Study of the Mass Media

2. Early Development of the World Press: read Sloan, Stovall, and Startt, *Media in America,* 3–23

3. Beginning of the Press in America (1690–1844): read Sloan, Stovall, and Startt, *Media in America,* 24–118

4. The Development of Newspapers

Weeks 3 and 4: The Impact of New Media

1. Era of the Telegraph (1844–60): read Knightley, *First Casualty,* 3–17, and Sloan, Stovall, and Startt, *Media in America,* 120–40.

2. Dilemmas of a Free Press.

3. The Era of Photography (1860–90): read Knightley, *First Casualty,* 19–64, and Sloan, Stovall, and Startt, *Media in America,* 142–215.

4. The Era of Motion Pictures (1890–1910): read Knightley, *First Casualty,* 65–67, and Sloan, Stovall, and Startt, *Media in America,* 216–41.

Weeks 5, 6, and 7: The Twentieth Century

1. The Era of Radio (1910–39), part 1: read Knightley, *First Casualty,* 79–170, Sloan, Stovall, and Startt, *Media in America,* 242–328, and Barnouw, *Tube of Plenty,* 1–67.

2. The Era of Radio (1910–39), part 2: read Knightley, *First Casualty,* 171–216, Sloan, Stovall, and Startt, *Media in America,* 330–64, and Barnouw, *Tube of Plenty,* 68–96.

3. World War II (1939–45): read Knightley, *First Casualty,* 217–334.

4. The Era of Television (1945–60), part 1: read Knightley, *First Casualty,* 335–56, Sloan, Stovall, and Startt, *Media in America,* 366–95, and Barnouw, *Tube of Plenty,* 97–172.

5. The Era of Television (1945–60), part 2: read Knightley, *First Casualty,* 357–72, Sloan, Stovall, and Startt, *Media in America,* 396–417, and Barnouw, *Tube of Plenty,* 172–260.

Weeks 8, 9, and 10: The Mass Media in Contemporary Life

1. Media during the 1960s: read Knightley, *First Casualty,* 373–426, and Barnouw, *Tube of Plenty,* 260–430.

2. The Cable Era (1970–), part 1: read Barnouw, *Tube of Plenty,* 430–90.

3. The Cable Era (1970–), part 2: read Barnouw, *Tube of Plenty,* 491–543.

4. Mass Media in Global Context.

5. Mass Media in the Future, Engaging Dilemmas: read Barnouw, *Tube of Plenty,* 545–47

Note

1. My research will lead to a trilogy on the history of U.S. feature films. The first book, which is nearly complete, will examine the history of the movie depiction of race and ethnicity. The second will focus on the history of the film treatment of interracial love and sex. The final volume will engage the history of the movie portrayal of foreign nations and world cultures.

Part 2

Multicultural Media as Text

The central feature of American identity is the experience of
migration, that Americans are in fact all descended from immigrants and that American selfhood is based on a seemingly paradoxical sense of shared difference. As Americans we partake
of a national identity, a communally determined and accepted
sense of self; at the same time, as Americans and ethnics all, we
define ourselves ancestrally.

—Mary Dearborn

7

A Different Image: Integrating Films by African-American Women into the Classroom

Gloria Gibson-Hudson

A cursory look at the image of black women in American movies conjures up a host of stereotypes.
   —Pearl Bowser

We [black women filmmakers] hope that with our films we can
create a new world, by speaking in our voice and defining ourselves. We hope to do this, one film at a time . . . to change
minds, widen perspectives and destroy the fear of difference.
   —Alile Sharon Larkin

The integration of films made by African-American women is critical to contemporary film pedagogy because these works communicate the visions of African-American women in their own voice. As
such, these provocative film texts redefine and celebrate African-
American womanhood, while their dynamic cinematic imagery challenges misrepresentations perpetuated by mainstream cinema. More
than "art for art's sake," the works of Alile Sharon Larkin, Zeinabu
irene Davis, Julie Dash, and many others redress historic and contemporary marginality. In so doing, their films create a new discourse of
identity cognizant of the commonalities and diversities in black wom-
en's lives. By integrating such films into the pedagogy, teachers expose students to the creative influences of African-American women
filmmakers and to their sociocultural insights.

African-American Film Courses

The study of film at Indiana University is part of the curriculum in a
number of different departments. The primary division, the Film

Studies Program, sits in the comparative literature department. Since the early seventies, members of the Afro-American studies department have developed and regularly taught several courses in black film, cross-listing them with film studies.[1]

The first course, developed by Phyllis Klotman, was Contemporary Black Film. The enrollment in this class (as in most black studies classes in the early seventies) remained predominantly black. I began working with Phyllis Klotman as an associate instructor (teaching assistant) in the early eighties. During that decade, the racial composition of the film classes, as well as other Afro-American studies classes, shifted, attracting a larger and more diverse segment of the student body. When I became a faculty member in the Department of Afro-American Studies in 1988, the racial mixture of the film classes was about 50 percent black, 50 percent white. During the spring 1992 semester, the Early Black Film class enrolled fifteen black students and seventy-five white students. We occasionally have Hispanic and Asian students.

The class's format is a seventy-five-minute morning lecture that the professor conducts, an evening screening the same day of the same film discussed in the morning lecture (7–9 P.M.), and a seventy-five-minute discussion period that an associate instructor conducts later in the week. The professor and the associate instructors prepare the discussion questions. Students purchase a textbook and a prepared reading packet that contain relevant articles. In addition, several special journal issues on black film are used, and students read assigned books and articles in Afro-American history and culture.[2] They are given a midterm and final examination (multiple choice and essay questions) and several quizzes. Finally, students must attend special lectures and film screenings and write critical analyses.

Because we analyze films not only from a cinematic standpoint, but also from a historic, cultural, and political perspective, the courses enable students (1) to analyze historic, cinematic images of African Americans as presented by independent and mainstream filmmakers; (2) to evaluate how cinematic images of African Americans have changed; and (3) to evaluate films critically and analytically. This focus directly relates to the Afro-American studies departmental philosophy and general mission, which emphasize the outreach applicability of academic knowledge.

Multiculturalism in Film

Multicultural pedagogy, in the truest sense of the concept, potentially enriches collective consciousness as it focuses on and teaches about our pluralistic society. By learning to appreciate heterogeneous representations of gender, race, and class, individuals gain better insight into the attitudes and behaviors of others. This pedagogical focus results in both short- and long-term consequences. It stimulates "cultural discovery" for students and teachers and also leads to meaningful, long-lasting social interchanges. Thus, a multicultural orientation fuses with a liberating pedagogy to embrace different worldviews and acknowledge the effects of oppression.

The eminent African-American scholar Cornel West, addressing the importance of acknowledging, teaching, and celebrating difference, explains the primary goal of the new cultural politics of difference as the eradication of the "monolithic and homogeneous in the name of diversity, multiplicity, and heterogeneity" (19). Moreover, he contends that the ultimate goal of such teaching is not "mainstream or malestream bashing," but rather the development of "distinct articulations of talented contributors to culture [artists, scholars, teachers] who desire to align themselves with demoralized, demobilized, depoliticized and disorganized people in order to empower and enable social action" (19). Because film is a pervasive, powerful, and persuasive medium in American society, it serves as an influential tool to educate and empower.

To maximize the educational potential of multiculturalism, the pedagogical approach must analyze and interpret African-American film in terms of its sociocultural interrelatedness to the larger American experience. A multicultural approach, therefore, must encompass more than the superficial inclusion of ethnic materials into the curriculum. To be an effective educational tool, ethnic materials need to sustain an in-depth integration into the curriculum and pedagogical approach. Consequently, the historical context and sociopolitical climate from which black film images emanate become key elements within the approach. African-American film images cannot be effectively taught with a multicultural emphasis without consideration of the cultural ethos and how that ethos is situated within society as a whole.

But far too often a multicultural perspective remains synonymous with a male cultural experience. Thus materials chosen to illustrate ethnic diversity, when closely examined, reveal a skewed diversity that excludes women. As educators increasingly incorporate images of ethnic pluralism, they must also be equally diligent to integrate the experiences of women. A multifaceted approach to multiculturalism in film pedagogy must, among other things, creatively combine film with historical context and systematically integrate and analyze gender-specific issues within that historical context.

Pedagogical Focus: The Historical and Cinematic Stereotypes of African-American Women

The cinematic image of black women did not materialize in a vacuum; cinematic representation, prescribed by racist attitudes, has bequeathed an enduring legacy of negative imagery. (This is the same legacy contemporary African-American women filmmakers strive to resist and to deconstruct.) A historical overview may be incorporated into a unit on the analysis of cinematic stereotypes of African-American women or as a preface to lectures focusing on films by contemporary African-American women to allow students to understand the interrelatedness of film to culture.

Black women as a group have historically experienced personal abuse and social invisibility. As bell hooks, an African-American feminist scholar, states, "A devaluation of black womanhood occurred as a result of the sexual exploitation of black women during slavery that has not altered in the course of hundreds of years" ("Ain't I a Woman," 53). To justify the violation of black women, Euro-America imposed a cultural identity upon African women slaves that dehumanized them. In addition to capitalizing on their physical labor, their reproductive ability was exploited for "breeding." To deny their humanity sanctioned all manner of physical, mental, and sexual cruelty. "White women and men justified the sexual exploitation of enslaved black women by arguing that they were the initiators of sexual relationships with men," bell hooks continues. "From such thinking emerged the stereotype of black women as sexual savages" (52). For African-American women slaves, there was little hope of escape from physical and sexual torment.

Even after slavery, white attitudes and behaviors toward black women barely changed; they continued to be viewed as sluts, mammies, or tragic mulattoes. These perceptions, which pervaded American society, legitimized harsh treatment of black women. Not only were they devalued, but also, because of societal perceptions, their subsequent film image held negligible cinematic value.

The cinema scholar Jacqueline Bobo, in "Black Women in Fiction and Nonfiction: Images of Power and Powerlessness," discusses the images that depict black women as one-dimensional: "Three notable characterizations of Black women that have been perpetuated over time are the sexually promiscuous Black woman, the overbearing Black matriarch, and the strident, domineering Black woman known as 'Sapphire.' Two other pervasive depictions are those of the domestic servant and the welfare mother" (73). Images of powerless black women became prevalent cultural icons, achieving pseudo power on the silver screen through coopting white values or at the expense of black males.

After students understand the historical background related to the development of social status among African-American women, they may proceed with the analysis of stereotypes in specific early films such as D. W. Griffith's *The Birth of a Nation* (1915), King Vidor's *Hallelujah* (1929), or Vincente Minnelli's *Cabin in the Sky* (1941). Close examination of these films clearly establishes the historical evolution of representations of African-American women. Moreover, films such as these perpetuate a destructive cycle of misrepresentation. Negative, one-dimensional societal attitudes structure demeaning, marginalized cinematic imagery and powerlessness, and cinematic icons feed and reinforce fallacious societal perceptions.

As students analyze these and other early films, the following questions may be addressed:

1. Are the cinematic representations of African-American women racist or sexist? How so?
2. Define and discuss the physical appearance, attitude, and behavior of the following characters: mammie, tragic mulatto, seductress/prostitute, matriarch.
3. How does the cinematic representation of black women, whether over- or undersexed, render them as depreciated sex objects?
4. Is upward mobility achieved by black women characters? If so, how?
5. Examine how acute dependency of African-American women characters results in their self-actualization being achieved only through "loving" relationships with their oppressor.
6. Even though many films are entertaining, (i.e., *Cabin in the Sky*), how are the cinematic images metaphorically enslaved by white patriarchal idealism?

The images of cinematic derision flourished during the following decades, with notable films such as *Carmen Jones* (1954), *Porgy and Bess* (1959), and *Imitation of Life* (1959). Images of black women continued to avoid genuine cultural nuances, simply ignoring any relationship to an authentic African-American sociocultural system. Most important, these stereotypes represent more than historical cinematic relics because contemporary cinema simply and persistently reembodies them.[3] However, the danger inherent in one-dimensional representations remains the same: "Representations of powerlessness have an effect on those in control: they give them the authority to continue to suppress collective resistance through force. Most importantly, images of powerlessness have an effect on those who would resist: rather than giving them incentive to further action, they may prompt an acceptance of the status quo" (Bobo 73).

The Cinema of African-American Women: Resistance to Marginalization

African-American women filmmakers have created a new discourse of black female identity cognizant of women's cultural and societal relationships and new political identities. Their films reflect the diversity and commonality of African-American women's life experiences. As such, their narratives diametrically oppose Euro-American film texts, which project patriarchal visions of womanhood.

One dominant element from my previous analysis of black women's film is consistent with research in black women's literary criticism: the female-centered narrative, which allows women to become the cinematic focal point. Their image is neither negotiated nor diffused through the eyes or perspective of men. It is not denigrated or subordinated to any other. Moreover, the female-centered narrative takes cognizance of the role of women in relation to the convergence of such issues as race, sex, and class. This cinematic perspective, in turn, provides an authentic historical and sociohistorical context to address specific thematic issues such as cultural identity, social invisibility, political impotence, and economic marginalization. In addition, within this cinematic structure evolves a framework in which individuals or characters subsequently exhibit a resilience to oppression and develop an increased sense of self.

Films made by African-American women have greatly increased since the 1970s. Moreover, the overwhelming success of Julie Dash's *Daughters of the Dust* (1991) heightened awareness of such work. Many of the films (1) articulate their vision of the relationships between black women, relationships between black women and their mates and family, and relationships between black women and society; (2) translate social, political, and cultural issues into cinematic statements; (3) integrate aspects of African-American history (African-American women's history); and (4) construct a didactic, cinematic narrative in which an empowering emancipatory esthetic undergirds the female voice.

Along with the advent and proliferation of films produced by African-American women came various types of analyses and interpretations of their work. Some examinations prove sadly superficial, exploring only broadly based thematic issues; others apply mainstream interpretations to films steeped in African-American consciousness and esthetics. Invariably, the incongruence of analysis with film content creates inaccurate interpretations of vital, culturally based artistic expression. Consequently, instructors must familiarize themselves with African-American history and culture because the integration of sociohistorical materials forces students to understand how black women's films represent a tangible manifestation of the creative artists' contemporary perceptions and historic perspectives. Moreover, with this knowledge the class moves beyond simply "showing a black woman's film" to comprehending how their works resist marginalization and misrepresentation.

Approaches to Teaching Alile Sharon Larkin's *A Different Image* (1982)

Alile Sharon Larkin's film, a serious work that "reimages" the African-American female cinematic icon, can be incorporated into a number of classes: Black Film, Women's Film, and Film and Social Issues. My goal is for students to understand how the film dramatizes and communicates a different image of a black female protagonist, representing a definite shift away from predetermined roles and stereotypes. The film also exposes students to Larkin's exploration of gender-based oppression and survival strategies. As such, it is a new way of seeing and filming womanhood. In studying the film, therefore, students experience a more encompassing visualization, one that captures the diversity and multiplicity of a woman's life experiences in a black voice. The lecture may cover one or all of the following conceptual areas: (1) filmmaker's objective; (2) social invisibility and cultural identity; (3) black feminist theoretical perspective; (4) cinematic technique (imagery and music); and (5) social issues such as rape, "sexploitation," and peer pressure.

Filmmaker's Objective

Students should discuss how Larkin restructures societal perceptions of African-American womanhood through authentic cinematic images. Teachers can achieve this by analyzing the film and Larkin's stated creative artistic philosophy. For example, she explains, "As a Black woman filmmaker, my objective is to contribute to the development of our own definitions" (158). Larkin's goal takes cognizance of her audience, exemplified by the use of the collective reference "our." As such, she acknowledges the potential function of film to enlighten, empower, and redress the cinematic and social invisibility of African-American women. This focus coincides with that of the feminist film scholar Teresa de Lauretis, who argues, "There has been a shift in women's cinema from an aesthetic centered on the text to what may be called an aesthetic of reception where the spectator is the film's primary concern" (141). The spectator (the class) becomes an active participant, not merely a passive viewer. This approach engages students, thereby encouraging critical thinking and generating provocative discussion.

Although in ideal situations the filmmaker would accompany the film screening, financial constraints often prohibit this. Thus, students should read interviews conducted with filmmakers or articles they have written. Larkin's article "Black Women Filmmakers Defining Ourselves: Feminism in Our Own Voice" provides in-depth social and historical commentary on her views on feminism, self-definition, and previous analysis of her films by scholars she found insensitive to her filmmaking objective and esthetic foundation. Students can assess how effective Larkin's stated filmmaking paradigm parallels her actual cinematic representations. Students might also be assigned interviews with African-American women filmmakers and selected chapters from Trinh T. Minh-hà's *When the Moon Waxes Red: Representation, Gender and Cultural Politics.*[4]

Social Invisibility and Cultural Identity

Many times we use terms such as *social invisibility* without exploring relevant experiential definitions. We must challenge students to understand the multifarious dimensions and ramifications of invisibility. What does it mean when African-American women contend that their voice is not heard or is misrepresented by white patriarchal structures, as in, for example, the Anita Hill–Clarence Thomas hearings? How does one interpret the criticism that many white women do not understand or embrace their intrinsic racism? Finally, do we understand African-American women who charge some African-American men with not recognizing how their attitudes and behaviors disempower black women? Because of these issues, black women still remain out of focus to the larger society and rank "insignificant" on the hierarchal scale of social valuation.

Larkin explains that "Alana [the film's central character] is never really seen as a person in her own right by men in the film, because Western society dictates that men view women as sex objects" (171). An early scene in the film provides the context for the class to explore invisibility. Alana and Vincent have developed a close, strictly platonic relationship. On one occasion their conversation centers around invisibility. Vincent reads a passage from Ralph Ellison's *The Invisible Man,* which examines negative perceptions of black Americans held by white society that render black people invisible. Alana states, "I can relate to that [invisibility]. All most brothers see is this [breasts] and this [hips]." Invisibility becomes more than an issue of race. For Alana, it specifically encompasses the issue of gender. To transform Alana's invisibility into a realistic self-portrait, Larkin restructures her cinematic representation through culturally based imagery and nuance. She thereby establishes a new discourse of identity that shatters one-dimensional stereotypes.

Students should examine how Alana's physical appearance and her feminist attitude translate into freedom and empowerment. In addition, her personal space functions as an extension of herself. The class should also understand that her freedom is not without cost. On the one hand, Alana wishes to be recognized as an American woman of African ancestry. On the other hand, she is a unique individual. She seeks to express her ethnicity and individuality. Alana's hairstyle, her brightly colored and sensual attire, and her outgoing personality all contribute to the image she wishes to project. She later discovers that her behavior, physical appearance, and demeanor are misinterpreted to communicate another message: sexual promiscuity. As Larkin juxtaposes culturally based individualism with preconceived stereotypic attitudes, she exposes societal contradiction and irony. Alana's resistance to invisibility entails identification with her African heritage and projection of a different, ultimately misunderstood, image.

A Different Image has the potential to broaden a student's perception of the historical and political magnitude of sexual oppression. Students should be assigned readings that impart a foundation for understanding social invisibility and cultural identity. Angela Davis's *Women, Culture and Politics,* bell hooks's *Ain't I a Woman: Black Women and Feminism,* and Hazel Carby's *Restructuring Womanhood* give students a background in black women's history and the politics of identity. Selected chapters in *Face Value: The Politics of Beauty,* written by Robin Lakoff and Raquel Scherr, provide in-depth analyses of the concept of "beauty" as well as the effects of negative self-perception.

Black Feminist Theoretical Perspective

Because black women's cinema still exists in a developmental stage as an emerging tradition, new and dynamic theoretical focuses to analyze the films are at an equally embryonic phase. Many approaches such as womanist perspective, black feminism, Afrocentric feminism, and Third World feminism are just now beginning to surface in the analysis of black women's film. The perspectives may vary, but at each core remains an objective of analysis that sets forth new parameters to critique and analyze society and artistic expression compatible with and germane to a black woman's sociohistoric reality. Moreover, the common threads that link each to the other acknowledge the effects of patriarchal imperialism and evaluate reconstructed texts to ascertain how they communicate empowering attitudes and behaviors of resistance.

The theoretical objective becomes defining salient, shared structures and common conceptual themes found in black women's cinema to establish a critical discourse. A "different [cinematic] image" requires a "different" analytical reading. A class in women's film or black women's film might begin to develop an analytical model that seeks to identify and understand specific aspects that qualify the films as African American and female. A challenging assignment for students in other classes could be a more detailed study of one or several aspects of a specific film; for example, they might analyze how Larkin constructs the "female body." Students could also address issues such as how Larkin constructs womanhood, how and why this construction might be considered a black feminist representation, and whether Larkin's challenge represents a powerful voice of resistance. The critical point is that analytical discourse should develop from the emerging body of work, not be imposed upon it. Several articles and books may be incorporated into this lesson focus, such as *Third World Women and the Politics of Feminism, Black Feminist Thought: Knowledge, Consciousness, and the Politics of Empowerment,* edited by Chandra Talpade Mohanty, Ann Russo, and Lourdes Torres, and *Multiple Voices in Feminist Film Criticism,* edited by Diane Carson, Linda Dittmar, and Janice Welsch.

Cinematic Technique (Imagery and Music)

The cinematic techniques used in *A Different Image* are intricately linked to the thematic content. Students should explore and discuss how Larkin's use of camera and editing techniques, color, imagery, and music become vital components to help communicate her message. Numerous scenes exist in which students may analyze the cultural significance of cinematic technique.

Throughout the film, Larkin highlights cultural connections between African and African-American culture. For example, an excerpt from the opening scene suggests a correlation between African and

African-American women. Larkin achieves this through montage, dissolves, and the accompanying music. The image of an African-American woman dissolves into a still photograph of an African woman wearing a decorative head wrap, which then dissolves into a photograph of her wearing a vividly colored wide shirt and sitting, open-legged, in the grass. The film's title appears next to her. Larkin uses the dissolve in this scene and in a later one to communicate cultural links among black women. The montage, primarily still photographs of girls and of African and African-American women, dramatizes their cultural similarities related to hair texture, skin color, and familial relationships. Moreover, it helps establish the structure of the film as a female-centered narrative. The images captured in the photographs communicate a reaffirmation of womanhood and reject traditional female passivity.

The pulsating rhythm of the opening music dissolves into an African folk song, "Modi Lama," which a woman sings a cappella. This musical theme continues as the stills are projected. With the montage, the music exposes further commonalities between the two worlds. Students' study of cinematic technique and music usage throughout the film can bring about the awareness of how Larkin intricately links them with thematic development. Supplementary readings in the historian Lawrence Levine's *Black Culture and Black Consciousness* or "Africanisms in African-American Music" by Portia Maultsby, an ethnomusicologist, acknowledge "the continuum of an African consciousness in America manifests itself in the evolution of an African-American culture" (Maultsby 185). The films of many contemporary independent African-American filmmakers reflect an African consciousness through cinematic structure and thematic development.[5]

Social Issues: Rape, Sexploitation, and Peer Pressure

Peer pressure, sexual exploitation, and rape are serious social problems that provide stimulating class discussion. Several scenes in *A Different Image* explore sensitive and potentially explosive issues that require openmindedness and maturity to discuss. The climactic scene demonstrates how peer pressure and sexism erode and destroy the friendship between Alana and Vincent. As they lie asleep on the floor after a long day of moving, Vincent awakens and begins to fondle Alana. He has finally succumbed to his friend Ralph's sexist attitudes regarding women as sexual objects. When Alana finally wakes, she is terrified. She doesn't understand why Vincent tried to "rape" her. Vincent, shocked, explains that he didn't try to rape her. Alana then asks,"What do you call it when my feelings don't matter. You have to learn to respect me!"

The sequence dramatizes the destructive force of sexism and peer pressure. Questions posed for discussion might include: Why is Alana afraid? Why is Vincent confused? Can men and women be friends? Do mainstream cinematic portrayals of women influence attitudes and behaviors? If so, how? What is date rape? Are present definitions of rape ambiguous? In what sense?

Final Reflections on Multicultural Pedagogy

A multicultural pedagogy encourages students to discuss interracial social interactions and intraracial cultural dynamics via film. Through the generation of stimulating dialogue and the formation of probing questions, students and teachers can move toward a liberating pedagogy. In addition, film can effectively address and promote discussion of issues related to race, sex, and class oppression. Teachers can also use film to introduce students to new voices of resistance. Most important, as a liberating pedagogical approach embraces those different voices, it encourages the advancement of critical thinking and consciousness-raising for students and teachers. The true test, of course, for the effectiveness of multicultural pedagogy begins in the classroom with the serious study of films such as *A Different Image,* but it ends with students and teachers embracing difference in their day-to-day lives.

Appendix 1: Discussion Questions for A Different Image

The following questions were compiled by Elizabeth Hadley Freydberg, Phyllis R. Klotman, and me:

1. How would you describe Alana's life-style? Her self-image? What is the significance of Alana sitting with her legs open and the little girl sitting at the bus stop in the same manner?
2. *A Different Image* uses actual billboards and magazines to show the sexism of popular American culture. Characters in the film react to these images in different ways.
   a. Do you feel that the billboard of the woman's behind affected the little boy's perception of Alana?
   b. Discuss Ralph's attitudes toward women as demonstrated by his reaction to Alana dancing down the street with Vincent.

    c. What types of societal pressures possibly shaped Ralph's attitudes?
3. *A Different Image* uses actual attitudes of American society with the dramatized responses of characters:
    a. Discuss Alana's reaction to the men's conversation outside her bathroom window.
    b. Discuss your reaction to the men's conversation. Did you find it humorous? Sexist? Offensive?
4. How does Alana define rape? How does Vincent define rape?
    a. Is rape always violent?
    b. Can rape occur between husband and wife? Between friends?
5. Discuss Vincent and Ralph's relationship. What types of societal pressures shape their attitudes and behavior in the film?
6. Sexism goes beyond the issue of woman as a sex object. It includes definitions of womanhood and manhood. Discuss those definitions.
7. What is the significance of the montage sequences of African women in film?
8. Discuss the issue of sexploitation in advertisement in Western culture and its effect on sexual attitudes.
9. Discuss Larkin's use of montage, stills, and dissolve.
10. How does music function in the film? What types of music are incorporated into the soundtrack?

Appendix 2: Syllabus for African-American Women Independent Filmmakers (Indiana University)

COURSE DESCRIPTION

This course is designed to introduce students to the cinematic images that African-American women create. Specifically, the course will investigate how African-American women independent filmmakers (1) articulate their vision of the relationship between black women and society; (2) translate social, political, and cultural issues into a cinematic statement; and (3) construct a didactic, cinematic narrative in which a female voice is undergirded by an empowering, emancipatory esthetic. The cinematic analysis takes cognizance of the political, social, and cultural forces that shape the creative processes of black women and demonstrates that as black women frame their own images they also call attention to the need to transform the circumstances of black women in American society.

RECOMMENDED READINGS

Donald Bogle, *Brown Sugar: Eighty Years of America's Black Female Superstars* (New York: Da Capo, 1990).

Julie Burchill, *Girls on Film* (New York: Pantheon, 1986).

Gina Dent, ed., *Black Popular Culture: A Project by Michele Wallace* (Seattle: Bay Press, 1992).

Manthia Diawara, ed., *Black American Cinema* (New York: Routledge, 1993).

Henry Louis Gates, ed., *Reading Black, Reading Feminist: A Critical Anthology* (New York: Meridian Books, 1990).

Molly Haskell, *From Reverence to Rape: The Treatment of Women in the Movies* (New York: Holt, Rinehart and Winston, 1974).

E. Ann Kaplan, *Women and Film: Both Sides of the Camera* (New York: Methuen, 1983).

Phyllis Klotman, ed., *Screenplays of the African American Experience* (Bloomington: Indiana University Press, 1991).

Chandra Mohanty, Ann Russo, and Lourdes Torres, eds., *Third World Women and the Politics of Feminism* (Bloomington: Indiana University Press, 1991).

DISCUSSION TOPICS, READINGS, AND SCREENINGS

Week 1

Course Introduction

Cinematic Stereotypes of African American Women, part 1

Readings: Thomas Cripps, *Black Film as Genre* (Bloomington: Indiana University Press, 1978), 1–63; Jacqueline Bobo, "Black Women in Fiction and Nonfiction: Images of Power and Powerlessness," *Wide Angle* 13, nos. 3–4 (1991): 72–81; Paula Giddings, *When and Where I Enter: The Impact of Black Women on Race and Sex in America* (New York: William Morrow, 1984), chs. 1–3.

In-class films: Thomas Edison's early images of black women.

Films: *Black Shadows on a Silver Screen* (1976); *Ethnic Notions* (1986).

Week 2

Cinematic Stereotypes of African-American Women, part 2

Readings: Donald Bogle, *Toms, Coons, Mulattoes, Mammies and Bucks: An Interpretive History of Blacks in American Films* (New York: Continuum Press, 1989), 1–34; Clyde Taylor, "The Re-Birth of the Aesthetic in Cinema," *Wide Angle* 13, nos. 3–4 (1991): 12–30; Robyn Wiegman, "Black Bodies/American Commodities: Gender, Race, and the Bourgeois Ideal in Contemporary Film," in *Unspeakable Images: Ethnicity and the American Cinema,* ed. Lester D. Friedman, 308–28 (Urbana: University of Illinois Press, 1991); Giddings, *When and Where I Enter,* chs. 4–6.

In-class clips: *Birth of a Nation* (1915).

Film: *Hallelujah!* (1929).

Week 3

Eloise Gist: An Early Pioneer

Readings: Pearl Bowser, "Sexual Imagery and the Black Woman in Cinema,"

in *Black Cinema Aesthetics: Issues in Independent Black Filmmaking*, ed. Gladstone Yearwood (Athens: Center for Afro-American Studies, Ohio University, 1982); Giddings, *When and Where I Enter*, chs. 7–14.
Films: *Hellbound Train; Verdict: Not Guilty* (both early 1930s).

Week 4

Madeline Anderson: An Early Documentary Filmmaker
Readings: Spencer Moon, "A Pioneer in Public Television: Madeline Anderson," *Black Film Review* 6, no. 4 (1991): 27–30; Giddings, *When and Where I Enter*, chs. 15–17.
Film: *I Am Somebody* (1970).

Week 5

The Literary/Cinematic Connection: Lorraine Hansberry and Maya Angelou
Readings: Gloria Gibson-Hudson, "African American Literary Criticism as a Model for the Analysis of Films by African American Women," *Wide Angle* 13, nos. 3–4 (1991): 44–54; Vattel T. Rose, "Afro-American Literature as a Cultural Resource for a Black Cinema Aesthetic," in *Black Cinema Aesthetics;* Claudia Tate, "Introduction," and "Maya Angelou," in *Black Women Writers at Work* (New York: Continuum, 1983); Margaret B. Wilkerson, "Lorraine Hansberry: The Complete Feminist," *Freedomways* 4th quarter (1979): 235–45; excerpts from *A Raisin in the Sun*.
Films: *A Raisin in the Sun* (1961); *Georgia, Georgia* (1972).

Week 6

Kathleen Collins: A Creative Trailblazer
Readings: David Nicholson, "A Commitment to Writing: A Conversation with Kathleen Collins Prettyman," *Black Film Review* 5 (Winter 1988–89): 6–15; Giddings, *When and Where I Enter*, chs. 18–20; Hazel Carby, "Woman's Era: Rethinking Black Feminist Theory," in *Reconstructing Womanhood: The Emergence of the Afro-American Woman Novelist* (New York: Oxford University Press, 1987); Gloria Gibson-Hudson, "Aspects of Black Feminist Cultural Ideology in Films by Black Women Independent Artists," in *Multiple Voices in Feminist Film Criticism* (Minneapolis: University of Minnesota Press, 1994).
In-class clips: *The Cruz Brothers and Miss Malloy* (1980).
Film: *Losing Ground* (1982).

Week 7

Music, Politics, and Film: Documentary Filmmaker Michelle Parkerson
Readings: Angela Davis, "Black Women and Music: A Historical Legacy of Struggle," in *Wild Women in the Whirlwind: Afra-American Culture and the Contemporary Literary Renaissance* (New Brunswick: Rutgers University Press, 1990); Gloria Gibson, "Michelle Parkerson IS the Eye of the Storm," *Black Film Review* 3 (Summer 1987): 16–17; Combahee River Collective, "A

Black Feminist Statement" and Audre Lorde, "The Master's Tools Will Never Dismantle the Master's House," both in *This Bridge Called My Back: Writings by Radical Women of Color,* ed. Cherrié Moraga and Gloria Anzaldúa (New York: Kitchen Table Press, 1983).
In-class film: *Storme: Lady of the Jewel Box.*
Films: . . . *But Then, She's Betty Carter* (1980); *Gotta Make This Journey: Sweet Honey in the Rock* (1983).

Week 8
A Different Image: Alile Sharon Larkin
Readings: Mark Reid, "Dialogic Modes of Representing Africa(s): Woman-ist Film," *Black American Literature Forum* 25 (Summer 1991): 2; Alile Sharon Larkin, "Black Women Filmmakers Defining Ourselves: Feminism in Our own Voice," in *Female Spectators: Looking at Film and Television,* ed. E. Deidre Primbram (New York: Verso, 1988), 157–73; Robin Lakoff and Raquel Scherr, "Beauty and Ethnicity," in *Face Value: The Politics of Beauty* (Boston: Routledge, 1984).
In-class film: *Dredlocks and the Three Bears.*
Film: *A Different Image* (1982).

Week 9
Exploring Women's Bodies and Emotions: The Work of Zeinabu irene Davis
Readings: Gloria Gibson-Hudson, "An Interview with Zeinabu irene Davis," (handout); Barbara Smith, "Toward a Black Feminist Criticism," in *Feminist Criticism and Social Change: Sex, Class, and Race in Literature and Culture* (New York: Methuen, 1985); Trinh T. Minh-hà, "Difference: A Special Third World Women Issue," in *Woman, Native, Other: Writing Postcoloniality and Feminism* (Bloomington: Indiana University Press, 1989).
Films: *Cycles* (1989); *A Powerful Thang* (1991).

Week 10
The Unique Documentary Style of Camille Billops
Readings: Angela Davis, "We Do Not Consent: Violence against Women in a Racist Society," in *Women, Culture, and Politics;* Valerie Smith, "Telling Family Secrets: Narrative and Ideology in *Suzanne, Suzanne* by Camille Billops and James V. Hatch," in *Multiple Voices in Feminist Film Criticism,* ed. Diane Carson, Linda Dittmar, and Janice Welsh (Minneapolis: University of Minnesota Press, 1994); Barbara Lekatsas, "Encounters: The Film Odyssey of Camille Billops," *Black American Literature Forum* 25 (Summer 1991): 395–408; Valerie Smith, "Reconstituting the Image: The Emergent Black Woman Director," *Callaloo* no. 11 (1988): 709–19.
Films: *Finding Christa* (1992); *Older Women and Love* (1988); and *Suzanne, Suzanne* (1982).

Week 11
Social-Historical Commentary: Filmmaker Ayoka Chenzira

Readings: Patricia Hill Collins, "The Social Construction of Black Feminist Thought," in *Black Women in America: Social Science Perspectives* (Chicago: University of Chicago Press, 1990); Joseph Holloway, "The Origins of African-American Culture," and Portia Maultsby, "Africanisms in African-American Music," both in *Africanisms in American Culture,* ed. Joseph Holloway (Bloomington: Indiana University Press, 1990); Alice Walker, "Oppressed Hair Puts a Ceiling on the Brain," *Ms. Magazine* 12 (June 1988): 52–53.

In-class film: *Hair Piece: A Film for Nappy-Headed People* (1985).

Films: *Secret Sounds Screaming: The Sexual Abuse of Children* (1986); *Zajota and the Boogie Spirit* (1989).

Week 12

Representation of Self: Black Lesbian Filmmakers

Readings: bell hooks, "Homophobia in Black Communities," in *Talking Back* (Boston: South End Press, 1984); Barbara Smith, "The Truth That Never Hurts: Black Lesbians in Fiction in the 1980s," in *Wild Women in the Whirlwind: Afra-American Culture and the Contemporary Literature Renaissance.*

In-class films: *Janine* (1991); *She Don't Fade* (1991; Cheryl Dunye).

Films: *Among Good Christian People* (1991; Jacqueline Woodson and Catherine Saalfield); *The Audre Lorde Project* (Michelle Parkerson).

Weeks 13 and 14

Retrospective: The Films of Julie Dash

Readings: Zeinabu irene Davis, "An Interview with Julie Dash," *Wide Angle* 13, nos. 3–4 (1991): 110–18; Trinh T. Minh-hà, "Questions of Images and Politics," in *When the Moon Waxes Red: Representation, Gender, and Cultural Politics* (New York: Routledge, 1991); Michele Wallace, "Variations on Negation and the Heresy of Black Feminist Creativity," and "Negative Images: Towards a Black Feminist Cultural Criticism," in *Invisibility Blues: From Pop to Theory* (New York: Verso, 1990); Gloria Gibson-Hudson, "The Ties That Bind: Cinematic Representations by Black Women Filmmakers," *Quarterly Review of Film and Video* 15, no. 2 (1994): 25–44; Julie Dash, *Daughters of the Dust: An African American Woman's Film.*

Films: *Diary of an African Nun* (1977); *Four Women* (1978); *Illusions* (1982); *Praise House* (1991); *Daughters of the Dust* (1991).

Week 15

Synthesis: Toward an Esthetic of Black Women's Films

Appendix 3: Selected Video/Filmography

Note: Distributors' names are abbreviated. See Appendix 4 for complete names and addresses.

Anita Addison
    Savannah (1989), 30 min., AD
    The Secret Space (1981), AD
    Sound of Sunshine, Sound of Rain (1983), AD
    Eva's Man (1978), AD
    The Guest (1977), AD
Madeline Anderson
    I Am Somebody (1970), 30 min., IU
    Integration Report I (1960), 24 min.
    Tribute to Malcolm X (1969), 15 min., IU
    Walls Came Tumbling Down (1975), 29 min., PF
Clair Andrade-Watkins
    The Spirit of Cape Verde (1986), 30 min., Eclipse
Mary Neema Barnette
    Sky Captain (1984), 65 min.
Camille Billops
    Finding Christa (1991), 55 min., WMM
    Older Women and Love (1988), 30 min., WMM
    Suzanne, Suzanne (1982), 25 min., TWN
Carroll Parrott Blue
    Conversations with Roy deCarava (1984), 28 min., First Run
    Varnette's World: A Study of a Young Artist (1979), 26 min.
    Smithsonian World: Nigerian Art—Kindred Spirits (1990; producer), 58 min.,
        PBS
Aarin Burch
    Dreams of Passion (1989), 5 min., WMM
    Spin Cycle (1991), 5 min., WMM
Ayoka Chenzira
    Alma's Rainbow (1993), 85 min.
    Five Out of Five (1987; director), 7 min., WMM
    Flamboyant Ladies Speak Out (1982), 30 min.
    Hair Piece: A Film for Nappy-Headed People (1984), 10 min., WMM & TWN
    On Becoming A Woman: Mothers and Daughters Talking Together (1987; ani-
        mator [film by Cheryl Chisholm]), 90 min., WMM
    Secret Sounds Screaming: The Sexual Abuse of Children (1986), 30 min., WMM
    Syvilla: They Dance to Her Drum (1979), 25 min., WMM & TWN
    Zajota and the Boogie Spirit (1989), 20 min., CG
Kathleen Collins
    The Cruz Brothers and Miss Malloy (1980), 54 min., Mypheduh
    Losing Ground (1982), 86 min., Mypheduh
Carmen Coustaut
    Extra Exchange (1987), 28 min.
    Justifiable Homicide, 5 min.
Julie Dash
    Daughters of the Dust (1991), 113 min., Kino International
    Diary of an African Nun (1977), 13 min.

Four Women (1979), 4 min., TWN
Illusions (1983), 34 min., TWN
Praise House (1991), 30 min., TWN
Zeinabu irene Davis
 Crocodile Conspiracy (1986), 13 min., TWN
 Cycles (1989), 17 min., WMM
 A Powerful Thang (1991), 58 min., WMM
 Recreating Black Women's Media Image (1987), 28 min.
Elena Featherston
 Visions of the Spirit: A Portrait of Alice Walker (1989), 58 min., WMM
Jacqueline Frazier
 Azz Ezz Jazz Ensemble
 Black Radio Exclusive Conference
 Curly Lock and The Three Brothers, 25 min.
 Hidden Memories
 Shipley Street (1981), 28 min.
Monica Freeman
 Learning through the Arts: The Children's Art Carnival (1979), 17 min.
 A Sense of Pride: Hamilton Heights (1977), 15 min.
 Valerie: A Woman, an Artist, a Philosophy of Life (1975), 15 min., Phoenix
  Films
Shirikiana Gerima
 Brick by Brick, 37 min., Mypheduh
Lorraine Hansberry
 Modern American Drama: A Raisin in the Sun, 18 min.
 Raisin in the Sun (1961; story and screenplay), 128 min.
Muriel Jackson
 The Maids! (1985), 28 min., WMM
Alile Sharon Larkin
 A Different Image (1982), 52 min., WMM
 Dreadlocks and the Three Bears (1991), Alile Prod.
 Miss Fluci Moses: A Video Documentary (1987), 22 min., Alile Prod.
 Your Children Come Back to You (1979), 27 min., WMM
Carol Munday Lawrence
 The Cotton Club (1982), 29 min., Beacon
 Oscar Micheaux, Film Pioneer (1981), 30 min., Beacon
 Sports Profile (1981), 30 min., Beacon
 When the Animals Talked (1982), 28 min., Beacon
O. Funmilayo Makarah
 Creating a Different Image: Portrait of Alile Sharon Larkin (1989), 5 min.,
  O.F.M.
 Define (1988), 5 min., O.F.M.
Jessie Maple
 Black Economic Power: Reality or Fantasy, 20 West
 Escape Artists (1982), 20 West
 Jimmy Carter—Plains, Georgia, 20 West

Methadone: Evil Spirit or Wonder? 20 West
Twice as Nice (1989), 70 min., 20 West
Will (1981), 80 min., 20 West
Barbara McCullough
Fragments (1980), 10 min., O.F.M.
Shopping Bag Spirits and Freeway Fetishes: Reflections on Ritual Space (1991),
10 min., O.F.M.
Water Ritual #1: An Urban Rite of Purification (1979), 4 min., O.F.M.
The World Saxophone Quartet (1980), 5 min., O.F.M.
Salem Mekuria
As I Remember It: A Portrait of Dorothy West (1991), 60 min., SM
Sidet: Forced Exile (1991), SM
Denise Oliver
Colour (1982; writer [produced and directed by Warrington Hudlin]), 30
min.
Ruby Oliver
Love Your Mama (1989), 94 min.
Michelle Parkerson
. . . *But Then, She's Betty Carter* (1980), 53 min., WMM
Gotta Make This Journey: Sweet Honey in the Rock (1983), 58 min., WMM
I Remember Betty (1987)
Litany: The Audre Lorde Film Project with Ada Griffin (in progress)
Odds and Ends (1993)
Storme: Lady of the Jewel Box (1987), 21 min., WMM
Debra Robinson
I Be Done Been Was Is (1983), 58 min., BFF
Kiss Grandmama Goodbye (1992), 70 min., WMM
Demetria Royals (and Louise Diamond)
*Mama's Pushcart: Ellen Stewart and Twenty-five Years of La MaMa Experimen-
tal Theatre Company* (1988), 54 min., WMM
Kathe Sandler
A Question of Color (1992), 58 min., CN
Remembering Thelma (1981), 15 min., WMM
Saundra Sharp
Back Inside Herself (1984), 5 min., WMM
Life Is a Saxophone (1985), 58 min., A Sharp Show
Picking Tribes (1988), 7 min., WMM
Jacqueline Shearer
A Minor Altercation (1977), 30 min., WMM
Ellen Sumner
Rags and Old Love (1986), 55 min., Mypheduh
Yvonne Welbon
The Cinematic Jazz of Julie Dash (1992), 26 min. TWN
Monique (1990), 3 min., TWN
Fronza Woods
Fannie's Film (1981), 15 min.
Killing Time (1979), 9 min.

Appendix 4: Distributors

Addison Productions (AD)
Washington Blvd., Room 210
Culver City, CA 90232

Alile Productions
4843 W. 17th St., No. 7
Los Angeles, CA 90019

Beacon
930 Pitner St.
Evanston, IL 60202

Beem Foundation (BF)
3864 Grayburn Ave.
Los Angeles, CA 90008

California Newsreel (CN)
149 Ninth St., Suite 420
San Francisco, CA 94103

Child Care Resource Center (CCRC)
3602 4th Ave. South
Minneapolis, MN 55409

Crossgrain (CG)
265 Bainbridge
Brooklyn, NY 11233

Eclipse Enterprises
P.O. Box 2053, Astor Station
Boston, MA 02123

First Run
335 W. 38th St., 5th Floor
New York, NY 10018

Indiana University (IU)
Audio/Visual Dept.
Franklin Hall
Bloomington, IN 47405

Kino International
333 W. 39th St.
New York, NY 10018

Salem Mekuria (SM)
19 Glade Ave.
Jamaica Plain, MA 02130

Mypheduh Film, Inc.
48 Q St., N.E.
Washington, D.C. 20002

O.F. Makarah (O.F.M.)
308 Westwood Plaza, No. 421
Los Angeles, CA 90024

PBS
1320 Braddock Place
Alexandria, VA 22314

Phoenix Films (PF)
468 Park Ave. South
New York, NY 10016

A Sharp Show
P.O. Box 75796, Sanford Station
Los Angeles, CA 90075

Third World Newsreel (TWN)
335 W. 38th St., 5th Floor
New York, NY 10018

20 West: Home of Black Cinema
20 West 120th St.
New York, NY 10018

Women Make Movies (WMM)
462 Broadway, Suite 500
New York, NY 10013

Notes

1. The courses developed and taught to date are: Early Black Film, Contemporary Black Film, and Racial and Ethnic Stereotypes in American Cinema. Topics courses (400 level) have also been taught, such as The Aesthetics of Black Cinema. Courses in the developmental stage include The Films of African-American Women, Black Women's Film Throughout the African Diaspora, and Black Film and Politics.

2. See *Black American Literature Forum* 25 (Summer 1991); and *Wide Angle: A Quarterly Journal of Film History, Theory, Criticism and Practice* 13 (July–Oct. 1991).

3. For further analysis of films that contain stereotyped representations of African-American women, see Robyn Wiegman, "Black Bodies/American Commodities: Gender, Race, and the Bourgeois Ideal in Contemporary Film"; Elizabeth Hadley Freydberg, "Prostitutes, Concubines, Whores, and Bitches: Black and Hispanic Women in Contemporary Film"; and Pearl Bowser, "Sexual Imagery and the Black Woman in Cinema."

4. See *Black Film Review* for interviews of several black women filmmakers such as Kathleen Collins (5 [Winter 1988–89]); Julie Dash (6, no. 1 [1991]); Madeline Anderson (6, no. 4 [1991]); and Michelle Parkerson (3, no. 3 [1987]).

5. See Haile Gerima's *Bush Mama* (1976), Larry Clark's *Passing Through* (1977), Ayoka Chenzira's *Zajota and the Boogie Spirit* (1989), and Zeinabu irene Davis's *A Powerful Thang* (1991).

8

Put Some Brothers on the Wall! Race, Representation, and Visual Empowerment of African-American Culture

Todd Boyd

Traditionally, courses in African-American or "Black Cinema" as they were often called had limited ability to present a strong body of films, due primarily to the lack of attainable or extant material in the area. With some notable exceptions, cinema courses concerning African-American film have been forced, in one way or another, into a somewhat submissive posture in that they focused on a detailed description of Hollywood's racist past, as opposed to a clear delineation of AFRICAN-AMERICAN cinema. Although films by Oscar Micheaux, Spencer Williams, and others existed, they were often difficult, if not impossible, to find for these courses. Thus, the classes usually reaffirmed the title of Donald Bogle's now canonical text *Toms, Coons, Mulattoes, Mammies, and Bucks* (1989).

Students of African-American cinema, for instance, often learned about the stereotypical religiosity of early sound films featuring African-American performers during the late 1920s and early 1930s, the social problem films of the 1940s and 1950s concerning African-American issues, the success of Sidney Poitier during the 1960s, and the degrading exploits of "pimps, pushers, and ho's" in the so-called Blaxploitation era of the 1970s. Much like the pedagogical tactics that emphasized how African-American existence begins with the slave trade and not in the "glorious" past of Africa, this teaching simply reaffirmed Hollywood's hegemonic posture over the representation of African-American imagery. As I have often argued, we learned more and more about America and less and less about Africa.

Yet, as the streets of Los Angeles went up in flames, so did the confines that limit the teaching of African-American cinema. There is not only a distinct shift in the number of popular African-American films, but also an increased awareness of racial issues in writings about cinema and culture as a whole. While on one hand the films of Spike Lee, the Hudlin brothers, John Singleton, and Robert Townsend garner a public audience, the more marginal works of Charles Burnett, Julie Dash, and Marlon Riggs also gain a certain amount of critical prestige. This increase in productivity and critical attention also presents the opportunity to formulate new ways of teaching courses on African-American cinema.

The current situation in cinema resembles contemporary discussions about the origins of the New World. Instead of assuming that America began with Columbus's arrival, many scholars have firmly articulated that a world existed long before he set sail. As a new critical journal, *Before Columbus Review,* indicates in its title, a world existed prior to and independent of the new world order that Columbus's arrival set in place. In similar fashion, this same political motivation underlies my approach to the concept of African-American cinema and the way it is traditionally taught. Why reaffirm Hollywood when you can articulate your own critically resistant and culturally empowered cinema?

My purpose is to explain the philosophy that underlies my approach to teaching and studying African-American cinema. From my perspective, the topic must be understood as an integral part of the cultural apparatus that comprises contemporary African existence in America. This cultural approach nullifies the need for extended discussions of stereotypes, which inevitably affirm Hollywood, and instead argues for empowerment through the ability to control one's own images. In essence, the traditional way of teaching the issue of race in cinema—discussions of stereotypes—remains useful to the extent that it demonstrates Hollywood's racist past and present. But such a pedagogical approach does little to inform students about crucial issues of representations, resistance, and empowerment. Thus, the move toward advancing discussion of the relevant issues requires the understanding of cinema as a vital component of African-American culture. Recent shifts in African-American cinematic production, as well as critical writing on the subject, demonstrate some of the possibilities that the addition of a cultural consciousness brings to this esthetic and political arena.

The Move Away from Stereotypes

Even in the early days of American cinema, one notices how it clearly operated on stereotypical images of racialized others in such films as *Uncle Tom's Cabin* (1903), *Ten Pickaninnies* (1904), *Wooing and Wedding of a Coon* (1905), the *Rastus* series (1910), and *Coon Town Suffragettes* (1914). The tendency toward demeaning stock characterizations has received a great deal of attention in several histories of African Americans in cinema, including Thomas Cripps's *Black Film as Genre* (1978) and *Slow Fade to Black: The Negro in American Films* (1976).

Donald Bogle and Daniel Leab also offer good examples of stereotype criticism. In *Toms, Coons, Mulattoes, Mammies, and Bucks,* for instance, Bogle focuses on performers—specifically upon actors and actresses and the roles they play: "The history of blacks in films remains one in which individual actors and actresses have often had to direct themselves; rather than *playing* characters, they have had to play *against their roles,* digging deep within themselves to come up with unexpected and provocative points of view" (4, emphasis in the original). While Bogle emphasizes the acting performance of African Americans—regarding their performances as sites of power—he optimistically disregards their historical placement within an institutionalized structure of capitalist cinema production.

In the opening chapter and thesis of *From Sambo to Superspade: The Black Experience in Motion Pictures* (1975), Leab argues that African-American characters have been denied humanity. Instead, he argues, Hollywood presented them as "subhuman, simpleminded, superstitious, and submissive" (4). Leab insists that "despite some progress on the part of the movies in depicting blacks naturally and despite a tendency of the industry to utilize them in the *mise en scene* and to publicize black actors and actresses as people not props; as yet, relatively few movies treat blacks as they treat other characters" (4–5). He sees the problem of stereotypes as the "unrealistic" character depiction of African-American life, especially to the extent that these characters are never offered the variety of roles given to white actors and actresses.

As Bogle and Leab accurately point out, American cinema has certainly relied on the formulaic characterizations of African Americans as its definition of race. Yet scholarly identification and discussion of these stereotypes often limits larger discussions of race and representation. Bogle and Leab both emphasize performance as resistance to cultural hegemony, but they ignore the economic and societal context in which performance takes place. They take the first step in "burning" Hollywood but fail to follow through with more complex discussions of cinema's ability to represent race. Unlike the rap group Public Enemy, they rely simply on discussing the negative implications of stereotypes in relation to society's knowledge of African Americans.

With cinema as one of the most powerful and ubiquitous means of representing African Americans to the dominant society, traditional criticism is limited to arguing inherently positive or negative individual stereotypes. It cannot examine how societal ideology uses these visual stereotypes to explain its position on race. In *Yearning: Race, Gender, and Cultural Politics* (1990), bell hooks observes that the practice of "placing cultural critique by black critics solely in the reformist realm of debate about good and bad images effectively silences more complex critical dialogue" (5).

These discussions of stereotypes mute cinema's function as a discursive institution using rhetorically powerful visual images to reinforce the power hierarchies explicit in a racist society. Michelle Wallace in "Negative/Positive Images" argues for a move beyond the negative-positive stereotype dichotomy (in *Invisibility Blues*). She claims that this type of analysis, other than simply reversing the terminology, never contends with how African-American culture constitutes an important variation on postcolonial discourse. According to Wallace, stereotype criticism does not distinguish between the visual and the textual, and it discourages discussions of production and audience reception of African-American mass and popular culture.

How then can teachers articulate a counter-cultural ideological theory of American cinema that will move beyond the discussion of stereotypes and open the classroom to explorations of race and visual representation? They can do it by foregrounding the racial foundation upon which American cinema and culture were built. In this sense, it becomes necessary to move beyond these traditional arguments about stereotypes to uncover the complexities of American cinema's relationship to the ideology of white supremacy.

This critical deconstruction of Hollywood cinema is imperative, initially, before students can achieve any understanding of the historical function of race and visual representation. Yet, in addition to an ideological analysis teachers must begin to investigate African-American culture and its impact on the resulting African-American cinematic product in order to achieve new levels of critical awareness regarding issues of race and representation. By using certain examples of African-American culture, and finally discussing African-American cinema itself as critical discourse on American cinema, the possibilities for a contemporary discussion of visual commentary on race can be expanded.

African-American Cinema

Having deconstructed certain moments in American film production, the teacher must next move to a level of criticism that involves cultural production. Consistently engaging in the debate over positive-negative images limits a potentially more fruitful discussion that comments on race and representation. Second, the emphasis on dominant cinema and culture alone leaves the class hanging theoretically in regard to understanding the political implications of an empowered African-American cinema.

Although rigorous critique of Hollywood does teach students the underlying ideological motivations of the film industry, it does not tell them much about a self-determined cinema that simultaneously attempts to resist the dominant culture and empower the margins through its own cultural production. Thus, the presence of a politically empowered African-American cinema helps to increase the student's critical awareness of Hollywood. In this regard, Manthia Diawara argues in *Black American Cinema* that "the development of black independent productions has sharpened the Afro-American spectator's critical attitude towards Hollywood films" (101). Yet, at the same time, this self-determined cinema offers a culturally specific series of representations that sets its own terms and creates its own rules, undermining the very nature of dominant cinema. Teachers can thus offer an argument that describes this culturally based African-American cinema as a response to the hegemonic model of dominant cinema.

Previous analysis of African-American cinema, such as the discussion of stereotypes, resisted the argument of culture as the primary determinant in cinema production. In addition to discussions of the positive-negative stereotype dichotomy, a recurring argument defines African-American cinema in the same terms as Hollywood. For instance, Thomas Cripps uses a traditional model for defining the subject in *Black Film as Genre,* arguing that it should be understood as using a series of narratives that rely on the exploits of an urban or pastoral hero. The narrative context of Cripps's definition posits that cinema may express itself across a number of "sub genres," for example, social drama, cautionary tales, musicals, documentaries, religious tracts, and romances. What ultimately makes genre the vehicle for the definition of African-American cinema is the presence of the primary theme, which he describes as the *aesthetique du cool:* "Outward detachment, composed choreographic strides, and self-posed enigmatic mask over inner urgency that have been admired in both Africa and Afro-America" (9).

Cripps outlines several films—*The Scar of Shame* (1927), *St. Louis Blues* (1958), *The Blood of Jesus* (1941), *The Negro Soldier* (1944), *Nothing but a Man* (1964), and *Sweet Sweetback's Baadasssss Song* (1971)— as examples that involve an integrated production situation and describe his definition of genre. The basis for this argument revolves around his idea that African-American cinema is inextricably connected to and influenced by the dominant white culture, and so no such product of this cinematic movement could be considered purely black. Cripps thus rejects the idea of an African-American cinema that involves "real" African-Americans in the production process, specifically in positions that can be associated with the production of meaning. He combines his specific definition of genre with what he sees as a limiting integrated social context in American society. "Black film must be seen as a genre, then for what its says and how it is said, rather than who is saying it" (10).

For Cripps, African-American cinema must be understood not by its esthetic factors, but by its "social and anthropological" dimensions. African-American genre films "may transmit social meanings beyond the conscious intention of the filmmaker, as well as meaning brought by the audience's own social and cultural history" (10). Thus, African-American cinema, although having no connection to a specific individual or group of individuals who provide authorial and racial identity, does have a relationship to the social to the extent that audiences assist in meaning production.

Although Cripps refutes traditional auteur theory, with its concern for authorship and its textual production of meaning, he ultimately removes African-American cinema from the cultural context that he wants to establish. Through this definition, the author of a particular text is irrelevant so long as the text meets the other generic requirements. In other words, African-American texts can be "authored" by whites if the generic conventions are maintained.

I am interested, however, in arguing for a definition of African-American cinema that requires not only that the author be African American but also, and more important, that the cinema emerge from an African-American cultural context. The racial identity of the author in African-American cinema is important, for one must have the knowledge and experience of the culture in question to articulate the discourse rooted in that particular cultural context.

With the most recent wave of African-American cinema (1986–92), audiences became increasingly aware of the multifaceted nature of the culture. Often neglected or totally denigrated, it is represented by the proliferation of images that affirm the dominant society's retrograde view of African Americans. Thus, the ability to represent oneself is a vital element in any attempt at cultural empowerment. The desire for self-representation is played out cinematically, for example, in Spike Lee's *Do the Right Thing* (1989). The central conflict in the film's narrative structure is Buggin Out's demand that Sal, the Italian owner of the neighborhood pizzeria, "put some brothers on the wall!" Buggin Out's argument, one of self-representation, can easily be translated into a larger demand for African-American self-determination. This quest, through visual representation, fuels African-American cultural production.

Yet, to investigate and use this cinema most effectively, teachers need a knowledge of African-American culture and an understanding of how it informs any artifact that emerges from its productive facilities. Most fundamental to this knowledge is a grasp of the history, esthetics, music, and politics that make up the culture. The extent to which these issues inform African-American visual imagery is the extent to which we begin to understand the cultural basis of cinema as another tool in the ongoing battle for empowerment.

African-American cinema must emanate from a cultural matrix that allows for a resistant and empowering cinematic voice. In this regard, August Wilson argues that one must be of the culture to produce the culture, stressing this argument in his request for an African-American director in the adaptation of his play *Fences* to film. "Someone who does not share the specifics of a culture remains an outsider, no matter how astute a student they are or how well-meaning their intentions. I decline a white director not on the basis of race but on the basis of culture. White directors are not qualified for the job. The job requires someone who shares the specifics of the culture of black Americans" (71).

I am not suggesting teachers need to present a utopian or essentialist cinema immune to the influence of the dominant society; this influence is undeniable. The production of an authentic text that terms itself "African" and "American" realizes, in the very naming, the tension and negotiation of Africans in American society. Yet this tension provides much of the content within African-American cultural artifacts and, in this case, cinema. As I have argued previously, "Just because the African American is produced under (white) American production circumstances, articulated in a dominant white society and discussed in ivory tower academic settings, does not mean that our only recourse to understanding this culture is to place it under a microscope which can only utilize and reaffirm the dominant discourse. The vernacular must be allowed to speak" ("The Meaning of the Blues," 58). The argument for a culturally specific, politically empowered cinema foregrounds its existence and determines its structure without having to imitate the model of dominant cinema. African-American cinema uses the technology of Western society in conjunction with the impulses of an oral culture. According to Gladstone Yearwood, African-American cinema "emanates from an essential cultural matrix deriving from a collective black socio-cultural and historical experience and uses black expressive traditions as a means through which artist languages are mediated" (70–71).

Furthering this argument for cultural specificity, Teshome Gabriel states that "black filmmakers break constraints and cross borders. . . . They create their own aesthetic terms in film discourse. Call them ethnobiographies, film essays, film poems, film lore or a combination thereof: they incorporate 'in clear rhythm with Africa' long-term memories and heritages" (71). This definition presents a cinema simultaneously resistant and empowering (breaking constraints, crossing borders) as well as culturally influenced by Africa. Thus, cinema becomes an effective tool in the struggle over creating one's own images. As Gabriel observes, African-American cinema has "its own discrete identity" and it revolves "on its own axis" (70).

Much of the discussion surrounding a contemporary use of African-American cinema as a culturally affirming tool in the struggle over representation involves the description of what many are calling a "new black aesthetic" (NBA). In a phrase coined by novelist Trey Ellis, the NBA "somehow synthesizes the last two art revivals; the Harlem Renaissance and the black arts movement. In the twenties blacks wanted to be considered as good as dominant culture. In the sixties we wanted no part of dominant culture at all. Today the NBA wants to dominate it. We feel separate but better" ("The New Black Aesthetic" 250).

Cornel West has also articulated a similar argument in describing what he refers to as a "new cultural politics of difference": "The new cultural politics of difference are neither simply oppositional in contesting the mainstream for inclusion, nor transgressive in the avant-gardist sense of shocking conventional bourgeois audiences. Rather they are distinct articulations of talented contributors to culture who desire to align themselves with demoralized, demobilized, depoliticized, and disorganized people in order to empower and enable social action" (19–20).

Ellis and West see the early, artistically motivated movements as a historical foundation; both are also interested in a diverse leftist, neonationalist, political agenda that embraces the many strands of African-American culture while simultaneously engaging in the process of self-critique. This movement rejects previously held ideas on, for example, essentialism and positive representation, fully understanding that there is neither a monolithic African-American culture nor a politically correct notion of blackness to represent. Instead, NBA argues for the complex, multifaceted nature of African-American culture that moves across race, class, and gender boundaries regardless of the contradictions incurred: "We no longer need to deny or suppress any part of our complicated and sometimes contradictory cultural baggage to please either white people or black" (Ellis 5). Thus the notion of a new black esthetic frees up the possibilities in cultural production because it removes many of the restricting boundaries associated with past attempts to establish a cultural arm of political activities in African-American society. Ellis concludes that "we can be more honest and critical of ourselves than ever before, and this open-minded far-sightedness may very well produce some of the greatest works of art the world has ever known" (251).

A good example of the NBA work that teachers could use would be the social criticism present in the comedy skits on "In Living Color." The ensemble cast routinely engaged in a critical exchange that saw little as sacred and privileged very few. "In Living Color" could critique Spike Lee for his multiple corporate relationships, which are seen as undermining his independent filmmaker status, while simultaneously deconstructing the image of the rapper Vanilla Ice to foreground his shameless exploitation of rap music. The character of Handyman can be seen simultaneously as an insensitive portrayal of a physically disabled African-American male, and at the same time can be regarded as the opportunity of a voice for disabled individuals. The purveyor of the character, Damon Wayans, who grew up disabled, has described the skit as the adventures of a handicapped superhero. "In Living Color" made Jesse Jackson as likely a target for criticism through humor as David Duke.

Another example of the practices of the NBA would be rapper Ice Cube, who on the album *Death Certificate* (1991) critiques the postmodern fascism of then Los Angeles police chief Daryl Gates in "The Wrong Nigga to Fuck Wit." In the song "Us," he urges African Americans to take on some of the responsibility for their oppressed status: "Sometimes I believe the hype, man / We mess it up ourselves and blame the white man." In times past, certain African-American images and icons were treated as sacred cows in the effort to maintain

a strong positive public image, but the emergence of the NBA demonstrates that for cultural production to be free of creative hindranc-
es, critical insight must be encouraged and undertaken.

The notion of a new black esthetic also expresses itself in cinema.
The proliferation of several African-American produced and directed films between 1986 and 1992 demonstrates the beginning of what
many hope will be an ever-developing body of work. Another example of the affirmation of culture in visual representation can be seen
in many politically minded rap music videos. Public Enemy's "Can't
Truss It" (1990) is a good example of the way in which history through
images repeats itself, specifically in terms of race. Slavery and contemporary circumstances are linked through black and white imagery to point out that the dominant society's liberal rhetoric has
changed little regarding institutionalized racial discourse. As the song
states, "Beware of the hand that's coming from the left." This defines
that which cannot be trusted—the liberal refiguration of racial discourse in contemporary society. With this visual affirmation of African-American culture embodying a significant amount of contemporary cultural space, teachers must begin to understand its function
in terms of the NBA as well. As the following examples demonstrate,
African-American cinema conceived in this cultural venue offers
numerous possibilities for teaching about race and representation.

At the base of the argument concerning cinema and the NBA is
the use of dominant means of distribution for what are otherwise
products of marginal economic production practices. Spike Lee's first
commercial release, *She's Gotta Have It* (1986), is a good example. Lee
assembled a minimal budget through grants and small investments
of time and capital from friends in a true cultural demonstration of
Malcolm X's often quoted phrase "by any means necessary." Greg Tate
sees these events as the pushing of "an uncompromising black vision
to blacks through mainstream distribution, exhibition, and media
channels" (7).

Traditionally, any association with the dominant society in a commodity selling venture has been deemed a co-optation of one's subjectivity, a dilution of the African-American voice to commodity culture. Yet, as Lee's film demonstrates, rules of identity have shifted to
the point that the presentation of the film can be seen as critiquing
the structure that makes its distribution possible. Tate says that "Lee's
making a success out of a film shot for jackshit with a collectivist cast
and crew demolishes Hollywood's megabudget mystique. Now, if
that's not culturally resistant, I don't know what is" (7).

Similar examples abound, with other African-American filmmakers having to rely on this "any means necessary" philosophy to have their products, and their political message, seen and heard on a mass scale. Robert Townsend, for example, encountered problems with the 1987 release of *Hollywood Shuffle*. He reportedly saved rejected film stock from the sets of previous movies in which he had acted, and he used credit cards for cash purposes to get this film produced, financed, and released.

The films that comprise this new movement in cinema, although made on the lowest of budgets, have become immensely profitable by earning exceptional box office returns. For example, John Singleton's 1991 film *Boyz 'N the Hood* according to *Entertainment Weekly* brought in the highest return on initial investment for any film released during the year. The film, budgeted at a mere $6.5 million, generated revenues of $56.1 million. Not only does this demonstrate contemporary culture's trendy infatuation with African-American culture, but it also clearly shows Singleton's ability to make "something out of nothing." It also demonstrates that he and other African-American filmmakers are good examples of what West has called "intellectual freedom fighters": "cultural workers who simultaneously position themselves within (or alongside) the mainstream while clearly being aligned with groups who vow to keep alive potent traditions of critique and resistance" (33).

In addition to African-American cinema functioning as an instance of resistant economic production, teachers can show how the narrative and formal qualities of the medium have become specific to the foregrounding and explanation of race. Using *She's Gotta Have It* as an example of the specificity of African-American culture in cinema, Teshome Gabriel praises the film for its "strong sense of place (New York's Bedford-Stuyvesant ghetto), its use of face-to-face address to the audience (in the tradition of oral discourse), and the resulting interactive mode which is obtained both between film and its audiences, and among audience members themselves" (74). In this sense, students can see how the film provides an example of cinema's ability to be culturally specific in using an oral address that emanates from an authentic cultural space in order to include the audience in the overall production of meaning. The film presents African-American culture as simultaneously metaphoric, verbal, and participatory, clearly demonstrating a visual affirmation of oral culture.

Yet not all African-American critics have seen this investment in visual imagery as the same, which demonstrates the multifaceted nature of the NBA. One particular concern has been the absence of an empowered female voice in African-American cinema. Instead, Jacquie Jones defines the new cinema as allowing African-American women the opportunity "to occupy two narrow categories in this cinema: that of the bitch and that of the ho" (39). African-American feminists argue for exposing the neglected role of gender and so avoiding the shortcomings of the black arts movement and subsequently the attempts at a black nationalist cinema during this same period. As Michelle Wallace observes, "The only way to avoid a renaissance of filmic black sexism would be to take on the field of sexual difference deliberately and oppositionally" (*Invisibility Blues,* 101–2).

Wallace, who is very critical of Spike Lee's handling of gender in his films, carefully does not link her criticisms with those of the dominant culture. She critiques Lee's films for reinscribing "the very thing they aim to dislocate, when they trivialize or deny the importance of women's oppression in general, and the problem of black women in particular" (109). Yet she celebrates "Lee's courage in making a film about 'racism' that, unlike *Betrayed, Mississippi Burning,* and *Places in the Heart,* is really about black people, and that doesn't end with whites and blacks linking arms to sing 'We Shall Overcome' as though Martin Luther King Jr. had never been shot" (107).

Wallace's argument describes African-American culture's ability to withstand often-needed critiques on the internal level, but she insists that the culture must continue to resist dominant culture and empower the margins at the external level. She would agree with West that "black cultural workers must constitute and sustain discursive and institutional networks that deconstruct earlier modern Black strategies for identity-formation, demystify power relations that incorporate class, patriarchal and homophobic biases, and construct more multi-valent and multi-dimensional responses that articulate the complexity and diversity of Black practices in the modern and postmodern world" (29). This critical situation is also similar to Malcolm X's assertion that "if you don't make it at home, you settle it at home; you get in the closet and argue it out behind closed doors, and then when you come out on the street, you pose a common front, a united front" (6). The potential of a united front embraces the cohesiveness as well as the contradictions. Ultimately, the stance empowers the entire African-American artistic and social community.

Therefore, the new cultural agenda foregrounds the questions of race in a visual context. In classrooms, this visual affirmation refutes Hollywood cinema and responds to traditional approaches to the study of African-American cinema. When understood from a perspective that emphasizes culture, the possibilities for teaching and discussing more complex issues on race and representation begin to become apparent. Cinema becomes a powerful tool in articulating a resistant response to dominant culture.

Conclusion

A deconstruction of American cinema in the style that I have described as the burning of Hollywood offers an illuminating opportunity for the intensive study of race and representation. The major problem is not one of positive or negative representations, but ultimately a question of who possesses the power to represent their culture through the cinematic medium. African Americans must be allowed the opportunity to define their existence from a culturally specific perspective. This perspective, currently undertaken in the move toward a new black esthetic, avoids previous ideas of essentialism and a hesitancy toward self-critique, favoring instead a cultural emphasis on the diversity permitted when one creates one's own representations. As opportunities to express this NBA continue through the cinema, it opens the possibilities for an empowered notion of representation that sets its own standards and creates its own rules as a vital tool in intellectual and political struggles.

Appendix: Syllabus for CNTV 407: African-American Cinema (University of Southern California)

COURSE OBJECTIVES

This course is designed as an intensive survey of African-American cinema and will engage questions of history, culture, politics, and the overall function of race and representation in American society. Recently, a great deal of media as well as scholarly interest has been focused on the popularity of filmmakers such as Spike Lee, the Hudlin brothers, John Singleton, Julie Dash, and others. The focus in this class is to understand these filmmakers and their respective films in addition to the films and filmmakers that preceded them. Discussion will also focus on cultural factors intrinsic to African-American society that assist in furthering knowledge of production and how cinema fits into this context. Finally, the class will evaluate the political landscape of American society throughout history and how African-American cinema participates in critiquing this history and forwarding its own political agenda.

WRITTEN ASSIGNMENTS

1. Research the critical reception of an in-class film. How was the film received in its time? What do the reviews say about that historical period?

2. Research the production history of an in-class film. How was the film conceived? What significant changes occur from start to finish? What does this research say about the historical period?

3. Analyze one of the in-class films with respect to its position on class and gender.

4. Compare one of the in-class films with another African-American cultural artifact, a book, music, or play.

DISCUSSION TOPICS, READINGS, AND SCREENINGS

Week 1

Silent Cinema

Films: *Body and Soul* (Micheaux, 1924); *Scar of Shame* (Peregrini, 1927).

Readings: Donald Bogle, *Toms, Coons, Mulattoes, Mammies, and Bucks: An Interpretive History of Blacks in American Films* (New York: Continuum Press, 1989), ch. 1, 1–19; Mbye B. Cham and Claire Andread-Watkins, eds., *BlackFrames: Critical Perspectives on Black Independent Cinema* (Cambridge: MIT Press, 1988), 16–25; Jane Gaines, *"Scar of Shame:* Skin Color and Caste in Black Silent Melodrama," *Cinema Journal* 26 (Summer 1987): 3–21.

Week 2

Early Sound Films and Hollywood's Appropriation of African-American Culture

Films: *Black and Tan* (Murphy, 1929); *Hallelujah* (Vidor, 1929).

Readings: Bogle, *Toms, Coons, Mulattoes, Mammies, and Bucks,* ch. 2, 19–35; Black Cinema Issue, *Wide Angle* 13, nos. 3–4 (1991): 12–31; Carter G. Woodson, *The Miseducation of the Negro* (Nashville: Winston-Derek, 1933 [repr. 1990]).

Week 3

Director, Auteurs

Films: *The Blood of Jesus* (Williams, 1940); *Lying Lips* (Micheaux, 1944).

Readings: Bogle, *Toms, Coons, Mulattoes, Mammies, and Bucks,* ch. 4, 101–9; Woodson, *The Miseducation of the Negro.*

Week 4

The African-American Star

Films: *The Emperor Jones* (Murphy, 1933); *Cabin in the Sky* (Minnelli, 1944).

Readings: Bogle, *Toms, Coons, Mulattoes, Mammies, and Bucks,* ch. 3, 35–94; Richard Dyer, *Heavenly Bodies: Film Stars and Society* (New York: St. Martin's Press, 1986), 67–140.

Week 5

Liberalism and the 1960s

Films: *Nothing but a Man* (Roemer, 1964); *The Cool World* (Clarke, 1963).

Readings: Bogle, *Toms, Coons, Mulattoes, Mammies, and Bucks,* chs. 5–7, 117–223.

Week 6

Cinema and Revolution

Films: *Sweet Sweetback's Baadasssss Song* (Van Peebles, 1971); *The Spook Who Sat by the Door* (Dixon, 1973).

Readings: Bogle, *Toms, Coons, Mulattoes, Mammies, and Bucks,* ch. 8, 231–64; Gladstone Yearwood, *Black Cinema Aesthetics* (Athens: Ohio University Press, 1982), 53–82.

Week 7

The "Blaxploitation" Film

Films: *Super Fly* (Parks, 1972); *The Mack* (Campus, 1973).

Readings: Yearwood, *Black Cinema Aesthetics,* 19–26; Iceberg Slim, *Pimp: The Story of My Life* (Los Angeles: Holloway House Publishing, 1969).

Week 8

Race, Gender, and the "Superwoman"

Films: *Coffy* (Hill, 1973); *Cleopatra Jones* (Starrett, 1973).

Readings: Michelle Wallace, *Black Macho and the Myth of the Superwoman* (New York: Verso, 1990).

Week 9

Music and Cinema (the Soundtrack)

Films: *Shaft* (Parks, 1972); *Trouble Man* (Dixon, 1972).

Readings: Nelson George, *The Death of Rhythm and Blues* (New York: Pantheon, 1988), 95–170.

Week 10

The Underground

Films: *Killer of Sheep* (Burnett, 1977); *Passing Through* (Clark, 1977).

Readings: Yearwood, *Black Cinema Aesthetics,* 9–41; Cham/Andread-Watkins, *BlackFrames,* 62–79; Manthia Diawara, "Black Spectatorship: Problems of Identification and Resistance," *Screen* 29 (Autumn 1988): 66–76.

Week 11

The Underground (cont.)

Films: *Street Corner Stories* (Hudlin, 1977); *Ashes and Embers* (Gerima, 1982).

Readings: Yearwood, *Black Cinema Aesthetics,* 92–118; Cham/Andread-Watkins, *BlackFrames,* 80–85; Clyde Taylor, "Black Films in Search of a Home," *Freedomways* (1985): 226–33.

Week 12

The Female Voice
Films: *Hair Piece: A Film for Nappy-Headed People* (Chenzira, 1984); *A Different Image* (Larkin, 1982); *Illusions* (Dash, 1983).
Readings: Yearwood, *Black Cinema Aesthetics,* 42–51; Black Cinema Issue, *Wide Angle* 13, nos. 3–4 (1991): 44–55, 72–81, 110–19.

Week 13

The New Black Aesthetic (NBA)
Films: *She's Gotta Have It* (Lee, 1986); *House Party* (Hudlin Bros., 1990).
Readings: Bogle, *Toms, Coons, Mulattoes, Mammies, and Bucks,* ch. 9, 267–98; *Wide Angle,* 56–61; Todd Boyd, "The Meaning of the Blues," *Wide Angle* 13, nos. 3–4 (1991): 56–61.

Week 14

The NBA (cont.)
Films: *To Sleep with Anger* (Burnett, 1990); *Malcolm X* (Lee, 1992).
Readings: Black Cinema Issue, *Wide Angle* 13, nos. 3–4 (1991): 32–43; Alex Haley and Malcolm X, *The Autobiography of Malcolm X* (New York: Ballantine, 1964).

9

Cultural Screens: Teaching Asian and Asian-American Images

Diane Carson

Let's try an experiment. Take a few minutes to list a representative cross-section of the Asian-Americans you recall from the vast array of Hollywood films, those works that have dominated screens worldwide almost since cinema's beginnings. Or try a somewhat easier task. Record those examples that spring to mind from recent offerings. Now briefly and honestly describe these characters—their values, their hopes, their fears, their psychological and emotional attributes, their physical appearance, and their fates within the film's story. Finally, survey the list; get an overview; and consider the number of examples cited, the relative ease or lack thereof in recalling Asian Americans in Hollywood films, and the two- or three-dimensional nature of their personas in the narratives. In class, this exercise can focus on film, literature, painting, politics, or many other subjects. Without exception, in my film classes the results poignantly and powerfully reveal the desperate need for assessing and addressing the images of Asian Americans and Asians perpetuated by visual media.

The deductions drawn from this experiment probably surprise no one. Students and educators alike usually produce short lists of stereotypical, circumscribed Asian characters with primarily negative, or at least strikingly limited, associations. Ironically, even if students (or their teachers) have not seen many older films, they probably share a cultural awareness of the nefarious Dr. Fu Manchu and his evil daughter the Dragon Lady (created by the British writer Sax Rohmer in 1913); the pithy, sage detective Charlie Chan; and "Chinese coolies," laundry and railroad workers, lustful defilers, opium den patrons, and cruel Asian (usually Japanese) captors who sadistically punish brave American and British soldiers in numerous World War II and Vietnam War films.[1]

Women are also represented by the subservient geisha girl, the sexually compliant Suzy Wong, deceitfully obsequious servants, or hard-working, barefoot farmers, such as those in *The Good Earth* (1937), with the leads played by Luise Rainer and Paul Muni. Others are patient, hard-working foreigners who adore the white man or woman, defer to the superior white culture, and, if redeemable, long to contribute or submit to its hegemony. We recognize these stock characters as the evil, exotic "other," in Edward Said's sense of the term, with "Orientalism" constructed to reinforce the West's ideological dominance.[2] Through filmic conflicts that often conflate race, gender, and class divisions, one monolithic threat emerges to all capitalist patriarchy. The predictable resolution defuses and reassures society's supporters.

As the independent film and television producer Loni Ding interprets the data, three common stereotypes continue to dominate the range of stock characters: "Asians as perpetual foreigners; as resigned, silent victims; and most recently, as successful 'model minorities' who 'contribute to America'" (47). In both Said's and Ding's discussions, "we" (Euro-American culture) serve as the sane norm against which to judge the other, the Orient and all the inscrutability we project onto it. As Said argues, we posit and accept an "absolute and systematic difference between the West, which is rational, developed, humane, superior, and the Orient, which is aberrant, undeveloped, inferior" (300). This translates into the feeling that, from a Western standpoint, "The Orient is at bottom something either to be feared (the Yellow Peril, the Mongol hordes, the brown dominions) or to be controlled" (Said 301). As Elaine Kim puts it, as this ideology finds its expression in film, there are really only two types, good and bad. "Bad" Asians are "sinister villains and brute hordes who cannot be controlled and must therefore be destroyed," and "good" Asians are those who are "helpless heathens, loyal sidekicks, docile servants, and seductive female partners" (100) who instinctively, films suggest, know how to please men and who reaffirm the virile white male's desirability.

This self-serving motif dominates films as different in style and temperament as *Sayonara* (1957), or *The World of Suzy Wong* (1960), and *Rambo: First Blood, Part II* or *Year of the Dragon* (both 1985). We might go on to argue, with tongue only slightly in cheek, that the popularity of *M Butterfly* and *The Wedding Banquet* (both 1993) reflects today's more liberated sexual mores in which the contemporary application translates into the white man's preference for Asian men as well and, further, that the Asian man has also become a feminized commodity. Consider, then, the perfect irony in Maggie Greenwald's *The Ballad of Little Jo* (1993) which is set in the Old West.

The most poignant sexual relationship in recent films develops between a woman, dressed and accepted as a man, who saves a Chinese man about to be hanged. Perhaps only a thoroughly transgressive individual can challenge and reverse the long-standing assertion of white male desirability.

The more formulaic presentation of patriarchy is, of course, not a recent phenomenon, but a paradigm stretching back to the earliest days of cinematic representation. In my courses, therefore, I approach the topic historically, hoping to avoid confrontational and often defensive reactions provoked by a detailed critique of contemporary shortcomings, our media's and our own. I have found that historically grounding the discussion generates a more positive student reception to analysis of Asian-American images. Approached from this perspective, it quickly becomes apparent that mainstream visual media still perpetuate derogatory images of Asian Americans and that they are still grossly under-represented in American films in proportion to their percentage of the population.

Once I establish this historical framework, rather than merely bemoaning the negative or rescuing some hope from the few positive images lost within the overwhelming accumulation of recurring stereotypes, I prefer to counter Hollywood images with recent, more complex, insightful, and three-dimensional works produced by Asian-American and Asian filmmakers. To narrow the field to manageable proportions, I limit my selections to those from the People's Republic of China. Although Asian Americans' own films certainly counter Hollywood's limited representation, an even more encompassing, cross-cultural perspective emerges with representative works from the PRC. In them, and in Asian-American films, alternatives to stock figures open a discussion of another way to present ethnicity, and the class can move to a more positive, although not naive, perspective. Asian-Americans should neither be idealized nor deferred to mindlessly, but rather recognized for the spectrum of their emotions and abilities, strengths and weaknesses.

An effective way to begin gaining insight into mainland Chinese and Asian-American cultures is to move quickly to their works, that is, let the individuals speak for themselves rather than stealing their voices. In studying complementary and complimentary images, new perspectives emerge, perspectives too often lacking in mainstream portrayals. I want to argue, then, for inclusion of units on Asian Americans and Asians, units that present their own images of themselves, images as diverse as the people who produce them. Through even a limited selection of such works, teachers are empowered to go beyond the stereotypes that they and their students can too easily list and too readily recognize.

In replacing the familiar with the unfamiliar through carefully designed learning units, teachers challenge students and themselves to redefine what they thought they knew. Students are asked to risk reexamination and reassessment of pseudo-knowledge, to complicate their mental lives by changing their minds—in the safety and supportive environment of the classroom. The task should not be underestimated. The sociologist Ashley Montagu recognized the difficulty of maintaining an open mind, an eagerness to learn new things, and a curiosity that drives people enthusiastically forward. He warned against the obverse, a "hardening of the mind—psychosclerosis."[3] Teachers can make a case for the importance of such units, and I will explain the catalyst for this position.

In the summer of 1993, I participated in an NEH seminar devoted to mainland Chinese Culture and Civilization and cosponsored by the East-West Center and the University of Hawaii. In the group of thirty-one community college and university professors, all with a keen curiosity about China, only a handful had seen more than one or two Chinese films, films from mainland China, Hong Kong, or Taiwan. Few had ever forcefully critiqued Hollywood's representations of Chinese or Chinese Americans in films, and fewer still had ever used film as a vehicle to teach about difference. (Although the focus of the seminar was China, these observations could be extended to most Asian and Asian-American images.) The reasons are obvious. Over the years and to this day, only the rare course devotes units to the important sociopolitical topics or the history of Chinese Americans or Chinese culture, that is, discussions that go beyond the nation's wartime engagements with and against Asians.

Because films bear their share of the blame for perpetuating many misimpressions about Asian countries and Asian Americans, what better way to work constructively to offer a range of alternatives to the numerous, lingering, wrongheaded ideas than through the very media that has, for too long, created and reinforced them. Athough never quite a perfect antidote to years of Hollywood's brainwashing, introducing works from—in my case—mainland China expands the narrow categories found in conventional films and humanizes a nation generally anonymous to students. Along with Asian Americans' own films and videos, mainland Chinese cinema supplements and enhances the circumscribed knowledge that most students carry with them.

The damage, in terms of negative representation, began in the earliest days of film, with such works as *Chinese Rubbernecks* (1903) or *The Yellow Menace* (1916). The years of anti-Chinese fervor and restrictive immigration laws found their emotional mirror in the xenophobic cinema. Even the more complex films fail to escape negative, unchallenged constructs. Lovers of early films, those who study the silent masterpieces, will remember D. W. Griffith's *Broken Blossoms* (1919) with "Yellow Man" Richard Barthelmess playing opposite the abused "Girl" (Lillian Gish).[4] Based on Thomas Burke's short story "The Chink and the Child," in *Broken Blossoms* the Chinese man proves his nobility by preparing for his own suicide after finding the chastely adored girl dead. Griffith minimized the miscegenation motif in favor of "poetic tragedy" (Tchen 136), but he still associates the Orient with the exotic, opium dens, and desexed rationality.

Cecil B. DeMille's *The Cheat* (1915) provides another classic example of the fear of the "Yellow Peril" and the hysteria that could be caused by the sexual and economic threat that nonwhites posed, a threat diverted into a melodramatic story. As Sumiko Higashi summarizes its plot, "Catastrophe results when socialite Edith Hardy ([Fannie] Ward) accepts $10,000 from a Japanese merchant (Sessue Hayakawa) to avoid ruinous disclosure after a stock market gamble in which she loses Red Cross funds raised for Belgian refugees" (127). Testimony to the obstacles to assimilating nonwhite immigrants, *The Cheat* offers further proof of the sexual brutality of Asians, especially the shocking scene in which Hayakawa brands Ward "with a hot iron bearing his trademark" (Higashi 123).

If we contextualize DeMille's popular film within the hysteria of the early decades of this century (as Higashi does), students see the transparent connection between sociohistorical conditions and their displacement into the stories we tell ourselves. "Since the ethnic and gender conflicts represented in *The Cheat* are far from resolved as the twentieth century comes to a close" (133), discussions quite easily segue to such an analytical interpretation of contemporary films. First one can supplement the picture of white women confronting Asian men with the portrayals of Asian women.

Early films present mysterious Asian female villains in the enduring portraits of Anna May Wong, most notably as the slave girl in *The Thief of Baghdad* (1924) and as the murderous vamp in *Shanghai Express* (1932). Or, reflecting the industry's careful representation of Asian-Caucasian relationships, heedful of charges of miscegenation and cautious in showing whites kissing Asians in studio films, we find Asian women played by Caucasian actresses, among them Myrna Loy, Lana Turner, Dorothy Lamour, and Loretta Young. In the anti-Japanese film *Dragon Seed* (1944), Katharine Hepburn and Agnes Moore-head played Chinese women in a town besieged by fiendish Japanese troops. And, in a ludicrous performance, Marlon Brando was the Asian interpreter to a serviceman (Glenn Ford) in *Teahouse of the August Moon* (1956), set in post–World War II Okinawa. It was not until 1954 that interracial marriage became an issue in Hollywood films, and then the plot inevitably dramatized the relationship of a white man and an Asian woman, with the exception of Sam Fuller's *The Crimson Kimono* (1959). In it, a Japanese-American L.A. detective agonizes over his divided identity and the white woman attracted to him. As usual, cultural friction becomes displaced onto gender conflict with a slippage of the cultural issues.

Leaping over a plethora of minor variations in the clichés, teachers can note the recent, albeit modest, increase in the number of Asian Americans on cinema screens. As in the past, this has brought a mixed bag of new and recycled images. *Rising Sun* (1993), based on Michael Crichton's 1992 novel, and Ridley Scott's *Black Rain* (1989) reinforce roguish gangster associations for Asians and Asian Americans. In both, Asian men commit the unpardonable crime of parading and ordering around their white mistress. Sexually charged scenes invite retaliation from the American representatives of law and order. Equally distasteful, the "bad" Asians are power-hungry, unethical Japanese executives.

In contrast, director Ang Lee's *The Wedding Banquet* (1993) humorously presents a likable New York gay couple, one Taiwanese and the other Anglo-American. With the aforementioned qualification—now gay whites want Asian men—*The Wedding Banquet* presents a Chinese American in a refreshingly unorthodox way. Lee's light touch complements the ambiance of the "closet drama" without trivializing the conflict. The pressure on real estate developer Wai-Tung/Winston Chao, who left Taiwan ten years earlier, to marry testifies to the lingering authority and influence of his parents and the pressure to succumb to a marriage of convenience with a painter-tenant who is having serious immigration problems.

Lee gently explores cross-cultural and cross-gender miscommunication; resourcefully avoids stereotypes of Asians, Americans, gays, or straights; and has produced a film worth discussing. Through the satisfying homosexual relationship of the Chinese American and the Anglo-American, through the tenant-landlord interaction, through the deference shown by Wai-Tung to his parents as well as his resistance to their desires, and through the wedding banquet itself, Ang offers scenes peopled with Asian characters atypical by Hollywood standards. Further, the comic collision of race, gender, and class exposes many of the tenets of our racist, sexist, elitist society in a palatable way. *Banquet* is reminiscent of first-generation struggles through its central Asian-American character's attempts to negotiate the demands of his parents as he makes the difficult transition to the modern American milieu. Avoiding the stock characters described earlier, the film provides students with a fuller spectrum of examples for their list of Asian-American images.

Similarly, the mainstream feature film *The Joy Luck Club* (1993), directed by Wayne Wang in consultation with Amy Tan, who wrote the novel, succeeds in infusing Chinese-American details into universal mother-daughter conflicts. It transcends the limitations of restrictive ethnicity, that is, ethnicity that emphasizes its "foreignness," without obfuscating significant cultural and historical details. Anchoring the film is the weekly mah-jongg gathering of four immigrant Chinese women; the death of one provides the catalyst for stories of the mothers and daughters of all four.

Grounded in specifics of Asian culture, *Joy Luck* includes one mother (June/Ming-Na Wen) with very strong traditional Chinese values; a daughter (Rose/Rosalind Chao) of another, who tries so desperately to assimilate that she denies her heritage; and another daughter (Lena/Lauren Tom), who is ashamed of her customs and must learn to assert herself and battle the reserve expected from her. One "auntie" (the affectionate term for close friends of one's mother) was, as she says in the film, "taught to desire nothing, to swallow other people's misery and eat her own bitterness." We watch the universal parent-child dynamics and conflicts, sibling rivalry, marriages and strained friendships intensified because of the women's shared Chinese cultural heritage and demands. *The Joy Luck Club* thereby interweaves a continuum of women, Asian or Anglo, rarely found in Hollywood films.

If time permits, earlier films directed by Hong Kong–born Wayne Wang will provide additional examples of the intergenerational and immigrant conflicts found in *Joy Luck*. Wang's first, low-budget film, *Chan Is Missing* ($22,000, 1982), parodies the American investigative detective genre with a different logic applied to the search for Chan. His *Dim Sum* (1984) and *Eat a Bowl of Tea* (1989) dramatize intercultural misunderstandings and immigrant family dynamics. *Dim Sum* in particular anticipates *Joy Luck* with its Chinese mother–American daughter discord at the center of the film. Director Peter Wang's (no relation to Wayne Wang) *A Great Wall* (1986, mainland China's first coproduction) offers another excellent dramatization of cross-cultural interaction.

What a film unit on Asian-American and Asian images in film study encourages, even requires, is for the class to move quickly to deeper critical analyses of Asian-American as well as Asian visual images. In *Banquet, Joy Luck,* and Wayne Wang's other films, Asian Americans speak for themselves, lending an authenticity to the images. Through "their films," comparisons and contrasts with Hollywood stereotypes easily emerge. In class, we can highlight the deep-seated universal resemblances without glossing over the ethnically specific differences. In setting up these areas of inquiry, teachers and students must critically inspect their facile assumptions about others of all types and hues. They must recognize that some differences loom large and should not be so cavalierly dismissed as merely insignificant details obscuring the really meaningful similarities. Films written and directed by Chinese Americans and thoughtfully analyzed and discussed can decisively accomplish this because their way of looking is somewhat familiar and yet shifts viewers' perspectives just enough to reinterpret the known.

The next step in expanding filmic horizons is to move to a comparison-contrast of images. Because the lion's share of mainstream images still offers objectionable reactionary stereotypes (see Clarence Spigner's discussion in this anthology), teachers must offer alternatives, both to the stereotypes and to the style of American films. My particular interest lies in countering the restrictive images of Asian women, a deplorable collection of exotic and subservient roles. To bridge the gap between Hollywood and independent films, to counter stereotypical with unconventional three-dimensional characters, two films provide a revealing contrast: the fictional *Year of the Dragon* and the documentary *Mississippi Triangle* (1989).

Gina Marchetti illuminates the regressive Hollywood reinforcement of white patriarchal dominance in *Year of the Dragon,* the Asian woman's obsequious doting on Mickey Rourke's character, her accepting emotional and physical abuse from him, and the masochistic submission of the Asian gangster. As Marchetti notes, "Once again the text obscures the issue of ethnicity by linking it intimately with questions of sexuality and sexual identity" (290). Most important for an expansion of Asian images, she completes her study with an informative distinction between Hollywood fare and a real-life case study.

In *Mississippi Triangle,* three directors document the social inequality of the interactions among Chinese, black-Chinese, poor blacks, and whites in the Mississippi Delta and create "a complex picture of the interrelation of class, race, ethnicity, and gender" (Marchetti 299).

Through "archival news footage, 'talking head' interviews, and cinéma-vérité slices of life" (301) from new immigrant as well as fourth- and fifth-generation Chinese, *Mississippi Triangle* offers a dramatic alternative look at Chinese Americans and the issues that involve them, especially the inequitable "patriarchal organization of sexuality" (303). It establishes another category of Asian-American images with which to inform our mental pictures.

Two Lies (1989), a short (twenty-five minute) piece by independent filmmaker Pam Tom, takes the effort to diversify filmic Asian-American images one step further. Two days before the plot of the film begins, Doris Chu, a divorced Chinese American, has had plastic surgery to make her eyes rounder. Her older daughter, Mei Ling, expresses her anger over her mother's hypocrisy and capitulation to white standards of beauty. Doris repeatedly tells her two daughters to feel pride for their Chinese culture, which, according to her, invented numerous important (the accordion) and unimportant (lipstick) items. Doris has cosmetic eye surgery. She also tells Mei that "Chinese children are to be seen and not heard during meals" and complains that she has "no respect for her elders."

Intercultural and generational conflicts again dominate the story, and several incidents illustrate the pressure to conform to white American standards. At a motel swimming pool, a child mocks the younger daughter's eyes by pulling back her own and laughing. Also at the pool, Mei Ling thinks that a white man is attracted to her, only to have him walk past to talk to a sunbather who is white. The resort the Chu family visits, Cabot's Old Indian Pueblo, is a product of a Boston man's fancy, that is, it is inauthentic culturally and exploited for capitalistic purposes. The wife of the founder would wear coolie hats when she visited Palm Springs, which led to her being called "the China Doll from Desert Hot Springs." The desire to fit in, to look attractive within the culture in which one lives, conflicts with the pride one continues to feel in one's heritage, as dramatized in *Two Lies*. Mei Ling eventually, reluctantly, accepts her mother's decision.

Amplifying several other works, the film returns to the mother-daughter conflict in a more honest, less Hollywood way because Pam Tom's style stimulates thought rather than emotion about difficult issues of identity and ethnicity. As with the women in *The Joy Luck Club* and *Dim Sum,* the mother and daughters in *Two Lies* also search for an elusive peace with each other, but their difficulties revolve more directly around their ethnic placement within white society. These women contend with prejudice against Asians, and any "other," in a more direct manner. With them, we confront the issue of Asian appearance and its relationship to identity and acceptance. Doing so adds several more nonstereotypical women to our list, women upon whom Hollywood does not focus.

Finally, already dependent on time and resources, an informative juxtaposition of American and foreign images can advance attempts to foster an intellectual diversity that will complement the multicultural diversity so desperately needed in all disciplines. By "intellectual diversity," I mean a recognition of the radically different ways of conceiving of experience. Truly constructive progressive education often begins with lack of understanding upon the first encounter with challenging and often mystifying, even befuddling, material. We learn, for example, through watching a Chinese film, that we may lack the conceptual wherewithal to grasp the cultural context and feel comfortable with the experience of the film. We need more information, but that is only a beginning. We need new frameworks and fresh approaches.

This is a good time to return to Edward Said's challenge in *Orientalism:* "None of this Orient is merely imaginative" (2) despite the fact that the Orient has been "politically, sociologically, militarily, ideologically, scientifically" (3), and systematically described from our understandably heretofore limited perspectives. Teachers should call for learners to open their minds to radically different ways of thinking about others among their immediate contacts as well as in more remote circles. To do this, it is necessary to first establish a critical perspective on Hollywood representations of Asian Americans and then move on to less familiar narrative patterns and cinematic styles. Part of this reassessment requires that people recognize and admit when they have reached the limits of comprehension and understanding.

If the class is guided to unique intellectual and emotional horizons, to a place where the commonplace is thrown into fresh relief, the conceptual journey is to uncharted personal territory, providing the opportunity to explore mental frontiers. This must entail more than abstract theorizing. The films chosen should shift focus to the unknown to allow a reconsideration of the known, to make viewers less sure of the assumed naturalness and universality of their ways of interpreting and seeing, and to invite an on-going reconsideration not only of American entertainment but also of sociopolitical structures.

Teachers as well as students often grapple hesitantly and unwillingly with what they consider "radically different," but multiculturalism means more than sampling ideas or food from others. It involves an intellectual conditioning that cultivates a disposition and strength of mind able to push beyond last week's knowledge.

If, as investigators such as the psychologists Robert Sternberg, J. P. Guilford, and Howard Gardner have proposed, human intelligence should be conceived of in the plural rather than the singular, then our multiple intelligences (MI) must surely also encompass many more ways of conceiving of cinematic narratives, images, and esthetics than most film study requires. If, as these researchers describe it, human intelligence is a mosaic of distinct abilities rather than a single whole, intellectual competence has gotten off too easily in most classes. What I am pointing to is another manifestation of diversity that can enrich us all—intellectual diversity that requires that we acknowledge different ways of conceiving, thinking about, and imagining the world. We can then push ourselves to envision and celebrate them. I am cheerleading for new theoretical maps for intellectual journeys, for new frontiers beyond established intellectual ports.

A brief overview of some of the philosophical tenets of Chinese thought and a quick rehearsal of some staggering statistics usually impress students (and their teachers) with the need to move beyond any parochial inclinations. For example, how many have noted that the Asia-Pacific region is America's largest market, "that the Asia-Pacific economies have grown at a rate unparalleled in the world" (6 percent for them versus 2 percent annually for the United States), and that China has the fastest growing economy in the world?[5] By the year 2010, eleven of the world's largest metropolitan centers will be located in the Asia-Pacific region (e.g., Tokyo, Seoul, Shanghai, and Taipei), and, at present, Asia is America's largest trading partner. Also by 2010, Asia will add another billion people to its population of 3.6 billion, and three-quarters of China's 1.2 billion people still live in the countryside, where only slightly more than a quarter of the population is literate. In China, repression and censorship continue at a time when living standards have improved. But accompanying this capitalist-type boom and mobility have also come unprecedented unemployment, a large migrant population, and severe environmental stress.

It should, then, prove provocative to look at the images that the Chinese regime has produced and permits its citizens to consume. How does China represent its culture to itself? Do its films reflect different concerns, different esthetic principles, and different narrative preoccupations? Even a brief sampling should demonstrate that this is indeed the case. China was never a colonizer of the Western world. It is a country that, until recently, closed its doors to outsiders as much as possible. Thus its films reflect a different sense of order and esthetics. The central idea of the social self, of the political self, dominates Chinese cinema as does the idea of fate, a determining force in an individual's life.[6]

Westerners conceive of the world differently. In the Chinese tradition, chaos has a positive value. Order inheres in the world, it is not transcendently independent of the world. The Chinese tradition is not cosmogonic; it has no beginning. The Western archic sense of order inclines us to look for underlying principles that make the world explainable. We think teleologically. In contrast, the Chinese do not believe that a god was needed as a first mover. Rather, the cause of the world is itself; it is autogenerative. In place of linear causality, the Chinese have conditionality: each event in the world can be described in the conditions that sponsor it. The worth of a human being is determined by his or her actions, and people are defined by the cluster of their relationships. Also of great importance, the principles of yin and yang are used to explain the relative dominance of one idea or quality over another in a person, an interaction, a moment, or an event.

In film, these principles are expressed in several ways that are different from Western tradition. Action may jump quickly over months, years, or decades and "include the ubiquitous use of poetic metaphors from nature."[7] Characters are types, as required, instead of unique individuated characters. Artistic unity, in the Western sense of the concept, may be freely sacrificed to draw attention to national events in the midst of intimate dramas. Lengthy digressions may pursue these secondary topics or occur as poetic interludes such as those provided by visual metaphors.

The mainland Chinese films available amply illustrate these concepts, and China's fifth-generation directors' films are particularly powerful and useful for prompting discussion.[8] Several works effectively illustrate the distinctive Chinese perspective discussed in the preceding paragraphs through stories focusing on women's predicaments within Chinese society. The prevalence of women protagonists suggests to E. Ann Kaplan that "the issue of sacrifice and the conflict between individual desire and the demands of the State is dealt with quite safely when put in terms of female love situations."

Conflicts between love and duty, repression and rebellion figure prominently in Chen Kaige's *Yellow Earth* (1984) and Zhang Yimou's *Red Sorghum* (1988), *Ju Dou* (1990), *Raise the Red Lantern* (1991), and *The Story of Qiu Ju* (1993). The best known of the Chinese directors, with two Academy Award nominations for best foreign film to his credit (*Ju Dou* and *Raise the Red Lantern*), Zhang Yimou uses, as Robert Sklar observes, a "carefully composed, highly symbolic style and historical settings" to create fictional narratives "rich in ethnographic and sociological detail [that are] above all politically astute."

All of these exemplary works, also now available on video, provide the necessary extension for a discussion of the monolithic Hollywood product. My personal choice is *Ju Dou,* Zhang Yimou's powerful and esthetically stunning work, set in "a small village somewhere in China in the 1920s." Ju Dou (Gong Li) is sold into marriage to Yang Jinshan (Li Wei), a man who runs a dye mill. He beats Ju Dou, who enters into a love affair with an adopted nephew, Tianqing (Li Boatian); they have a son, Tianbai (Zheng Jian), who accidentally kills Jinshan and then deliberately murders his father, Tianqing. The film focuses on the violent repression of Ju Dou, the abusive patriarchal system, and the price one pays for rebellion. Gong Li, the lead actress in Zhang's works, is a charismatic presence who personifies the clash between a tyrannical, inflexible framework and the rebellious individual trapped within it. What students can be lead to recognize is that the at times platitudinous precepts and, at other times, real-life solutions that work for us may be totally inapplicable to Chinese culture. This leads us nicely to the ability to particularize students' developing sensitivity to ethnic and gender issues, exactly the realization that units on multicultural topics aim to develop.

However, although I argue that focusing attention on images of Asian-Americans and Asians is a worthwhile undertaking, it must do more than increase awareness and analytical ability. It must also translate into positive action. Let's not fetishize some myth of a classless melting pot, with all ethnic, gender, and economic differences magically transformed into irrelevant details. Let's not practice intellectual colonization any more than market-place exploitation.[9] But let's also not ignore the profound influence on behavior of film and video, and let's recognize that cinema literacy includes developing understanding of cultural, artistic diversity.

As the National Leadership Conference on Media Literacy's report explains, everyone must attain a level of media literacy in today's media-saturated environment, and being a media-literate person includes "aesthetic appreciation and expression, social advocacy, self-esteem, and consumer competence." Media images have political and ideological implications that influence and determine behavior. My hope is that in gaining an informed perspective on Asian and Asian-American images teachers and students can move proactively toward a healthier, more functional participation in the world community.

Appendix 1: Syllabus for Images of Asian-Americans and Asians in American and Mainland Chinese Films and Videos (St. Louis Community College at Meramec)

COURSE OBJECTIVES

The following objectives will be met through comparing and contrasting American, Asian-American, and mainland Chinese (PRC) films and videos:

1. To critique images of Asians and Asian-Americans in past and contemporary Hollywood films;

2. To analyze representations of Asians and Asian Americans in their own films and videos made in America;

3. To contrast studio/mainstream films with independent works, conventional narratives with more experimental dramas, and fictional films with documentaries;

4. To explore, compare, and contrast American films and videos with several examples from mainland China;

5. To demystify the filmic apparatus and thereby to provide critical tools for stylistic and thematic inquiry; and

6. To explore relevant topics in all the films and videos, for example, the representation of women and the nature of self, relationships within the family and the community, and the esthetics of representation.

READINGS

As time permits, readings will be selected from the following:

Chris Berry, ed., *Perspectives on Chinese Cinema* (Bloomington: Indiana University Press, 1991).

> This anthology of twelve articles plus several translated documents, an appendix of major directors, and a historical-cinematic chronology presents a useful overview of Chinese film history and contemporary fifth-generation directors.

W. A. Callahan, "Gender, Ideology, Nation: *Ju Dou* in the Cultural Politics of China," *East-West Film Journal* 7 (January 1993): 52–80.

> A provocative, insightful analysis of director Zhang Yimou's *Ju Dou.*

Lester D. Friedman, "Celluloid Palimpsests: An Overview of Ethnicity and the American Film," in *Unspeakable Images: Ethnicity and the American Cinema,* ed. Lester D. Friedman (Urbana: University of Illinois Press, 1991), 11–33.

> An excellent introduction to American film representation and ethnicity.

Elaine Kim, "Asian Americans and American Popular Culture," *Dictionary of Asian American History* (New York: Greenwood Press, 1986), 99–115.

> A discussion of the negative, stereotypical aspects of Asian-American representation in American popular culture.

Jenny Kwok Wah Lau, "*Judou*—A Hermeneutical Reading of Cross-cultural Cinema," *Film Quarterly* 45 (Winter 1991–92): 2–10.

————, "Towards a Cultural Understanding of Cinema: A Comparison of Contemporary Films From the People's Republic of China and Hong Kong," *Wide Angle* 11 (July 1989): 42–49.

Russell Leong, ed., *Moving the Image: Independent Asian Pacific American Media Arts* (Los Angeles: UCLA Asian American Studies Center and Visual Communications, Southern California Asian American Studies Central, Inc., 1991).

   An anthology of fifty short pieces on independent Asian-American films and videos.

Gina Marchetti, "Ethnicity, the Cinema and Cultural Studies," in *Unspeakable Images: Ethnicity and the American Cinema* (Urbana: University of Illinois Press, 1991).

   Specifically contrasting *Mississippi Triangle* and *Year of the Dragon*.

Sumiko Hagishi, "Ethnicity, Class, and Gender in Film: DeMille's *The Cheat*," in *Unspeakable Images: Ethnicity and the American Cinema* (Urbana: University of Illinois Press, 1991).

Yuejin Wang, *"Red Sorghum:* Mixing Memory and Desire," in *Perspectives on Chinese Cinema,* ed. Chris Berry (Bloomington: Indiana University Press).

Esther C. M. Yau, "Cultural and Economic Dislocations: Filmic Phantasies of Chinese Women in the 1980s," *Wide Angle* 11, no. 2 (1989): 6–21.

Yingjin Zhang, "Ideology of the Body in *Red Sorghum:* National Allegory, National Roots, and Third Cinema," *East-West Film Journal* 4, no. 2 (1990): 38–53.

FILMS AND VIDEOS

As time permits, screenings will be selected from the following. See appendix 2 for addresses and telephone and fax numbers of rental sources.

Ju Dou (1991), directed by Zhang Yimou and Yang Fengliang, color, 93 min., starring Gong Li, Li Boatian, and Li Wei, film: New Yorker, video: Cheng and Tsui or Facets Multimedia.

   The esthetically powerful story of a woman sold to a cruel husband, her rebellion against him, and the dire consequences that follow.

Mississippi Triangle (1984), codirectored by Christine Choy, Worth Long, and Allan Siegel, 120 min., Third World Newsreel.

   This socially critical political documentary explores complex racial and ethnic identities in the Mississippi Delta through archival news footage, "talking head" interviews, and cinema-verité slices of life. It directly addresses the ideology of race, ethnicity, class, and gender in contemporary American society through a study of the Chinese and black Chinese (Choy), black (Long), and white (Siegel) communities. Topics include music, the sharecropping system, perpetuation of racism, class divisions, education, interracial sexuality, and family relations. (See Marchetti's contrast with *Year of the Dragon*.)

Red Sorghum (Hong Geoliang, 1988), directed by Zhang Yimou, color, 91 min., Xi'an Film Studio, New Yorker. Based on Mo Yan's novella (same title).

Set in northern China, the story, told in flashback with voice-over narration, begins with the arranged marriage of Jiu'er to a leper, thirty years her senior, who runs a winery. The narrative involves several bandit attacks, kidnappings, a ransom, the Japanese invasion, and an anti-Japanese ambush. The film powerfully addresses issues of desire, sexuality, and transgression. Its detractors in China attacked it as mindless, violent sensationalism; its supporters praise its confrontation of repression and rebellion. It is visually gorgeous.

Slaying the Dragon (1988), Deborah Gee, color, 60 min., video: CrossCurrent Media or Women Make Movies.

From *The Thief of Bagdad* to *Year of the Dragon,* this video critiques Hollywood's one-dimensional images of Asian-American women through film clips, interviews with media critics, and Asian-American actresses. It also discusses the social and psychological impact these stereotypes have on Asian-American women and the way contemporary society regards them. This is a very engaging video that interweaves film clips with analysis with personal commentary.

Small Happiness (1984), 58 min., documentary, New Day Film, Long Bow series, Carma Hinton and Richard Gordon.

Interviews with women in a small village (Long Bow) on marriage, birth control, work, and daily life.

Two Lies (1989), directed by Pam Tom, black and white, 25 min., 16mm, video: Women Make Movies.

Doris Chu, a recently divorced Chinese-American woman, has had plastic surgery on her eyes before the film's narrative begins. Her teenage daughter Mei objects; the younger daughter observes. During Doris's recuperation, the family journeys to a desert pueblo (a tourist trap stereotyping Native Americans) and confrontations ensue. The film raises complex issues of standards of beauty, generational conflict, and implicit and explicit prejudice.

Year of the Dragon (1985), directed by Michael Cimino, 136 min., MGM-UA, Facets Multimedia and many other sources have the video, starring Mickey Rourke, Ariane, and John Lone.

Uncorrupted lawman Stanley White (Rourke) is assigned to clean up New York's Chinatown, pitting him against the young, ambitious gangster Joey Tai (Lone), who is moving in on Italian and Southeast Asian drug trafficking. Factored in is a romance between White and Tracy Tzu (Ariane), a young Chinese newswoman. The film raises and then obscures issues of race, gender, class, and ethnicity in eradicating the villain and allowing romance to triumph. Chinatown emerges as violent and corrupt; the white, male, heterosexual ideal triumphs.

Yellow Earth (Huang Tudi, 1984), directed by Chen Kaige, color, 90 min., Guangxi Studio.

Set in the 1930s in the "unliberated" western highlands of Shaanbei. An Eighth Route Army soldier arrives to collect folk tunes to transform to army songs and observes a feudal marriage. Inspired by what she learns, the daughter of the peasant who houses the soldier rejects her own arranged marriage, runs away to join the army, and drowns. Shot on location in Shaanxi Province in northwestern China, *Yellow Earth* is visually and ideologically stunning. It won several international awards and provoked heated debate in China. If using this film, add for reading (both from *Perspectives on Chinese Cinema,* ed. Chris Berry): Esther C. M. Yau, *"Yellow Earth:* Western Analysis and a Non-Western Text," 62–79, and Chris Berry, "Market Forces: China's 'Fifth Generation' Faces the Bottom Line," 114–40.

Appendix 2: Film and Video Sources

Cheng and Tsui Company
25 West St.
Boston, MA 02111
Tel.: 617-426-6074; fax: 617-426-3669
This company lists a variety of books, laserdiscs, and videotapes, including audio tapes and paperback books on the Japanese and the Chinese (Mandarin) languages, "The Silk Road" (volumes 1–12), and Chinese and Japanese television and feature film videos.

China Film Import & Export (L.A.), Inc.
2500 Wilshire Blvd., Suite 1028
Los Angeles, CA 90057
Tel.: 213-380-7520; fax: 213-487-2089
This company lists Chinese films available in 35mm and some in 16mm. The listing includes running time, year of production, a brief (one to two sentences) description, the director, stars, producer, and awards (if any).

China Video Movies Distributing Co., Inc.
1718 Broadway
Redwood City, CA 94063
Tel.: 415-366-2424; fax: 415-365-2523
This listing of videos includes the title of the film and its running time. Those marked with an asterisk have English subtitles. They are not alphabetized, but are listed by catalog number.

Cross Current
346 Ninth St., 2d Floor
San Francisco, CA 94103
Tel.: 415-552-9550; fax: 415-863-7428
An excellent source for Asian-American films and videos, including *Slaying the Dragon.*

Facets Multimedia
1517 W. Fullerton
Chicago, IL 60614
Tel.: 312-281-9075; 800-331-6197
They rent and sell videotapes and have an extensive listing of foreign films.

Kino International Corporation
333 West 39 St., Suite 502
New York, NY 10018
Tel.: 212-629-6880; fax: 212-714-0871
Feature-length films, 16mm and 35mm, for rental from China, Hong Kong, and Japan.

Nan Hai Co.
510 Broadway, Suite 300
Millbrae, CA 94030
Tel.: 415-259-2100; fax: 415-259-2108
They have eighty to ninety Chinese films on video.

New Day Film
22D Hollywood Ave.
Hohokus, NJ 07423
Tel.: 201-652-6590; fax: 201-652-1973

New Yorker Films
16 West 61st St.
New York, NY 10023
Tel.: 212-247-6110; fax: 212-307-7855
They rent Zhang Yimou's films: *Ju Dou, Raise the Red Lantern,* and *Red Sorghum.*

Third World Newsreel
335 West 38th St., 5th Floor
New York, NY 10018
Tel.: 212-947-9277; fax: 212-594-6417

Women Make Movies
462 Broadway, Suite 501
New York, NY 10013
Tel.: 212-925-0606; fax: 212-925-2052

Notes

1. Dr. Fu Manchu appeared in at least thirteen novels, translated into a dozen languages, and in scores of films and radio programs. See Kim, "Asian Americans and American Popular Culture." Forty-seven Charlie Chan mov-

ies were made in which six different non-Chinese actors starred. Chan's creator, Earl Derr Biggers, wrote six Charlie Chan novels between 1925 and 1932, published as books after serialization in *The Saturday Evening Post.* See Kim for a debate on the positive or negative dimensions of Chan and the reaction to him.

2. See Said for a thorough discussion of the ways in which the West has defined and colonized the Orient through our ideology of it as "other."

3. In "Reaching the Child within Us," Montagu explores the mental resistance to new ideas and the compelling need for flexibility and openness.

4. See Tchen for a discussion of the ambiguity of the images in this film.

5. Information from the *East-West Center Annual Report 1992,* Oksenberg, "The Asian Century," and speeches to the 1993 NEH Institute on Chinese Culture and Civilization by Michael Oksenberg, president of the East-West Center, in which he elaborated upon the severe consequences of isolationist mentality.

6. One of the clearest and most helpful books explaining Chinese philosophical perspectives and tenets is Hall and Ames's *Thinking Through Confucius;* a very readable full history is Spence's *The Search for Modern China.*

7. See Rayns and Meek, *Electric Shadows: Forty-five Years of Chinese Cinema,* in which the provocative and illuminating differences to be found, in general, in Chinese film are discussed.

8. The fifth-generation filmmakers are those who graduated from film school during the 1980s. The Cultural Revolution, beginning in 1966, shut down virtually all film production for a decade. In *Chinese Cinema,* Clark provides a thorough history of Chinese film, and Berry's anthology contains expert analyses of a range of specific works.

9. A provocative debate over the aims of multiculturalism is contained in the June 1993 issue of *American Quarterly* devoted to multiculturalism (volume 45, number 2).

10

Analyzing Latino Stereotypes: Hispanic Images/Counterimages in Hollywood Film and Television

Charles Ramírez Berg

Teaching an undergraduate course on the stereotyping of Latinos in Hollywood film and television has been a formidable challenge and a great opportunity, and I hope that my comments either will help teachers add stereotyping units to their courses in any number of liberal arts areas (anthropology, sociology, history, government, ethnic studies, Latin American studies, Spanish, literature, and communication) or help them develop stereotyping courses of their own. Stereotyping is the topic of my course, Hispanic Images and Counterimages in Hollywood Film and Television. My focus is on the depiction of Latinos in Hollywood media, but the concepts can be expanded or focused to suit any group that is marginalized and stereotyped.

Teaching Qualifications

Because stereotyping analysis offers an excellent way to introduce the history of the marginalization of ethnic groups, Latino teachers are well equipped to teach it. But anyone—Latino or not—who makes a sensitive, well-prepared, and open-minded presentation of the material should be allowed to do so, regardless of their race, class, or ethnicity. For me, the prerequisites to teaching about stereotyping are a genuine concern about the issues and an honest and well-prepared approach to them in the classroom, not ethnic membership. It seems axiomatic that a course about the understanding and toleration of differences be flexible enough pedagogically to practice what it preaches.

Moreover, everyone, whatever their race, class, or ethnic affiliations, has some personal experience of otherness. One of the more insidious aspects of stereotyping is the pernicious way that the dominant ideology goes beyond the construction of denigrating images of out-group others (most often by creating ethnic and racial caricatures). It also stereotypes all manner of in-group members as well— women, the working class, the poor, rural America, intellectuals, and anyone else who falls outside of what is considered the norm in lifestyle, sexual preference, body type, health, age, and intelligence. Most people identify with several groups that fall outside this constructed norm and suffer from stereotyping.

Stereotyping in the media involves everyone as consumers, spectators, and victims. What better way to demonstrate this than to show that although the teacher or some students may be Anglo the media stereotypes them, too, in one way or another and consequently distances them from the mainstream. Furthermore, demonstrating that everyone—Anglo and minority—is a target of the stereotyping machine helps dispel impressions that a course about stereotyping is a semester-long exercise in Anglo-bashing.

The Course

Hispanic Images and Counterimages, an upper-level undergraduate course, contains historical, theoretical, writing, and critical thinking components. I divide class periods between lecture and discussion, in addition to a separate film screening once a week. Because the enrollment of the University of Texas at Austin hovers around fifty thousand, classes tend to be large. I have taught Hispanic Images to a class of fifty upper-division students (with the assistance of a graduate teaching assistant), but the ideal class is half that size. In a typical class, about one-third of the students are Latino and students of color, and two-thirds are Anglo. Because I teach in Texas, my Latino students are primarily Mexican American, and I focus on images of Mexicans and Mexican Americans in film and television.

The Course as a Writing Workshop

The first of four writing assignments spaced throughout the semester asks students to find and describe a stereotype—any stereotype— in the media. In this short exercise (800 to 1,000 words) students must spot, describe, and explain in detail the ways their stereotype simplistically represents and denigrates otherness.

The second assignment is a full-fledged analysis (1,000 to 1,500 words) of Latino stereotypes in one film. I hand out an annotated list of Hollywood films that are available in our library's video collec-

tion and at local video rental shops and either have Latino characters or deal with Latinos in some significant way. Among these are
The Big Steal (1949), *Boulevard Nights* (1982), *The Border* (1982), *Border Incident* (1949), *The Brave One* (1956), *Colors* (1988), *Five Came Back*
(1939), *The Fugitive* (1947), *Giant* (1956), *Internal Affairs* (1990), *The
Lawless* (1950), *Juarez* (1939), *The Magnificent Seven* (1960), *The Mark
of Zorro* (1920 and 1940), *A Medal for Benny* (1945), *My Man and I*
(1952), *One-Eyed Jacks* (1961), *Requiem for a Heavyweight* (1962), *Revenge*
(1990), *Right Cross* (1950), *The Ring* (1952), *Stakeout* (1987), *The Three
Caballeros* (1945), *Three Godfathers* (1948), *The Treasure of the Sierra
Madre* (1948), and *West Side Story* (1961). I save films made by Chicano filmmakers for the last assignment.

One part of the assignment requires students to find periodical
reviews of their study film. I ask them to comment on how contemporary reviewers discussed (or failed to discuss) marginalized groups.
This is a simple but effective way to give students a sense of the film's
reception and provides them with evidence of the degree of social
awareness of minority issues at the time of the film's release.

Toward the end of the semester we as a class can generally agree
that stereotyping exists, is denigrating to the stereotyped group,
harmful to the social fabric, incompatible with America's egalitarian
principles, and needs to be avoided. In preparation for a final critical term paper, students prepare a three-to-four-page proposal that
includes title, topic, thesis statement, an abstract of their argument,
a list of sources (readings and films) they intend to use, and a tentative outline. In this way I can check their ideas, research questions,
and methodology before they embark on the long essay (2,500 to
3,000 words).

In this assignment students are asked to propose practical solutions
to stereotyping in film and television and demonstrate the efficacy
of their suggestions by citing (where possible) successful instances of
antistereotyping or describing original ways to avoid and counter it.
Here I use the Latino-made films and ask students to assess whether
they successfully counter stereotyping. If so, how? If not, why do they
fail?

Film Screenings

Hispanic Images and Counterimages is also an overview of U.S. film
and television history. I teach the historical material chronologically, beginning with silent film and proceeding to the present. Weekly
screenings follow this chronology. In the class period before the

screening, each film is briefly introduced. A longer discussion takes place on the class day following the viewing of the film. The following discussion details the films I use, my reasons for doing so, and my suggestions for alternatives.

Why Worry? (1923) with Harold Lloyd culminates classroom lectures and discussions on early film stereotyping, which usually include in-class screenings of such short films from the silent era as Edwin S. Porter's *The Watermelon Patch* (1905), J. Stuart Blackton's *Humorous Phases of Funny Faces* (1906), and the so-called greaser films, for example, *Broncho Billy and the Greaser* (1914). These films are available from the Museum of Modern Art.

Why Worry? is a good way to begin the semester because it is one of Lloyd's more entertaining comedies and easily accessible to students who have little familiarity with film analysis, silent feature films, or both. It also has the virtue of being relatively short—just over an hour's running time. At the same time, it effectively demonstrates that Latino stereotypes enjoyed mass currency early in film history.

Another silent film of interest is *The Four Horsemen of the Apocalypse* (1921), with Rudolph Valentino playing an Argentinian Latin lover, a smoldering combination of tenderness and violence. Valentino's legendary tango scene made him a star and began a national dance craze, but it serves as a typical example of Hollywood's ignorance of Latin-American culture. Valentino and his partner actually dance the flamenco.

The Mark of Zorro (1920), one of Douglas Fairbanks's most entertaining comedy-adventures, raises a number of interesting issues related to stereotyping. First, it exhibits the way Hollywood follows the path of least resistance in its treatment of others. It avoids them when it can; otherwise it narratively marginalizes them as minor characters and stereotypes. In those rare instances where an other is the protagonist, as in *The Mark of Zorro,* he (the protagonist is almost always male) is played by a star with recognizable Anglo features to make him palatable to a mass audience. Furthermore, Fairbanks's Zorro is a well-heeled member of the upper class, making him even less threatening and less alien to Anglos. The film's treatment of class is of interest as well, because Zorro is engaged in an elitist power struggle between two aristocratic factions, a struggle that completely ignores the plight of the peons. Finally, because Zorro's foppish alter ego can be read as a gay stereotype, *The Mark of Zorro* presents an opportunity to raise and discuss the representation of gender and sexuality.

Bordertown (1935), with Paul Muni and Bette Davis, is an example of an early Hollywood attempt to treat Chicanos sympathetically.

Because it is a prototypical assimilation narrative and Chicano social problem film, I always screen it.

The Ox-Bow Incident (1943), with Henry Fonda and Anthony Quinn, is still a powerful film about mob violence. Ideologically it offers a rare instance of Hollywood countering the dominant ideology and critiquing Anglo power structures. I elicit this in class discussions by noting the many ways the film overturns long-standing conventions of the western genre. To take just one generic element, posses in westerns have symbolized community unity and righteousness—the best that the dominant ideology has to offer—since Edwin S. Porter's *The Great Train Robbery* (1903). But *The Ox-Bow Incident*'s posse is a band of immoral hotheads, egomaniacs, and weak-willed conformists. In addition, the film provides an opportunity to introduce the reprehensible and little-known history of the lynching of blacks in the South and Mexicans and Mexican Americans in the Southwest.

Furthermore, Anthony Quinn's portrayal of the proud and knowing vaquero is a striking reversal of the *bandido* stereotype. The fact that his character hides behind the stereotype is a sign of his intelligence. Iconographically he looks like the *bandido,* but the film goes beyond stereotyping by furnishing him with a social and cultural background, precisely the sort of information that most Hollywood films omit. In giving the vaquero a reason for his actions—survival in a hostile environment—the film is a useful example of how story, scripting, acting, and direction can all counter stereotyping.

Viva Zapata (1952), with Marlon Brando and Anthony Quinn, directed by Elia Kazan, and screenplay by John Steinbeck, is a look at the Mexican Revolution. The discussion can center around the film's depiction of the revolution, an Anglo actor's (Brando's) characterization of a Mexican versus a Latino's (Quinn's), and Steinbeck and Kazan's Zapata compared to the real-life rebel leader.

The film also introduces the post–World War II social problem films and the House Un-American Activities Committee's Hollywood witch hunt. Kazan bridges both topics, having directed some of the better-known examples of the social problem genre, such as *Pinky* (1949) and *Gentlemen's Agreement* (1947, I show clips from these in class), as well as being a friendly witness and "naming names" to the committee.

High Noon (1952) allows, via the character of Katy Jurado's Helen Ramírez, consideration of a portrayal of a Mexican-American woman. The film's production history is also interesting, having been written by blacklisted writer Carl Foreman and produced by Stanley Kramer, who would later gain fame as a producer-director of social problem films, for example, *The Defiant Ones* (1958) and *Guess Who's Coming to Dinner* (1967).

I use *Touch of Evil* (1958), directed by Orson Welles, to discuss Hollywood's depiction of the Southwest, Mexico, and Latin America. Welles's stylistics (long takes, moving camera, deep focus photography, complex mise-en-scène) blend to create a richly evocative border town. To what extent is the portrayal evenhanded, to what extent essentialist and stereotypical?

A number of Chicano social problem films could be profitably substituted for *High Noon* and *Touch of Evil: Right Cross* (1950, directed by John Sturges), *My Man and I* (1952, directed by William Wellman), *The Lawless* (1950, directed by Joseph Losey), *A Medal for Benny* (1945, directed by Irving Pichel), *The Ring* (1952, directed by Kurt Neumann), *Trial* (1955, directed by Mark Robson), and *Giant* (1956, directed by George Stevens). I have used them all and find *The Ring, Giant,* and *My Man and I* to be the most popular and useful.

Salt of the Earth (1954) is a must, and the documentary short *A Crime to Fit the Punishment* (1982) provides an informative companion piece. *Salt* begins the second, self-representational, phase of the course. As an example of committed collective filmmaking, it is a counter-imagery model that the students will refer to again and again.

I have found it best to prepare students beforehand about what to expect (and not expect) from *Salt.* If they know that it was a renegade production, purposely made outside the Hollywood system by blacklisted filmmakers with very little funding and that its actors were largely nonprofessionals who lived the film's story, they will be more receptive and forgiving. Otherwise they may be initially put off when the film doesn't provide Hollywood's realism and slick production values. *Salt's* creative alternative to the Hollywood paradigm is, of course, one of the central points to be made by screening it.

El Teatro Campesino is an early PBS (it was an NET Playhouse presentation) documentary on Luis Valdez's guerrilla theater and its support of Cesar Chavez's mobilization of the farm workers. It provides a stirring starting point from which to trace Valdez's career, which takes the class from the fields of Delano to *La Bamba* (1987). Once they know Valdez's theatrical and political roots, they are in a better position to appreciate *Zoot Suit* (1981) and to say whether or not *La Bamba* represents a sell-out. The film includes a performance of Valdez's best known *acto* (political skit), "Los Vendidos," which speaks directly to the question of stereotyping and to the conformity that assimilation can bring. Here I assign the Chicano filmmaking manifestos from Noriega's *Chicanos and Film.*

For the second part of the program, I use *Chulas Fronteras* (1976), a documentary directed by Les Blank. It captures the Tejano (a Texan of Mexican heritage) experience that many of the Chicano students live and with which many Anglo students are unfamiliar. This remarkable film tells its story from inside the culture, taking viewers from makeshift recording studios to dancehalls to backyard *barbacoas* (barbecues). In addition, because Blank is an Anglo, the film raises knotty cross-cultural problems. Can a filmmaker who is not a member of a cultural group render that group honestly and accurately? What are the risks of such a venture? How can they be overcome? Aren't there advantages to being an outsider? At this point in the class, we read excerpts from Franz Fanon's *The Wretched of the Earth* and Paulo Freire's *The Pedagogy of the Oppressed* for clues as to how— or even if—cross-cultural film projects should be approached.

I next select a program of shorts to show the breadth and originality of Chicano nonfeature filmmaking. A nice program consists of Isaac Artenstein's *Ballad of an Unsung Hero* (1983), Sandra P. Hahn's *Replies of the Night* (1989) or *Slipping Between* (1991), Frances Salomé España's *Anima* (1989) or *El Espejo* (The Mirror, 1991), Lourdes Portillo and Susana Muñoz's *La Ofrenda: Days of the Dead* (1989), and Robert Rodriguez's award-winning student film *Bedhead* (1990) (Appendix 3).

Alambrista! (1979), directed by Robert M. Young, begins a two-week, two-film unit on immigration. *Alambrista!* is remarkable on several counts. First, it presents the story of a Mexican man crossing the border into the United States from his point of view. Viewers gradually identify with him and see the Land of Opportunity from the perspective of a newly arrived, Spanish-speaking laborer. From that vantage point what we see is a pattern of exploitation and abuse. Because the director of this fascinating film is an Anglo, class discussions return to issues of ethnography and cross-cultural film production.

El Norte (1983), directed by Gregory Nava, continues the immigration unit and illustrates another way of representing the Latin-American immigrant experience. If *Alambrista!* uses semidocumentary realism, *El Norte* approximates the magic realism of Gabriel García Márquez and other Latin-American authors. In this way, the film's form gives a native slant to its emigrant-immigrant narrative.

Zoot Suit, directed by Luis Valdez, starring Edward James Olmos, is another must. A mixture of courtroom drama and stage musical, *Zoot Suit* depicts the events surrounding the infamous Sleepy Lagoon trial from a Chicano point of view. The film makes few concessions to an Anglo (or even a middle-class, Mexican-American) audience, and, in an unusual twist of standard Hollywood practice, *Zoot Suit*'s youths speak *caló* (Chicano dialect) mixed with English. This alienating effect turns the tables on mainstream audiences and gives them a taste of how it feels to be marginalized by a Hollywood feature film.

The Ballad of Gregorio Cortez (1983), another film directed by Robert M. Young, was produced by Moctezuma Esparza and stars Edward James Olmos. Based on Américo Paredes's *With His Pistol in His Hand,* the film's subject is the tragic consequences of cross-cultural misunderstanding. It is an inverted western in which a Chicano hero is pursued by a posse of Texas Rangers. The film elicits interesting reactions. Some students compare it to Hollywood westerns and praise it for what they see as a significant—and refreshing—departure from the genre formula. Others grant the film its genre-busting due but fault its depiction of Gregorio Cortez as a skittish and weak-willed hero, a view that Paredes has told me he shares.

A number of other films might be included here—*La Bamba* (1987), *Born in East L.A.* (1987), *Stand and Deliver* (1988), *The Milagro Beanfield War* (1988), Isaac Artenstein's *Break of Dawn* (1988), *American Me* (1992), and Robert Rodriguez's *El Mariachi* (1993). Because these are readily available on video (*Break of Dawn* may be more difficult to find, but is available; see Appendix 3), I do not screen them, but encourage students to use them for their final papers if they wish. I do, however, show clips from some of these films in class. Edward James Olmos's performances in *Stand and Deliver* and "Miami Vice," for example, offer interesting contrasts to his role in *Zoot Suit.* And Cheech Marin's *Born in East L.A.* puts an interesting spin on the immigrant narrative.

Class Discussions

In addition to weekly discussions on the screened films and analysis of the stereotyping or counterimagery they reveal, I have two topics especially designed for class discussion. The first, the recounting of personal experiences of otherness, I use very early in the semester to break the ice. I ask students to describe a time in their lives when they realized they were different from the norm and felt marginalized as a result—a time when they were marked as an other. I let everyone in the class relate their experiences. What emerges are remembrances that run the gamut from being the new kid in school, to being from "the wrong side of the tracks," to blatant cases of racism. The goal for this early discussion is to demonstrate a number of notions about otherness.

1. Otherness can take many forms and is based on a number of criteria. Some of them have to do with visible characteristics, others with beliefs, creeds, culture, nationality, life-style, language, and the like.

2. Although some markers of otherness (language, socioeconomic class) can be overcome, others (skin color) cannot.

3. Life on the margin is uncomfortable. In this way I try to have everyone in the class relate to—and, I hope, empathize with—the plight of the marginalized.

4. We can use the normative criteria I mentioned in the first point—which the dominant uses to define the margin—as a means of defining the dominant. Knowledge of the norm, the dominant, or the mainstream is something we know, having internalized its rules and precepts. To formulate a more explicit understanding of the dominant, I ask students to think of the many ways it is defined—by age, education, class, religion, skin color, language skills, intelligence, body type, health, nationality, gender, sexual preference, and so forth.

The second extended discussion is on immigration, and it begins during the weeks that I screen *Alambrista!* and *El Norte*. After presenting a brief history of the immigrant experience in American history, I focus on the articles in the course packet (Appendix 2) by Rodolfo Alvarez and Dale McLemore and Ricardo Romo that describe the three-generation immigration-to-assimilation model and give a history of the Chicano population in the United States. Students are then asked to trace both sides of their family trees back to the immigrant generation. They relate what they discover about their family's genealogy over the next several class meetings. The goals for this teaching unit include:

1. Situate stereotyping within the broader dividing practice of nativism. Looked at from this perspective, stereotyping is part of a larger maintenance myth that glorifies "us" and dehumanizes "them."

2. Uncover the central contradiction in the melting pot myth: Although America officially proclaims an open door policy, it has continually resisted including and amalgamating foreigners.

3. See immigration not as a recent phenomenon, but as a universal practice of global migration that has existed since the dawn of time and has been a permanent feature of American history. Viewed in this way, the recent furor surrounding the migration to this country by Mexicans, Cubans, Haitans, Asians, Irish, and Latin Americans is only the latest chapter in an ongoing national debate about how to resolve the melting pot contradiction.

4. Discover how immigrant labor is an integral—but largely in-

visible—part of the national economy. It contributes to lower costs of everything from produce to construction, however, its darker side is the routine exploitation, maltreatment, and abuse that migrant workers undergo. Because they have no mechanism in place to defend themselves or even to register grievances, they are completely vulnerable.

5. Celebrate the first, migrant generation. Wherever they came from and whenever they did it, uprooting themselves and moving to a different country took grit and gumption. And once they arrived, they endured the travails and humiliations concomitant with being at the bottom of the American socioeconomic structure. Appreciating the bravery of the first generation gives the class a fresh perspective on today's immigrants, who are equally courageous.

6. Remember that we are an immigrant nation, a nation of cultural transplants. Having students discover their own immigrant roots reminds them that at one time in their family's history their ancestors were outsiders and were probably reviled, targeted as scapegoats, and exploited just as immigrants and illegal aliens are now. Equipped with this ancestral memory, I hope that students will look upon today's immigrants more compassionately.

Finally, I try not to make ethnic and minority students into spokespersons for their groups during class discussions. When a question arises about their group, I hope they will volunteer information but do not call on them to do so. Many students feel awkward in a school like the University of Texas at Austin, where they are always the minority in the classroom. They are justifiably suspicious about how their ideas will be received. As the semester goes along, I try to make them more at ease by creating as relaxed and informal a classroom atmosphere as possible, one that promotes mutual respect among all students and in which all comments are welcome and accepted courteously.

To encourage introverted students, those for whom volunteering during a class discussion is an ordeal, I pose nondirected questions and take responses from those who raise their hands. Unfortunately, this means that some students may never participate. Although that is far from ideal, I make it clear at the beginning of the course that I encourage class participation, which I define as attending class and making comments when students feel they have something to say. As the semester proceeds and we have gotten to know each other better, I comment that some students have not yet participated and that we look forward to their comments during the rest of the semester. Still, some students never say a word. I have learned to respect their silence. In their own ways these students are thinking about the issues and arriving at conclusions. I make it a point to find some other time to talk to them, before or after a class or a screening, just to let them know that I value them, their thoughts, and their ideas (as they have expressed them in their written assignments).

Hispanic Images and Counterimages in Hollywood Film and Television is a difficult and demanding class. But to the extent that it can contribute something to multicultural understanding, its rewards far outweigh its costs. I invite teachers to join with their students in grappling with and learning about racism, prejudice, stereotyping, and ethnocentrism—the most perplexing, confounding, and gut-wrenching issues of our time.

Appendix 1: Syllabus for Hispanic Images and Counterimages in Hollywood Film and Television (The University of Texas at Austin)

COURSE OBJECTIVES

This course will investigate stereotyping in the American media by looking at how Hollywood films and television have portrayed Hispanics. The focus will be on Mexican Americans, but discussion will also include Hollywood's treatment of other Hispanic groups. The concepts covered are applicable to other stereotyped groups. The aims of the course are to seek answers to the following questions:

1. What is the history of Hispanic representation in Hollywood movies and on television?

2. What Hispanic stereotypes have developed?

3. What are the key sociological, psychological, and ideological theories about stereotyping?

4. Why has the Hispanic been represented in these ways?

5. What does such representation signify about America, its movies and its minorities?

TEXTS

One packet of readings (Appendix 2), class handouts, and the following books:

Gary D. Keller, ed., *Chicano Cinema: Research, Reviews, and Resources* (Binghamton: Bilingual Press, 1985).

Chon Noriega, ed., *Chicanos and Film: Essays on Chicano Representation and Resistance* (Minneapolis: University of Minnesota Press, 1992).

Arthur G. Pettit, *Images of the Mexican American in Fiction and Film* (College Station: Texas A & M Press, 1980).

WRITTEN ASSIGNMENTS

Students will write several one-page responses to readings; two critical essays of approximately four to six typed pages (1,000 to 1,500 words); a term paper proposal (three to four pages); and one longer term paper (ten to twelve pages, 2,500–3,000 words). The screened films are the laboratory for this course (see film list in main text).

DISCUSSION TOPICS

Weeks 1, 2, 3, and 4

Otherness in early American cinema; "greaser" films; Hispanics in films in the 1930s and 1940s.

Weeks 5 and 6

Theories of stereotyping: sociological, psychological, and ideological.

Weeks 7 and 8

The 1950s: Hollywood focuses on the Hispanic; television and the Hispanic image.

Weeks 9 and 10

The roots of Chicano counterimagery; early films; El Teatro Campesino and Luis Valdez.

Weeks 11, 12, and 13

Chicanos and the immigrant experience.

Weeks 14 and 15

Counterimagery problems: cooptation and the depiction of women. What constitutes a positive image? What can filmmakers do to avoid stereotypical imagery?

Appendix 2: Course Packet of Readings

Alvarez, Rodolfo, "The Psycho-historical and Socioeconomic Development of the Chicano Community in the United States," in *The Mexican American Experience: An Interdisciplinary Anthology,* ed. Rodolfo O. de la Garza, 33–56 (Austin: University of Texas Press, 1985).

Artel, Linda, and Susan Wengraf, "Positive Images: Screening Women's Films," in *Jump Cut: Hollywood , Politics, and Counter Cinema,* ed. Peter Steven, 199–202 (New York: Praeger, 1985).

Berg, Charles Ramírez, "Images and Counterimages of the Hispanic in Hollywood," *Tonantzin* 6, no. 1 (1988): 12–13.

————, "Immigrants, Aliens and Extraterrestrials: Science Fiction's Alien 'Other' As (among *Other* Things) New Hispanic Imagery," *CineACTION!* 18 (Fall 1989): 3–17.

————, "Stereotyping in Films in General and of the Hispanic in Particular," *Howard Journal of Communications* 2 (Summer 1990): 286–300.

Dyer, Richard, "Rejecting Straight Ideals: Gays in Film," in *Jump Cut: Hollywood, Politics, and Counter Cinema,* ed. Peter Steven, 286–95 (New York: Praeger, 1985).

————, "Stereotyping," in *Gays and Film,* ed. Richard Dyer, 27–39 (New York: Zoetrope, 1984).

————, "White," *Screen* 29, no. 4 (1988): 44–64.

Excerpts from Frantz Fanon, *The Wretched of the Earth* (New York: Grove Press, 1961).

Excerpts from Paulo Freire, *Pedagogy of the Oppressed* (New York: Continuum Publishing, 1970).

Gilman, Sander L., Introduction. In *Difference and Pathology: Stereotypes of Sexuality, Race, and Madness* (Ithaca: Cornell University Press, 1985).

Lippmann, Walter, *Public Opinion* (New York: Macmillan, 1922). Excerpts.

McLemore, S. Dale, and Ricardo Romo, "The Origins and Development of the Mexican American People," in *The Mexican American Experience: An Interdisciplinary Anthology,* ed. Rodolfo de la Garza, 3–32 (Austin: University of Texas Press, 1985).

Mulvey, Laura, "Visual Pleasure and Narrative Cinema" [1975], repr. in *Narrative, Apparatus, Ideology: A Film Theory Reader,* ed. Phillip Rosen, 179–209 (New York: Columbia University Press, 1986).

Pages 47–54 in Anya Peterson Royce, *Ethnic Identity: Strategies of Diversity* (Bloomington: Indiana University Press, 1982).

Subervi-Vélez, Federico A., "The Mass Media and Ethnic Assimilation and Pluralism: A Review and Research Proposal with Special Focus on Hispanics," *Communication Research* 13, no. 1 (1986): 71–96.

Chapters 2–4 in Clint C. Wilson and Félix Gutiérrez, *Minorities and Media* (Beverly Hills: Sage, 1985).

Excerpts from Allen L. Woll, *The Latin Image in American Film* (Los Angeles: University of California Los Angeles, Latin American Center Publications, 1980).

Wood, Robin, "An Introduction to the American Horror Film" [1979], repr. in *Movies and Methods,* ed. Bill Nichols, 2: 195–219 (Berkeley: University of California Press, 1987).

Appendix 3: Sources for Selected Films

Most of the Hollywood feature films mentioned are available in 16mm through commercial film rental companies. Many are also available on videotape. The following is a list of distributors of the Chicano features and shorts cited, together with a short list of other Chicano films of interest.

Alambrista! (1979)
Unfortunately, this film is extremely difficult to find; contact the East Los Angeles Public Library, 213-825-0755.

Anima (1989, 3 min., directed by Frances Salomé España)
Frances Salomé España
1704½ Edgewood Dr.
Alhambra, CA 91803

Ballad of an Unsung Hero (1983, 28 min., directed by Isaac Artenstein)
The Cinema Guild
1697 Broadway, Suite 506
New York, NY 10019
212-246-5522

Bedhead (1990, 8 min., 47 sec., directed by Robert Rodriguez)
Included on the video of *El Mariachi.*
Columbia/TriStar Home Video
3400 Riverside Dr.
Burbank, CA 91505
818-972-8686

Break of Dawn (1988, directed by Isaac Artenstein)
A feature film version on the subject of *Ballad of an Unsung Hero,* musician and activist Pedro J. Gonzalez.
Platform Releasing
627 8th Ave.
San Diego, CA 92101
619-696-9822

Broncho Billy and the Greaser (1914)
Museum of Modern Art
Dept. of Film
11 West 53d St.
New York, NY 10019
212-708-9530

Chicana (1979, directed by Sylvia Morales)
Sylvan Productions
12104 Washington Pl.
Los Angeles, CA 90066
310-391-0070

Chicano Park (1989, 60 min., directed by Marilyn Bulford, produced by Mario Barrera and Marilyn Bulford)
The Cinema Guild
1697 Broadway, Suite 506

New York, NY 10019
212-246-5522

Chulas Fronteras (1976)
Les Blank
Flower Films
10341 San Pablo Ave.
El Cerrito, CA 94530

Despues del Terremoto (1979, 24 min., directed by Lourdes Portillo and Nina Serrano)
Xochil Film Productions
981 Esmeralda St.
San Francisco, CA 94110
415-824-5850

El Espejo (The Mirror) (1991, 5 min., video, directed by Frances Salomé España)
Frances Salomé España
1704½ Edgewood Dr.
Alhambra, CA 91803

El Mariachi
Columbia/TriStar Home Video
3400 Riverside Dr.
Burbank, CA 91505
818-972-8686

El Teatro Campesino (60 min., NET Playhouse)
El Centro Campesino Cultural
P.O. Box 1278
San Juan Bautista, CA 95045

Esperanza (1985, 60 min., directed by Sylvia Morales)
Sylvan Productions
12104 Washington Pl.
Los Angeles, CA 90066
310-391-0070

Faith Even to the Fire (1991, 60 min., directed by Sylvia Morales)
Sylvan Productions
12104 Washington Pl.
Los Angeles, CA 90066

Las Madres de la Plaza de Mayo (1985, 58 min., directed by Lourdes Portillo)
Xochil Film Productions

981 Esmeralda St.
San Francisco, CA 94110
415-824-5850

Los Mineros (1991, 60 min., directed by Hector Galán)
Galán Productions
5524 Bee Caves Rd.
Austin, TX 78746
512-327-1333

Neighbors: The United States and Mexico (1985, 60 min., directed by Jesús Salvador Treviño and José Luis Ruiz)
The Cinema Guild
1697 Broadway, Suite 506
New York, NY 10019
212-246-5522

La Ofrenda: Days of the Dead (1989, 50 min., directed by Lourdes Portillo and Susana Muñoz)
Xochil Film Productions
981 Esmeralda St.
San Francisco, CA 94110
415-824-5850

Replies of the Night (1989, 10 min., video, directed by Sandra P. Hahn)
Sandra P. Hahn
12416 Pellisier Rd.
N. Whittier, CA 90601
213-695-1843 (telephone and fax)

Slipping Between (1991, 3 min., video, directed by Sandra P. Hahn)
Sandra P. Hahn
1216 Pellisier Rd.
N. Whittier, CA 90601
213-695-1843 (telephone and fax)

Yo Soy Joaquín (1967, production of El Teatro Campesino)
El Centro Campesino Cultural
P.O. Box 1278
San Juan Bautista, CA 95045

11

Power/Knowledge/Pleasure in the Multicultural Classroom: A Pedagogy for Media Studies

Serafina Bathrick and Louise Spence

> . . . [I]t is not those differences between us that are separating us. It is rather our refusal to recognize those differences.
>   —Audre Lorde

Our relationship to the mass media involves a flux of intimacy and distance, safety and insecurity, fascination and criticism. Although our daily lives are fully intertwined with the media, we often must convince colleagues that the popular and the pleasurable are worthy of serious consideration and persuade students that the popular and the pleasurable are worthy of critical investigation. Looking closely at print, film, and broadcast media in the classroom offers teachers and students the opportunity to question the multiple, contradictory, experiences of living in society. This questioning can lead to exploring identities; to envisioning new possibilities for media production, representation, and reception; and to addressing the larger issues of difference, truth, power, and pleasure.

We taught media studies for many years at Hunter College (part of the City University of New York, a public institution with a liberal admissions policy), an enclave of racially and ethnically diverse students and faculty situated in the wealthiest white neighborhood on the island of Manhattan.[1] This is a very lively community, made up of people with a variety of experiences and distinct material realities. Among the students, there are differences in abilities, political consciousness, age, class, gender, health, race, and sexual identification, as well as a variety of educational agendas and motives—both explicit intentions and those more hidden. Many students identify with subordinated groups and must grapple with social contexts and institutional practices that deny and distort their cultural lives. Seventy percent are women; the majority are more than twenty-five. A large percentage are the first of their families to attend college.

In our teaching, we cannot assume a homogeneous educational or family background; we must, therefore, treat students as individuals and encourage self-expression and self-definition. We suggest that an idea of struggle be built into courses—a struggle to understand, appreciate, and learn from our differences, our diversity, and even our disagreements. We must not be diverted by a politics of unity or a pedagogy of assimilation and standardization. The heterogeneity of the multicultural classroom has an existential, political, and intellectual variety that challenges teachers and students to redefine and recast the meanings of solidarity and individual freedom.[2]

Media studies is an increasingly popular area of study at Hunter because students seek job-related education and are so drawn to the mass media. In a culturally diverse classroom, what students often have in common is their familiarity with the mass media, a shared "American" identity. Because their lives so enjoyably integrate with media sounds and images, most students have an affectionate cynicism; however, they seldom have a focused critique. What criticism they do bring might be characterized as enthusiastic; that is, the questions they raise are mostly those the media ask in the promotional loop of game shows, bloopers, satires, documentaries on media issues, and nostalgic reviews of highlights.

The students' knowledge about the media is most often fact-based and seldom social or theoretical. Therefore, when we teach about the media, we encounter, and perhaps contribute to, a tension between students' comfort with their own authority and familiarity with the mass media and our efforts to complicate this relationship. How can we work with this tension? The resistance—these contradictions and collisions—actually yield a rich ground for dialogue, analysis, and personal empowerment. How can we explore this terrain in a nonthreatening manner, keeping students engaged and willing? How can the classroom be the place to break down the media's notions of consumer groups as community, consumption as participation?

We work to help students see themselves as historical subjects, as active participants in their lives, as contestants of historical memory.[3] This must entail an ongoing critique of media images—"unreal" fictions and "real" news reports—and absences as they suppress the variety and the specifics of daily practices and collective history. Because the media tend to present history as technologically determined rather than a process of social struggle, and because they reduce the complexity of people's social and psychological lives, to declare one's own historical identity may be fraught with conflict. After discussing the representation of Puerto Ricans in the media, Blanca Vásquez asks, "What does it mean to be Puerto Rican if the society does not reflect you or reflects you pathologically? What does it mean to *choose* to be called Puerto Rican, to self-identify, if to do so is to line up with working class people, 'inferior' people of color, confined to projects and poor housing, expected to fail in school and to end up in prison or on welfare?" (7).

While asking students to define their relationships to the mass media, instructors should point out that the transparent style of the media thwarts critique and mythologizes history.[4] The apparent naturalness of the image, the seeming neutrality of a particular point of view, and the invisibility of stylistic devices and techniques all discourage spectators from seeing the media as constructs. Representation appears as presentation; the present subsumes the past; difference is erased; and contradiction is denied. Media images often impose a singular perspective on character and environment. This simplification inflects the ways in which we see or describe ourselves: our appetites, desires, race, gender, and social world. Such reduction makes it difficult to construct independent self-definitions or understand how people may experience commonalities differently.

Teachers can expose this transparency and the exclusionary and reductive tendencies of mainstream media by presenting films and videos that represent the perspectives of historically specific peoples in a language that reflects the complexity of their experiences. Including many works by women and people of diverse cultures provides an example and inspiration to students and also demonstrates the abundance of interesting and provocative works available.[5] However, it is important to avoid the kind of "enlightened" pedagogy that offers twelve weeks of mainstream media followed by a postscript of "third world" or feminist alternatives. It is necessary to look at the special problems and opportunities of women and "minorities" as scholars and as media makers and yet not marginalize them as alternatives or essentialize their work as examples of "special" experiences. To avoid this, we suggest combining mainstream and experimental works that deal with the same subject or address the same theoretical issue. For example, *The Birth of a Nation* (D. W. Griffith, 1915) and *De cierta manera* (One Way or Another, Sara Gómez, 1974–77) both deal with race, nation, and manliness. The sentimental treatment of victims in "Harvest of Shame" (a "CBS Reports" segment, 1960) contrasts with the self-conscious politics of representation in

Luis Valdovino's *Work in Progress* (1990). A study of Marilyn Monroe and Madonna might also include *The Body Beautiful* (Ngozi Onwurah, 1991);[6] and Kate Farrell and Trish Rosen's fragmented and destabilized video production *The Most Dangerous Place* might complement ABC's September 17, 1991, episode of "20/20" on domestic violence ("Pushed to the Edge").

This integrated plan allows outsiders or subordinated groups not to remain silent until after those with access to power have their say. In addition, although teachers should seek ways to discuss how the media represents others, this should not be the only time they show works by women and people of nonprivileged cultures. For example, rather than spending one week on the Latina experience, why not use Blanca Vásquez's article as an introduction to a unit on reception? Indu Krishnan's video *Knowing Her Place* (1990) might be an example of a reflexive documentary practice rather than a "testimony" on the cultural displacement of Asian-American women.[7] The integration of films and readings by peoples not generally represented in the canons is essential for both the curriculum and the learning environment in such survey classes as Introduction to Mass Media, Film History, Melodrama, and Documentary Media. Any media studies program would also offer more focused courses, such as "Third World" Media, Women and Media, and Latin- or African-American Filmmaking.

The classroom can be a secure environment that encourages students to draw on their diverse standpoints, interests, personal histories, and expressive strategies. If we approach history and identity as always-emerging constructs, then part of knowing ourselves is knowing others and acknowledging how they see, and have seen, us. As Audre Lorde writes, "I am who I am, doing what I came to do, acting upon you like a drug or a chisel to remind you of your me-ness, as I discover you in myself" ("Eye to Eye," 147). Identity is not fixed, not an essence, and not monolithic. Identity is always in the process of becoming, of being redefined and rearticulated—and may contain contradictions. For example, students often encounter some conflict between their pleasures in media sounds and images and the demand for critical engagement. How can they be encouraged to address these contradictions? Teachers must work with and within the tension that exists between students' confident familiarity with the media and the questioning needed to develop a critique.

One way to do this is a classroom exercise early in the semester. We project slides of magazine advertisements and ask students to respond to each image and write down their associations and reactions.[8] Leaving each slide on the screen for several minutes, isolating it, daring students to disrupt the power, "perfection," and ephemeral nature of the image, we ask them to create their own interpretive texts. The lesson shows students that they can be—indeed *are*—critical thinkers and, as important, that there are many different ways to see and analyze any one image. Most likely no two people will agree on what a slide actually shows, much less means. The multiplicity of meanings produced, the various ways to see and analyze our differing relationships to the media, are related to the diverse experiences of the students. It is not a matter of identifying a correct or insider reading of the images, characters, and issues, because we all have multilayered subjectivities; it is not only a matter of the plurality of personal stories, but often a multitude of perspectives within individual students as well. In "Age, Race, Sex, and Class," Lorde discusses the many different ingredients of her identity; yet, she says that she is "constantly being encouraged to pluck out some one aspect of [herself] and present this as the meaningful whole" (20). At times one may feel specific connections with other women, other workers, grandmothers, Spanish-speaking students, or other people of color.[9]

When students read the responses to the advertisement's images aloud, what is normally an individual experience becomes the basis for examining the constructed nature of meaning. This alerts students to the difficulties and frustrations of trying to imagine an essential truth. By emphasizing the contingent and provisional nature of meaning, we encourage students to search and explore instead of waiting for the singular, unchanging, authoritative answer.

When teachers try to pull students away from their uncritical attachments to mass media and introduce them to the value of critical inquiry, they must be attuned to the students' discomforts. Part of their resistance lies in the fear of losing their emotional investment in the idealized media image, a world where everything turns out all right. This dependency may be experienced at an unconscious level as the risk of losing an important part of one's self. Jessica Benjamin's perspective on the intrapsychic conflicts of mutual recognition between parent and child might explain other attachments. Noting both the necessity and difficulty of establishing a "paradoxical balance between the recognition of the other and the assertion of self," Benjamin suggests that when "the conflict between dependence and independence becomes too intense," we abandon the effort and seek refuge in the familiarity of easy oppositions (46–50).

The unconscious resistance to establishing relationships that allow for both dependence and autonomy, oneness and separateness, sameness and difference, may explain our solace in the familiar and binary oppositions. The difficulties we have letting go of our attachment to the media are fostered by images of "perfection" and "absoluteness" and by stories that reduce historical complexity to the conflict of opposites, resolvable in twenty-three minutes. However, a break with this polarized mode is essential to restructuring our relationships to the media—and to overcoming our fears of cultural difference as well. In order for students to address their dependency (and the security and comforts that come with it) we propose a pedagogy that recognizes the simultaneity, reciprocity, and integration of sameness and difference, rather than tries to disentangle them, and that encourages a relationship to the mass media in which both enjoyment and critique, belonging and detachment, are possible.

In order to do this, we look at how different people experience the mainstream media; we must also examine some of the specific dynamics of media reception. For the post–World War II generation of students, television is the most familiar medium, offering both continuity and comfort, a complete and self-sustaining world. At the center of home life, our most private space, television presents the public as a nonthreatening intrusion. Community is reduced to family, and groups are reduced to an unproblematized category, such as "Asian." Facts are decontextualized, homogenized, presented as evident and universal truths.

One reason we find television so comfortable is that the generic character of the medium makes the viewing experience very predictable. Although competitive necessity calls for some novelty, the familiar is seldom lost or even disrupted. Just as important, we experience television as contiguous with the everyday. The television set, generally positioned in the family or living room, often sits among portraits of relatives. The people on the screen also seem familiar because we saw them last week, or because we recognize their stereotypical characteristics. This is one of the ways we learn to value sameness. As viewers, we feel situated and secure.

Given the depth and scope of these investments and their affirmation of daily life, we must not pathologize the pleasures. Nor can we deny the displeasure in misrecognition. (Isn't there always both comfort and unease in our viewing "enjoyment"?) However, we must not analyze these representations as simply incorrect, wrong, or negative images, as if there existed some single true way people should be represented.

Part of the pleasure of stereotypes is their easy recognition. We see them and feel flattered to think that we know whole characters and how they will behave. Indeed, the grossness of the media's stereotypes assumes that these traits are well known, taken for granted, and yet, paradoxically, need constant reinforcement.[10]

Analyzing these images in the classroom can be complex because students' individual interpretations, memories, conflicts, and desires produce a web of intervening contexts and discourses. Students often need to be encouraged to examine the specific contexts that shape their interpretations. Either in discussions or written assignments they are asked to consider some of the ways in which they view and experience mass media at home. For instance, how and when do they watch television? What kinds of shows do different family members like or dislike? Who gets to select what to watch or record? Who controls the remote? Which representations are experienced as offensive? Absurd? Amusing? This may be the moment when a student begins to look critically at the dynamics of his or her home life and personal history. The politics of the family and everyday life may gain an important resonance as students begin to identify roles and power relations within the family structure. As they write about these things, students move toward a relationship to family and personal history that becomes more differentiated.

This process of separation can be uncomfortable and may disrupt the social order of the family. Students have varying relationships with their families and homelands. Some are new immigrants (sometimes identifying themselves as exiles or refugees), others have immigrant parents but were born in this country and still have strong ties to their families. At Hunter, a large number of students do not speak English at home. Because many are the first generation to be educated in the United States and are closely tied to their families, we must realize that our ideas may be frightening or challenging to their traditional values and mores, their dreams of America, and the media's representations of the "American way of life." Other students are third generation in the North or in the United States; some are exploring their roots, searching for some meaningful relationship with their grandparents' experiences; others were raised by their grandparents and seek ways to integrate the lessons of their elders with the modern urban environment.[11] The critiques we offer in class are often carried beyond the classroom and may disturb or displace ideas already invested with conflicted feelings.

How do we work with this "community of discomfort"? In a multicultural classroom in which the character and expressions of discomfort may differ in sometimes subtle ways, this can be particularly challenging. We must encourage an atmosphere where autonomy and dependence derive from strength, not fear and insecurity, where students can engage with each other's differences, and where they experience education as an assertive and engaging act. We do this through assignments and class exercises that invite individual expression. Scholarship can become a place to explore power and subjectivity. In a course about Women and the Media, for example, we have asked students to audio-tape interviews with a "wise" woman, an older family member, acquaintance, or friend.[12]

These interviews form the bases for oral histories, semester-long projects in which students reflect on and wrestle with the moral and political issues around representation and reception. In such a project, students must consider their responsibilities in the selection of a subject; the approach and contract; the intervention of recording, transcription, and editing; and the ethics of structuring and re-telling of another's story.[13] How do you choose to re-present a person whose memories you have elicited? How do you respond to and interpret their recollections?

> After I had prepared the questions that I wanted to ask my mother, I had to decide when would be the best time for me to actually sit down and actually start the interview. I would say to my mother, "I can't wait for you to help me out with my oral history project, it's going to be great. You will have a lot of information to give me." She would just look at me, smile, and ask, "What kinds of questions are you going to ask me?" I would reply, "Oh, general questions about your life in Jamaica and your life in New York." She would say, "You know, I don't understand why you are so interested in that. Remember I'm not going to answer any personal questions, so don't even think about it." My mother said all this with a smile on her face. I think she was very surprised that I would ask her to take an official part in my assignment. (Opal Reid)

For constructive assistance, students might work in teams or form small groups to discuss the selection of interviewees, the process of interviewing, and the kinds of questions asked. In a multicultural environment, these support groups provide helpful exchange, enabling students to see how differences in approach relate to dissimilarities in lived experiences and ethnic sensibilities. Oral histories recognize the importance of gesture, language, speech patterns, and inflection and confirm the validity of memories, recollection, and different storytelling traditions.

The subject I have chosen is my mother. When I first told her that I wanted to do an interview with her about her story, she seemed perplexed. "Why?" was written all over her face. She "warned" me that there was nothing extraordinary about her life. . . . Many weeks passed after [our] initial talk. It was difficult trying to set up a time, because none seemed appropriate, until one night very recently I told her, "We really have to start this soon." We went into her room. I sat on her bed with a small tape recorder on cue and my questions. Since she had to put in 10 hours at work that day she lay down on the bed. This is where we usually have our talks so it was very comfortable and natural. She asked me if it was O.K. to be lying down. I said sure, "I know you will get excited soon." I was right, within twenty minutes she was sitting up on the bed her hands flying in all directions. (Daisy Severino)

This assignment is one way to record differences and commonalities among first, second, and third generations of migrants and immigrants, or between different groups, and for students to discover their own sense of history. This dialogue between the student and her or his narrator is grounded in the self-identity of each: "This paper has taken a turn that I never expected. At first I thought it was going to be a straight history of my grandmother's life. With a focus on the war years and Rita's feeling about herself as a worker. But instead, the focus changed to me defining myself as a woman in relation to my grandmother's own definition of herself" (Ericka Roszko).

These collaborations also validate personal life as an essential part of history. Subjective experience emerges as important as the more visible events. The interviews reveal not only what people did, but also what they wanted to do, what they believed they were doing, and what they felt about having done it. What someone believes—or believes happened—is important historically. The text may tell quite a bit about imagination, feeling, needs, hopes, and aspirations. Judged in this way, errors reveal more than factually accurate accounts. Faulty memory can tell us how people *wished* they had led their lives (Portelli 100). Self-aggrandizement can reveal quite a bit about needs and desires. We should not view oral histories as another Truth, but as another narrative universe—perhaps another symbolic framework— a descriptive mode that may be related to different folk traditions and ways of life.[14]

The oral history projects encourage students to view their chosen narrators and themselves as historical subjects. Helping to undermine the myth of historical inevitability students claim history as their own, by seeing themselves as both active interpreters and part of historical life. These assignments allow students to experience their agency in the act of representing and to use their differing experiences to produce understanding and knowledge, to generate new questions and new language. As George Lipsitz observes, "What we choose to remember about the past, where we begin and end our retrospective accounts, and who we include and exclude from them—these do a lot to determine how we live and what decisions we make in the present" (34). What we choose to remember and acknowledge also helps shape how we identify ourselves.

In some courses, we assign weekly journals (the students' responses to the week's readings, screenings, and class discussion or to questions suggested by the instructor). We pose the assignment in terms that are as open as possible. For example, we may simply ask each student to write two or three pages each week on an aspect of the film, reading assignment, lecture, and/or classroom discussion that particularly interested him or her.[15] In another class, more directive questions may be appropriate; for instance, following the week when we discussed the "cult of true womanhood" in nineteenth-century novels, magazines, sermons, and melodramas, students were asked to find and reflect on a contemporary example that reinforced, modified, or challenged that ideal of womanhood.[16]

The diverse experiences and realities of the students may stimulate different epistemological and political approaches to the journal assignments and other course material. Different people have dissimilar ways of producing and validating knowledge. People also have varying notions of methodological adequacy. The kinds of questions asked, and the types of explanations found satisfying, reflect distinct practices, needs, and expectations. It is possible, for instance, that "consistency" as a standard might be based on masculine Eurocentric criteria. Other people may be more comfortable with ambiguities and contradictions; for them, gaps and incompleteness prove fertile. Some kinds of knowledge are surely suppressed by coherence.

It may also be that the tradition of scholarly distance and objectivity developed out of necessity from the situation of white males studying an other. Pierre Bourdieu writes that this de facto exclusion has been turned into an academic methodology (10). Some students will refuse to objectify, to devalue their feelings, or will see less of a separation between their emotional and intellectual faculties. (James Baldwin's writing is one model; see, for instance, *The Fire Next Time*.) Journals can function as safe spaces for students to explore the subjective aspects of scholarship and find a voice to articulate resistance to class material.

What we think of as "academic resources" can actually thwart a student's creativity. Some find practical experience a better example of evidence than official statistics and use an inductive logic to assess knowledge claims. For example, the story of an immigrant Jewish bride borrowing the oriental carpets from the local movie palace to decorate the basement of the shul for her wedding reception may be more resonant to some than demographics about film audiences in the late teens and early twenties. Oral histories also provide material to provoke historical or historiographic reflection.

Teachers must learn to read different kinds of classroom demeanor, talking back as well as silence. As bell hooks points out, back talk can be an act of risk and daring, especially for those who have been taught to hold their tongue before elders or authority figures.[17] For some, speaking one's mind is not only an act of expressive power but also an open challenge to a system that prefers opposition to be voiceless. However, for others, silence may not be submission, repression, paralysis, an absence, or a lack; silence can be an act of courage, a will to resist, a political and creative decision, a statement that is clear and loud.

In order to encourage students to apply their diverse standpoints, interests, and modes of expression to the course material, we have some practical suggestions. These represent an approach to teaching more than specific strategies. They are culled mainly from our experiences teaching in a multicultural setting at Hunter College, particularly teaching films and videos made by "third world" peoples in both regularly offered courses and special topics courses such as "Third World" Media.

We try to establish a sense of dialogue in the classroom. This includes struggling with differences among ourselves and between us and the ideas in the reading assignments and films. A teacher should not pose as *the* authority on the "third world," "third world peoples," or "third world film and video." Not only is the instructor not the expert on the subject, but the instructor must also admit that many students may know more than she or he does about some of the issues discussed. (This is especially likely when talking about television, music videos, and other aspects of popular culture.) We work to distribute power, authority, and control in order to create an atmosphere in which we learn from our students. This may be particularly difficult for those educated by teachers claiming to hold "the truth" and expecting a single correct answer to any question. Many instructors and their students were raised to obey and respect adults, to deny individual authority and assign it to those in control. Teachers should

recognize the difficulty students have in assuming authority and acknowledge this hesitation as detrimental to creative learning. Teachers must also honestly admit that in denying students' authority, they
foster their dependency. This takes place at both conscious and unconscious levels.

We also make it clear that we do not speak *for* "third world" people or groups. It is important that the students know who is speaking to them, because our opinions and lectures on "third world"
peoples and their cultures are always a dialogue between our identities and subjectivities and those of the peoples and cultures about
whom we are speaking. (For instance, as an educated white person,
one enjoys a certain privilege in society; however, as a Jew or as a
woman, one may be speaking from the margins.)[18] In a dynamic
where cultural differences reciprocally inflect each other, we should
understand these differences not as oppositions but as part of a constant to-and-fro movement. Trinh T. Minh-hà's writing illuminates this
subject. See, for example, "Of Other Peoples: Beyond the 'Salvage'
Paradigm."[19]

Critics sometimes discuss limiting who should speak about or study
different cultures. This grossly limits what we can learn. (We would
never think of declaring the reverse: Native Americans, for example,
can only study Native-American films.) As Ella Shohat observes in
"Can the Non-Subaltern Speak?" "Rather than ask who can speak, we
should ask what are the different modes of speech." What we learn
from diverse cultures is an important part of how we know ourselves
and offers us a chance to affirm the different roots of much of what
we know as the dominant discourse. On the other hand, we also have
to acknowledge that the empowered group's ideologies and representations may have so penetrated the disempowered sectors that, in
some cases, their representations of self may not differ greatly from
those the dominant culture produces.

Likewise, we do not expect a student to represent an ethnic group,
a sexual preference or orientation, a gender, a social class, a generation, a disease, a physical challenge, or a specific ability. Although we
should encourage our students to speak from their personal histories (Simon Watney's *Policing Desire* is a good model of this), we cannot expect them to speak for a group. Drawing from our experiences is not the same as being "the authentic voice" of a group or offering
"the official version" of a social constituency. This expects too much
from anyone and is based on the false premise of a monolithic, for
example, "Asian-American experience," or an essential ethnic sub-

ject.[20] We have to respect, indeed, savor, diversity not only between groups but also within groups. And of course there exists some diversity within any individual, a multiple-voiced subjectivity.

Can the mainstream media's construction of the multiethnic nation as "melting pot" do justice to the variety, hybridity, richness, complexity, and contradictions of our daily experiences? We suggest a move away from the idea of universals that tie us together and toward a posture of using differences creatively and productively. Let us work to build political solidarity, alliances, and trust among different groups that are based on ongoing and committed interdependence.[21] The aim should not be universal harmony, but an inclusionary dissonance.

Appendix 1: Syllabus for Media/Women Studies 384: Women and Media, Hunter College (Serafina Bathrick)

COURSE OBJECTIVES

This course will explore the social, psychological, and political issues that inform the representation of woman by the mass media in America. In an effort to investigate the gaps that exist between stereotypic images of woman and the wide diversity of women's lived experiences, we will also consider the work of feminists who offer a challenge to mainstream genres. With a historical perspective on the development of different forms of media, the course will consider the production, distribution, and reception of images from both mainstream and alternative sources, including print, photography, film, and television/video. At several points during the semester, we will have in-class guest speakers, primarily women involved in media production.

Students are encouraged to develop their critical and creative skills in weekly journal assignments related to class discussions and readings throughout the semester. They will also be asked to produce an oral history project based on conversations with a wise woman whom they know. Every other week they will meet with a small group to discuss their involvement in the process of producing an oral history. There will be an in-class midterm examination and a final examination.

REQUIRED TEXTS

Note: Supplementary handouts will be distributed weekly.
Linda Brent, *Incidents in the Life of a Slave Girl,* ed. L. Maria Child (1861, repr. New York: Harcourt, Brace and Jovanovich, 1973).
Carol Hymowitz and Michaele Weissman, *A History of Women in America* (New York: Bantam, 1978); assigned readings noted weekly.

DISCUSSION TOPICS, READING, SCREENINGS, AND GUEST LECTURERS

Week 1

Feminist Approaches to Women's Culture

Readings: Johnnetta Cole, ed., *All American Women: Lines That Divide, Ties That Bind* (New York: Free Press, 1986); Michael Frisch, *A Shared Authority: Essays on the Craft and Meaning of Oral and Public History* (Albany: State University of New York Press, 1990); Ynestra King, "Ecofeminism: On the Necessity of History and Mystery," *Women of Power* (Spring 1988); Tillie Olsen, *Silences* (New York: Dell, 1978); Adrienne Rich, "Compulsory Heterosexuality," in *Powers of Desire: The Politics of Sexuality,* ed. Ann Snitow, Christine Stansell, and Sharon Thompson (New York: Monthly Review Press, 1983); Alice Walker, "In Search of Our Mothers' Gardens," in *Working It Out,* ed. Sara Ruddick and Pamela Daniels (New York: Pantheon, 1977); Linda Nochlin, "Why Have There Been No Great Women Artists?" *Women, Art, and Power and Other Essays* (New York: Harper and Row, 1988); (the first two are relevant to oral history projects).

Week 2

Women as "Weavers of Speech"

Readings: Hymowitz and Weissman, *A History of Women,* 2–37; bell hooks, *Talking Back: Thinking Feminist, Thinking Black* (Boston: South End Press, 1989); Dale Spender, *Man Made Language* (London: Routledge and Kegan Paul, 1981); Ann Barry, "Quilting Has African Roots, a New Exhibition Suggests," *New York Times,* Nov. 16, 1989; Patricia Robinson, *Poor Black Women* (Boston: New England Free Press, 1968); Elaine Hedges, "Quilts and Women's Culture," and Alice Walker, "Everyday Use," both in *In Her Own Image: Women Working in the Arts,* ed. Elaine Hedges and Ingrid Wendt (Old Westbury: Feminist Press, 1980); Melissa Meyer and Miriam Shapiro, "Femmage: Waste Not/Want Not: An Inquiry into What Women Saved and Assembled," *Heresies,* no. 4 (Winter 1978).

Week 3

The Image of True Womanhood in Nineteenth-century Print Media

Readings: Hymowitz and Weissman, *A History of Women,* 40–76; Barbara Welter, "The Cult of True Womanhood: 1820–1860," *American Quarterly* 17 (Summer 1966); Charlotte Perkins Gilman, *The Yellow Wallpaper* (Old Westbury: Feminist Press, 1973); Gayle Davis, "Women's Frontier Diaries: Writing for Good Reason," *Women's Studies: An Interdisciplinary Journal* 14 (1987).

Week 4

The Slave Narrative

Readings: Hymowitz and Weissman, *A History of Women,* 76–155; Brent, *Incidents in the Life of a Slave Girl;* Marilyn Richardson, "Literacy and Resistance: Black Women in the Ante–Bellum South," *Radical Teacher,* no. 22 (1982).

Week 5

Journalism: Contemporary Feminist Approaches

Readings: Hymowitz and Weissman, *A History of Women,* 156–90; selected essays from "The Media and Women without Apology," special issue of *Media Studies Journal* (Winter-Spring 1993).

Week 6

Méliès's Magic Films and Women as Producers and Spectators of Early Cinema

Readings: Hymowitz and Weissman, *A History of Women,* 192–233; Lucy Fischer, "The Lady Vanishes: Women, Magic and the Movies," *Film Quarterly* (Fall 1979); Elizabeth Ewen, "City Lights: Immigrant Women and the Rise of Movies," *Signs* 5 (1980): 545–66; Martin Norden, "Women in the Early Film Industry," *Wide Angle* 6 (1984): 58–67.

Films: Méliès, Blaché, D. W. Griffith films in class.

Week 7

Female Stereotypes and Woman as Sign

Readings: Hymowitz and Weissman, *A History of Women,* 234–84; Judith Williamson, "Woman Is an Island: Femininity and Colonization," in *Studies in Entertainment,* ed. Tania Modleski (Bloomington: Indiana University Press, 1986); Gloria Joseph and Jill Lewis, *Common Differences: Conflicts in Black and White Feminist Perspectives* (Boston: South End Press, 1981); Rosalind Coward, *Female Desires: How They Are Sought, Bought and Packaged* (New York: Grove Press, 1984); Blanca Vásquez, "Puerto Ricans and the Media: A Personal Statement," *Centro* 3 (Winter 1990–91).

Week 8

The Rise of the Female Star

Readings: Hymowitz and Weissman, *A History of Women,* 234–84; Charles Eckert, "The Carole Lombard in Macy's Window," Karen Alexander, "Fatal Beauties: Black Women in Hollywood," and Andrea Weiss, "'A Queer Feeling When I Look at You': Hollywood Stars and Lesbian Spectatorship in the 1930s," all in *Stardom: Industry of Desire,* ed. Christine Gledhill (London: Routledge, 1991); John Boles, "Let the Screen Stars Teach You How to Make Love," *Serenade: The Illustrated Love Magazine* (June 1934); Gloria Steinem, *Marilyn* (New York Holt, 1986); bell hooks, *Yearning: Race, Gender and Cultural Politics* (Boston: South End Press, 1990).

Slides: Hollywood glamour photographers (George Hurrell, etc.) in class.

Week 9

Hollywood Melodrama and the "Woman's Film"

Readings: Hymowitz and Weissman, *A History of Women,* 285–322; Molly Haskell, *From Reverence to Rape: The Treatment of Women in the Movies* (New York: Holt, 1973); E. Ann Kaplan, "Mothering, Feminism, and Representation: The Maternal in Melodrama and the Woman's Film, 1910–40," in *Home Is Where the Heart Is: Studies in Melodrama and the Woman's Film* (London: BFI, 1987); Laura Mulvey, "Visual Pleasure and Narrative Cinema," in *Visual and Other Pleasures* (Bloomington: Indiana University Press, 1990).

Clips: from *Imitation of Life* (Sirk, 1959) in class (view VHS copy on reserve in library).

Week 10

Race and Ideals of Beauty in Feminist Fiction Film

Readings: Hymowitz and Weissman, *A History of Women*, 322–end; Alice Walker, "Beauty: When the Other Dancer Is the Self," in *In Search of Our Mothers' Gardens* (New York: Harcourt, Brace, 1983); Lois Banner, *American Beauty* (Chicago: University of Chicago Press, 1983); Emma Knight, "Miss U.S.A.," in *American Dreams: Lost and Found*, ed. Studs Terkel (New York: Pantheon, 1980); Alile Sharon Larkin, "Black Women Film-makers Defining Ourselves: Feminism in Our Own Voice," in *Female Spectators*, ed. Dierdre Pribam (London: Verso, 1988); Julie Dash and Sharon Larkin, "New Images: An Interview with Julie Dash and Alile Sharon Larkin," *The Independent* (Dec. 1986).

Screenings: *Illusions* (Dash, 1982), *The Body Beautiful* (Onwurah, 1953), *Hair Piece: A Film for Nappy-Headed People* (Chenzira, 1984) in class.

Week 11

Latina Documentary-Film/Video

Readings: Liz Kotz, "Unofficial Stories: Documentaries by Latinas and Latin Women," *The Independent* (May 1989); Olivia M. Espin, "Cultural and Historical Influences on Sexuality in Hispanic/Latin Women," in *All American Women*, ed. Johnnetta Cole (New York: Free Press, 1986).

Guest lecturer: Marta Bautis, with her documentary/fiction video *Home Is Struggle* (1992).

Week 12

Domestic Violence: Network Television and Feminist Video

Readings: Selections from *Felix* (Spring 1992); Alex Juhasz, Indu Krishan, and Kelly Anderson, "Shifting Communities/Forming Alliances," *Felix* (Spring 1992); Elizabeth Hess, "Pictures from the Combat Zone," *Women's Review of Books* 9 (March 1992).

Guest lecturer: Trish Rosen, with her experimental video *The Most Dangerous Place* (1991); also a segment from "20/20," fall 1991.

Week 13

Lesbian Film, Video, and Oral History

Readings: Edith Becker et al., "Lesbians and Film," in *Jump-Cut: Hollywood, Politics, and Counter-Cinema*, ed. Peter Steven (Toronto: Between the Lines, 1985).

Guest lecturer: Tami Gold, with her experimental/documentary *Juggling Gender* (1992).

Week 14
Working Women: Documenting Their History
Readings: Julia Lesage, "Political Aesthetics of the Feminist Documentary Film," in *Films for Women*, ed. Charlotte Brunsdon (London: BFI, 1986).
Guest lecturer: Andrea Vasquez, with her video *Heaven Will Protect the Working Girl* (1993).

Appendix 2: Syllabus for the Documentary Tradition, Hunter College (Louise Spence)

COURSE DESCRIPTION

This course looks at and questions some of the major epistemological, esthetic, and political concerns of documentary film, video, and still photography (photojournalism and family snapshots). It is designed to introduce a variety of documentary principles, methods, and styles in order to explore a series of documentary problems. The work is arranged around theoretical issues, with photos, films, and videos chosen to provoke discussion about those issues. By juxtaposing different documentary forms and agendas, we will investigate such issues as how we define "documentary"; the distinctions between fiction and nonfiction; played and nonplayed material; notions of "truth," objectivity, responsibility, and intervention; the practical and theoretical implications of esthetic choices; how the illusion of reality is created; different methods of argument and storytelling; the use of narrators and commentary; problems in representing an other; potential contradictions in the interests of media makers, funders, their subjects, and viewers; and the relation of documentary discourses to power.

REQUIRED TEXTS

Barnouw, Erik, *Documentary: A History of the Non-fiction Film* (New York: Oxford University Press, 1974).
Rosenthal, Alan, ed., *New Challenges for Documentary* (Berkeley: University of California Press, 1988).

DISCUSSION TOPICS, READINGS, AND SCREENINGS
Week 1

Introduction to Documentary Truth, Objectivity, Responsibility, and Fame: How the Act of Observation Affects the Observed, and How Interpretation Is a Part of the Process of Documenting

Film: *Broken Noses* (1987, Bruce Weber).
Reading: Jay Ruby, "The Ethics of Imagemaking," in *New Challenges for Documentary*, ed. Rosenthal.

Week 2

Introduction to Modes of Investigation and Representation, Objectivity and Responsibility
Documentary photography: photojournalism and family snapshots; "Harvest of Shame" ("CBS Reports," 1960); *Work in Progress* (1990, Luis Valdovino).
Readings: Alan Trachtenberg, "From Image to Story," in *Documenting America, 1935–43*, ed. Carol Fleischauer and Beverly Brannan (Berkeley: University of California Press, 1988); Brian Winston, "The Tradition of the Victim," in *New Challenges for Documentary*, ed. Rosenthal; Barnouw, *Documentary*, 213–28.

Week 3

Modes of Investigation and Representation, Objectivity and Responsibility
Clips: from network news and "60 Minutes."
Readings: Stuart Hall, "Media Power: The Double Bind," and Michael Arlen, "The Prosecutor," both in *New Challenges for Documentary*, ed. Rosenthal.

Week 4

Introduction to the Illusion of Reality
Film: *The War Game* (1966, Peter Watkins).
Readings: Alan Rosenthal, *"The War Game:* An Interview with Peter Watkins," in *New Challenges for Documentary*, ed. Rosenthal; "The War Game" (dossier of criticism), and James Blue and Michael Gill, "Peter Watkins Discusses His Suppressed Nuclear Film, *The War Game," Film Comment* 3, no. 4 (1965): 14–19.

Week 5

The Illusion of Reality
Film: *Law and Order* (1969, Frederick Wiseman).
Readings: Carolyn Anderson and Thomas Benson, "Direct Cinema and the Myth of Informed Consent," in *Image Ethics: The Moral Right of Subjects in Photographs, Film, and Television*, ed. Larry Gross, John Katz, and Jay Ruby (New York: Oxford University Press, 1988); Calvin Pryluck, "Ultimately We Are All Outsiders: The Ethics of Documentary Filming," in *New Challenges for Documentary*, ed. Rosenthal; Barnouw, *Documentary*, 231–53.

Week 6

The Illusion of Reality
Film: *Who Says It's Fate?* (1979, Helga Reidemeister).
Readings: Bill Nichols, "The Voice of Documentary," and Jay Ruby, "The Image Mirrored: Reflexivity and the Documentary Film," both in Rosenthal, *New Challenges for Documentary;* Barnouw, *Documentary*, 253–62.

Week 7

Representing Ourselves

Films: *Joyce at 34* (1972, Joyce Chopra and Claudia Weill); *Sari Red* (1988, Pratibha Parmar).

Readings: E. Ann Kaplan, "Theories and Strategies of the Feminist Documentary," in *New Challenges for Documentary*, ed. Rosenthal; Barnouw, *Documentary*, 3–81; Julia Lesage, "Political Aesthetics of the Feminist Documentary Film," in *Films for Women*, ed. Charlotte Brunsdon (London: BFI, 1986), 14–23; and The Heresies Collective's interview "If I Ever Stop Believing," *Heresies*, no. 16 (1983): 68–72.

Week 8

Representing Ourselves

Film: *Handsworth Songs* (1986 John Akomfrah).

Readings: Coco Fusco, "An Interview with Black Audio Film Collective," in *Young, British, and Black;* Kobena Mercer, "Recoding Narratives of Race and Nation," and Stuart Hall, "New Ethnicities," both in *Black Film/British Cinema* (London: Institute of Contemporary Arts, 1988).

Week 9

Representing an Other

Film and clips: *Reassemblage* (1982, Trinh T. Minh-hà); clips from a National Geographic special on Bali and *The Sky Above, the Mud Below* (1961, Pierre-Dominique Gaisseau).

Readings: James Roy MacBean, "Two Laws from Australia, One White, One Black," in *New Challenges for Documentary*, ed. Rosenthal; Claudia Springer, "Ethnographic Circles: A Short History of Ethnographic Film," *The Independent*, Dec. 1984, 13–18; *"Reassemblage* (Sketch of a Sound Track)," *Camera Obscura*, nos. 13–14 (1979): 104–11; Trinh T. Minh-hà, "Questions of Images and Politics," *The Independent*, May 1987, 21–23; and Harriet Hirshorn, "Interview with Trinh T. Minh-hà," *Heresies*, no. 22 (1987): 14–17.

Week 10

Storytelling and Narrative Materials

Films: *Langston Hughes: The Dream Keeper* (1988, St. Clair Bourne); *Looking for Langston* (1989, Isaac Julien).

Readings: Jeffrey Youdelman, "Narration, Invention, and History," in *New Challenges for Documentary*, ed. Rosenthal.

Week 11

Storytelling and Narrative Materials

Films: *The River* (1937, Pare Lorentz); *Prelude to War* (1942, Frank Capra).

Readings: Willard Van Dyke, "Letters from the River," *Film Comment* 3 (Spring 1965): 38–56; Walt Whitman, "Song of the Broad-Axe," in *Leaves of Grass; "The River,"* in Robert Snyder, *Pare Lorentz and the Documentary Film* (Norman: University of Oklahoma Press, 1968); Barnouw, *Documentary*, 85–212.

Week 12

Storytelling and Narrative Materials
Film: *The Life and Times of Rosie the Riveter* (1980, Connie Field).
Readings: Barbara Zheutlin, "The Politics of Documentary," in *New Challenges for Documentary,* ed. Rosenthal; Barnouw, *Documentary,* 262–315; Robert Rosenstone, "History, Memory, and Documentary," *Cineaste* 17, no. 1 (1984): 12–15.

Week 13

Storytelling and Narrative Materials
Film: *The Ties That Bind* (1984, Su Friedrich)
Readings: Su Friedrich, "Artist's Statement," program notes, Whitney Museum of American Art, 1987, and "Does Radical Content Deserve Radical Form?" *Millennium,* no. 22 (1989–90): 118–23.

Week 14

Documentary Storytelling, Illusion, Responsibility, and Truth?
Film: *Lightning over Braddock: A Rust Bowl Fantasy* (1988, Tony Buba).

Notes

Many of the ideas in this essay were developed for presentations given at workshops on pedagogy and race at the Society for Cinema Studies Conferences in 1990 and 1991 and in discussions with Bill Luhr when he was visiting professor at Hunter College. We wish to thank our students at Hunter College and Sacred Heart University for the challenges that made this chapter possible.

1. The Board of Trustees of the City University of New York recently described the student body as reflecting "perhaps the broadest ethnic, racial, and generational diversity in the United States."
2. Cornel West, in "The New Cultural Politics of Difference," elaborates on these points.
3. George Lipsitz writes about Jesse Jackson and Ronald Reagan mixing "myth and history in ways that dramatically illustrate the contested nature of historical memory in our time." *Time Passages* 33.
4. Roland Barthes reminds us that myth "transforms history into nature." *Mythologies* 129.
5. A wide range of films and videos can be rented from such distributors as Women Make Movies (462 Broadway, New York, NY 10013, 212-925-0606), Black Filmmakers Foundation (375 Greenwich St., New York, NY 10013, 212-941-3944), Third World Newsreel (335 West 38th St., New York, NY 10018, 212-947-9277), New Yorker Films (16 West 61st St., New York, NY 10023, 212-247-6110), African Diaspora Images (71 Joralemon St., Brooklyn, NY 11201, 718-852-8353), and California Newsreel (149 Ninth St., San Francisco, CA 94103, 415-621-6196).

6. Gloria Steinem's chapter "The Body Prison" from her book *Marilyn* (1988, with George Barris's photographs) is an interesting reading assignment.

7. This relates to larger questions of the politics of course organization seldom discussed in the discipline. For example, what constitutes an historical approach to media? What are the advantages of organizing a course around historicized theoretical issues rather than chronology?

8. These are written on unsigned file cards, collected, passed out randomly, and read aloud. Anonymity often produces honest and energetic responses.

9. See her essay, "Age, Race, Class, and Sex," 120.

10. This dynamic is discussed in terms of different structural relationships in Johnetta Cole's essay "Commonalities and Differences" (in *All American Women*). This might be a good assignment at the beginning of a course, encouraging students to interrogate any future readings or screenings about how texts represent and express different ideological interests. What are the authors' assumptions? Who is speaking about whom?

11. For further discussion of stereotypes, see James Snead, "The Visual Rhetoric of Black Independent Film."

12. Much literature exists on intergenerational relations, especially between mothers and daughters. See, for example, Elizabeth Ewen, *Immigrant Women in the Land of Dollars,* Cherríe Moraga, "What Is Left," Maxine Hong Kingston, *The Woman Warrior,* and Nellie Wong, "When I Was Growing Up." Gloria I. Joseph discusses generational issues in "Black Mothers and Daughters." See also *Double Stitch: Black Women Write about Mothers and Daughters,* edited by Patricia Bell-Scott et al. and Alice Walker, "Everyday Use."

13. Although we recommend inexpensive and readily accessible technology, other circumstances may allow for videotaping. However, we suggest that the tape not be the final project, that students engage in a self-reflexive, written analysis.

14. Bret Eynon from The City University of New York's American Social History Project has been helpful in this work. For more information on oral histories, see Alessandro Portelli, "The Peculiarities of Oral History," Michael Frisch, *A Shared Authority,* Virginia Yans-McLaughlin, "Metaphors of Self in History," Sherna Berger Gluck and Daphne Patai, *Women's Words,* and Paul R. Thompson, *The Voice of the Past.*

15. Throughout the semester, we also assign letters, diaries, poems, short stories, and independent films and videos that reinforce the importance of the first person and personal experience for people whose race, class, sexual identity, health, or gender has put them outside dominant representations. These encourage students to realize that they are working within a valuable historical tradition that, until recently, has rarely been included in social or literary histories, seldom validated by commercial media industries, or acknowledged by the academic or critical establishment.

16. When commenting on students' journals, we tend to raise questions about their observations, their arguments, and their language, rather than correcting their opinions or thoughts. Evaluations are based on thoughtful-

ness and conceptualization, the extent to which the student has begun to integrate abstract concepts and concrete experience, and the willingness to deal with substantial issues.

17. Students may, for example, relate the ideals to the norms of *marianismo* in some Latin-American cultures. See Evelyn P. Stevens, *"Marianismo."* For the cult of true womanhood, see Barbara Welter, "The Cult of True Womanhood: 1820–1860," Mary Ryan, *Cradle of the Middle Class,* and Linda M. Perkins, "The Impact of the 'Cult of True Womanhood' on the Education of Black Women."

18. Berenice Reynaud spoke in these terms in "Three Asian Films."

19. See also Trin T. Minh-hà, *Woman, Native, Other* (Bloomington: Indiana University Press, 1989).

20. Some recent film and videomakers have insisted that they do not speak for a people but *from* a particular experience (Sankofa Collective, for instance) or, as Trinh T. Minh-hà puts it in *Reassemblage* (1982), not *about* a people, just *nearby.*

21. bell hooks's writing is helpful on this as well; see, for instance, "Sisterhood." Norma Alarcón has also written eloquently on these issues in "The Theoretical Subject(s) of *This Bridge Called My Back.*"

Part 3

Multicultural Media as Product

I define conflict very simply as political and social hostility rooted in different systems of moral understanding. The end to
which these hostilities tend is the domination of one cultural
ethos over all others. Let it be clear, the principles and ideals
that mark these competing systems of moral understanding are
by no means trifling but always have a character of ultimacy to
them. They are not merely attitudes that change on a whim but
basic commitments and beliefs that provide a source of identity,
purpose, and togetherness for the people who live by them. It
is for precisely this reason that political action rooted in these
principles and ideals tends to be so passionate. . . . Whatever
else may be involved, cultural conflict is about power—a struggle to achieve or maintain the power to define reality.

    —James Davison Hunter

12

Multicultural Learning through Documentaries: Focus on Latin-American Women

Julia Lesage

When educators decide to teach about Latin-American women and film, they often have just one or two feature fiction films in mind—perhaps *Lucía* (1969) or *Salt of the Earth* (1954) or an older film with Carmen Miranda. They may not know about the wide range of documentary media made by and about Latin Americans or the particular appropriateness of studying this film genre in depth. In fact, documentary media has historically had a long and lively life as an art form in Latin America (see Burton, *Cinema and Social Change in Latin America* and *The Social Documentary in Latin America*).

Documentaries are within the financial reach of many Latin-American media makers, whereas feature fictions are not. And documentary's argumentative and persuasive strategies convey the urgency that many Latin-American intellectuals feel in dealing with acute social problems and political oppression. In the United States, such documentaries are frequently made within the independent film-video-making sector as an act of solidarity with Latin-American struggles. Furthermore, in the classroom, documentary films and video provide a way to teach how inadequately U.S. news deals with foreign countries. When the issue of representing reality is dealt with in an intellectually sophisticated way, it also provides an occasion for classes to examine larger ethical and epistemological issues (Nichols, 1988). Ethnography, testimony, and oral history or personal narratives often comprise the material studied in a multicultural curriculum, especially insofar as that curriculum is about the other or the oppressed. The power relations inherent in the use of such material need to be examined within the curriculum itself. This essay describes a course on documentary within a film studies program, with the term focus on Latin-American women.

The educator who decides to teach material about Latin-American women may have a special reason for dealing with this topic. He or she may be in a school with many Latina students, know Spanish, or have traveled in Latin America. He or she may also be a person of color. In contrast, an educator who knows little about cultural perspectives different from his or her own often hesitates to use creative material from other cultures or subcultures. Both kinds of instructors, those who are familiar with a culture or subculture and want to introduce it to their class and those who are unfamiliar with a culture and want to learn about it while teaching it, can use representations by and about "others" for a new pedagogical purpose. They and their classes can explore such material in a way that investigates what multicultural education might be, perhaps creating such an educational experience for the first time for them all.

Students who are not in the strongest social and economic position within a culture constantly have to negotiate their ethnic, gender, and cultural identities. The limited representations of them that circulate in the dominant media reinforce oppressive institutions and ideology. Artistic representations by and from such groups help students of color build and sustain resistance cultures and renew their sense of cultural identity. Typically, a class on Latin-American women's media will contain Latino students—both women and men, other students of color, Anglo women students, and probably fewer Anglo men students. A class on racial representation in the media or one on documentary film might have a different mix. Beyond that, the students' mixed ethnic identities, differing relations to language and skin color, different sexual orientations, and different backgrounds make them very useful resources. Their shifting, individualized relations to the cultural representations presented in class should be a part of what the class studies.

To facilitate students' analysis of their relation to the material studied, my course uses a major pedagogical strategy, student journal writing. The central focus for writing assignments is the journal. I pose specific questions to focus the writing, and the entries then become an integral part of daily discussion. In particular, the journals give insights into how the course material is received as familiar or not (e.g., it is familiar to the degree that it uses fiction or documentary media conventions, oral history, social science discourse). The shifting intellectual and emotional topographies of student responses, as recorded in their journals, reveal how viewers and readers in the United States use material by and about other cultures. The students (and the media and literature studied) make the foreign familiar. While doing that, they may also have to be taught how to respect, not efface, difference. Furthermore, because students come from different ethnic backgrounds, their perspectives and analyses will vary in a fruitful way.

By allowing the journal writing to be private and shared in an obligatory way only with the teacher, instructors can establish a space in which students decide what of their written work they want to talk about in class. Such a tactic is particularly important in making the class a welcoming place for students of color. It allows them a safe place to express the anger and bitterness that they might feel too vulnerable to express openly. The teacher must explicitly indicate in the syllabus that students of color are free to bring their experiences to bear on the discussion at hand but are not responsible for teaching white students about racism and race.

For students outside of Latino culture, one of the most common reactions to seeing media by and about Latin-American women will be, "I never knew about this before. I am glad to have the chance to learn all this." Obviously, media from Latin America convey a great deal of information about people's situations and ways of thinking. Some students will receive the documentary films and videos as transparent conduits of such information. The teacher should accept this kind of media reception as a partial good but should teach additional conceptual tools. First, the class should deal explicitly with the limits of mainstream news representations of Latin America and analyze why such representations predominate. The students not from a Latino background should reflect on the limited information they seek about Latin America and the lack of any profound effect from the information they do receive. For example, people often set implicit limits on their curiosity. Have students write in their journals what kinds of questions they normally ask of people they know, in contrast to what they could ask and expect an answer to. Journal entries can also probe how students may have unquestioningly accepted institutional authority about what is important to know.

Studying and learning from those other than oneself is the beginning of all intercultural understanding. However, such study must also be accompanied by an understanding of how one uses the other to construct oneself and one's sense of social process. What kind of discourse, what kind of language, what kind of power relations structure that learning? It is not sufficient to consider alternative media merely as a better, somehow more authentic, source of information. Students in a media class must consider the construction of media representation itself, the shaping of the communication in all its facets—including the artist's milieu and resources, the film or tape as a text, and the context of the work's reception.

Michel Foucault has written about the regime of truth, asking us to analyze the power structures that organize the production, regulation, circulation, and operation of statements. When we see or read a work about the oppressed, we do so within structures of reception established by transnational capitalist institutions. In particular, at this time in history there is an uneven international flow of knowledge. "In terms of power relations," students should query their journals, "who wrote, filmed, edited, translated, distributed, and has used this work?" There is no objective overview from which to represent the world, but there are choices to be made at any stage of production and reception. Keeping a journal during the course means learning how to analyze the parameters of such choice.

Documentary, Ethnography, and Oral History

Documentary films have a strong tie to both ethnography and oral history. Students should do reading that sets out the theoretical issues at stake in the three intersecting modes of discourse. The teacher should introduce some of the best texts in feminist ethnography and discuss ways ethnographers have developed to study individual lives and social structures cross-culturally. Here I use material that sets out social issues in ways particularly relevant for media studies, even if that material is not specifically about Latin America. For example, Carol Stack's *All Our Kin: Strategies for Survival in a Black Community* (1974) describes a structure too often ignored in feminist analyses—the extended family as one of the major ways women have for organizing social relations and distributing scarce resources. The family sustains and recreates patriarchy, but among poor women it also establishes a woman's supportive relations with the other women in her extended family. Stack describes participant-observation methodology and demonstrates how white feminist academics can work as committed outsiders in a less-privileged community.

Although Stack's focus is on black family structure in the United States, her book is a succinct and valuable resource for discussing participant-observation methodology, which is especially useful for students who might wish to make documentaries. Stack eschews cultural relativism. Rather, she demonstrates how to take social and personal responsibility for her privileged class position, her relations with the subjects of her study, and the kind of book she wrote. These issues are very important in a film or video course. Media *about* or *with* a socially disadvantaged group can never simply be assumed to be *of* that group. Those who make media, no matter what their origin, are almost always upwardly mobile in class terms (Kleinhans).

Beyond the concerns of whom a documentary film represents, or who made it, is the issue of viewership. In particular, because U.S. viewers of media about the third world often see such films in a privileged college environment, the teacher must lead U.S. students to interrogate their relation to media that they consume from and about poorer countries or cultures in the United States. Students must also be led to interrogate their relation to the cultures depicted, which have been captured and exhibited on film and which they learn about in a relatively passive way. According to Bill Nichols, the institutional conditions of news and documentary viewership, as well as certain aspects of documentary film form, lead to a viewing habit of "epistephilia," or the desire to know more and more in this controlling, comforting, and passive way (*Representing Reality*).

Similar in function and genesis to the feminist documentary film, oral histories are useful to study alongside documentary media. Daphne Patai's *Brazilian Women Speak* (1988) offers a model of verbal "documentary" construction. In this collection, ordinary Brazilian women from Rio and the rural northeast and from many walks of life tell about their everyday lives, dreams, limitations, and rebellions. Extensive notes provide background information and biographical details, as well as brief analyses of women's legal status, education, health conditions, economic possibilities, black and feminist activism, and participation in religion both through liberation theology and Afro-Brazilian cults. In her introductory essay, "On Constructing a Self," Patai, as author and outsider, analyzes how she collects, uses, and interprets women's oral histories. Later Patai coedited *Women's Words: The Feminist Practice of Oral History* (1991), a useful collection of essays dealing with the methodology and ethics of gathering personal narratives. She challenges her earlier work in an essay entitled "U.S. Academics and Third World Women: Is Ethical Research Possible?" Because she answers no to her own question, both essays should be required reading for the course Latin-American Women and Documentary Media.

Economic and social structures are determining factors in people's lives. Understanding these factors explains much about what lies under the surface of phenomena and images. However, U.S. media almost always eschew presenting structure. The structures and historical conditions that shape women's lives in particular areas of the southern hemisphere include women's paid and unpaid labor; reproduction; socialization; the extended family and male migration to seek work in the capital city or the United States; women's participation in markets, industry, and farming in specific countries; migration histories within the United States; and political oppression and resistance (see Nash and Safa). At best, social analyses of women's lives in Latin America deal with the complexities of a situation and explain social circumstances that might not be self-evident. Lourdes Arguelles and B. Ruby Rich's articles on gays and lesbians in Cuba provide a model of such writing.

Students should also be informed about the range of issues being debated in anthropology, media studies, and writings by feminists of color. Bill Nichols's *Representing Reality: Issues and Concepts in Documentary* (1991) deals extensively with documentary media's formal structures, as well as with processes of production and reception. Nichols synthesizes the epistemological issues related to documentary from the point of view of a theorist who takes seriously media's possible contribution to social change.

Within the discipline of anthropology, *Writing Culture*, edited by James Clifford and George Marcus, examines the textual strategies that ethnographers use to write about cultures and the power held or reinforced by the people who write and film such texts. Media students can use such an approach to analyze how media style or the representational tactics of film and video confer an unwarranted authority on the filmmaker and filmic text. Talal Asad's essay, "The Concept of Cultural Translation in British Social Anthropology," in *Writing Culture* challenges those who assume that they are entitled to apprehend directly, in an unmediated fashion, institutions and cultural meaning that are historically or socially distant. This may mean that viewers or media makers assume that they and those people depicted in television, video, or film share similar worlds. Or it may mean seeing the others as less well defined, less well developed, or less fully formed. It may especially result in idealizing or pitying poor people (e.g., in elegies for vanishing cultures or pessimistic visions of urban life). The people whose lives are interpreted in the mass media can rarely challenge their representation effectively. Even more insidious, the international authority of writing published and media distributed in a European language is such that texts by outsiders often reinscribe a people's memory itself.

Film theory, too, must change to deal with racial representation. The Cuban-born author Edmundo Desnöes has written about how images of his native country have circulated in the international press, which is always hungry for exotica from the "underdeveloped" world

("The Photographic Image of Underdevelopment"). He challenges
the cultural reduction and international marketability of photographs
from around the world that emotionally convey the concept of the
"family of man." Coco Fusco has offered a trenchant critique of the
ways in which white feminist film critics have liberally taken up the
topics of race and the "third world" ("Fantasies of Oppositionality").
Those critics have celebrated works by artists of color, reifying the
artists into an essential ethnic position while refusing to analyze critics' own ethnocentrism of privileging white subjectivity as the main
reference point for film criticism. These feminists, says Fusco, must
analyze their own white ethnicity and not treat ethnicity as a quality
or subject position that belongs to people of color alone. Continuing this argument, Isaac Julien and Kobena Mercer ("Introduction:
De Centre and De Margin") point out that filmmakers of color have
such limited funds and access to making media that they often do not
have the luxury of presenting an individualized or particular perspective, as do white artists. Rather, these artists of color feel pressured
to represent the experience and problems of their entire ethnic
group, subculture, or race. When they do succeed in speaking for
their community, their action feeds into tokenism. It is as if their one
film or tape could somehow speak for "an entire social category which
is seen to be 'typified' by its representative" (Julien and Mercer 5).
Julien and Mercer challenge the concept of "otherness." They analyze how the use of that term in cultural criticism shapes discourse
in terms of a binary relation. It vests authority in the voice of the
person speaking, writing, or filming from a central perspective. It
relegates all other perspectives or modes of cultural production to a
position of marginality, as something which occurs elsewhere or far
away.

Finally, although I grant ethnography and oral history a privileged
space in my course, it is important to teach the limits of such material. It is often difficult for students to learn the impossibility of trans-
lating culture directly. Oral history and testimonials seem to do just
that. We grant authority to writers, filmmakers, or ethnographers who
have an intense engagement with their subjects, a knowledge of the
language and region, and participant-observation methodology. But
then, when we are recipients of a text, it seems as if personal narrative and personal guarantees of authenticity establish the validity of
a text as an unmediated and transparent vehicle for communicating
"social reality." The immediacy of eyewitness testimony and the sin-
cerity and lived experience of writers and filmmakers seem to guar-
antee that the text will reveal everything we could or should know

about these people's lives. It seems all to be there on the surface, just waiting for us to apprehend it by reading the book or watching the film or tape.

This issue of transparency and communicability raises a question students should address in their journals at different times and in relation to different works: What is or is not the universality of women's concerns? Ethnicities are not based on identical historical structures or ways of life. In this shrinking world, all women are shaped by intercultural influences, and many women, especially women of color, acutely feel multicultural, contradictory layers of self. Cross-culturally, women often share bonds of solidarity and intimacy. They also may share common ideas, on the basis of what they mutually interpret as common sense, or they may have had similar experiences in their lives, especially in the domestic sphere. Feminist scholarship and feminist activism need to generalize about women's lives, albeit imperfectly, in order to contest restrictive, exclusionary codes in all areas of social, economic, and cultural life. For some women, including myself, "feminism" refers to a utopian project of collectively reconstructing women's experience on the basis of our commonalties and differences. B. Ruby Rich, in "The Crisis of Naming in Feminist Film Criticism," has summarized different esthetic approaches taken by both critics and filmmakers who call themselves feminist.

Key writings by women of color attack such an enterprise. Placing issues of "first" and "third world" feminism in specific historical contexts is Gayatri Chakravorty Spivak's *In Other Worlds* (1987). Even more emphatically than Spivak, Chandra Talpade Mohanty challenges the universalizing tendency of the words *feminism* and *woman* ("Under Western Eyes"). In many of her writings, Trinh T. Minh-hà attacks the racism and patriarchal bias of anthropology as a discipline and also the concept of the third world (a concept that Ella Shohat defends in "Notes on the Post-Colonial" and "Gender and the Culture of Empire"). Trinh rejects realist representation and an essentialist notion of women's writing, but her prose style has the decentered and lyrical form familiar to contemporary feminist readers of women's prose.

Documentary Practice

Because I often teach film and videomaking students, I find it useful to structure a course around documentary practice and documentary texts. Because of the critique of realism in contemporary film and literary theory, many writers look for the degree to which documentary filmmakers represent themselves in their work. In other words, a clear critical distinction is often made between cinema verité and self-reflexive cinema, the latter also including the interrogation of cinematic process within the film. For film students, however, these critical distinctions are less useful. Media makers are used to seeing all media representations as artifacts. When seeing a film, they often understand what its makers' relations were with its subjects, evidenced by such audio and visual traces as composition within the frame, or microphone, or lens choice. Whether or not a filmmaker appears within the film seems more a conceit to prove his or her authenticity to viewers later on.

In fact, most documentaries create an other, for they reify, interpret, and simplify the people filmed. During the time of scripting, the preproduction phase, and the moment of filming, film and videomakers readily acknowledge what anthropologists do not. A documentary filmmaker is always looking for drama, people to interview who are lively subjects and have good screen presence, and dramatic moments to capture. The mise-en-scène should have good light, minimal traffic and wind noise, and a visual environment that can be shot so as to "speak" for the persons in it. People are chosen to appear in an interview if they are "contemporary" and "interesting," talk succinctly, use imagistic language, and know how to deliver a punch line. Many media makers would prefer to avoid using an oppressed group's leaders on screen if these leaders do not have good screen presence, the kind that makes someone a star witness. In this light, students' journal entries can interrogate the works seen in terms of a comparison with their own production experience, or with a projection about what they as media makers could or would have done with the same topics or locales.

I know from the experiences of my peers that many media makers who wish to make oppositional tapes and films and work with groups who do not have access to making media often have struggles with these groups based upon the issue of acknowledging painful realities and contradictions within the tape or film. A common example would be a film's depiction of the degree to which the women still are subordinate to the men within a militant group. Media makers know the value of depicting contradictions to lend a work drama and credibility. *Political* media makers know that although contradictions are painful to recognize, they are the points of social movement, the pressure points leading to change, and the places where the future is already visible within the present.

Each documentary shown should be subject to close textual analysis. In their journals, students can examine the various works' representations of (and assumptions about) subjectivity and objectivity. Who is given the voice? What is the relation of voice to image? Is the voice emotional? Which social structures does it take for granted and which does it explicitly teach? Are multiple voices respected in the editing? To what degree is difference enhanced and preserved? To what degree are other cultural constructions of the person and of commonsense flattened out and reinterpreted so as to communicate to U.S. viewers? Do individual speakers or people seen on the image track reveal their multiple social roles or discontinuous layers of self? Does the film or tape show people (on the sound or image track) in the multiple, constantly shifting positions from which one person's subjectivity can be expressed?

More likely, the people interviewed become characters, used for their typicality. An illusion of fairness may come from incorporating interviews that "show both sides," but films rarely challenge their most emotionally convincing or eloquent interviewees. One of the advantages of using self-reflexive formal tactics both in the scripting and the editing stages is that doing so allows filmmakers to locate their vision as separate from the people speaking in the film. Experimental documentaries strive to find ways to represent their own process as they re-present the lives of others. But it is difficult to balance both tasks at the same time—to show how the media operates and to give others "the voice."

The systematic aspects of documentary structuration can be examined explicitly for what they reveal about the vantage points from which media looks at people's lives. For example, how does the camera move through time and space, and how is the film edited? To what degree do details about and from people's daily lives remain part of the background, and to what degree are the systems of meaning that shape these details made explicit? For example, one can usefully interrogate documentary images by asking, "In contrast to the camera work here, or the edited construction of time and space, how would these people move through time and space? What would they say is important to know about what we see?" In their journals, students should analyze what audiences rarely do: the selection and framing of images and the ambient sound and music tracks. Students can also examine television images of life in other countries. These documentary images often prove reductive in predictable ways, expressing the "family of man," "poverty," "exotic beauty," or "chaotic rage" stereotypes.

The teacher must be careful not to grant the insider's voice a kind of primal innocence as an interviewee. People who appear in documentaries have an emotional stake in being interviewed. There may even be a reciprocal kind of transference relation between filmmaker and interviewee in which each projects his or her assumptions and needs onto the other. Being interviewed often inspires a person to "pull herself or himself together" and speak from a more coherent persona than usual. Who can understand what is or what is not contained in the kind of partial truths commonly spoken in an interview? The person interviewed might not have seen the larger perspective and have spoken out of a restricted vision. Furthermore, filmmakers edit according to their own esthetic and social vision. Frequently in an intercultural situation a filmmaker may not understand the context of the words that she or he recorded and used. It is common among oppressed peoples that those interviewed may have a more complex perspective than they choose to present. While speaking, they may evaluate and modify information, feeling that listeners would reject certain ideas divergent from their own dominant ideology.

Published interviews with film and videomakers may reveal the time spent and the social process of making a media project, as well as the economic and institutional resources available to the maker. Because documentary media, especially in video format, is a less expensive genre, poor artists often choose it. Latina and Latino artists, Latin-American filmmakers, and artists working for social change often have limited means. As a documentary videomaker who has worked in Latin America, I bring up my own practice for the class to analyze. My practice is to try to establish equitable processes for making media with underrepresented groups. I gather the broadest possible input during the preproduction and scripting stages and give the people I have taped veto power over their self-representation at the rough edit stage. But I know that people's imagination about the kind of media they might like about themselves has been shaped by feature fiction and television. I also feel a social urgency to finish the tape in a timely fashion and know how impossible it is to do collective editing. For these reasons, I say openly at the beginning of our joint venture that I will be in charge of the piece from the time of shooting through the rough edit. Stylistically, the esthetic theories of Bertolt Brecht have had a great influence on me, so I often work in an experimental documentary mode, which means the final structure is often elaborated at the editing stage. This esthetic commitment to experimental forms also has political and economic consequences, for an inverse relation often exists between formal innovation in documentary work and successful commercial distribution.

Institutional mechanisms for distributing documentaries are different in the United States than in Latin America. Film festivals have played a major role in letting works from both regions be seen. Still, the reception of militant documentaries has to be considered in terms of their use within specific struggles, and there is only a partial record of Latin-American and U.S. reception of such works. Neither is much known about who has seen these films and tapes, and under what circumstances. Usually such details come out in interviews with the director. In the United States, a few socially committed distribution companies distribute almost all militant documentaries.

Some Documentaries and Their Use

Some documentaries can profitably be matched with others in various units analyzing the relations between media-making practice, textual structures, and modes of reception. A first category is cinema verité, which should be reexamined not only in order to critique cinematic realism (which is perhaps too easy) but also to look at relations among the maker, the people filmed, and the potential audiences. *The Mexican Tapes* (1987) were shot over a number of years in a San Diego housing complex where video artist Louis Hock lived and taped his neighbors' conversations with him and also their ongoing daily lives. The people in the tapes are undocumented immigrant families. Hock tapes them as they work San Diego, are deported to Mexico, and then return. Significantly, Hock and his neighbors speak together in both Spanish and English. *Carmen Carrascal* (1982) is one of the first self-consciously feminist films widely seen in Latin America. The women from Bogota who made this tape about the life of a rural basket weaver on Colombia's Atlantic Coast have formed the major production and distribution company run by women in South America, CineMujer (see Lesage, "Women Make Media"). *Miles from the Border* (1987) is a brief film of special interest to Latino students in the United States because it depicts the intergenerational immigrant experience of a Mexican-American family, with the scholastically capable daughter unable to cope with the expectations for success that she and her family have for her.

Cinema verité made by Latin-American filmmakers indicates the special advantage of the insider's eye and the different social relations evoked in front of the camera when media makers are *of* the culture they film or tape. Among the works listed here, a striking difference exists between those cinema verité–style documentaries that strive to give a sense of timeless struggle and those fascinated with the contradictions unique to a given moment. *The Brick Makers* (1972), a pioneering work by two Colombian ethnographic filmmakers, Marta Rodríguez and Jorge Silva, is a study of the barrenness and isolation faced by a family doing the hardest kind of backbreaking labor to just get by. They all make bricks in an arid area on the outskirts of a big city. *Look at My People How They Struggle* (1985) documents an extraordinary testimonial from women prisoners in El Salvador as they bring their wounded close to the prison walls, where they scream out about abuses. The film was videotaped by women demonstrating outside the prison walls with El Salvador's Comadres, the organization of the mothers of the disappeared. *Don't Forget Me* (1988), a beautifully composed and edited work by the Chilean video artist Tatiana Gaviola, documents a street theater demonstration in which masses of people brought life-sized cardboard cutouts of the dead and disappeared to stand against walls and telephone poles in Santiago's city center. Clearly the demonstration was organized with the idea of making the videotape. Gaviola's achievement is thus the culmination of a larger project of public art.

If such works have a sense of age-old struggle enacted again and again, *Time of Women* (1988), by Monica Vásquez, both conveys and ruptures that sense of timelessness as it shows the tilling of the fields in an Ecuadoran Andean village being done by women and then demonstrates that all the men have migrated to the United States to look for work. *Women's Town Hall Meeting* (1987) is a U.S.-distributed excerpt from a weekly Sandinista television program, "Cara al pueblo" (Facing the People), which taped various town meetings across Nicaragua where citizens gathered to meet with national leaders and ask questions. In the time of the Sandinista Revolution, the meetings and this very popular television show emphasized the role of contradiction in the political process. In this segment, the contradictions are particularly bitter and acute. The episode documents part of a long public meeting at which women confronted Daniel Ortega and other leaders in the time before Nicaragua's constitutional convention. It shows the kinds of lively discussions about family violence, the double day, and abortion that took place on television during the Sandinista era. In *Susana* (1980), the filmmaker Susana Blaustein-Muñoz, a young Argentine lesbian, discusses family strife and homophobia as she looks back on family life from the perspective of her current position in the United States.

Related to cinema verité are films and videotapes that have a more synthetic structure, often using a collection of interviews but sometimes employing other narrative devices to give an overview of life in Latin America. These projects are usually made with a sense of urgency. The media makers and the people they represent want to teach repressed or ignored social structures to a larger audience that is crucial to reach within the context of an ongoing organizing effort or political struggle. The media made for such specific purposes often has a longer life than the original struggle, because the kinds of structures and contradictions brought out in one struggle can often teach the participants in another.

Especially useful for class discussion are documentaries about labor. Like *Harlan County, U.S.A.* (1976), these often follow organizing struggles that document people's lives over a long period of time and introduce a number of real-life characters whom we follow, whose circumstances change, and who explain the conditions of oppression and the people's collective response. Three films, *Land for Rose* (1987), *My Life, Our Struggle* (1979), and *We Are Not Asking for the Moon* (1986), show different kinds of life-and-death organizing efforts among the poor in the third world: land take-overs, shantytown communal organizing, and labor union formation. *Land for Rose* follows Brazilian peasants who try to occupy fallow farm land so that they can lay claim to it. *My Life, Our Struggle* was made with women trying to organize a slum community outside of Sao Paolo. In *We Are Not Asking for the Moon,* Mexican seamstresses organize to recover bodies from their workplace after the earthquake in Mexico City. Then they form a seamstresses' union, facing constant opposition from the bosses, the government, and the official union hierarchy. The film project began as a documentation of the earthquake and, over the course of time, became a collaborative project to help the seamstresses' organizing campaign. Noteworthy in all these films is the relation between media maker and subject, a relation of intimacy because they are working together in adversity over a long period for a mutual cause.

Two films have particular relevance in the face of the North American Free Trade Agreement because they specifically elicit a discussion of the relation between international economic structures and the quality of human life. Focusing on the human devastation that results from multinational corporations' dependence on a cheap labor force and the hazardous labor conditions that those corporations perpetuate, *Love, Women, and Flowers* (1988) presents the relationship between the European flower market and the industrialized growing of these flowers in Colombia, where the intense use of pesticides greatly endangers workers. The visual motif of flowers, usually a symbol of love and beauty, ironically symbolizes inhumane and murderous labor conditions under which a third world work force dies while producing the luxuries used elsewhere by the affluent. *The Global Assembly Line* (1986), a more analytic work, presents the *maquilas* (assembly factories) in Mexico, just across the border from the United States. Although the film is dated, it remains the best introduction to the labor issues surrounding the Free Trade Agreement, demonstrating that when a documentary teaches an understanding of persistent social structures it does not soon go out of date.

Other films with this synthetic form present issues of interest to feminists but set them in the context of a specifically Latin-American interpretation. As with feminist documentaries in the United States (see Lesage, "The Feminist Documentary"), these documentaries were made as part of an alternative media structure because they raise questions not considered valid or important by the mass media or by mainstream intellectuals in the film's country of origin. *Miss Universe in Peru* (1984), made by a small leftist media collective in Lima, protests beautifying the city for the Miss Universe finals, held at the same time as a national conference of Andean peasant women organizers. The latter group comments on the real conditions of rural women's lives in contrast to European standards of femininity. *With or Without War* (1986), a coproduction of a Nicaraguan and a U.S. feminist videomaker, uses street theater and dramatic reenactments to dramatize the ongoing problem of wife abuse. The title indicates Nicaragua's need to deal with the problem even while fighting the Contras. Finally, a Chilean filmmaker living in exile, Valeria Sarmiento, has made a highly controversial documentary, *A Man, When He Is a Man,* about Latin-American machismo, which she punctuates with a humorous deconstruction of the Latin tradition of the romantic love ballad (Lesage, "Women Make Media").

I have found two films especially effective for demonstrating the clear impact of U.S. imperialism on the lives of people in Latin America. Somehow these two works are among the most eye-opening and persuasive for otherwise conservative students. *La Operación* (1982) analyzes how and why one-third of Puerto Rican women have been sterilized by U.S.-imposed family planning. *Roses in December* (1982) tells of the life of Jean Donovan, one of four Catholic religious women from the United States murdered by the Salvadoran military, and the lack of U.S. government support as her family tried to investigate and redress her death.

Experimental documentaries by Latin-American women media makers take up issues of racial mixture and intercultural penetration. In *The Darkness of My Language* (1989) Silvana Afram employs a complex audio mix of voices to demonstrate the difficulty of communicating across language barriers when people are forced to migrate. *Unfinished Diary* (1986), the most esthetically accomplished of all the documentary films discussed here, is a semiautobiographical study of a Chilean woman artist's multilayered experience of self. Marilu Mallet presents aspects of herself in exile in Canada, a person possessing no cultural space of her own. The work must be seen on film and not video because its use of various film stocks and precise composition, often at the edges of the frame, are some of the subtle ways in which it expresses the collisions of culture within one person's experience.

In contrast to Mallet's film esthetic, the tapes for Brazilian television by the feminist Lilith Video Collective are made in a fast-paced televisual style that owes nothing to film. For example, *Black Women of Brazil* (1986) depicts the lives of women who discuss Brazil's racially segregated class system, women's condition, and the validation they find in traditions of music and religion. *A Kiss on the Mouth* (1987) lets Brazilian prostitutes speak for themselves. Students sufficiently sophisticated in their knowledge of modern critical theory or the artistic avant-garde can usefully devote journal writing to a contrastive cross-cultural study of either self-reflexive or realist media tactics. For example, none of the works listed reject emotion, characterization, or typage in the way that such experimental media often does in the United States. Here, for example, the editing goal is not to fragment narrative structure. Latin-American artists use forms that oppose realism in the United States and Europe, but for many cultural reasons these forms are used in subtly different ways (see Lesage, "Creating History in *The Other Francisco* and *One Way or Another:* Dialectical, Revolutionary, Feminist").

Only a small amount of the solidarity media made in the United States uses an experimental documentary form. My tape, *Las Nicas* (1984), made with Carole Isaacs, conveys Nicaraguan women's euphoric view of women's role in the new Nicaragua shortly after the revolution as they contrast their lives then to their suffering under Somoza. The tape looks at sexual politics, the family, religion, education, prostitution, and work. In *El Crucero* (1988), I use four different documentary styles to present four segments, each of which delineates a different aspect of daily life on one farm in Nicaragua. Each style also provokes a different level of analysis and a different structuration of possibilities for viewer response. *Los Hijos de Sandino* (1982) is a euphoric, lyrical collage shot in Managua during the first anniversary of the Nicaraguan revolution. The three works are examples of low-budget media, the first being a video adaptation of a slide show, the second shot in VHS video and edited onto three-quarter-inch U-matic, and the third shot originally on super-8 film and transferred to video.

Finally, the class should consider the creative use of artistically mixing documentary, history, news reportage footage, and national legend within feature fiction films because this occurs frequently in all of Latin America. Some films continue in the Italian neorealist tradition. *Salt of the Earth* (1954) is a U.S.-Mexican-American classic of collaborative filmmaking by Hollywood filmmakers. Based on a real-life story of how mining women took over a strike when the men were legally enjoined from doing so, it was made in collaboration with the real-life strikers. Although anticommunist forces in the media industry effectively blocked its distribution, the feminist movement of the seventies rediscovered the film (Rosenfelt, Biberman). *Vera* (1987) offers a complex view of an orphaned, teenaged, cross-dressing lesbian in Rio. Also in the pessimist, naturalist vein is *Iracema* (1979), a cinema verité–style fiction about an indigenous adolescent in the Amazon River basin, her fall into prostitution, and her decline as she moves from riverfront city to the deforested areas of Brazil. A documentary that looks like a polished feature fiction, and which was not advertised as a documentary but as the story of a Guatemalan woman, is *When the Mountains Tremble* (1983). Made by U.S television journalists working independently in the dangerous war zones in Central America, it traces the genocide of the peasants in Guatemala, narrated in the film through the perspective of an indigenous organizer, Rigoberta Menchu. Because Menchu has won the Nobel Peace Prize, much to the dismay of established politicians in her country, the film is of interest, as is her autobiography, *I . . . Rigoberta Menchu.*

Susana Amaral, a Brazilian feature filmmaker, bases her film *Hour of the Star* (1985) on a well-known Brazilian novel of the same name by Clarice Lispector. Both rework the naturalist tradition by incorporating overt fantasy elements to depict a poor young urban woman's "doomed" life and her subjectivity. *Macu: The Policeman's Wife* (1986) is based on a news story in the Venezuelan press and developed into a fiction about a woman who is married off as a child and grows up dissatisfied in that relationship. It is an unusually candid study of girlhood sexuality and a family's complicity in child sexual abuse, one containing a mix of fantasy and realist styles. In contrast to the pessimistic tone of these films, the Cuban feature directed by Sara Gómez, *One Way or Another* (1974), is filled with revolutionary optimism; a middle-class schoolteacher and a working-class factory worker in Havana fall in love and deal with gender-based and workplace conflicts. In general, Latin-American women directors who use narrative fictions to focus on sexual politics present observations about gender intertwined with observations about the country's society and politics, and they use these two poles of observation to qualify and explain each other.

More material has been presented in this chapter than can possibly be taught in a semester. Admittedly, a utopian burden has been placed on the journal as a learning tool. However, it is not utopian but challenging for a teacher to stop using films and videotapes as self-explanatory illustrations of "life in other cultures" and instead teach them as complex examples of a process of intercultural media production and reception. Such processes must not remain invisible, but can and must be taught.

Appendix 1: Media List

Black Women of Brazil (Mulheres Negras),(Brazil, 1986), 25 min., video, Silvana Afram and Lilith Collective, Women Make Movies.

The Brick Makers (Chircales), (Colombia, 1972), 42 min., film/video, Marta Rodríguez and Jorge Silva, Cinema Guild.

Carmen Carrascal (Colombia, 1982), 30 min., subtitles, film/video, Eulalia Carrizosa, Women Make Movies.

El Crucero (United States, 1988), 59 min., video, Julia Lesage, Facets.

The Darkness of My Language (Canada/Brazil, 1989), 4 min., video, Silvana Afram, Women Make Movies.

Don't Forget Me (Chile, 1989), 13 min., video, Tatiana Gaviola, Women Make Movies.

The Global Assembly Line (U.S., 1986), 60 min., film/video, Lorraine Gray, English, New Day.

Los Hijos de Sandino (U.S., 1982), 42 min., film/video, Fred Barney Taylor and Kimberly Safford, Third World Newsreel.

Hour of the Star (La Hora de la Estrella), (Brazil, 1985), 96 min., Suzana Amaral, video: Facets, film: Kino.

Iracema (Brazil, 1979), 90 min., Jorge Brodansky, video, Cinema Guild.

A Kiss on the Mouth (Brazil, 1987), 28 min., Jacira Melo and Lilith Video, video, Women Make Movies.

Land for Rose (Terra para Rose), (Brazil, 1987), 90 min., Teté Moraes, video, New Day.

Look at My People How They Struggle (El Salvador, 1985), 27 min., video, El Salvador Media, c/o Third World Newsreel.

Love, Women, and Flowers (Colombia, 1988), 58 min., Marta Rodríguez and Jorge Silva, film/video, Women Make Movies.

Macu: The Policeman's Wife (Venezuela, 1986), 90 min., Solveig Hoogesteijn, film/video, Macu Films.

The Mexican Tapes (U.S., 1987), four 54-min. tapes, subtitles, Louis Hock, Facets.

Miles from the Border (U.S., 1987), 16 min. Ellen Frankenstein, video, Bellars.

Miss Universe in Peru (Peru, 1986), 32 min., Grupo Chaski, subtitles, film/video, Women Make Movies.

My Life, Our Struggle (Brazil, 1979), 43 min., subtitles, Susana Amaral, video, Third World Newsreel.

Las Nicas (U.S., 1984), 45 min., Julia Lesage and Carole Isaacs, video, English and Spanish versions, purchase: Julia Lesage, Facets; rental: Foreign Images.

One Way or Another (De Cierta Manera), (Cuba, 1974), 78 min., Sara Gómez, film: New Yorker, video: Center for Cuban Studies.

La Operación (U.S., 1982), 40 min., Ana Maria Garcia, film/video, Cinema Guild.

Roses in December (U.S., 1982), 56 min., Ana Carrigan and Bernard Stone, film/video, First Run/Icarus.

Salt of the Earth (U.S., 1954), 94 min., Herbert Biberman, film, Facets.

Susana (U.S., 1980), 25 min., Susana Blaustein-Muñoz, English, film/video, Women Make Movies.

Time of Women (Ecuador, 1988), 20 min., subtitles, Monica Vásquez, film/video, Women Make Movies.

Unfinished Diary (Journal Inachévé), (Canada, 1986), 55 min., Marilu Mallet, film, Women Make Movies.

Vera (Brazil, 1987), 87 min., subtitles, Sergio Toledo, film, New Yorker.

We Are Not Asking for the Moon (Mexico, 1986), 58 min., Mari Carmen de la Lara, film, First Run/Icarus.

When the Mountains Tremble (U.S., 1983), 83 min., Pamela Yates and Thomas Sigel, video, Skylight Pictures; film, New Yorker.

With or Without War (Nicaragua/U.S., 1986), 28 min., Martha Wallner and Miriam Loaisiga, video, XChange TV.

Women's Town Hall Meeting (Nicaragua, 1987), 10 min., Ann Crenovich, part of videotape collection, TV Sandino, Video Data Bank.

Appendix 2: Distributors

Center for Cuban Studies
124 West 23rd St.
New York, NY 10011
212-242-0559

The Cinema Guild
1697 Broadway, Suite 506
New York, NY 10019
212-246-5522; 800-723-5522

Facets Multimedia
1517 West Fullerton
Chicago IL 60614
312-281-9075; 800-331-6197

Films, Inc.
5547 North Ravenswood Ave.
Chicago, IL 60640-1199
800-323-4222

First Run/Icarus
153 Waverly Pl.
New York, NY 10014
212-727-1711; 800-876-1710

Full Frame Film and Video
  Distributors
394 Euclid Ave., Number 201
Toronto, Ont. M6G 2S9
Canada
416-925-9338; fax 416-324-8268

IDERA Films
2524 Cypress St.
Vancouver, B.C. V6J 3N2
Canada
604-738-8815

Julia Lesage Video
3480 Mill St.
Eugene, OR 97405
503-344-8129

Kino International
333 West 39th St., Number 503
New York, NY 10018
212-629-6880

Macu Films C.A. and Cinearte C.A.
Sabana Grande
Calle Villaflor
Edif. Asunción, Piso 3, Ofic. 302
Caracas, Venezuela
71-02-65; 443-25-26

Maryknoll World Video and Film
  Library
Media Relations
Maryknoll, NY 10545
800-227-8523

Moraes, Teté, Vemver Comuniçacao
Rua Joa Borges 83
Gavea 22
415 Rio de Janeiro, Brasil
55-21-266-7245

New Day Films
22D Hollywood Ave.
Hohokus, NJ 07423
201-652-6590

New Yorker Films
16 West 61st St.
New York, NY 10023
212-247-6110

Paper Tiger Television Collective
339 Lafayette St.
New York, NY 10012
212-420-9045

Karen Ranucci
124 Washington Pl.
New York, NY 10014
212-463-0108

Skylight Pictures
330 West 42nd St.
New York, NY 10036
212-947-5333

Third World Newsreel
335 West 38th St., 5th Floor
New York, NY 10018
212-947-9277

Video Data Bank
School of the Art Institute of
  Chicago
112 S. Michigan
Chicago, IL 60603
312-345-3550

Martha Wallner
750 Ocean Avenue
Apartment 5B
Brooklyn, NY 11226
718-768-1829

Women Make Movies
462 Broadway, Suite 500
New York, NY 10013
212-925-0606; fax 212-925-2052

13

The Perfect Take: Multiculturalism in the Production Classroom

Steve Carr

For educators like myself, talking about a new pedagogy is one thing. Doing it is quite another. Although we believe in education's inherently liberating process, we often avoid confronting the breach between what Jane Tompkins calls "our practice in the classroom" and "the values we preach" (653). I wonder how many teachers, especially those in film and video production, in spite of their best intentions, inadvertently reinforce a situation in which students "have been unjustly dealt with, deprived of their voice, cheated in the sale of their labor" (Freire 34–35). Are teachers doomed, in the words of Louis Althusser, "to turn the few weapons [they] find . . . against the ideology, the system and the practices in which [they] are trapped" (157)?

If teachers sincerely want to liberate students from their institutionally based education, they should turn to examining their own film and video production pedagogy. With a potential to encourage exploration and creativity, these classes could restore voices that the educational system otherwise methodically seeks to erase. Some might argue that these classes already encourage exploration and creativity. Yet in the studio and field production classes I have taught, the voices that have spoken provide little comfort to me.

Students' projects as well as their day-to-day remarks often reveal an unabashed racism, sexism, and heterosexism. For example, one student project involved a white male dressing up as a lower-class black woman. During the taping of a demonstration on how to make sushi, a student remarked on how much he hated the Japanese, and called them "a bunch of bastards." Many times, even female students jokingly called one another "bitch," "whore," or "slut" in class. Another student project was entirely devoted to showing a man handcuffing a woman to a fence and then raping her. The same semester, another project had a detective tracking down a gay hairdresser who, after assaulting his victims, would redo their hair.

Although it is tempting to perceive these students as racist, sexist, or homophobic, the shortcoming here lies squarely with an institution failing to educate students adequately about the images they see and reproduce in the classroom. In addition to the oppressive and discriminatory practices of this country's educational system (which boasts abysmal percentages of minorities and women and denies access to a college degree for those who cannot afford spiraling educational costs), film and television departments have embraced a mission of becoming glorified trade schools. The departments disproportionately invest thousands of dollars in equipment that only a few advanced students will use; they provide a clearinghouse for area media outlets and production houses to hire our students as unpaid interns; and they ask students to work on sponsored projects for which outside agencies will determine the subject and content.

The day-to-day teaching of an industry esthetic compliments this message. The introductory television labs I teach, for instance, inevitably emphasize well-honed formats (a demonstration show or an interview), or how to focus, compose, and frame a shot. I end up teaching a particular format and a way of seeing that someone in a classroom down the hall is probably critiquing, and that I myself have critiqued many times over.

The unnatural separation between the classroom and the studio legitimizes what production teachers do and the departments within which they exist (Hemingway 13–14). Instead of calling attention to the ideology of the image, teachers like me blandish the myth of Hollywood success to students. Outside the history, theory, or criticism classroom, who instills within students the dream that they may one day sign a contract with a big studio? Who falters in puncturing this myth? After all, what kind of teachers would discourage students from achieving their goals? Students are told, implicitly or explicitly, "Take our classes, learn our aesthetic, and you too may be one of the lucky ones to get a job in Hollywood." Simon Hemingway compares today's aspiring film and video student to the soda jerk of yore "who flirts with 'discovery'" (Hemingway 19). If students then emulate the same racist, sexist, and homophobic content they see on mainstream television and film images, who else but their teachers are to blame?

The production lab environment offers tremendous potential for teaching. Completely different from a classroom, where students sit at their desks and absorb information imparted to them during lecture, the lab allows a great deal of freedom for student interaction. Students get hands-on experience with equipment, but, even better, they have an opportunity to use this praxis by articulating their own ideas. But the constricted pedagogy of these introductory classes, parochial gateways to Hollywood, quells any desire to find an individual and personal voice outside the conventions of mainstream media. Worse still, little opportunity exists to discuss and critique this mainstream esthetic in lab. Unlike a classroom, where teacher and student can interrupt the class to discuss or comment on an idea, the lab is a place where students are only expected to function in their assigned role, serving in the greater good of the finished project. Because each student's project is taped, and the goal of each project is to obtain a "perfect take," it would be highly inappropriate for either the teacher or anyone else in the class to stop someone's production and launch into a discussion of the ideological component of esthetics.

The larger issue here involves the obsolescence of the studio mode of production. With the rise of small, lightweight, and affordable consumer video, a whole new style of image-making has displaced the stodgier, obligatory concerns of moving a three-wheeled behemoth across the studio floor. Three-point lighting, the rule of thirds, and carefully composed closeups are neither pertinent nor useful to understanding images like the videos of Rodney King being beaten by the Los Angeles Police Department. People are using video in their own way and taking it into the streets, regardless of what is taught in $100,000 complexes. It is necessary to rethink film and video production pedagogy completely, and to teach it in such a way that can encourage students to think differently about the images they produce.

In the spring of 1991, I taught an undergraduate field video production class at the University of Texas at Austin that forever changed my view of video production. Because I wanted to make the course different from the typical production class, I redesigned it to encourage a more critical perspective of the media. Unique in its focus, the class neither emphasized the technical aspects of video, nor did it falsely give hope of Hollywood employment. Instead, the class emphasized issues of ethnicity, color, gender, and sexual orientation, struggling with how one would represent these things in video. My partisan support of multiculturalism's emphasis on these issues remained the guiding sensibility for developing the class. In addition to some of the more inappropriate projects I had seen, and an inability to discuss the issues these projects raised adequately, the campus itself had undergone a heated debate over multiculturalism. The time for a production class to treat the issues raised by multiculturalism was long overdue.

Four projects formed the backbone to the class. In addition to teaching technical skills, each project taught something about representation as well. These projects were inspired by the "unlearning racism" workshops of New Bridges, a grass-roots organization focusing its work in communities across the country. In one of their activities, called a speakout, a group of people stands in front of an audience. One person will ask the group a question, such as, "What would you like us to know about you and your people," and "What do you never want to hear about you and your people again?" Members of the group answer each question. Members of the audience then repeat back, word for word, the answers the people at the front of the room have given. The activity is painful, moving, revealing, and always educational; the questions, I felt, were sufficiently incisive to warrant their becoming the basis for class projects. (I have since parted ways with New Bridges over philosophical differences, although I believe exercises like the speakout have immense value [Carr].)

I also discussed the course at great length with Bernard Timberg, who was teaching a similar class that incorporated production and criticism at Rutgers University. Early in the semester, Bernard had his students bring in and exchange pictures of themselves. I found this exercise extremely valuable; it served as a kind of icebreaker, it stimulated discussion about issues of representation, and it introduced the first project. Because I used John Berger's *Ways of Seeing* to start students thinking about different way of looking at images, having students exchange snapshots encouraged them to think of pictures "in a highly personal way to match and express [their] experience" (Berger et al. 30).

For their first project, I then asked the students to collect images on video that expressed themselves in a similarly personal way. Many felt confined by the project. Some wanted to use sound. For others, finding self-expressive images proved a bewildering experience. In a unique way, however, it brought up the difficulties and ambiguities of representation. If it is so difficult to represent one's own self through pictures, how can we even begin to represent other people? To a certain extent, the frustration and dissatisfaction many experienced on this first project inspired a greater awareness of the issues raised in subsequent images.

I based the second project on one of the questions asked in New Bridges's speakout: What do you never want to see or hear about you and your people again? Students edited both images and sounds, although they could not use any synchronized sound (such as dialogue). They instead created a kind of audio and video collage of all of the things they had seen and heard about themselves for years. Everyone shied away from multicultural issues, although a few students used the assignment to produce intensely personal statements. One student, continuing to employ snapshots and home video footage, created an incredibly moving picture about being seen as a head-injury survivor. Another student cut images from a fraternity and sorority party to an original song about phoniness and appearances. Although the projects failed to address multicultural issues overtly, their candid, unpretentious style represented an important development in these students' voices. If multiculturalism teaches anything, it is mutual respect for the diversity of experience. By first finding a candid and unpretentious voice for their own experience, students would then be better equipped to represent the experience of others.

The third project asked students to represent a group other than their own. I divided the class into teams of three, allowing each team to define a different group however they liked. This would allow students the latitude to represent anyone however they pleased. In the discussion section, the class would then view all of the projects and discuss their images and meaning. At the time, I thought this project would be useful to discuss the stereotypes that had come up in earlier classes. But students were unclear about the concept of differences defining a group, and the structured nature of the class and the project perhaps made people wary of engaging in overt stereotypes.

All three team projects failed to take chances, as the individual projects had done. One project satirized university officials; another was a straight documentary on Zendik Farms, a cooperative that had just moved to Austin; a third went for shock value in its depiction of devil worshipers. In the way they defined a different group, and the manner in which each team presented these differences, the production teams deftly avoided the issues of stereotyping and representation I hoped to raise. Even more important, however, I failed to communicate the nature and purpose of the difficult assignment—one that attempted to confront the day-to-day construction of difference.

This issue did appear in the fourth project. In this project, each team produced a video of a person or group of people as that person or those people would want to be represented. Each team had to meet twice with their subjects: first, before shooting, to determine the way in which their subjects wanted to be represented, and, second, after project completion, to review the edited tape. Two of the teams had their preliminary meetings but did not follow the instructions for the project, which required that they reach consensus with their subjects on an appropriate style of representation. Instead, the teams decided one thing with their subjects and then did something completely different once they got into the editing room. One team interviewed members of a gay choir. In one sequence, the team had taped footage of a gay man "camping it up" before the camera. The man, however, had been unaware that the camera was rolling. When the team had their second meeting, their subjects confronted them with a great deal of anger. The second meeting allowed my students to learn firsthand what it is like to face someone betrayed by a misrepresentation. Although the students failed to follow the instructions for the project, they still learned from the invaluable experience of being confronted by their subjects.

Another project, however, raised far more uncomfortable issues that I could not resolve in class. This video intercut sexist images of nude women with interviews of female strippers. The students had not discussed this strategy with their subjects although, when they showed the video in the second meeting, the women did not object to it. To complicate matters, on the day the class viewed the project I had invited a friend to observe. I often invited guests to attend my classes for both their ideas and feedback. These visits usually occurred without incident. On that day, however, a bitter debate erupted between my friend and one of the male students who had worked on the project. The student felt the intercut images were entirely in keeping with the wishes of the women interviewed. My friend, on the other hand, found the intercutting yet another example of a man dictating control over the representation of women's bodies. In previous class discussions, the student tended to be abusive toward other students, particularly women in the class. When the male began to assert his territory, women usually backed down. The student became increasingly agitated, however, when he saw my friend, an articulate, strong, and outspoken woman, fail to relent.

The incident raised troubling issues that address multicultural concerns. During class discussions, how does a teacher handle interaction between a hostile and defensive male and an independent, outspoken female? There is no easy answer. In theory, the teacher should provide a role model and interrupt male obnoxiousness. Yet this interruption might send an unintended message: Women are incapable of handling these situations themselves and the benevolent authority figure—in my case, male—must rescue the woman from dire discursive circumstances?

I also found myself stifling my own contributions to the discussion. Because my friend articulated many of my own objections to the project and because, as a woman, she set an example for other women in the class to deal with a particularly difficult student, I decided to remain silent. Yet the discussion failed to address one major issue:

If the strippers didn't object to the intercut images after the fact, why should anyone else worry? Although I wanted to address this point, I decided that it was more important to let students see a woman stand up to a verbally abusive male.

Despite these difficulties, this and other projects followed a useful trajectory, each exercise posing a different technical and ideological challenge. With the first project, for instance, students had to represent themselves using only silent images. With the second, they had to think about different uses of sound and how it feels to be misrepresented. For the third, they were introduced to synchronized sound and the representation of difference. And for the fourth, they had to relinquish their control to the voice they were trying to represent.

The class readings paralleled issues raised by this trajectory. In addition to discussing John Berger's *Ways of Seeing*, students also read *Women's Ways of Knowing* by Mary Belenky et al. I used this latter book in a video production class because the different levels of knowledge that it outlines encourage students to integrate the information covered in the class into their own voice. The chapter on silence, which discusses women who find themselves "mindless and voiceless," parallels the restrictions of the first project. Chapters on received knowledge, in which women conceive of themselves as passive receptacles for learning, and procedural knowledge, in which women see learning as a set of "objective procedures for obtaining and communicating knowledge," highlights the question of teaching a class that ultimately relies on students' proficiency in understanding video technology and operating equipment (15).

Although *Women's Ways of Knowing* clearly extends beyond the realm of women, many male students had difficulty accepting it. One referred to it, in class, as "just a bunch of bitches pissing and moaning." Others expressed hostility and lack of sympathy toward the voices of lesbians and abused women interviewed in the book. At the same time, however, the book empowered many of the women in the class, who were able to argue and talk back to the men when they interrupted or used abusive language in discussions. For many of the students, Belenky's book and the discussions that ensued offered their first exposure to women-oriented concerns.

In every aspect of the course, I emphasized the importance of students' personal experience and insights. Half of both the midterm and final examinations required students to integrate material from *Women's Ways of Knowing* and *Ways of Seeing* into present-day and personal settings. In the midterm, for instance, one of the essay questions asked students at what level of knowledge would they place themselves with regard to the Gulf War and Iraq. Another question asked students how they would feel had someone else done their second project (something they never wanted to hear or see about themselves again). Another prompted students to reflect on one of their projects, what it taught them technically as well as ideologically.

Students also kept a journal that discussed the various readings, speakers, class discussions, and their own work. Not graded, the journal only needed a minimum number of entries for the student to earn credit. Similarly, students needed only to complete the first project to earn an A, which took some of the pressure of producing a highly personal first project off them. In all of the discussions, I encouraged students to share their personal frustrations with the educational system. Students often told horror stories in which other professors had made insensitive remarks or had belittled them in class. Yet in some ways, I too reproduced the same authoritarian models that denigrate students. For one thing, I lectured to the class. This entailed standing up in front of a seated audience and trying to play the expert on everything from *Women's Ways of Knowing* to videotape editing. Jane Tompkins calls it the performance model of education:

> I had always thought that what I was doing was helping my students to understand the material we were studying. . . I had finally realized that what I was actually concerned with and focused on most of the time were three things: a) to show the students how smart I was, b) to show them how knowledgeable I was, and c) to show them how well-prepared I was for class. I had been putting on a performance whose true goal was not to help the students learn but to perform before them in such a way that they would have a good opinion of me. (654)

Production classes provide fertile ground for this performance model. What is taught, and consequently, what students expect, is a certain technology and esthetic. Teachers present themselves as the experts on operating a camera or framing a close-up. Hence, they must perform in front of the class to demonstrate their proficiency. Worse still, students are expected to perform, too. Even in the class I taught, I could not escape the pedagogical compulsion to assign grades. On my project evaluations, I assessed students' performance on the categories of "direction," "videography/sound," "editing," "organization," and "effort." Grading student performance in these areas, although common, nonetheless rated projects against my own esthetic and technical ideal. Although teachers often tell students not to be so concerned about grades, they only help conceal the ideological force that grades exert. Short of refusing to assign grades, perhaps teachers can at least recognize this concealment and instead show more empathy for the pressure students experience when they are evaluated.

Although I devoted a great deal of time to class discussion, something I had never experienced in the production classes I took, both I and the students would have been a lot better off had I sat down, pulled up a chair, and let other students talk. As the semester continued, I soon discovered that I was talking too much, even in discussion. I refrained from presenting the "nontechnical" information, a term I now regret having used when I referred to the multicultural readings, and instead encouraged other people to speak. Unfortunately, however, I still stood at the front of the class and called upon various people. Not only did this reinforce the power dynamic of an insecure graduate student lording over his undergraduate subjects, but facilitating discussions also hindered my own contributions to discussions.

In designing and teaching this class, I had been careful not to take advantage of my role as instructor and supplant the opinion of students with my own. On the other hand, students would often ask me in class what I thought about a particular issue we were discussing. I would refuse to say anything, instead asking the students what they thought. In trying to empower a student voice in the classroom, I had in fact reinforced the power of my own voice through maintaining my silence in discussions. It is one thing to perform a well-articulated opinion in front of a classroom audience, quite another to sit with the audience and talk with them. By refraining from participating in discussions, and instead maintaining my silent position of power in front of the class, I created a rather precarious situation. As a result, the class would often end up tolerating the racist, sexist, and heterosexist attitudes I had intended to combat. In confronting these attitudes, teachers must allow people to express themselves freely, no matter how disdainful we may find them. But teachers should also speak themselves, if only to provide and inspire alternative voices within students. If, for example, I had asked another student to facilitate a discussion, I could both speak and avoid taking advantage of my position of power as facilitator.

After the class was over, I asked for student feedback. Many of the comments were overwhelmingly positive. "I sure wish more of my classes had been this good," wrote one student on an anonymous evaluation. "This was probably the greatest experience I had at [the University of Texas]." "Got a lot from this class," another wrote, stressing that their "technical skills and communication skills have both been sharper due to the course." One student, critical of the class, even admitted that "in hindsight . . . the amount and diversity of the non-technical issues discussed in class were beneficial and important to the overall success of the course."

Many students, however, stressed a need for more hands-on knowledge of the equipment. "Great course!" wrote one, but added that it "needs more attention to teaching technical proficiency." Another student wrote that the "weakness of the course is the way in which the technical information is presented. We need more hands-on experience." One of the harsher critics of the class wrote that the non-video issues "commanded way too much attention." The student wanted more of a balance between technical and nontechnical discussion: "A discussion about some of today's newer video tech[nologie]s would have been just as worthwhile, relevant, and timely as a discussion on the topic of women's issues, or homophobia, or racism, or any of the other multicultural issues covered."

These students had picked up on my central dilemma. Given that this was a production class, and that students had enrolled in it based on an expectation that they would get hands-on experience learning how to operate video equipment, how reasonable was it for me to redesign the course and place much more emphasis on multiculturalism? Put more bluntly, was I cheating students out of something they had every reasonable right to expect? The answer to this question lies not with finding some perfect balance between production and criticism, but in the manner that classes are taught.

Teachers need to find creative ways of relinquishing their control over the classroom, so that students, motivated by their own interests, can present material on new technologies, lead discussions on multiculturalism, offer critiques of one another's work, and even demonstrate how to operate equipment. Is the issue whether students should receive more hands-on experience and technical information, or is it that classroom dynamics take away student initiative to make the educational process relevant to their own interests?

The desire for students to receive more technical knowledge indicates their reliance on the performance model of education. After all, this model is something they have come to expect after years of schooling. Had I allowed students to sign up for various topics and then make presentations to the class, I could have increased student involvement. Students would have felt more control over the material. As an educator, I can have innumerable readings, discussions, projects, and the like on multiculturalism. But if the performance model reinforces a power dynamic, what good are the values that I preach? To a certain extent, what I do undermines what I say.

Something else I would have done differently is to have shown more examples of alternative film and video. All too often, when I discuss objectionable content with a student, the defense is that "it's no worse than anything we see on TV." As much as showing these images can take time to order and money to rent, teachers need to demonstrate that a whole host of images exists beyond "Saturday Night Live" and "In Living Color." Just as important as showing the work of established alternative film and video makers, educators who bring multiculturalism into the production classroom can exchange their students' work with one another. Many of the projects my students did were too good to be shown only in class. Teachers can show each other's student work as a way of stimulating new ideas and discussions in class, and as an antidote to the mainstream media.

In conclusion, production pedagogy could stand improvement in two areas. First, class content needs to change. Exercises should show students how to do more than press the right buttons, or compose an aesthetically pleasing shot. Discussions of technology should include a more critical emphasis upon its function in society. Teachers should actively encourage students to ask who benefits most from improved technology. Teachers should ask students to question prime-time television, not emulate it. Through creative and stimulating projects, teachers can encourage students to find their voice, independent of mainstream media.

To implement these changes, however, teaching must reflect upon the classroom power dynamic. As long as educators continue to wield authority over students, the educational system remains at odds with the values giving rise to multiculturalism. Teachers are not imparters of knowledge, but facilitators encouraging students to explore their own identities, to create the images they want, to find their own voices within the context and community of other voices. This difficult process requires a certain relinquishing of control. Some may find the results objectionable or distasteful. But this is a small price for the many creative and mature voices I have seen and heard—voices not often heard in traditional production classes.

Unlike the typical classroom, the production classroom offers a tremendous opportunity for teaching. Particularly in labs, where students interact freely with one another and get plenty of hands-on experience with equipment, the teacher can put these conditions to use. By changing the focus of these classes and labs to one that asks students to become more critical of the images they produce, the educator can make them more aware of the ideological issues that have traditionally been left within the safe confines of the classroom. Finding ways to empower students to learn without the traditional pressures of the classroom, and finding ways to encourage students to articulate their own voice, can help bring about the multicultural revolution in the production classroom.

Appendix 1: Syllabus for RTF 366K: Television Field Production (University of Texas, Austin)

Required Texts
Berger, John, et al., *Ways of Seeing* (London: BBC-Penguin Books, 1988).
Belenky, Mary Field, et al., *Women's Ways of Knowing* (New York: Basic Books, 1986).
Selected readings from Coursepak

COURSE OBJECTIVES

RTF 366K is an intensive introduction to single-camera videotape production. Technical emphasis will be placed on the single-camera shooting technique, including lighting, writing, directing, and editing. This course is also multicultural; the class will highlight issues of ethnicity, color, gender, and sexual orientation in readings, discussions, and projects. The class will cover issues of representation as they pertain to both the media in general, as well as to the images we produce in this class. Students' personal experience and insights are crucial. To help articulate these thoughts, keep a weekly journal. Both the journal and all projects, including the final examination, will require that students reflect upon how they represent themselves and others using the video medium.

REQUIRED PROJECTS

Project 1
Using only edited images, how would you represent yourself?
Format: Three minutes; silent only; shooting limit: one thirty-minute videotape.
Objectives: familiarization with camcorders; production planning; shooting techniques; editing; self-representation.

Project 2
A representation of yourself that you never want to see or hear again. Tell what people say about you and your identity that is incorrect and unfair.
Format: Three minutes; wild sound only (no music or narration); shooting limit: one thirty-minute videotape.
Objectives: familiarization with camcorders; production planning; shooting techniques; editing; sound recording; mis-representation.

Project 3

How you see a person or people in a group other than your own. Define that person's or people's group however you like, but be prepared to articulate why that group is different from your own.

Format: Three minutes; narrative; sound and dialogue only (no music or narration); shooting limit: one thirty-minute videotape.

Objectives: familiarization with camcorders; production planning; shooting techniques; editing; sound recording; multicultural representation.

Project 4

How you see a person or people in a group other than your own, as they would want to be seen. By working closely with your subject(s), find out how they would like you to represent them. Like project 3, be prepared to articulate why this person belongs to a group different from your own.

Format: Three minutes; documentary; sound, dialogue, and voiceover only (no music); shooting limit: one thirty-minute videotape.

Objectives: familiarization with camcorders; production planning; shooting techniques; editing; sound recording; multicultural representation; working with subjects.

Final Project

Format: Ten minutes; narrative, documentary, or public service; to be shot and edited according to approved script and storyboard developed by group members; shooting limit: two hundred minutes of raw footage; must have writer/director, videographer, sound recordist/editor; must include titles, credits, mixed soundtrack, original music, and material clear of all copyright infringements.

14

Good-bye Hollywood: Introductory Filmmaking and Difference

Patricia R. Zimmermann

Battle Lines

If you crave a good definition of that old Marxist-infused term *over-determination*, then teach introductory filmmaking for a semester. Imagine, if you will, an unreal place criss-crossed with hyperbole: the dominant ideology, media business practices, Hollywood hallucinations, stars, big money. Imagine that place deflecting departmental quests for survival, multinational media organizations, upward mobility myths, technology, creative blocks, nineteenth-century romantic fantasies of creativity, and adolescent dreams of salvaging identity and power through expression. This place is so ideologically congested you can't see a 16mm Bell and Howell camera for the discourses encircling it like a wagon train in a John Ford film shot in Monument Valley. This place is the beginning film production classroom.

A teacher ensconced in this situation requires more than guns and ammunition; she needs strategies to outsmart these invisible, discursively bound adversaries. She needs to turn these ideologies and discourses inside out, like a pair of old, worn blue jeans, exposing their seams and ripping open their homogenizing agendas with the differences incumbent in all filmmaking students. To sling a metaphor, she needs to turn those old jeans into a mini skirt with studs and embroidery, for a different and more diverse clientele.

Rather than concentrating on those ephemeral, ill-defined, ideological constructs about preparing students for postgraduation jobs or, put differently, commodifying them into reproducible parts for the "industry" that hover like a ghost around most introductory filmmaking classes, she instead needs to focus on how students can make affordable films in their voices. To be an advocate for and a facilitator of the diversity in students rather than a conduit for outside industrial, corporate, or even experimental agendas, is, in today's climate, a radical, and, yes, multicultural act. Students, parents, the culture, college administrators, or "Entertainment Tonight" install those phantasms about the happy and wealthy futures of students, not film production teachers whose fantasies about student success often involve the less lofty goals of focus, exposure, and composition. Students who can master those skills and then express their difference have accomplished quite a bit in any introductory production class.

Filmmaking prevails as one of the most expensive classes on any college campus, given the sheer cost of film stock compared to books. When you couple this appalling economic reality with students' $40 million filmmaking fantasies fueled by multinational media corporate propaganda, you end up with a formidable pedagogical conundrum: How do you detoxify students from the inaccessible Hollywood dream to produce work in their own voices? How do you convince them that their differences are what matter most, not their slavish conformity to Hollywood plots, desires, and representational systems? Although not all Hollywood filmmaking is quite the ideological monolith that might be implied in these statements, its image grips the imaginary horizons of student creativity. Indeed, it is quite monolithic, even petrifying—especially to people whom Hollywood never addresses adequately: women, students of color, gays, and students from different regions and different classes.

When difference is concretely confronted in screening both student and established work, multiculturalism generates practical ways of organizing classes and critiques. Multiculturalism emerges not as some sort of pluralistic, postmodern theory lashing out against master narratives, but as an extremely specific offensive strategy to produce films out of one's experiences. In my more political take on this, multiculturalism is denuded of its true radical potential if it simply revels in a pluralist-inspired arrangement of difference and neglects the central issue: power. Instead, I define multiculturalism as multiple representations of race, class, gender, sexual preference, and regional differences in continual confrontations with both overt and covert power.

A truly radical multiculturalism destroys these larger cultural imperatives toward sameness and erasure of all conflict, ideological and personal. And it is exactly this manufacturing of sameness—typified in the teaching of classical Hollywood narrative style, in the reliance on male genres like horror or detective films for plot lines, and in an adherence to an ideology that all filmmaking practices are politically neutral—that immobilizes large portions of beginning filmmakers, especially women and people of color. Beginning students become paralyzed; they assume they lack talent if they don't conform to these standards or don't tell "those kind of stories." Some students devalue their films about their mother's Italian immigrant family in the Adirondacks, or about their experiences with depression, as not "real narrative films." They have never encountered stories like these at "the real movies" in suburban shopping mall multiplex theaters.[1]

We have to avoid becoming seduced by utopian, multicultural dreams about some pluralized paradise where all differences are equal and where the production classroom waxes into some idealized, "We Are the World," Disney-style zone of unproblematic creativity and unfettered productivity. Feminist film production teachers can be neutralized, metaphorically transformed into reenacting *Snow White and the Seven Dwarfs* during critiques. They should not presume that showing more diverse films and creating assignments focused on students' experiences will create a media revolution that will annihilate racism, sexism, and homophobia. It is not that easy.

The larger educational and social context of film production courses begets a conflictual situation. A filmmaking professor must be prepared for bloodshed with administrators, students, and even other faculty if she or he decides to deviate from homogenizing structures of media production into more multicultural domains. The former supplies an easy set of reproducible, standardized norms—continuity action and male-centered plots, for instance. These rules are easy to teach; students only need to mimic. The latter blasts open a whole set of difficulties; every student's vision compels different, distinctive filmic strategies. A film production teacher, then, needs a large arsenal of film styles, theories, strategies, and skills to guide students through the murky, landmined jungle of articulating their own filmic voice.

Battlegrounds: A Case Study

With film programs across the country embattled by declining budgets, and with some programs even disbanding during the recession, the beginning filmmaking course can convert from a creative conservatory into a highly charged battleground. In my program, some administrators are interminably distressed over the declining pool of eighteen-year-olds in the economically embattled Northeast who can afford our nearly $20,000 tuition, room, and board. Consequently, the beginning film production class has been transformed. In the 1970s it was a creative outpost; now it is a potent marketing tool to decimate our competitors. Students are required to enroll in film production their first year, a big selling point for high school students eager to get their hands on actual 16mm filmmaking equipment. Consequently, "intro" endures the most criticism and debate when it detours from these prescribed fantasies of assimilation into dominant media practice.

So *how* introductory filmmaking is taught, and *what* is taught, becomes entangled and almost indiscernible from what is marketed, which most of the time has nothing at all to do with teaching students how to thread cameras, edit, and produce meaningful work. The ideological and marketing function of introduction to film production for our target clientele is so charged that my school set up a Freshmen Experience Committee to assess how production courses can better accommodate entering students. Production is then privileged as the dominant mode of thinking; critical and theoretical courses are framed as necessary adjuncts of legitimation, not primary areas of inquiry. This move manifests both the marketing demands of higher education in the 1990s and an accommodation to the unformulated, uncritical pleasures of eighteen-year-olds to ensure their continued fealty to our highly competitive, expensive program.

In my experience teaching introductory filmmaking for more than a decade at Ithaca College, administrators, departmental chairs, other faculty, students not enrolled in the class, teaching assistants, and parents will fret like undercover agents from the National Endowment for the Arts or Jesse Helms about whether the professor teaches "classical Hollywood narrative" or "marketable, professional, filmmaking skills" in the classroom. These foes establish a false causality between traditional narrative forms and securing entry-level jobs in the commercial film industry.

To run the risk of reiterating the obvious like a whining, pessimistic radical, let me quickly outline the concrete practices these foes would have teachers forget to install in this supposedly ideologically pure form of film production. Forget about academic freedom. Forget that the golden age of Hollywood no longer exists, transmuted into a hydra-headed multinational media monster. Forget you are the one gulping down aspirin for headaches induced from watching thousands of feet of underexposed, overexposed, out of focus, poorly composed, shaky student footage on the Steenbeck. Forget you dispense Kleenex in your office to students sobbing because their film "didn't turn out." Forget your intellectual and artistic needs to construct some semblance of a democratic public sphere in your production classroom where all can argue and debate in spite of the new academic etiquette that frames debate and argument as organizationally dysfunctional. Debates on film content and form disrupt the anesthetic required to produce obedient workers for the multinational media industry.

As Dan Quayle, Jesse Helms, the NEA, and Donald Wildmon from the American Family Association have argued, the war between those fighting for social justice and the right to difference and those old white patriarchs straining to hold on to their declining power has moved from picket lines to television sets, art galleries, movie theaters, and now the introductory film production classroom. Culture is the new battleground.[2] The instrumental approach of teaching specific styles in introductory filmmaking is much less threatening than the more dialogical and messy idea of opening the production classroom to diverse models, films, and producers that support and encourage, rather than inhibit, difference.

How to Organize a Strong Defense and Offense

In years of teaching feminist media theory and political documentary, no one has ever criticized my assignments, my film or book selections, or my intellectual goals. However, film production—in comparison a lower-level course focused on skills, strategies, and surveys—looms more like San Francisco. Perched on the fault line between ideology and expectation, it is subject to earthquakes precipitated by rejecting "Hollywood" (a completely vague term) or "narrative" (an amorphous term redefined by postmodernism). Although these discontented rumblings often remain underground, small eruptions like reduced film rental budgets, complaints by a few students of "intolerance," discussions relating educational missions to post-graduation jobs, and invocations to please a few disgruntled white male students who consider *Batman* filmic exploration telegraph the political struggles in which I am engaged.

A certain irony lurks around these "criticisms." Compared to almost any other introductory film production class anywhere else, our course neither advocates one style of filmmaking nor sanctions a specific content area, such as feminist, narrative, or avant-garde. My colleague, Marcelle Pecot, and I want students to experience a wide swathe of filmic strategies as methods to be appropriated, reworked, and recombined to produce powerful and significant work. Our theoretical operating model is that filmmakers continually interact in concrete ways with films, crossing borders, borrowing, and unearthing ways to assert one's identity and voice. This involves a precipitous ideological and esthetic position.

As the experienced authority figures, teachers want to explain work and guide students toward border crossings into all sorts of difference and critiques of power. Yet they also do not want these various traverses over the border to privilege one identity over another. Otherwise, every white male Wasp in the classroom will presume he can't make a film because he is not oppressed, black, female, or gay. Identity politics only answers half of the question that multiculturalism poses. The other side of multiculturalism—the dismantling of power—is often overlooked. Its destabilizations can provide openings for making work in coalitions across differences.

It is important to serve as a rigorous tour guide through these different terrains. But it is also mandatory that teachers communicate their own political and esthetic positions so students know their viewpoints and can argue with them. Some film teachers camouflage their own positions. I consider this tactic unethical and dishonest; it assumes neutrality and plurality. It de-skills faculty, wrapping them in pedagogical abstention and mystery. Ultimately, this stance destroys democratic participation. Many teachers in the "neutrality" school also prefer the more technical version of film production techniques to simplify interactions with students. This presumed neutrality derails conflicts over work or anything bordering on the political. A good film production teacher should function as a lightning rod, sparking ideas and creating space for debate. While this means explaining one's positions, it also means accepting that although not all students will agree with the teacher, they still need adequate space to express themselves.

One semester I taught a film by Winnipeg Film Group feminist filmmakers Tracy Traeger and Shawna Dempsey called *We're Talking Vulva.* Borrowing from music video styles, the film features a singer dressed up as a vulva, singing a song about her various functions. The film's frank, feminist discussion of female genitalia disturbed some male students, yet the rock video format negotiated more familiar and less threatening territory. As most educators know, male students generally feel less anxiety in speaking vigorously in discussions. However, this short, three-minute piece opened a different kind of public sphere that featured female students explaining that the film worked through combining commercial form with radical content.

The students know I also teach a course in feminist media theory. After thirty minutes of debate, one male student inquired why I programmed this film. I answered that its combination of different esthetic strategies to express a bold feminist content was intriguing. The film itself did not inject students with feminist consciousness, but instead opened a public sphere for women to speak that was typically unavailable in society. The discussion exploded. Because the film raised the specter of the female body, women students served as discursive experts while male students occupied a different, less dominant power relation to the film. The students learned that teachers can have definite theoretical orientations. Given the high pitch of the debate, at least students responded vociferously, rather than operating within a lobotomized, pluralistic, never-never land based on therapeutic models.

For a text, we use Bruce Kawin's *How Movies Work*, a general survey of film styles, genres, theory, filmmaking techniques, and the Hollywood industry. Because students advance into specialty theory and production classes in experimental, narrative, and documentary film, it remains vital to curricular health to guide them beyond their horizons. Over the years, we dumped texts stressing filmmaking techniques and equipment for three reasons: first, the equipment these books meticulously describe never matches our own 16mm gear; second, these texts overemphasize technology and technique beyond the reach of beginners; and third, they neutralize political and theoretical issues into fairly instrumental technical problems. We focus on how students can wield technology to find their own filmic voice, rather than privileging equipment and technical proficiency as the mark of a "good filmmaker."

We prefer a more critical, theoretical book that provides an overview of as many aspects of film production as possible, including film exhibition and distribution, to a more technical text driven by machinery. However, I should caution that employing a more critically oriented textbook for a production class places more demands on teachers. They must dispense a wide array of technical and esthetic "prescriptions" to students during critiques tailored to their individual ideas, their production problems, and their ideological snafus. Consequently, we never need to highlight the relationship between theory and practice. Our textbook epitomizes this dialectic, offering a critical language that can then be deployed by student and teacher alike in critiques. As one of my first-year students chirped, Kawin's text is really a Berlitz language guide to a foreign country called filmmaking.

The most successful introductory filmmaking classes spend more time on critique of student work than on explication of technology. Students arrive intimidated by 16mm technologies, so we try to frame cameras and editors as machines to be used for the student's own ends rather than as objects of fetishistic desire endemic to film students. The decentering of film technology (a politically charged intervention in the extremely well-equipped, state-of-the-art Roy H. Park School of Communications at Ithaca College) is a much more effective way to empower women students, who are often phobic about technology. We bolster student confidence in operating equipment through individualized tutorials with our teaching assistants, a more effective way to develop minimal exposure and focus skills than large group sessions, where women and minority students in particular can feel like outsiders.

Within this more democratic framework, a concept of struggle replaces the outmoded concept of professionalism. Students struggle with operating equipment, learning equipment check-out, dealing with the laboratory, generating an idea, and submitting to critiques. This terrain is volcanic. There will be pitched battles with students in the initial classes about whether they will ever learn "real," that is, classical Hollywood-style, filmmaking. That style is so tattooed into our unconscious that students cannot even see it. A film in the classical narrative style of seamless editing, changes in image size and camera angle, and cuts on action is perhaps the most difficult, complex task for a student still learning how to thread film into a Bell and Howell Filmo. Yet my students have enormous psychological and political investments, whether consciously or unconsciously, in Hollywood-style filmmaking. Therefore, our first assignment is a short narrative continuity film shot in our communications building. Amazingly, nearly all students find it difficult to grasp this style. After the first assignment (see Appendix), most prefer expressing themselves to imitating narrative rules.

This rather blasé assignment teaches students that the basic ingredient of filmmaking is not the rules, but who they themselves are and how they see the world through the camera. Most students have problems executing narrative. It looms over them so naturally—almost like the weather—that they never consider how it is constructed. Consequently, I have discovered that emphasizing composition and how one sees through the camera constitutes the first step toward liberating and then legitimating their differences in multiculturalism and difference. Most students, even the most media savvy, have no concept of composition and its ability to convey their subjectivity. We ask them to think of cameras and lights as chisels, sculpting order out of chaos and subjectivity out of commodification.

We foreground form and technique rather than content. I have found that the worst way to instill some sort of collective responsibility in students is to tell them to do it. Instead, we ask students to concentrate on the much more accessible formal issues of composition and editing. The films raise all sorts of issues about race, class, gender, sexual preference, and regionalism. By structuring assignments to progress from formal and craft issues to more specific personal explorations, the covert goal of the course becomes the development of one's own, distinctive filmmaking vision.

Skirmishes

In the larger political context of extreme antagonism toward creativity and difference in American culture, with rollbacks on civil rights and abortion, I do not want to overstate the effectiveness of these strategies for creating a classroom more attuned to race, class, sex, regionalism, and sexual preference. The marketing agendas of higher education impinge on introductory classes in complicated ways, weaving conservative ideologies of acquiescence to commercial media into the classroom. My professional context is much more dialectical and complicated than simply rejecting this marketing emphasis on "professional communications," a term defined differently by each one of my forty-five colleagues.

Precisely because the very marketing I abhor generates great demand, the Department of Cinema and Photography has been able to integrate theory and production and reconceptualize college-level filmmaking along more fine arts lines. Consequently, cinema faculty, like all workers in late capitalism, occupy a contradictory position with respect to this hype and simulation. As an intellectual, I find the marketing of conformity to the dominant media industry repulsive and antagonistic to critical inquiry. As a worker in the academy, I find its successful recruitment for our program bulwarks my department from the vicissitudes of recessionary fiscal times in the Academy.

The Roy H. Park School of Communications has always positioned itself as a hands-on professional program, which ultimately sanctions access to equipment rather than critical thinking. However, if you visited my workplace and asked anyone from the dean on down to the faculty and technical support staff, they would divulge their commitment to critical thinking and imaginative artmaking. Yet the smoke of "professional media education" infuses almost every agenda. This marketing extends into all Park School literature, underscoring small, intimate production classes in comparison to larger, impersonalized state universities. After all, the high cost of Ithaca College ensures access to professors and equipment, often referred to as "equivalents." This selling of intimacy and hands-on has direct consequences for production pedagogy. These conditions function as both ideological discourses and capitalization practices; they surround my introductory film production course like a fleet of Stealth bombers.

Our cinema curriculum reflects a much more traditional humanities and artistic tradition, which, in the swiftly changing media environment of the 1990s, provides the broadest intellectual and artistic skills to deal with a dramatically reconfigured media industry. Like media faculty everywhere, we have agitated for and implemented a program integrating theory and practice. On the most obvious level, no student may enroll in any film production course without a semester of a companion theory course. For instance, nonfiction film theory serves as the prerequisite for nonfiction production. Introduction to Film Aesthetics and Analysis is the prerequisite for beginning filmmaking. Linking theory and practice is so much a part of our everyday operations and curricular assumptions that we rarely debate it any more, a significant paradigm shift from the more argumentative early 1980s. As one of my newer colleagues, John Hess, puts it, whether you are making a film or writing a paper, we assume that you are engaged in some sort of intellectual inquiry.

Critiques: Bloodshed and Armistice

Nothing is debated more vigorously in cinema programs than how to manage critiques of student work. In my workplace, several schools of thought on critique strategies compete with one another: the supportive role, the mentor, the peer group of artists, the experienced critic, the artist, the theoretician, the agitator. A program resplendent with a wide array of production courses will flourish with diverse approaches to critique sessions. In smaller programs, a medley of critique styles may not be possible.

Student evaluations of production courses comment most frequently and exuberantly on critique sessions. In reviewing other faculty and in scrutinizing my evaluations, one of the most common complaints that students raise in the Park School is that the critiques are not "hard enough," suggesting, it seems to me, that students prefer learning openly about their problems and successes. Students often are so consumed with executing projects on the micro-level that they cannot access the more macro-levels of ideology and esthetics. When I deploy a more theoretical language to explain the political issues of representation and power raised when a student photographs the small black community in Ithaca with a traveling surveillance shot from the inside of a new Volvo, the students listen more intently. No longer "just my opinion," my comments become part of a larger argument on culture and representation that includes them as participants.

Some of my colleagues, in contrast, conceive of the production classroom as a therapy group that nurtures students' individual, artistic, emotional expression, an idiosyncrasy of art schools and photography programs mired in nineteenth-century conceptions of the artist as an isolated artisan exploring subjectivity. In the context of an extremely industry-oriented professional school like the Park School, this position is not as reactionary as it might initially seem. Any focus on individuality and personal expression combats the more robotic approach of conditioning students in the proper execution of media forms for entry-level jobs. These more "artistically oriented" classes use theory to figure out how "feelings" could become more authentic and to raise issues of representation when feelings entice students into more politically volatile representations, such as nudes or images of people with AIDS. Such courses privilege making media as an exploration of individuality and emotion, tropes proffering terms like *intuition, inspiration, creativity,* and *emotional responsiveness* that constitute very conservative, elitist, and often inaccessible structures of art making.

Although the construct of "artist" resists commodity capitalism and mass production, it unfortunately foregrounds an obsession with narcissistic individuality and solipsistic creativity rather than empowerment of students through collective experiences and responsible participation in the world. Too much reliance on individuality as a structuring concept in film production classes isolates students, enforcing competition in a mode of production requiring the cooperation of other people to hold lights, move dollies, and serve as actors. Too much of an obsession with creativity, in my experience, erects a covert class system. Only upper-class students who have had access to camcorders, rental video, and well-heeled suburban schools that taught media production are deemed "creative." Women and minority students are alienated and shop for a new major. A more productive orientation seizes these individualized, emotional, and personal feelings as starting points and then integrates them within more contextual modes, such as interrogating how women are positioned within student narratives.

We toss out terms like *creativity, individual expression, talent, feelings,* and *searches for authenticity* and instead concentrate on helping students find their own voice. We work to make the classroom a participatory, team environment where different sections possess what one

student terms "section pride," a way to replace competition with collective identity. Our film production classrooms are charged yet supportive arenas for struggle over skills acquisition, generation of ideas
specific to each student's experience, and execution of technical and
creative skill.

In critiques, the easiest way to broach difficult issues of politics and
representation is actually to concentrate on the formal and technical construction of the students' work first. We analyze composition,
lighting, exposure, focus, and editing as specifically as possible. Then,
we find remedies. We always focus on whether the student's concept
is conveyed clearly. If a film crosses into a racist representation, students can draw on the formal parts of the critique to explain how and
why rather than to simply assert. Ironically, this inversion of form over
content actually can spark much more complex discussions about the
politics of representation.

Partial Victories and Small Liberations

Filmmaking classes have a simple goal: to make filmmaking, one of
the most inaccessible and expensive of all the arts, accessible. Mistakes
like exposure problems cannot be repaired as easily as argumentative errors in film theory papers. Films require money, a scarce resource for most students. Therefore, we rarely suggest reshooting.
Rather, we direct students to forge a film from out-takes in the bins.
This strategy concentrates on editing, rather than reshooting, and
does not require money for film stock. Some student and faculty
detractors denigrate the resulting films as avant-garde compilations.
However, filmmaking students see them as inexpensive, fascinating
solutions to production problems.

One phrase my teaching partner Marcelle Pecot and I repeat over
and over again is "turn your liabilities into your asset." If you don't
have lots of lights, use what you have. If you can't deal with actors,
make a film without them. If you can't figure out narrative continuity, find a new style you understand. If your film is overexposed, hand
color it. If your voice-over sounds stilted, reedit your footage. We focus
on process, not product. No matter how creative our students want
to be, we institute limitations on how much footage they can shoot
for each of the three assignments. We limit them in the first assignment to fifty feet and in the final two assignments to two hundred
feet of rushes. These restrictions foreground ideas and flatten out
class privilege that allows some students to not even have to think
about how much it costs to shoot a thousand feet of reversal. Besides

equalizing financial and class differences, students can feel more empowered editing smaller amounts of footage.

In 1991 I had the somewhat unsavory and time-consuming task of revising the introductory course from its total focus on conventional narrative style based on murder films (a legacy of my film school over the past twenty-five years) toward a survey of different styles to prepare students better for upper-division specialty courses. Marcelle Pecot and I emphasized two simple goals in our revision: first, concentrating on film craft and form to make sure everyone could focus, expose, and compose with comfort and ease; and second, emphasizing that each student should explore something in themselves, rather than copying from Hollywood narrative or fretting about creativity.

Our Introduction to Film Production course has been team taught for more than a decade. Our commitment to including more international and multicultural films stems as much from our experiences dealing with alienated, despairing film students as it does from our intellectual and political commitments to advancing production as an empowering experience for more than Hollywoodized white males from the New York City suburbs. Both Marcelle Pecot and I are interested in theory and production. I have a Ph.D. and write about documentary film history; she has a M.F.A. and makes films. I serve as the film scholar, while Marcelle is the working filmmaker. Marcelle has extensive professional postproduction, commercial editing experience and works as an experimental filmmaker and animator. Before joining the academy, I worked as a television producer for an affiliate of the Spanish International Network and as a researcher for an independent documentary production house in Madison, Wisconsin.

Our professional and academic experience grounds two claims: first, the fluidity of filmic modes and strategies in one's life practice; second, the intricate maze of constantly shifting relationships among theory and practice, mass cultural practice, and a culture celebrating difference. We continually emphasize that this theoretical concept of difference informs the practical structure of the course: filmmaker and scholar, senior faculty person and junior faculty person, documentary and avant-garde, independent and commercial cinema, and different regions of the country (no small issue of cultural difference in the myopic Northeast—Marcelle is from Louisiana and Creole, I am from Chicago and Irish and German). We are firmly committed to a conflict between all of these different forms so as not to foreground narrative or documentary, and to encourage students to find their way by piecing together parts of these various practices. We insist that this diversity among the faculty will open a realm of undiscovered possibilities in students, recasting filmmaking from socialization into the dominant apparatus into an activity of creative discovery of individual specificity and interconnection with larger political and social issues.

Truce

The goals of a film production teacher are much simpler than the discursive framework attempting to control film production itself: to help each student produce something meaningful that they would want to show to other people in public. Filmmaking teachers should provide skills and strategies, not recipes for reproducing either the dominant ideology (increasingly difficult to locate in this multinational, postmodern age) or the politically correct line on race, class, sex, or the avant-garde. All films, particularly student films, are not static constructs awaiting deconstruction. They are vital, living things, engaged in a continual process of interaction—not always polite—with their audiences. Perhaps the student film is the most exciting film genre of all because it is the most open to interaction and change. Students produce films within engaged communities: the small, often competitive community of the film school or the production class. Most film schools swallow Hollywood competitiveness as a common-sensical norm. Every teacher knows that this ideology suffocates students who could only fantasize about making movies because their families were not wealthy enough to own camcorders.

If Marcelle Pecot and I have implemented anything in our teaching from critical film theory from the 1960s onward, it is to always maintain a dialectical stance toward student work, accepting it in a constant state of metamorphosis. Although we raise many issues about the representation of women and people of color, we never advocate a politically correct style or content. Instead, we concentrate on compositional design to elaborate concepts and emphasize detail to avoid reproducing cheap imitations of television.

To preempt the fascination with Hollywood, we screen a wide range of experimental, documentary, and narrative film to provide different role models and artistic strategies. We screen shorter films rather than features because longer narrative and documentary films depend so much on structure that their visual and conceptual strategies can be hard for beginners to decipher. Screening lots of different kinds of films not available in video stores positions spectatorship as something more than recreational viewing. We use a multicultural framework in our selection of films screened for the course (for example, we are always searching for shorts by women and people of color), but we rarely discuss the term *multicultural*. We have screened everything from Yugoslavian animation, to Soviet documentaries, to African-American alternative rap films, to Marlon Riggs's *Tongues Untied*, to the early works of Gus Van Sant, to alternative animation by Joanna Priestly, to a British black feminist film called *The Body Beautiful*, to clips from *The Godfather*, to *Meshes of the Afternoon*.

During the lectures, we stress perceiving visual and conceptual strategies. We compare them to other work screened in the course, assessing their content, argumentative, and visual differences. We often use the consumerist-inflected metaphor of "shopping for strategies" to describe how students should engage the work as active filmmakers rather than as passive viewers.

Working under this new system of diversification for several years, we have never had a student complaint about screenings. Because students do not wish to miss a screening of something to which they would have no other access, attendance is high. It is important to acknowledge the particular perks of working within the financially stable environment of the Roy H. Park School of Communications, where we enjoy sizable film rental budgets. Also, our course is organized with two seventy-five-minute lectures and screenings before the laboratory sessions, so time is not pinched between screening and critiques.

Postwar Fallout

In May 1992, Marcelle Pecot and I publicly screened seventy-five student films produced in our beginning filmmaking class. The screening culminated our introductory production class; more advanced juniors and seniors, as well as friends and parents, attended. The two-hundred-plus-seat auditorium bulged with people. The last film assignment, dubbed the personal explorations film project, requires a three-minute film revealing a unique personal story. Our only guideline is that at least two different filmmaking strategies, such as documentary and narrative or experimental and diary, are combined.

For this assignment, most of the students fashion films from their immediate lives: mononucleosis, their parents' divorce, a friend who died in high school, their fears about college, sports, a deceased parent, accidents, lost loves, or black consciousness. In explaining our expectations for the assignment, we emphasize the students' unique point of view. As they admit trepidation about revealing themselves on film, we say, "Take us where we can't go without you."

Nearly all of the films shown in May 1992 combined many different genres and strategies, but essentially they all told stories concretely located in the students' lives. One woman made a powerful film about her inability to deal with her mother's mastectomy. One animated film chronicled a young man in the dormitory trying to avoid eating ice cream. One film explored the anxiety of looking for a book in the library for a research paper, shot entirely in hand-held point-of-view shot with eerie music. The most successful deployed innovative, well-focused, and well-exposed shooting to relate a very detailed, unique story. However, all was not well in paradise.

Two white male students produced films criticizing us and our assignments. Their critique vindicates our success. The second assignment is called "visual explorations and montage rhythms," an assignment focusing specifically on composition, lighting, and editing to resolve the esthetic deficiencies of the continuity exercise. No story line is allowed; projects must use composition and lighting to convey a feeling or concept. Each term, a few students, generally those already possessing a certain amount of media proficiency from high school, balk at the assignment as overly avant-garde. They exclaim that they know how to shoot well and continually overrate their compositional skills.

The two contentious films were produced by filmmakers continually distressed that we were not teaching horror, war, and detective film style and special effects. The films contended that the Park School censored creativity by prohibiting narrative filmmaking and enforcing the production of avant-garde feminist films. Ironically, both interventions depended on documentary and avant-garde techniques: analytical intertitles, direct address, metaphorical imagery, and montage editing. One beautifully photographed and viscerally edited film featured two men clad in military attire and fighting each other, interrupted by intertitles decrying the Roy H. Park School as a rabid censor. The second film featured a young man walking around campus and encountering various roadblocks (like groups of people or construction barriers), with a voice-over excoriating the "ban on regular filmmaking." His film used extremely surrealistic shooting and mise-en-scène.

What interested me about these projects was not their protest, which in some perverse way I actually enjoyed, but how it betrayed the embattled nature of any attempt to decenter the dominant mode.

When experimental, feminist, documentary, international, third world, and independent narrative films were profusely screened to create a more multicultural, pluralistic framework, an extremely small group of white males unwilling to explore other avenues of filmmaking was the most threatened. Ironically, more than 55 percent of the lectures in the course explore narrative film. We also screen a broad array of international narrative films in many different filmmaking styles. Clearly, these two male students equated Hollywood with narrative. Everything else was avant-garde junk to them.

What we learned from the experience is that when other genres and producers diversify the more traditional mix of Hitchcock and Coppola (filmmakers we actually screen), the perception among some students and even colleagues is that our survey of film strategies had veered into the avant-garde ether. When two feminists teach introductory film production, male colleagues position the entire terrain of introductory film production as unstable and dangerous. When white male students addicted to classical narratives featuring macho fight scenes became class rebels, we knew that our pluralizing of film screenings and extension of the range of debates in critiques had been effective. In my undergraduate days, the class rebels were the one or two women who ventured into film production.

Despite the proliferation of pedagogical theories, despite the national debates on political correctness and multiculturalism, despite the attempts of Whittle Communications to create a plan for a new private school system aimed at solving the problems of the public schools, teachers still learn how to teach on a micro level. New faculty in my department never ask how to be more multicultural in their classrooms. They ask what films to show or how to deal with a racist film project characterizing a black man as a drug-dealing criminal. Teaching film production weaves theory into the classroom and the student through immersion, debate, and interaction. A good class also accomplishes something else for students: a utopian zone where they can create and argue without punishment. That something else is often hard to define, and even more difficult to predict, but it occurs when the class, with the professor as leader and authority and the students as explorers, discovers something that changes how all will think about visual representation and theory. It is something that makes the debates feel physical, worth fighting for, and part of one's life. For those who teach filmmaking at the beginning level, focus and exposure, in a technical as well as ideological sense, are the goals.

Appendix: Syllabus for 22-210: Introduction to Film Production (Ithaca College)

COURSE OBJECTIVES

This course is organized as a studio course. During the first class each week there will be lectures focusing on technical, theoretical, esthetic, and economic aspects of film; the second class each week will feature film screenings and discussion relevant to the previous class's lecture. Labs will concentrate on in-class critiques of student work.

This course is designed to introduce the student to a focused yet diverse experience of filmmaking. It provides a broad overview of all aspects of the film process: technique, esthetics, theory, economics, and social and political issues. A primary goal of the course is to demystify filmmaking and to empower students to produce their own unique vision. To ensure that this goal is met, the course will stress basic techniques of film production, from concept, composition, lighting, and editing.

As a survey of filmmaking techniques, the course will introduce the student to a broad and diverse survey of filmic strategies: narrative continuity, new narrative, documentary, documentary essay, experimental, animation, and mixed genres. Students should achieve basic competence in the use of basic filmmaking equipment, including 16mm cameras, lenses, light meters, lights, sound recorders, microphones, editing benches, and upright moviolas.

REQUIRED TEXT

Bruce Kawin, *How Movies Work* (Berkeley: University of California Press, 1992).

SUGGESTED READING

Arthur L. Gaskill, and David A. Englander, *How to Shoot a Movie Story,* 4th ed. (Dobbs Ferry: Morgan Press, 1985).
Spike Lee, *Do the Right Thing: A Spike Lee Joint* (New York: Simon and Schuster, 1989).
Lenny Lipton, *Independent Filmmaking* (New York: Simon and Schuster, 1983).
Gerald Millerson, *The Technique of Lighting for Television and Motion Pictures,* 3d ed. (Stoneham: Butterworth, 1991).
John Sayles, *Thinking in Pictures,* 3d ed. (New York: Houghton Mifflin, 1987).
Shawn Slovo, *A World Apart* (London: Faber and Faber, 1990).
Douglas Underdahl, *16mm Help Book* (New York: Media Logic of New York, 1993).

FILMMAKING REQUIREMENTS

1. Students must shoot at least thirty feet of camera tests using all three lenses and changing film speed for slow or fast motion.

2. Students must shoot with a partner.

3. Students must shoot a narrative film for continuity style.

4. Students must shoot an activity that shows overlapping action.

5. Each short film must contain a minimum of four scenes.

6. Each short film must maintain proper screen direction and proper screen continuity.

7. Each short film must vary image size and camera angle for every shot.

8. Each short film must contain a cutaway to a scene outside the ongoing action.

DISCUSSION TOPICS, READINGS, SCREENINGS, AND LAB WORK

Week 1

1. Introduction to course and lab assisting; student films; film versus video, *Buzz Box;* read Kawin, *How Movies Work,* 120–56.

2. Film handling/threading; projectors; groups assigned; exposure self-help assigned; exposure/editing exercise assigned.

Week 2

1. Camera/exposure/continuity editing; pictorial continuity; Hitchcock clip; read Kawin, *How Movies Work,* 157–77.

2. Short narrative films: *Great Train Robbery, Trip to the Moon, Life and Death of a Hollywood Extra, Java Junkie, Trouble with Fred;* read Kawin, *How Movies Work,* 178–90.

3. Light meters/B&H cameras; editing bench procedures.

Week 3

1. Frame composition (slides from films); read Kawin, *How Movies Work,* 201–42.

2. Composition analysis; clips of *The Godfather,* parts 1 and 2; read Kawin, *How Movies Work,* 243–63.

3. Lighting exercises (low key, high key, people, places).

Week 4

1. Films illuminating light as form: *Lemon, New York, Near Sleep;* read Kawin, *How Movies Work,* 264–85.

2. VPMR film assignment explained; classical film lighting; read Kawin, *How Movies Work,* 539–57.

3. Critique camera/editing exercise.

Week 5

1. Montage rhythms: quoting and stealing, part 1: narrative and montage; *La Jetée, Meshes of the Afternoon,* read Kawin, *How Movies Work,* 2–44.

2. Montage rhythms: quoting and stealing, part 2: Hollywood style; *Flashdance;* read Kawin, *How Movies Work,* 45–58.

3. Critique camera exposure/editing exercise; critique VPMR film rushes.

Week 6

1. U.S. animation; *Rubber Stamp Film;* Pooh Kaye film, *Wake Up Call;* read Kawin, *How Movies Work,* 59–96.
2. International animation; *Broken Down Film, Fly, Pica Don, Resistance, Darkness Light Darkness.*
3. Critique VPMR film rushes and VPMR film rough-cuts.

Week 7

1. New narrative cinema: tales from the Winnipeg Film Group; read Kawin, *How Movies Work,* 97–117.
2. Experimental film: ways of seeing; Jane Campion shorts; read Kawin, *How Movies Work,* 191–200.
3. Critique VPMR film rushes and VPMR film rough-cuts.

Week 8

1. Experimental film: personal explorations in cinema; *The Body Beautiful;* read Kawin, *How Movies Work,* 288–301.

Week 9

1. U.S. documentary film; video: cinema department student documentaries; read Kawin, *How Movies Work,* 302–26.
2. International documentary film; Glasnost Film Festival (thirty minutes on punks); read Kawin, *How Movies Work,* 327–61.
3. Sound room demonstration; VPMR film rough-cut critique.

Week 10

1. VPMR film festival; read Kawin, *How Movies Work,* 362–409.
2. VPMR film festival; read Kawin, *How Movies Work,* 410–80.
3. Critique PE film and sound rough-cuts.

Week 11

1. Lagniappe: everything but production (funding, censorship, grants, film festivals, distribution); *Hairway to the Stars.*
2. Lagniappe screening: censored films; *Tongues Untied;* read Kawin, *How Movies Work,* 481–521.
3. Critique PE film and sound rough-cuts.

Week 12

1. Before you go to Hollywood: early work of Gus Van Sant; *The Discipline of D.E., Fly Elaine, Nightmare Typhoon, My Friend, My New Friend.*
2. Economics and politics of Hollywood.
3. Critique PE film and sound rough-cuts; PE fine-cuts due.

Week 13

1. International film scene; *Island of Flowers, TAUW.*

2. Emerging international cinema.
3. PE fine-cuts due.

Week 14

1. The cutting edge, part 1; Park School senior films.
2. Four shorts by the Brothers Quay.
3. PE fine-cuts due.

Week 15

1. Preprofessional opportunities: profit corporation internships.
2. Preprofessional opportunities: nonprofit institution internships.
3. Final critique of all groups to check for screening.

Week 16

1. Final film screening (replaces written final).

Notes

The ideas developed in this chapter owe much to my past and present colleagues in the Department of Cinema and Photography, who have debated and discussed the meaning of teaching film production with me. For their help in thinking through these ideas, I would like to thank Marcelle Pecot, R. William Rowley, Skip Landen, Steve Tropiano, Deborah Fort, Ann Skinner-Jones, John Hess, and Scott Nygren.

1. My theoretical ideas on multiculturalism and pedagogy are informed by feminism, poststructuralism, and civil rights, For more thorough and systematic discussions, see bell hooks, *Yearning;* Paulo Freire, *The Politics of Education;* Henry Giroux, ed. *Postmodernism, Feminism, and Cultural Politics;* and Henry Giroux, *Border Crossings.*
2. There has been an outpouring of popular magazine articles and books on political correctness, multiculturalism, and the curriculum. These rightwing attacks on higher education assumed to be polluted by hordes of radicals constitute a much wider and more philosophically damaging deliberate disintegration of public spaces, public culture, and the public sphere by neoconservatives. As education becomes one of the last domains for open public discussion in a society where almost all communication is controlled by multinational media corporations, the debates on culture have become particularly pitched.

It is my contention that as U.S. economic power declines and shifts into other sites of production around the world, U.S. hegemony grips more tightly to culture and education. In other words, as the economy shifts from a national manufacturing to a transitional information economy, social control of the superstructure of the arts, culture, and education becomes more urgent for conservatives. For three very different discussions of these movements of social control, see Dinesh D'Souza, *Illiberal Education;* Mas'ud Zavarzadeh, *Seeing Films Politically;* and Herbert I. Schiller, *Culture Inc.*

Bibliography

Ahmad, Aijaz. "Jameson's Rhetoric of Otherness and the 'National Allegory.'" *Social Text* 17 (1986–87).

Alarcón, Norma. "The Theoretical Subject(s) of *This Bridge Called My Back* and Anglo-American Feminism." In *Making Faces, Making Soul, Haciendo Caras: Creative and Critical Perspectives by Women of Color*. Edited by Gloria Anzaldúa. San Francisco: Aunt Lute Foundation Books, 1990.

Alcoff, Linda. "Cultural Feminism versus Poststructuralism: The Identity Crisis in Feminist Theory." *Signs: Journal of Women in Culture and Society* 13, no. 3 (1988): 405–36.

———. "The Problem of Speaking for Others." *Cultural Critique* (Winter 1991–92): 5–32.

Alexander, Karen. "Fatal Beauties: Black Women in Hollywood." In *Stardom: Industry of Desire*. Edited by Christine Gledhill. London: Routledge, 1991.

Allouache, Merzak. "The Necessity of a Cinema Which Interrogates Everyday Life." In *Film and Politics in the Third World*. Edited by John Downing. New York: Autonomedia, 1987.

Althusser, Louis. "Ideology and Ideological State Apparatuses (Notes Towards an Investigation)." In *Lenin and Philosophy and Other Essays*. 1971. Translated by Ben Brewster. New York: Monthly Review Press, 1972.

Alvarez, Rodolfo. "The Psycho-historical and Socioeconomic Development of the Chicago Community in the United States." In *The Mexican American Experience: An Interdisciplinary Anthology*, 33–56. Edited by Rodolfo O. de la Garza. Austin: University of Texas Press, 1985.

Anderman, Janusz. *The Edge of the World*. New York: Reader's International, 1988.

Anderson, Carolyn, and Thomas Benson. "Direct Cinema and the Myth of Informed Consent." In *Image Ethics: The Moral Right of Subjects in Photographs, Film, and Television*. Edited by Larry Gross, John Katz, and Jay Ruby. New York: Oxford University Press, 1988.

Appadurai, Arjun, and Carole Breckenridge. "Buying the Nation: Advertising and Heritage in Contemporary India." Paper presented to the Social Science Research Council Symposium on Advertising, Consumption and the New Middle Class in India, 1991.

Arguelles, Lourdes, and B. Ruby Rich. "Homosexuality, Homophobia, and Revolution: Notes toward an Understanding of the Cuban Lesbian and Gay Male Experience. Part 1." *Signs* 9 (Summer 1984): 683–99; "Part 2." *Signs* 11 (Autumn 1985): 120–36.

Arguelles, Lourdes, and B. Ruby Rich. "Reply to Montaner." *Signs* 11 (Winter 1986): 416.

Arlen, Michael. "The Prosecutor." In *New Challenges for Documentary*. Edited by Alan Rosenthal. Berkeley: University of California Press, 1988.

Aronowitz, Stanley, and Henry A. Giroux. *Education under Seige: The Conservative, Liberal and Radical Debate over Schooling.* New York: Bergin and Garvey, 1985.

Artel, Linda, and Susan Wengraf. "Positive Images: Screening Women's Films." In *Jump Cut: Hollywood, Politics and Counter Cinema*, 199–202. Edited by Peter Steven. New York: Praeger, 1985.

Asad, Talal. "The Concept of Cultural Translation in British Social Anthropology." In *Writing Culture: The Poetics and Politics of Ethnography*. Edited by James Clifford and George Marcus. Berkeley: University of California Press, 1986.

Asante, Molefi Kete. "Multiculturalism: An Exchange." *American Scholar* 60 (Spring 1991): 267–76.

Aufderheide, Patricia, ed. *Beyond PC: Toward a Politics of Understanding.* St. Paul: Graywolf Press, 1992.

———."The Maghreb." Arab Film Festival (handout). Washington, D. C., 1991.

Bakhtin, M. M. *Speech Genres and Other Late Essays.* Translated by V. W. McGee. Edited by C. Emerson and M. Holquist. Austin: University of Texas Press, 1986.

Banks, James A. *Teaching Ethnic Studies.* 5th edition. Boston: Allyn and Bacon, 1991.

Banner, Lois. *American Beauty.* Chicago: University of Chicago Press, 1983.

Barnouw, Erik. *Documentary: A History of the Non-fiction Film.* New York: Oxford University Press, 1974.

———. *Tube of Plenty: The Evalution of American Television,* 2d ed., rev. New York: Oxford University Press, 1990.

Barry, Ann. "Quilting Has African Roots, a New Exhibition Suggests." *New York Times,* November 16, 1989.

Barthes, Roland. *Mythologies.* New York: Hill and Wang, 1972.

Becker, Edith, Michelle Citron, Julia Lesage, and B. Ruby Rich. "Lesbians and Film." In *Jump-Cut: Hollywood, Politics and Counter-Cinema.* Edited by Peter Stevens. Toronto: Between the Lines, 1985.

Belenky, Mary Field, et al. *Women's Ways of Knowing.* New York: Basic Books, 1986.

Bell-Scott, Patricia, et al., eds. *Double Stitch: Black Women Write about Mothers and Daughters.* Boston: Beacon Press, 1991.

Benjamin, Andrew, ed. *The Lyotard Reader.* London: Blackwell, 1989.

Benjamin, Jessica. *The Bonds of Love: Psychoanalysis, Feminism, and the Problem of Domination.* New York: Pantheon, 1988.

Berg, Charles Ramírez. "*Bordertown:* The Assimilation Narrative and the Chicano Social Problem Film." In *Chicanos and Film: Representation and Resistance.* Edited by Chon Noriega. Minneapolis: University of Minnesota Press, 1992.

————."Images and Counterimages of the Hispanic in Hollywood." *Tonantzin* 6, no. 1 (1988): 12–13.

————. "Immigrants, Aliens, and Extraterrestrials: Science Fiction's Alien 'Other' as (among *Other* Things) New Hispanic Imagery." *Cineaction* 18 (Fall 1989): 3–17.

————."Stereotyping in Films in General and of the Hispanic in Particular." *Howard Journal of Communications* 2 (Summer 1990): 286–300.

Berger, Arthur Asa. *Media Analysis Techniques.* Revised edition. Newbury Park: Sage Publications, 1991.

Berger, John. *Ways of Seeing.* London: BBC-Penguin Books, 1988.

Berger, John, and Jean Mohr. *Another Way of Telling.* New York: Pantheon Books, 1982.

Berry, Chris. "Market Forces: China's 'Fifth Generation' Faces the Bottom Line." In *Perspectives on Chinese Cinema,* 114–25. Edited by Chris Berry. Bloomington: Indiana University Press, 1991.

Berube, Michael. "Untitled." In *Beyond PC: Toward a Politics of Understanding.* Edited by Patricia Aufderheide. St. Paul: Graywolf Press, 1992.

Bhabha, Homi. "Signs Taken for Wonders." *Critical Inquiry* 12, no. 1 (1985): 144–65.

Biberman, Herbert. Salt of the Earth: *The Story of a Film.* Boston: Beacon Press, 1965.

Blue, James, and Michael Gill. "Peter Watkins Discusses His Suppressed Nuclear Film, *The War Game.*" *Film Comment* 3, no. 4 (1965): 14–19.

Bobo, Jacqueline. "Black Women in Fiction and Nonfiction: Images of Power and Powerlessness." *Wide Angle* 13, nos. 3–4 (1991): 72–81.

————. *"The Color Purple:* Black Women's Responses." *Jump Cut* 33 (February 1988): 43–51.

Bogle, Donald. *Brown Sugar: Eighty Years of America's Black Female Superstars.* New York: Da Capo, 1990.

————. *Toms, Coons, Mulattoes, Mammies, and Bucks: An Interpretive History of Blacks in American Films.* New York: Continuum Press, 1989.

Boles, John. "Let the Screen Stars Teach You How to Make Love." *Serenade: The Illustrated Love Magazine* (June 1934).

Bourdieu, Pierre. *Outline of a Theory of Practice.* Cambridge: Cambridge University Press, 1977.

Bowser, Pearl. "Sexual Imagery and the Black Woman in Cinema." In *Black Cinema Aesthetics: Issues in Independent Black Filmmaking.* Edited by Gladstone Yearwood. Athens: Center for Afro-American Studies, Ohio University, 1982.

Boyarin, Jonathan. *Storm from Paradise: The Politics of Jewish Memory.* Minneapolis: University of Minnesota Press, 1992.

Boyd, Todd. "The Meaning of the Blues." *Wide Angle* 13, nos. 3–4 (1991): 56–61.

Brauchli, Marcus W. "Cost of Growth: China's Environment Is Severely Stressed as Its Industry Surges." *Wall Street Journal,* July 25, 1994, A1, A5.

Breckenridge, Carole, and Peter Van der Veer. *Orientalism and the Post-Colonial Predicament.* Philadelphia: University of Pennsylvania Press, 1993.

Brent, Linda. *Incidents in the Life of a Slave Girl.* Edited by L. Maria Child. New York: Harcourt, Brace, 1973.

Brooks, Peter. "Fictions of the Wolf Man: Freud and Narrative Understanding." In *Reading for the Plot.* New York: Random House, 1984.

Broughton, James. *Seeing the Light.* San Francisco: City Lights, 1977.

Burch, Noel. *To the Distant Observer: Form and Meaning in the Japanese Cinema.* Berkeley: University of California Press, 1979.

Burchell, Julie. *Girls on Film.* New York: Pantheon, 1986.

Burroughs, William. "Screenwriting and the Potentials of Cinema." In *Writing in a Film Age: Essays by Contemporary Novelists.* Edited by Keith Cohen. Niwot: University Press of Colorado, 1991.

Burton, Julianne, ed. *Cinema and Social Change in Latin America: Conversations with Filmmakers.* Austin: University of Texas Press, 1986.

———, ed. *The Social Documentary in Latin America.* Pittsburgh: University of Pittsburgh Press, 1990.

Caldarola, Victor. "Reading the Television Text in Outer Indonesia." Paper presented at the meeting of the American Anthropological Association, 1991.

Callahan, W. A. "Gender, Ideology, Nation: *Ju Dou* in the Cultural Politics of China." *East-West Film Journal* 7 (January 1993): 52–80.

Campbell, Bebe Moore. "Myths about Black Female Sexuality." *Essence* 19 (April 1989): 71–72, 108, 113.

Carby, Hazel. *Restructuring Womanhood: The Emergence of the Afro-American Woman Novelist.* New York: Oxford University Press, 1987.

Carelli, Vincent. "Video in the Villages: Utilization of Videotapes as an Instrument of Ethnic Affirmation among Brazilian Indian Groups." n.d. [photocopy].

Carr, Steven. "Attack Theory: Re-Evaluating P.C." *The Polemicist* 3 (1992): 3.

Carson, Diane, Linda Dittmar, and Janice Welsch, eds. *Multiple Voices in Feminist Film Criticism.* Minneapolis: University of Minnesota Press, 1994.

Cham, Mbye D., and Claire Andrade-Watkins, eds. *Blackframes: Critical Perspectives on Independent Black Cinema.* Cambridge: MIT Press, 1988.

Chametzky, Jules. "Beyond Melting Pots, Cultural Pluralism, Ethnicity—or *Deja Vu* All Over Again." *Melus* 16 (Winter 1989–90): 3–17.

Clark, Paul. *Chinese Cinema: Culture and Politics since 1949.* Bloomington: Indiana University Press, 1991.

Clifford, James, and George Marcus, eds. *Writing Culture: The Poetics and Politics of Ethnography.* Berkeley: University of California Press, 1986.

Cohen, Keith. *Film and Fiction: The Dynamics of Exchange.* New Haven: Yale University Press, 1979.

———, ed. *Writing in a Film Age: Essays by Contemporary Novelists.* Niwot: University Press of Colorado, 1991.

Cole, Johnnetta. *All American Women: Lines That Divide, Ties That Bind.* New York: Free Press, 1986.

Collins, Patricia Hill. "The Social Construction of Black Feminist Thought." In *Black Women in America: Social Science Perspectives.* Edited by Micheline R. Malson. Chicago: University of Chicago Press, 1990.

Combahee River Collective. "A Black Feminist Statement." In *This Bridge Called My Back: Writing by Radical Women of Color.* Edited by Cherríe Moraga and Gloria Anzaldúa. New York: Kitchen Table Press, 1986.

Corso, P. J. "Sexist Language in the Press." *Editor and Publisher* (October 1991).

Cortés, Carlos E. "Hollywood Interracial Love: Social Taboo as Screen Titillation." In *Plot Conventions in American Popular Film.* Edited by Paul Loukides and Linda K. Fuller. Bowling Green: Bowling Green State University Press, 1991.

———. "Pride, Prejudice and Power: The Mass Media as Societal Educator on Diversity." In *Prejudice, Polemic, or Progress.* Edited by James Lynch, Celia Modgil, and Sohan Modgil. London: Falmer Press, 1992.

———. "The Societal Curriculum: Implications for Multiethnic Education." In *Education in the Eighties: Multiethnic Education.* Edited by James A. Banks. Washington, D.C.: National Education Association, 1981.

Coward, Rosalind. *Female Desires: How They Are Sought, Bought and Packaged.* New York: Grove Press, 1984.

Crary, Jonathan. *Techniques of the Observer: On Vision and Modernity in the Nineteenth Century.* Cambridge: MIT Press, 1990.

Crawford, Peter, and David Turton, eds. *Film as Ethnography.* Manchester: University of Manshester Press, 1992.

Cripps, Thomas. *Black Film as Genre.* Bloomington: Indiana University Press, 1978.

Dasenbrock, Reed Way. "The Multicultural West." In *Beyond PC: Toward a Politics of Understanding.* Edited by Patricia Aufderheide. St. Paul: Graywolf Press, 1992.

———. "Teaching Multicultural Literature." In *Understanding Others: Cultural and Cross-Cultural Studies and the Teaching of Literature.* Edited by Joseph Trimmer and Tilly Warnock. Urbana: National Council of Teachers of English, 1992.

Dash, Julie. Daughters of the Dust: *The Making of an African American Woman's Film.* New York: New Press, 1992.

Dash, Julie, and Sharon Larkin. "New Images, and Interview with Julie Dash and Alile Sharon Larkin." *The Independent* (December 1986).

Davis, Angela. *Woman, Culture, and Politics.* New York: Random House, 1989.

———. "Black Women and Music: A Historical Legacy of Struggle." In *Wild Women in the Whirlwind: Afra-American Culture and the Contemporary Literary Renaissance.* New Brunswick: Rutgers University Press, 1990.

Davis, Gayle. "Women's Frontier Diaries: Writing for Good Reason." *Women's Studies: An Interdisciplinary Journal* 14 (1987): 5–14.

Davis, Zeinabu irene. *"Daughters of the Dust:* Interview with Julie Dash." *Black Film Review* 6, no. 1 (1991): 12–19.

———. "An Interview with Julie Dash." *Wide Angle* 13, nos. 3–4 (1991): 110–19.

Dearborn, Mary. *Pocahontas's Daughters: Gender and Ethnicity in American Culture.* New York: Oxford University Press, 1986.

DeFleur, Melvin L., and Sandra Ball-Rokeach. *Theories of Mass Communication.* 4th edition. New York: Longman, 1982.

De Lauretis, Teresa. *Technologies of Gender: Essays on Theory, Film, and Fiction.* Bloomington: Indiana University Press, 1987.

Dent, Gina, ed. *Black Popular Culture: A Project of Michelle Wallace.* Seattle: Bay Press, 1992.

Desnöes, Edmundo. "Cuba Made Me So" and "The Death System." In *On Signs.* Edited by Marshall Blonsky. Baltimore: Johns Hopkins University Press, 1985.

————. "The Photographic Image of Underdevelopment." *Jump Cut* 33 (1988): 69–81.

Diawara, Manthia. *Black American Cinema.* New York: Routledge, 1993.

————. "Black Spectatorship: Problems of Identification and Resistance." *Screen* 29 (Autumn 1988): 66–76.

————. "Oral Literature and African Film: Narratology in *Wend Kuuni.*" In *Questions of Third Cinema.* Edited by Jim Pines and Paul Willemen. London: BFI Publishers, 1989.

Ding, Loni. "Strategies of an Asian-American Filmmaker." In *Moving the Image: Independent Asian Pacific American Media Arts.* Los Angeles: UCLA Asian American Studies Center and Visual Communications, Southern California Asian American Studies, Central, Inc., 1991.

Dissanayake, Wimal, and Malti Sahai. *Sholay: A Cultural Reading.* Delhi: Wiley Eastern, 1992.

Dittmar, Linda. "Inclusionary Practices: The Politics of Syllabus Design." *Journal of Thought* [special issue on feminist education], 20, no. 3 (1985): 37–47.

Doane, Mary Ann. "The Economy of Desire: The Commodity Form in/of the Cinema." *Quarterly Review of Film and Video* 11 (1989): 23–33.

Dower, John W. *War without Mercy: Race and Power in the Pacific War.* New York: Random House, 1986.

Downing, John D. H., ed. *Film and Politics in the Third World.* New York: Autonomedia, 1987.

D'Souza, Dinesh. *Illiberal Education: The Politics of Race and Sex on Campus.* New York: Vintage, 1992.

Dunbar, Roxanne. *Poor White Woman.* Boston: New England Free Press, 1968.

Dyer, Richard. *Heavenly Bodies: Film Stars and Society.* New York: St. Martin's Press, 1986.

————. "Rejecting Straight Ideals: Gays in Film." In *Jump Cut: Hollywood, Politics, and Counter Cinema,* 286–95. Edited by Peter Steven. New York: Praeger, 1985.

————. "Stereotyping." In *Gays and Film,* 27–39. Edited by Richard Dyer. New York: Zoetrope, 1984.

————. "White." *Screen* 29, no. 4 (1988): 44–64.

Eckert, Charles. "The Carole Lombard in Macy's Window." In *Stardom: Industry of Desire.* Edited by Christine Gledhill. London: Routledge, 1991.

Ehrenreich, Barbara. "Teach Diversity—with a Smile." *Time,* April 8, 1991, 84.

Eidsvik, Charles. "Mock Realism: The Comedy of Futility in Eastern Europe." In *Comedy/Cinema/Theory*. Edited by Andrew Horton. Berkeley: University of California Press, 1991.

Eisenstein, Sergei. *The Film Sense.* New York: Harvest, 1947.

Ellis, John M. "The Origins of PC." *Chronicle of Higher Education,* January 15, 1992, B1–B2.

Ellis, Trey. "The New Black Aesthetic." *Before Columbus Review,* May 15, 1989, 4–23.

Epstein, Barbara. "Political Correctness and Identity Politics." In *Beyond PC: Toward a Politics of Understanding.* Edited by Patricia Aufderheide. St. Paul: Graywolf Press, 1992.

Espin, Olivia M. "Cultural and Historical Influences on Sexuality in Hispanic/Latin Women." In *All American Women.* Edited by Johnnetta Cole. New York: Free Press, 1986.

Ewen, Elizabeth. "City Lights: Immigrant Women and the Rise of Movies." *Signs* 5 (1980): 545–66.

———. *Immigrant Women in the Land of Dollars: Life and Culture on the Lower East Side, 1890–1925.* New York: Monthly Review Press, 1985.

Fabian, Johannes. *Time and the Other: How Anthropology Makes Its Object.* New York: Columbia University Press, 1983.

Fanon, Frantz. *The Wretched of the Earth.* New York: Grove Press, 1961.

Fawcett, E., and T. Thomas. "A Rich and Varied Sameness: Regions and People." In *The American Condition.* New York: Harper and Row, 1982.

Fischer, Michael M. J. "Ethnicity and the Postmodern Arts of Memory." In *Writing Culture: The Poetics and Politics of Ethnography.* Edited by James Clifford and Gregory Marcus. Berkeley: University of California Press, 1986.

———. "Figuring (Indian) Ads in Translocal Spaces: Towards a Transnational Anthropology of Advertising." Paper presented to the Social Science Research Council Symposium on Advertising, Consumption, and the New Middle Class in India, 1991.

———. "Towards a Third World Poetics: Seeing through Short Stories and Film in the Iranian Culture Area." *Knowledge and Society* 5 (1984): 171–241.

Fischer, Michael M. J., and Mehdi Abedi. *Debating Muslims: Cultural Dialogues in Postmodernity and Tradition.* Madison: University of Wisconsin Press, 1990.

Fiske, John. "British Cultural Studies and Television." In *Channels of Discourse.* Edited by Robert Allen. Chapel Hill: University of North Carolina Press, 1987.

Forester, E. M. *Aspects of the Novel.* New York: Harvest, 1954.

Freire, Paolo. *Pedagogy of the Oppressed.* New York: Continuum Press, 1970.

———. *The Politics of Education: Culture, Power, and Liberation.* Translated by Donaldo Macedo. Granby: Bergin and Garvey, 1985.

Freydberg, Elizabeth Hadley. "Prostitutes, Concubines, Whores, and Bitches: Black and Hispanic Women in Contemporary American Cinema." In *Women of Color: Perspectives on Feminism and Identity.* Edited by Audrey T.

McCluskey. Bloomington: Women's Studies Department, Indiana University, 1985.

Friedman, Lester D., ed. *Unspeakable Images: Ethnicity and the American Cinema.* Urbana: University of Illinois Press, 1991.

Friedrich, Su. "Does Radical Content Deserve Radical Form?" *Millennium,* no 22 (1989–90): 118–23.

Frisch, Michael. *A Shared Authority: Essays on the Craft and Meaning of Oral and Public History.* Albany: State University of New York Press, 1990.

Fusco, Coco. "Fantasies of Oppositionality." *Screen* 29 (Autumn 1988): 80–93.

———. "An Interview with Black Audio Film Collective." In *Young, British and Black.* Buffalo: Hallways, 1988.

Gabriel, Teshome H. "Thoughts on Nomadic Aesthetics and the Black Independent Cinema." In *Black Frames: Critical Perspectives on Black Independent Cinema.* Edited by Mbye D. Cham and Claire Andrade-Watkins. Cambridge: MIT Press, 1988.

Gaines, Jane. *"The Scar of Shame:* Skin Color and Caste in Black Silent Melodrama." *Cinema Journal* 26 (Summer 1987): 3–21.

Gaskill, Arthur L., and David Englander. *How to Shoot a Movie Story,* 4th ed. Dobbs Ferry: Morgan Press, 1985.

Gates, Henry Louis, Jr. "'Authenticity,' or the Lesson of Little Tree." *New York Times Book Review,* November 24, 1991, 1, 26–30.

———, ed. *Reading Black, Reading Feminist: A Critical Anthology.* New York: Meridian, 1990.

George, Nelson. *The Death of Rhythm and Blues.* New York: Pantheon, 1988.

Giannetti, Louis. *Understanding Movies.* 6th edition. Englewood Cliffs: Prentice-Hall, 1993.

Gibson-Hudson, Gloria. "African-American Literary Criticism as a Model for the Analysis of Films by African-American Women." *Wide Angle* 13, nos. 3–4 (1991): 44–54.

———. "Aspects of Black Feminist Cultural Ideology in Films by Black Women Independent Artists." In *Multiple Voices in Feminist Film Criticism.* Edited by Diane Carson, Linda Dittmar, and Janice Welsch. Minneapolis: University of Minnesota Press, 1994.

———. "Michelle Parkerson IS the Eye of the Storm." *Black Film Review* 3 (Summer 1987): 16–17.

———. "The Ties That Bind: Cinematic Representations by Black Women Filmmakers." *Quarterly Review of Film and Video* 15, no. 2 (1994): 25–44.

Giddings, Paula. *When and Where I Enter: The Impact of Black Women on Race and Sex in America.* New York: William Morrow, 1984.

Gilman, Charlotte Perkins. *The Yellow Wallpaper.* Old Westbury: Feminist Press, 1973.

Gilman, Sander L. Introduction. In *Difference and Pathology: Stereotypes of Sexuality, Race, and Madness.* Ithaca: Cornell University Press, 1985.

Giroux, Henry. *Border Crossings: Cultural Workers and the Politics of Education.* New York: Routledge, 1992.

————, ed. *Postmodernism, Feminism, and Cultural Politics: Redrawing Education-al Boundaries*. Albany: State University of New York Press, 1991.

Giroux, Henry A., et al. *Popular Culture: Schooling and Everyday Life*. Granby: Bergin and Garvey, 1989.

Gitlin, Todd. "Prime-Time Whitewash." *American Film* 9 (November 1983): 36–38.

Glazer, Nathan. "Additional Comments." In *One Nation, Many Peoples: A Declaration of Cultural Interdependence*. The Report of the New York State Social Studies Review of Development Committee (June 1991), 35–36.

Glicksman, Marlene. "Black Like Who?" *Film Comment* 25 (May–June 1989): 75–76.

Gluck, Sherna Berger, and Daphne Patai, eds. *Women's Words: The Feminist Practice of Oral History*. New York: Routledge, 1991.

Gordon, Robert. "People of the Great Sandface." *CVA Review* (Spring 1990): 30–34.

Grazzini, Giovani. *Federico Fellini: Comments on Film*. Fresno: The Press at Cal State, 1988.

Greenberg, Bradley S. "Minorities and Mass Media." In *Perspectives on Media Effects*. Edited by Jennings Bryant and Dolf Zillman. Hillside: LEH Publishers, 1988.

Guerrero, Ed. *"The Color Purple, Brother from Another Planet:* The Slavery Motif in Recent Popular Cinema." *Jump Cut* 33 (February 1988): 52–59.

Haley, Alex, and Malcolm X. *The Autobiography of Malcolm X*. New York: Ballantine, 1964.

Hall, David L., and Roger T. Ames. *Thinking through Confucius*. Albany: State University of New York Press, 1987.

Hall, Stuart. "Media Power: The Double Bind." In *New Challenges for Documentary*. Edited by Alan Rosenthal. Berkeley: University of California Press, 1988.

————. "New Ethnicities." In *Black Film/British Cinema*. London: Institute of Contemporary Arts, 1988.

Haskell, Molly. *From Reverence to Rape: The Treatment of Women in the Movies*. New York: Holt, 1973.

Hatchett, David. "The State of Race Relations." *The Crisis* 96, no. 9 (1989): 14–19, 47.

Hedges, Elaine. "Quilts and Women's Culture." In *In Her Own Image: Women Working in the Arts*. Edited by Elaine Hedges and Ingrid Wendt. Old Westbury: Feminist Press, 1980.

Hemingway, Simon. "Notes on the Ideology of University Film and Television Production Education." Unpublished essay, 1990.

The Heresies Collective. "If I Ever Stop Believing." *Heresies,* no. 16 (1983): 68–72.

Hess, Elizabeth. "Pictures from the Combat Zone." Review of *Living with the Enemy* by Donna Ferrato. *The Women's Review of Books* 9 (March 1992): 7.

Higashi, Sumiko. "Ethnicity, Class, and Gender in Film: DeMille's *The Cheat.*" In *Unspeakable Images: Ethnicity and the American Cinema*. Edited by Lester D. Friedman. Urbana: University of Illinois Press, 1991.

Himley, Margaret. *Shared Territory: Understanding Children's Writing as Works.* New York: Oxford University Press, 1991.

Himley, Margaret, and Delia C. Temes, eds. *The Study and Practice of Narratives.* Boston: Copley, 1991.

Hirshorn, Harriet. "Interview with Trinh T. Minh-hà." *Heresies,* no. 22 (1987): 14–17.

Holloway, Joseph. "The Origins of African-American Culture." In *Africanisms in American Culture.* Edited by Joseph Holloway. Bloomington: Indiana University Press, 1990.

hooks, bell. *Ain't I a Woman? Black Women and Feminism.* Boston: South End Press, 1981.

———. "Homophobia in Black Communities." In *Talking Back: Think Feminist, Thinking Black.* Boston: South End Press, 1989.

———. "Sisterhood: Political Solidarity between Women." *Feminist Review* 23 (June 1986).

———. "Talking Back." *Discourse* 8 (Fall–Winter 1986–87): 123–28.

———. *Talking Back: Think Feminist, Thinking Black.* Boston: South End Press, 1989.

———. *Yearning: Race, Gender, and Cultural Politics.* Boston: South End Press, 1990.

Hunter, James Davison. *Culture Wars: The Struggle to Define America.* New York: Basic Books, 1991.

Hymowitz, Carol, and Michaele Weissman. *A History of Women in America.* New York: Bantam, 1978.

Jackson, Kenneth T. "A Dissenting Opinion." In *One Nation, Many Peoples: A Declaration of Cultural Interdependence.* The Report of the New York State Social Studies Review of Development Committee (June 1991), 39–40.

Jameson, Fredric. "Regarding Postmodernism." *Social Text* 17 (1987–88): 29.

———. "Third World Literature in the Era of Multinational Capital." *Social Text* 15 (1986): 65–88.

Jay, Gregory S. "The First Round of the Culture Wars." *Chronicle of Higher Education,* February 26, 1992, B1–2.

Jeffords, Susan. "The New Vietnam Films: Is the Movie Over?" *Journal of Popular Film and Television* 13, no. 3 (1986): 186–94.

Jewell, K. Sue. "Black Male/Female Conflicts: Internalization of Negative Definitions Transmitted through Imagery." *Western Journal of Black Studies* 17, no. 1 (1983): 43–48.

Jones, Jacquie. "The New Ghetto Aesthetic." *Wide Angle* 13, nos. 3–4 (1991): 32–43.

Joseph, Gloria I. "Black Mothers and Daughters: Their Roles and Functions in American Society." In *Common Differences: Conflicts in Black and White Feminist Perspectives.* Edited by Gloria I. Joseph and Jill Lewis. Boston: South End Press, 1981.

Joseph, Gloria, and Jill Lewis. *Common Differences: Conflicts in Black and White Feminist Perspectives.* Boston: South End Pess, 1981.

Juhasz, Alex, Indu Krishan, and Kelly Anderson. "Shifting Communities/ Forming Alliances." *Felix* (Spring 1992).

Julien, Isaac, and Kobena Mercer. "Introduction: De Margin and De Centre." *Screen* 29 (Autumn 1988): 2–10.

Kaplan, E. Ann. "Mothering, Feminism and Representation: The Maternal in Melodrama and the Woman's Film, 1910–40." In *Home Is Where the Heart Is: Studies in Melodrama and the Woman's Film*. London: BFI, 1987.

———. "Problematizing Cross-Cultural Analysis: The Case of Women in the Recent Chinese Cinema." *Wide Angle* 11, no. 2 (1989): 40–50.

———. "Theories and Strategies of the Feminist Documentary." In *New Challenges in Documentary*. Berkeley: University of California Press, 1988.

———. *Women and Film: Both Sides of the Camera*. New York: Methuen, 1983.

Kawin, Bruce. *How Movies Work*. Berkeley: University of California Press, 1992.

Keen, Sam. *Faces of the Enemy: Reflections of the Hostile Imagination*. New York: Harper and Row, 1986.

Keith, Stephen N., Robert M. Bell, August G. Swamson, and Albert P. Williams. "Effects of Affirmative Action in Medical Schools: A Study of the Class of 1975." *New England Journal of Medicine* 313, no. 24 (1985): 1519–25.

Keller, Gary D., ed. *Chicano Cinema: Research, Reviews, and Resources*. Binghampton: Bilingual Press, 1985.

Kessler-Harris, Alice. "Cultural Locations: Positioning American Studies in the Great Debate." *American Quarterly* 44 (Spring 1992): 299–312.

Kim, Elaine. "Asian Americans and American Popular Culture." *Dictionary of Asian American History*. New York: Greenwood Press, 1986.

Kinder, Marsha. "Ideological Parody in the New German Cinema: Reading *The State of Things, The Desire of Veronica Voss,* and *Germany Pale Mother* as Postmodernist Rewritings of *The Searchers, Sunset Boulevard,* and *Blonde Venus.*" *Quarterly Review of Film and Video* 12 (1990): 73–103.

King, Ynestra. "Ecofeminism: On the Necessity of History and Mystery." *Women of Power* (Spring 1988).

Kingston, Maxine Hong. *The Woman Warrior*. New York: Vintage, 1975.

Kleinhans, Chuck. "Forms, Politics, Makers and Contexts: Basic Issues for a Theory of Radical Political Documentary." In *Show Us Life! Toward a History and Aesthetics of the Committed Documentary*. Edited by Thomas Waugh. Metuchen: Scarecrow Press, 1984.

Klotman, Phyllis, ed. *Screenplays of the African American Experience*. Bloomington: Indiana University Press, 1991.

Knight, Emma. "Miss U.S.A." In *American Dreams: Lost and Found*. Edited by Studs Terkel. New York: Pantheon, 1980.

Knightly, Philip. *The First Casualty: From the Crimea to Vietnam, the War Correspondent as Hero, Propagandist, and Mythmaker*. New York: Harcourt Brace, 1987.

Koedt, Anne. *The Myth of the Vaginal Orgasm*. Boston: New England Free Press, 1968.

Kotz, Liz. "Unofficial Stories: Documentaries by Latinas and Latin American Women." *The Independent* 12 (May 1989): 21–27.

Lakoff, Robin, and Raquel Scherr. *Face Value: The Politics of Beauty*. Boston: Routledge, 1984.

Lang, Andrew. *The Blue Fairy Book.* New York: Dover, 1965.

Lant, Antonia. *Blackout: Reinventing Women for Wartime British Cinema.* Princeton: Princeton Unversity Press, 1991.

Larkin, Alile Sharon. "Black Women Filmmakers Defining Ourselves: Feminism in Our Own Voice." In *Female Spectators: Looking at Film and Television.* Edited by E. Deidre Pribram. New York: Verso Press, 1988.

Lau, Jenny Kwok Wah. *"Judou:* A Hermeneutical Reading of Cross-Cultural Cinema." *Film Quarterly* 45 (Winter 1991–92): 2–10.

———. "Towards a Cultural Understanding of Cinema: A Comparison of Contemporary Films from the People's Republic of China and Hong Kong." *Wide Angle* 11 (July 1989): 42–49.

Leab, Daniel. *From Sambo to Superspade: The Black Experience in Motion Pictures.* New York: Houghton Mifflin, 1976.

Lee, Richard B. "Art, Science, or Politics? The Crisis in Hunter-Gatherer Studies." *American Anthropologist* 94 (March 1992): 31–54.

Lee, Spike. *Do the Right Thing: A Spike Lee Joint.* New York: Simon and Schuster.

Lekatsas, Barbara. "Encounters: The Film Odyssey of Camille Billops." *Black American Literature Forum* 25 (Summer 1991): 395–408.

Leong, Russell, ed. *Moving the Image: Independent Asian Pacific American Media Arts.* Los Angeles: UCLA Asian American Studies Center and Visual Communications, Southern California Asian American Studies, Central, Inc., 1991.

Lesage, Julia. *"The Other Francisco:* Creating History.*" Jump Cut* 30 (1985): 53–58.

———. "The Feminist Documentary: Politics and Aesthetics." In *Show Us Life! Toward a History and Aesthetics of the Committed Documentary.* Edited by Thomas Waugh. Metuchen: Scarecrow Press, 1984.

———. *"One Way or Another:* Dialectical, Revolutionary, Feminist." *Jump Cut* 20 (1979): 20–23.

———. "Political Aesthetics of the Feminist Documentary Film." In *Films for Women.* Edited by Charlotte Brunsdon. London: BFI, 1986.

———. "Women Made Media: Three Modes of Production." In *The Social Documentary in Latin America.* Edited by Julianne Burton. Pittsburgh: University of Pittsburgh Press, 1990.

Levine, Lawrence. *Black Culture and Black Consciousness.* New York: Oxford University Press, 1977.

Lichter, S. Robert, et al. "Prime-Time Prejudice: TV's Images of Blacks and Hispanics." *Public Opinion* 10 (July–August 1987): 13–16.

Lippmann, Walter. *Public Opinion.* New York: Macmillen, 1922.

Lipsitz, George. *Time Passages: Collective Memory and American Popular Culture.* Minneapolis: University of Minnesota Press, 1990.

Lipton, Lenny. *Independent Filmmaking.* New York: Simon and Schuster, 1983.

Loizos, Peter. *Innovation in Ethnographic Film: From Innocence to Self-Conciousness.* Chicago: University of Chicago Press, 1993.

López, Ana. "Parody, Underdevelopment, and the New Latin American Cinema." *Quarterly Review of Film and Video* 12 (1990): 63–71.

Lorde, Audre. "Eye to Eye." In *Sister Outsider.* Trumansburg: The Crossing Press, 1984.

———. The Master's Tools Will Never Dismantle the Master's House." In *This Bridge Called My Back: Writings by Radical Women of Color.* Edited by Cherríe Moraga and Gloria Anzaldúa. New York: Kitchen Table Press, 1983.

———. *Sister Outsider.* Trumansburg: The Crossing Press, 1984.

Lubiano, Wahneema. "Multiculturalism: Negotiating Politics and Knowledge." *Concerns* 22, no. 3 (1992): 11–21.

Lull, James. *China Turned On: Television, Reform, and Resistance.* London: Routledge, 1991.

Lyotard, Jean-François. "The Dream-Work Does Not Think," and "Figure Foreclosed." In *The Lyotard Reader.* Edited by Andrew Benjamin. London: Blackwell, 1989.

MacBean, James Roy. "Two Laws from Australia, One White, One Black." In *New Challenges for Documentary.* Edited by Alan Rosenthal. Berkeley: University of California Press, 1988.

Malti-Douglas, Fedwa. *Women's Body, Woman's World: Gender and Discourse in Arabo-Islamic Writing.* Princeton: Princeton University Press, 1991.

Marable, Manning. "Do the Right Thing." *Black Issues in Higher Education* 6, no. 11 (1989): 4.

Marchetti, Gina. "Ethnicity, the Cinema, and Cultural Studies." In *Unspeakable Images: Ethnicity and the American Cinema.* Edited by Lester D. Friedman. Urbana: University of Illinois Press, 1991.

Marcus, George, and Michael M. J. Fischer. *Anthropology as Cultural Critique: An Experimental Moment in the Human Sciences.* Chicago: University of Chicago Press, 1986.

Maultsby, Portia. "Africanisms in African-American Music." In *Africanisms in American Culture.* Edited by Joseph Holloway. Bloomington: Indiana University Press, 1990.

May, Larry. *Screening Out the Past: The Birth of Mass Culture and the Motion Picture Industry.* London: Oxford University Press, 1980.

Mayer, David. *Eisenstein's Potemkin: A Shot-by-Shot Presentation.* New York: Grossman Publishers, 1972.

McLemore, S. Dale, and Ricardo Romo. "The Origins and Development of the Mexican American People." In *The Mexican American Experience: An Interdisciplinary Anthology,* 3–32. Edited by Rodolfo de la Garza. Austin: University of Texas Press, 1984.

Menand, Louis. "School Daze." *Harper's Bazaar* 125 (September 1992): 380–81, 400–404.

Menchu, Rigoberta. *I . . . Rigoberta Menchu: An Indian Woman in Guatemala.* Translated by Ann Wright. Edited by Elisabeth Burgos. New York: Verso Press, 1984.

Mercer, Kobena. "Recoding Narratives of Race and Nation." In *Black Film/ British Cinema.* London: Institute of Contemporary Arts, 1988.

Mernissi, Fatima. *The Veil and the Male Elite: A Feminist Interpretation of Women's Rights in Islam.* New York: Addison-Wesley, 1987.

Meyer, Melissa, and Miriam Schapiro. "Femmage: Waste Not/Want Not: An Inquiry into What Women Saved and Assembled." *Heresies* 1 (Winter 1978): 66–69.

Miller, Seymour M. "Race in the Health of America." In *The Nation's Health.* Edited by Phillip R. Lee and Carroll L. Estes. Boston: Jones and Bartlett, 1990.

Millerson, Gerald. *The Technique of Lighting for Television and Motion Pictures.* Stoneham: Butterworth, 1991.

Mishra, Vijay, Peter Jeffery, and Brian Shoesmith. "The Actor as Parallel Text in Bombay Cinema." *Quarterly Review of Film and Video* 11 (1989): 49–67.

Mohanty, Chandra Talpade. "Under Western Eyes: Feminist Scholarship and Colonial Discourse." *Feminist Review,* no. 30 (Autumn 1988): 61–88.

Mohanty, Chandra Talpade, Ann Russo, and Lourdes Torres, eds. *Third World Women and the Politics of Feminism.* Bloomington: Indiana University Press, 1991.

Montagu, Ashley. "Reaching the Child within Us." *Utne Reader* (January–February 1990): 87+.

Moon, Spencer. "A Pioneer in Public Television: Madeline Anderson." *Black Film Review* 6, no. 4 (1991): 27–30.

Moraga, Cherríe. "What Is Left." In *Pleasure and Danger: Exploring Female Sexuality.* Edited by Carole S. Vance. Boston: Routledge, 1985.

Morris, Rosalind. *New Worlds from Fragments: Film, Ethnography, and Representation of the Northwest Coast Cultures.* Boulder: Westview, 1994.

Mulvey, Laura. "Visual Pleasure and Narrative Cinema." In *Narrative, Apparatus, Ideology: A Film Theory Reader,* 198–209. Edited by Phillip Rosen. New York: Columbia University Press, 1986.

Naficy, Hamid. "Exile Discourse and Televisual Fetishization." *Quarterly Review of Film and Video* 13, nos. 1–3 (1988): 85–116.

Nandy, Ashis. "An Intelligent Critic's Guide to Indian Cinema." *Deep Focus* 1, nos. 1–3 (1987–88): 68–72, 53–60, 58–61.

Nash, June, and Helen Safa. *Women and Change in Latin America.* South Hadley: Bergin and Garvey, 1988.

Nichols, Bill. *Representing Reality: Issues and Concepts in Documentary.* Bloomington: Indiana University Press, 1991.

———. "The Voice of Documentary." In *New Challenges for Documentary.* Edited by Alan Rosenthal. Berkeley: University of California Press, 1988.

Nicholson, David. "A Commitment to Writing: A Conversation with Kathleen Collins Prettyman." *Black Film Review* 5 (Winter 1988–89): 6–15.

Nochlin, Linda. "Why Have There Been No Great Women Artists?" In *Women, Art, and Power and Other Essays.* New York: Harper and Row, 1988.

Norden, Martin. "Women in the Early Film Industry." *Wide Angle* 6 (1984): 58–67.

Noriega, Chon, ed. *Chicanos and Film: Representation and Resistance.* Minneapolis: University of Minnesota Press, 1992.

O'Connor, John E., ed. *Image as Artifact: The Historical Analysis of Film and Television.* Malabar: Robert E. Kreiger Publishing Company, 1990.

O'Connor, John E., and Martin A. Jackson, eds. *American History/American Film: Interpreting the Hollywood Image.* New York: Frederick Ungar, 1979.

Oksenberg, Michel. "The Asian Century." *Honolulu Advertiser,* July 11, 1993, B1, B4.

Olsen, Tillie. *Silences.* New York: Dell, 1978.

Omi, Michael, and Howard Winant. *Racial Formation in the United States.* New York: Routledge, 1989.

Patai, Daphne. *Brazilian Women Speak: Contemporary Life Stories.* New Brunswick: Rutgers University Press, 1988.

Patai, Daphne, and Sherna Berger Gluck. *Women's Words: The Feminist Practice of Oral History.* New York: Routledge, 1991.

Peacock, James. *Rites of Modernization.* Chicago: University of Chicago Press, 1968.

Perkins, Linda M. "The Impact of the 'Cult of True Womanhood' on the Education of Black Women." *Journal of Social Issues* 39, no. 3 (1983): 17–28.

Pettit, Arthur G. *Images of the Mexican American in Fiction and Film.* College Station: Texas A & M Press, 1980.

Pines, Jim, and Paul Willemen, eds. *Questions of Third Cinema.* London: BFI Publishers, 1989.

Portelli, Alessandro. "The Peculiarities of Oral History." *History Workshop* 12 (Autumn 1981): 96–107.

Powers, John. "Saints and Savages." *American Film* 9 (January–February 1984): 38–43.

Pryluck, Calvin. "Ultimately We Are All Outsiders: The Ethics of Documentary Filming." In *New Challenges for Documentary.* Edited by Alan Rosenthal. Berkeley: University of California Press, 1988.

Rabine, Leslie. "Romance in the Age of Electronics." In *Feminist Criticism and Social Change,* 246–67. Edited by Judith Newton and Deborah Rosenfelt. New York: Methuen, 1985.

Ravitch, Diane. "Diversity and Democracy: Multicultural Education in America." *American Educator* 14 (Spring 1990): 16–20, 46–48.

Raybon, Patricia. "A Case of 'Severe Bias,'" *Newsweek,* October 2, 1989, 11.

Rayns, Tony. "Breakthroughs and Setbacks: The Origins of the New Chinese Cinema." In *Perspective on Chinese Cinema.* Edited by Chris Berry. Bloomington: Indiana University Press, 1991.

Rayns, Tony, and Scott Meek. *Electric Shadows: Forty-five Years of Chinese Cinema.* Dossier Number 3. London: British Film Institute, 1980.

Readings, Bill. *Introducing Lyotard.* London: Routledge, 1991.

Reid, Mark. "Dialogic Modes of Representing Africa(s): Womanist Film." *Black American Literature Forum* 25 (Summer 1991): 375–88.

Reynaud, Bérénice. "Three Asian Films: For a New Cinematic Language." Paper presented to the Columbia Seminar on Cinema and Interdisciplinary Interpretation, Museum of Modern Art, September 27, 1990. [A shortened version published in *Cinematograph* 4 (1991).]

Rich, Adrienne. "Compulsory Heterosexuality." In *Powers of Desire: The Poli-*

tics of Sexuality. Edited by Ann Snitow, Christine Stansell, and Sharon Thompson. New York: Monthly Review Press, 1983.

Rich, B. Ruby. "The Crisis of Naming in Feminist Film Criticism." In *Jump Cut: Hollywood, Politics and Counter Cinema.* Edited by Peter Steven. Toronto: Between the Lines, 1985.

Richardson, Marilyn. "Literacy and Resistance: Black Women in the Ante-Bellum South." *Radical Teacher,* no. 22 (1982): 17.

Rickels, Lawrence. *The Case of California.* Berkeley: University of California Press, 1991.

Robinson, Patricia. *Poor Black Women.* Boston: New England Free Press, 1968.

Rollins, Peter C., ed. *Hollywood as Historian: American Film in a Cultural Context.* Lexington: University Press of Kentucky, 1983.

Rollwagen, Jack. *Anthropological Film and Video in the 1990s.* Brockport: The Institute Press, 1993.

Rose, Vattel T. "Afro-American Literature as a Cultural Resource for a Black Cinema Aesthetic." In *Black Cinema Aesthetics: Issues in Independent Black Filmmaking.* Edited by Gladstone Yearwood. Athens: Center for Afro-American Studies, Ohio University, 1982.

Rosen, Miriam. "Cinemas of the Arab World." Arab Film Festival (handout). Washington, D.C., 1991.

Rosenbaum, Jonathan. "Mapping the Territory of Raul Ruiz." *Cinematograph* 3 (1988): 166–78.

Rosenfelt, Deborah Silverton. "Commentary on *Salt of the Earth.*" [In the screenplay *Salt of the Earth.*] Edited by Deborah Silverton Rosenfelt. Old Westbury: Feminist Press, 1978.

Rosenstone, Robert A. "History in Images/History in Words: Reflections on the Possibility of Really Putting History onto Film." *American Historical Review* 93 (December 1988): 1173–85.

———. "History, Memory, and Documentary." *Cineaste* 17, no. 1 (1989): 12–15.

Rosenthal, Alan. *New Challenges for Documentary.* Berkeley: University of California Press, 1988.

———. "*The War Game:* An Interview with Peter Watkins." In *New Challenges for Documentary.* Edited by Alan Rosenthal. Berkeley: University of California Press, 1988.

Roszak, Theodore. *Flicker.* New York: Bantam, 1991.

Rothenberg, Paula. "Integrating the Study of Race, Gender, and Class: Some Preliminary Observations." *The Feminist Teacher* 3, no. 3 (1988): 37–42.

Rouve, Pierre. "Reel to Real: The Cinema as Technological Co-Reality." In *Art and Technology.* Edited by Rene Berger and Lloyd Eby. New York: Paragon, 1986.

Royce, Anya Peterson. *Ethnic Identity: Strategies of Diversity.* Bloomington: Indiana University Press, 1982.

Ruby, Jay. *The Cinema of John Marshall.* New York: Harwood, 1993.

———. "The Ethics of Imagemaking." In *New Challenges for Documentary.* Edited by Alan Rosenthal. Berkeley: University of California Press, 1988.

———. "The Image Mirrored: Reflexivity and the Documentary Film." In

New Challenges for Documentary. Edited by Alan Rosenthal. Berkeley: University of California Press, 1988.

Ryan, Mary. *Cradle of the Middle Class: The Family in Oneida County, New York, 1790–1865.* New York: Cambridge University Press, 1981.

Said, Edward. *Orientalism.* New York: Pantheon Books, 1978.

Santer, Eric. *Stranded Objects: Mourning, Memory and Film in Postwar Germany.* Ithaca: Cornell University Press, 1990.

Sato, Tadao. *Currents in Japanese Cinema.* Tokyo: Kodansha International, 1982.

Sayles, John. *Thinking in Pictures.* New York: Houghton Mifflin, 1987.

Schiller, Herbert I. *Culture Inc.: The Corporate Takeover of Public Expression.* New York: Oxford University Press, 1989.

Schlesinger, Arthur M., Jr. "The Disuniting of America." *American Educator* 15 (Winter 1991): 14–33.

———. "Report of the Social Studies Syllabus Review Committee, A Dissenting Opinion." In *One Nation, Many Peoples: A Declaration of Cultural Interdependence.* Albany: New York State Education Department, 1991.

Scott, Joan Wallach. "Campus Communities beyond Consensus." In *Beyond PC: Toward a Politics of Understanding.* Edited by Patricia Aufderheide. St. Paul: Graywolf Press, 1992.

Seoull, Michael S. "Labor Pains." *Time,* June 27, 1994, 14–18.

Shaheen, Jack G. "The Hollywood Arab: 1984–1986." *Journal of Popular Television* 14 (Winter 1987): 148–57.

Shohat, Ella. "Can the Non-Subaltern Speak? Cinema Studies, Multiculturalism, and Questions of Representation." In *Postmodern Occasions.* Edited by Roman Della Campa, E. Ann Kaplan, and Michael Sprinkler. New York: Verso Press, in press.

———. "Gender and the Culture of Empire: Towards a Feminist Ethnography of Cinema." *Quarterly Review of Film and Video* 13 (May 1991): 45–50.

———. "Notes on the 'Post Colonial.'" *Social Text* 31–32 (1992): 99–113.

Silverman, Kaja. *The Subject of Semiotics.* New York: Oxford University Press, 1983.

Sklar, Robert. *"The Story of Qiu Ju." Cineaste* 20, no. 1 (1994): 41, 63.

Slim, Iceberg. *Pimp: The Story of My Life.* Los Angeles: Holloway House Publishing, 1969.

Sloan, William David, James G. Stovall, and James D. Startt, eds. *The Media in America: A History,* 2d ed. Scottsdale: Publishing Horizon, 1993.

Slovo, Shawn. *A World Apart.* London: Faber and Faber, 1990.

Smihi, Moumen. "Moroccan Society as Mythology." In *Film and Politics in the Third World.* Edited by John Downing. New York: Autonomedia, 1987.

Smith, Barbara. "Toward a Black Feminist Criticism." In *Feminist Criticism and Social Change: Sex, Class, and Race in Literature and Culture.* New York: Methuen, 1985.

———. "The Truth That Never Hurts: Black Lesbians in Fiction in the 1980s." In *Wild Women in the Whirlwind: Afra-American Culture and the Contemporary Literary Renaissance.* New Brunswick: Rutgers University Press, 1990.

Smith, Valerie. "Reconstituting the Image: The Emergent Black Woman Director." *Callaloo,* no. 11(1988): 709–19.

————. "Telling Family Secrets: Narrative and Ideology in *Suzanne, Suzanne* by Camille Billops and James V. Hatch." In *Multiple Voices in Feminist Film Criticism.* Edited by Diane Carson, Linda Dittmar, and Janice Welsh. Minneapolis: University of Minnesota Press, 1994.

Snead, James. "The Visual Rhetoric of Black Independent Film." Program notes, "Recoding Blackness" film series. New York: The Whitney Museum of American Art, 1985.

Snyder, Robert. *Pare Lorentz and the Documentary Film.* Norman: University of Oklahoma Press, 1968.

Sollors, Werner. *Beyond Ethnicity: Consent and Descent in American Culture.* New York: Oxford University Press, 1986.

Sorlin, Pierre. *European Cinemas, European Societies 1939–1990.* New York: Routledge, 1991.

Southwestern Alternate Media Project. *Media Bulletin* (Fall-Winter 1993–94): 3.

Special Issue on Multiculturalism. *American Quarterly* 45 (June 1993).

Spence, Jonathan D. *The Search for Modern China.* New York: W. W. Norton, 1990.

Spender, Dale. *Man Made Language.* London: Routledge, 1981.

Spigner, Clarence. "Black Impressions of People of Color: A Functionalist Approach to Film Imagery." *Western Journal of Black Studies* 15, no. 2 (1991): 69–78.

Spivak, Gayatri Chakravorty. *In Other Worlds: Essays in Cultural Politics.* New York: Methuen, 1987.

Springer, Claudia. "Ethnographic Circles: A Short History of Ethnographic Film." *The Independent* (December 1984): 13–18.

Stack, Carol. *All Our Kin: Strategies for Survival in a Black Community.* New York: Harper and Row, 1974.

Stam, Robert. "Hitchcock and Buñuel: Desire and the Law." In *The Cinematic Text: Methods and Approaches.* Edited by R. Barton Palmer. New York: AMS Press, 1989.

————. *Subversive Pleasures: Bakhtin, Cultural Criticism and Film.* Baltimore: Johns Hopkins University Press, 1989.

Stanley, Robert H., and Charles S. Steinberg. *The Media Environment: Mass Communications in American Society.* New York: Hastings House, 1976.

Steinem, Gloria. *Marilyn.* New York: H. Holt, 1986.

Stember, C. H. *Sexual Racism.* New York: Elsevier, 1976.

Steven, Peter, ed. *Jump Cut: Hollywood, Politics, and Counter Cinema.* Toronto: Between the Lines, 1985.

Stevens, Evelyn P. "Marianismo: The Other Face of Machismo in Latin America." In *Female and Male in Latin America.* Edited by Ann Pescatello. Pittsburgh: University of Pittsburgh Press, 1973.

Stoller, Paul. *The Cinematic Griot: Ethnography of Jean Rouch.* Chicago: University of Chicago Press, 1992.

Subervi-Vélez, Federico A. "The Mass Media and Ethnic Assimilation and Pluralism: A Review and Research Proposal with Special Focus on Hispanics." *Communication Research* 13, no. 1 (1986): 71–96.

Tajima, Renée. "I Just Hope We Find a Nip in This Building That Speaks English." *Village Voice,* December 5, 1989, 104.

———. "Lotus Blossoms Don't Bleed: Images of Asian Women." In *Making Waves.* Edited by Asian Women United of California. Boston: Beacon Press, 1989.

Tate, Claudia. "Introduction" and "Maya Angelou." In *Black Women Writers at Work.* New York: Continuum, 1983.

Tate, Greg. "The Return of the Black Aesthetic: Cult-Nats Meet FreakyDeke." *Village Voice Literary Supplement* (December 1986): 5–7.

Taylor, Clyde. "Black Films in Search of a Home." *Freedomways* 26 (1986): 226–33.

———. "The Re-Birth of the Aesthetic in Cinema." *Wide Angle* 13, nos. 3–4 (1991): 12–30.

Taylor, Lucien. *Visualizing Theory: Selected Essays from Visual Anthropology.* London: Routledge, 1993.

Tchen, John Kuo Wei. "Modernizing White Patriarcy: Re-viewing D. W. Griffith's *Broken Blossoms.*" In *Moving Image: Independent, Asian Pacific, American Media Arts,* 133–43. Edited by Russell Leung. Los Angeles: UCLA Asian American Studies Center and Visual Communications, Southern California Asian American Studies Center, Inc., 1991.

Thompson, Paul R. *The Voice of the Past: Oral History.* New York: Oxford University Press, 1978.

Tomaselli, Keyan, et al. "People of the Great Sandface." *Visual Anthropology* 5 (1992): 153–66.

Tompkins, Jane. "Pedagogy of the Distressed." *College English* 52, no. 6 (1990): 653–60.

Toplin, Robert Brent. "The Filmmaker as Historian." *American Historical Review* 93 (December 1988): 1210–27.

———, ed. *Hollywood as Mirror: Changing Views of "Outsiders" and "Enemies" in American Movies.* Westport: Greenwood Press, 1993.

Trachtenberg, Alan. "From Image to Story." In *Documenting America, 1935–43.* Edited by Carol Fleischauer and Beverly Brannan. Berkeley: University of California Press, 1988.

Traweek, Sharon. *Lifetimes and Beamtimes.* Cambridge: Harvard University Press, 1988.

Trinh T. Minh-hà. "Of Other Peoples: Beyond the 'Salvage' Paradigm." In *Discussions in Contemporary Culture.* Edited by Hal Foster. Seattle: Bay Press, 1987.

———. "Questions of Images and Politics." *The Independent* (May 1987): 21–23.

———. "*Reassemblage* (Sketch of a Sound Track)." *Camera Obscura,* nos. 13–14 (1985): 104–11.

———. *When the Moon Waxes Red: Representation, Gender, and Cultural Politics.* New York: Routledge, 1991.

————. *Woman, Native, Other: Writing Postcoloniality and Feminism.* Blooming-ton: Indiana University Press, 1989.

Turner, Terence. "Representing, Resisting, Rethinking: Historical Transforma-tions of Kayapo Culture and Anthropological Consciousness." In *Colonial Situations: Essays on the Contextualization of Ethnographic Knowledge.* Edited by George W. Stocking. Madison: University of Wisconsin Press, 1992.

"The Twenty-something Generation." *Time,* July 1990, 57–63.

Tyler, Steven. *The Unspeakable: Discourse, Dialogue and Rhetoric in the Postmod-ern World.* Madison: University of Wisconsin Press, 1986.

Underdahl, Douglas. *16mm Help Book.* New York: Media Logic of New York, 1993.

United States Department of Health and Human Services. *Healthy People 2000* [Conference Edition]. Washington, D.C.: U.S. Government Printing Of-fice, 1990.

Van Dyke, Willard. "Letters from *The River." Film Comment* 3 (Spring 1985): 38–56.

Vásquez, Blanca. "Puerto Ricans and the Media: A Personal Statement." *Centro* 3 (Winter 1990–91).

Virilio, Paul. *War and Cinema: The Logistics of Perception.* New York: Verso Press, 1984.

Walker, Alice. "Beauty: When the Other Dancer Is the Self." In *In Search of Our Mothers' Gardens.* New York: Harcourt, Brace, 1983.

————. "Everyday Use." In *In Her Own Image.* Edited by Elaine Hedges and Ingrid Wendt. Old Westbury: Feminist Press, 1980.

————. "In Search of Our Mothers' Gardens." In *Working It Out.* Edited by Sara Ruddick and Pamela Daniels. New York: Pantheon, 1977.

————. "Oppressed Hair Puts a Ceiling on the Brain." *Ms.* 12 (June 1988): 52–53.

Wallace, Michelle. *Black Macho and the Myth of the Superwoman.* New York: Verso Press, 1990.

————. *Invisibility Blues: From Pop to Theory.* New York: Verso Press, 1990.

————."Variations on Negation and the Heresy of Black Female Creativity" and "Negative/Positive Images: Towards a Black Feminist Cultural Criti-cism." Both in *Invisibility Blues: From Pop to Theory.* New York: Verso Press, 1990.

Walters, Ronald. "A Different View: 'Afrocentrism' Means Providing the Neglected Black Perspective." In *The Disuniting of America.* Edited by Arthur Schlesinger. New York: Norton, 1992.

Wang, Yuejin. *"Red Sorghum:* Mixing Memory and Desire." In *Perspectives on Chinese Cinema.* Edited by Chris Berry. Bloomington: Indiana University Press, 1991.

Weiss, Andrea. "'A Queer Feeling When I Look at You': Hollywood Stars and Lesbian Spectatorship in the 1930s." In *Stardom: Industry of Desire.* Edited by Christine Gledhill. London: Routledge, 1991.

Welter, Barbara. "The Cult of True Womanhood: 1820–1860." *American Quarterly* 18 (Summer 1966): 151–74.

West, Cornel. "The New Cultural Politics of Difference." In *Out There: Marginalization and Contemporary Cultures*. Edited by Russell Furguson, Martha Gever, Trinh T. Minh-hà, and Cornel West. Cambridge: MIT Press, 1990.

Wiegman, Robyn. "Black Bodies/American Commodies: Gender, Race, and the Bourgeois Ideal in Contemporary Film." In *Unspeakable Images: Ethnicity and the American Cinema*. Edited by Lester Friedman. Urbana: University of Illinois Press, 1991.

Wilkerson, Margaret B. "Lorraine Hansberry: The Complete Feminist." *Freedomways* 19, no. 4(1979): 235–45.

Wilkinson, Doris, and Gary King. "Conceptual Methodological Issues in the Use of Race as a Variable: Policy Implications." *Millbank Quarterly* 1 (1987): 47–61.

Williams, Raymond. "Cinema and Socialism." In *The Politics of Modernism*. Edited by Tony Pinkney. New York: Verso Press, 1985.

Williamson, Judith. "Women Is an Island: Femininity and Colonization." In *Studies in Entertainment*. Edited by Tania Modleski. Bloomington: Indiana University Press, 1986.

Wilson, August. "I Don't Want to Hire Nobody Just 'Cause They're Black." *Spin* 6 (October 1990): 70–71.

Wilson, Clint C., and Félix Gutiérrez. *Minorities and Media*. Beverly Hills: Sage Publications, 1985.

Winston, Brian. "The Tradition of the Victim." In *New Challenges for Documentary*. Edited by Alan Rosenthal. Berkeley: University of California Press, 1988.

Woll, Allen L. *The Latin Image in American Film*. Los Angeles: University of California Los Angles, Latin American Center Publications, 1980.

Wong, Frank F. "Diversity and Community: Right Objectives and Wrong Arguments." *Change* 23 (July–August 1991): 48–54.

Wong, Nellie. "When I Was Growing Up." In *This Bridge Called My Back: Writings by Radical Women of Color*. Edited by Cherríe Moraga and Gloria Anzaldúa. New York: Kitchen Table Press, 1983.

Wood, Robin. "An Introduction to the American Horror Film." In *Movies and Methods*. Volume 2, 195–220. Edited by Bill Nichols. Berkeley: University of California Press, 1985.

Woodson, Carter G. *The Miseducation of the Negro*. Nashville: Winston-Derek, 1933. Reprint, 1990.

Woodward, C. Vann. "Freedom and the Universities." In *Beyond PC: Toward a Politics of Understanding*. Edited by Patricia Aufderheide. St. Paul: Graywolf Press, 1992.

Xian, Chen. "Shadow Play: Chinese Film Aesthetics and the Philosophical and Cultural Fundamentals." In *Chinese Film Theory*. Edited by G. Semsei, Xia Hong, and Hou Jiaou Ping. New York: Praeger, 1990.

Yans-McLaughlin, Virginia. "Metaphors of Self in History." In *Immigration Reconsidered: History, Sociology, and Politics*. Edited by Virginia Yans-McLaughlin. New York: Oxford University Press, 1990.

Yau, Esther C. M. "Cultural and Economic Dislocations: Filmic Phantasies of Chinese Women in the 1980s." *Wide Angle* 11, no. 2 (1989): 6–21.

————. *"Yellow Earth:* Western Analysis and a Non-Western Text." In *Perspectives on Chinese Cinema,* 62–79. Edited By Chris Berry. Bloomington: Indiana University Press, 1991.

Yearwood, Gladstone. *Black Cinema Aesthetics: Issues in Independent Black Filmmaking.* Athens: Center for Afro-American Studies, Ohio University, 1982.

Youdelman, Jeffrey. "Narration, Invention, and History." In *New Challenges for Documentary.* Edited by Alan Rosenthal. Berkeley: University of California Press, 1988.

Zavarzadeh, Mas'ud. *Seeing Films Politically.* Albany: State University of New York Press, 1991.

Zhang, Yingjin. "Ideology of the Body in *Red Sorghum:* National Allegory, National Roots, and Third Cinema." *East-West Film Journal* 4, no. 2 (1990): 38–53.

Zheutlin, Barbara. "The Politics of Documentary." In *New Challenges for Documentary.* Edited by Alan Rosenthal. Berkeley: Univeristy of California Press, 1988.Zizek, Slavoj. *Looking Awry: An Introduction to Jacques Lacan through Popular Cinema.* Cambridge: MIT Press, 1991.

Zizek, Slavoj. *Looking Awry: An Introduction to Jacques Lacan through Popular Cinema.* Cambridge: MIT Press, 1991.

Contributors

SERAFINA BATHRICK, associate professor in the Communications Department at Hunter College, teaches Women in the Media, Introduction to Media Studies, and Propaganda and the Mass Media. Her articles have appeared in *Jump Cut* and in various collections of essays on contemporary mass media. She is working on a book about the representation of women in mass culture.

CHARLES RAMÍREZ BERG, associate professor at the University of Texas at Austin, teaches film studies in the Department of Radio-Television-Film. He has published numerous articles on Hispanic images in Hollywood film and on Mexican cinema. His articles have appeared in *Spectator, Jump Cut,* and in the anthology *Chicanos in Film.* He is the author of *Cinema of Solitude: A Critical Study of Mexican Film, 1967–1983.*

TODD BOYD, assistant professor at the University of Southern California, teaches in the School of Cinema-Television. He has published numerous articles on African-American images and esthetics in film. He is working on a book concerning the question of race and contemporary culture, specifically analyzing the mediated rhetoric of Louis Farrakhan, the politics of rap music, and the cinema of Spike Lee.

STEVE CARR, assistant professor at Indiana University–Purdue University (Fort Wayne), completed his dissertation on the accusation of Jewish control over the media. His article on the Smothers Brothers won first place in the Society for Cinema Studies Student Essay Contest and was published in *Cinema Journal.* In the past, he has taught classes in radio, television, and film at the University of Texas and Austin Community College.

DIANE CARSON, professor of media studies at St. Louis Community College at Meramec, teaches film studies and film production. She is coeditor of *Multiple Voices in Feminist Film Criticism,* as well as numerous articles and presentations on pedagogy and feminist theory. She writes weekly film reviews for St. Louis's *Riverfront Times,* coproduced the video *Bonnie and Clyde Remembered,* and is completing a project on images of Asians and Asian Americans in film.

CARLOS E. CORTÉS, professor of history at the University of California (Riverside), has lectured widely throughout the world on such topics as race and ethnicity, media literacy, multicultural and social studies education, and the implications of global diversity for education, government, and private business. His publications include *Three Perspectives on Ethnicity: Blacks, Chicanos, and Native Americans* and *Understanding You and Them.* He is at work on a three-volume study of the history of U.S. motion picture treatment of ethnic groups, foreign nations, and world cultures.

LINDA DITTMAR, professor of English at the University of Massachusetts (Boston), teaches courses in English, film, women's studies, and American studies. A coeditor of *From Hanoi to Hollywood: The Vietnam War in American Film* and *Multiple Voices in Feminist Film Criticism,* she has written widely on film, modern fiction, and pedagogy. She is a member of the *Radical Teacher* editorial group.

LESTER D. FRIEDMAN, who teaches humanities at the SUNY, Health Science Center and film at Syracuse University, offers courses such as Multiculturalism and the American Cinema, Medicine in Film and Literature, and Contemporary British Film. His books include *American-Jewish Filmmakers: Traditions and Trends* (with David Desser) and *Unspeakable Images: Ethnicity and the American Cinema.* He is currently exploring the relationships between film and health care.

MICHAEL M. J. FISCHER, formerly professor of anthropology and director of the Center for Cultural Studies at Rice University, now teaches at MIT, where he is professor of science and technology studies and continues to teach the course described in this book. His publications include coauthorship of *Debating Muslims: Cultural Dialogues in Post Modernity* and *Tradition* and *Anthropology as Cultural Critique.* Among his projects is a book on cultural change in Iran, India, and Poland.

GLORIA J. GIBSON-HUDSON, associate professor of Afro-American Studies and assistant director of the Black Film Center–Archive at Indiana University, teaches a variety of courses, including Early Black Film, The Cinema of African-American Women, World Folk Music Traditions, and Contemporary Black Cinema. Her articles have appeared in *Wide Angle, Black Film Review, Uhura Magazine,* and *Quarterly Review of Film and Video.* She is completing a book on black women filmmakers of the African diaspora.

MARGARET HIMLEY, associate professor in the English-Writing Program at Syracuse University, teaches classes in writing theory and research, reading sexuality, radical pedagogy, and the rhetoric of AIDS. Her books include *Shared Territory: Understanding Children's Writing as Works* and *Political Moments in the Classroom: Teachers Talking Toward Knowledge and Action* (with Delia Temes). Her research centers around queer theory.

JULIA LESAGE, associate professor of English at the University of Oregon (Eugene), teaches film criticism and screenwriting. She is coeditor and founder of *Jump Cut: A Review of Contemporary Media* and a videomaker and director of *Las Nicas, El Crucero, Troubadours,* and *In Plain English.* She has published extensively on documentaries, Latin-American cinema, and feminist film criticism.

LOUISE SPENCE taught at Hunter College for five years and now teaches media and cultural studies at Sacred Heart University. She teaches classes in film history, women in popular culture, third world film, and cultural identity. Her work has appeared in many journals, including *Screen* and *Quarterly Review of Film Studies.* She has completed a study of women who watch soap operas and is collaborating on a book about the silent films of Oscar Micheaux.

CLARENCE SPIGNER was an assistant professor of community health, with joint appointments in the Ethnic Studies Program and the Department of Anthropology at the University of Oregon (Eugene), where he taught film classes about race and gender representations. Currently, he is associate professor in the School of Public Health and Community Medicine, University of Washington (Seattle). His work has appeared in the *Western Journal of Black Studies* and the *Journal of Multicultural Counseling and Development.*

DELIA C. TEMES designs and teaches composition and literature courses in the Liberal Arts in Sciences Department at the SUNY, Health Science Center. Previously, she taught junior and senior writing studios, developed curriculum, and participated in teacher-research projects in the Writing Program at Syracuse University, where she also coordinated program publications and teacher journals. Her writings include articles on gender and the professions, the varieties of collaborative experience, strategies for writing across the curriculum, and interdisciplinary approaches to teaching the western.

PATRICIA R. ZIMMERMANN, associate professor in the Department of Cinema and Photography of the Roy H. Park School of Communications at Ithaca College, teaches courses in documentary film and feminist film theory. She has written extensively on documentary film theory, amateur film history, and feminist film. She is the author of *Reel Families: A Social History of the Discourse on Amateur Film.*

Index

Note: Film titles are followed by names of directors; books are followed by authors' names in parentheses; and television programs and songs are indicated by quotation marks.